Political Science

For UGC-NET/SLET/JRF

Paper I, II and III

Previous Years' Papers with Key

Atlantic Research Division

PUBLISHERS & DISTRIBUTORS (P) LTD

Published by

ATLANTIC

PUBLISHERS & DISTRIBUTORS (P) LTD

7/22, Ansari Road, Darya Ganj,
New Delhi-110002
Phones : +91-11-40775252, 23273880, 23275880, 23280451
Fax : +91-11-23285873
Web : www.atlanticbooks.com
E-mail : orders@atlanticbooks.com

Branch Office
5, Nallathambi Street, Wallajah Road,
Chennai-600002
Phones : +91-44-64611085, 32413319
E-mail : chennai@atlanticbooks.com

ISBN 978-81-269-1954-3

Disclaimer:

The author and the publisher have taken every effort to the maximum of their skill, expertise and knowledge to provide correct answers to questions in the book. Even then if some mistakes persist in the content of the book, the publisher does not take responsibility for the same. The publisher shall have no liability to any person or entity with respect to any loss or damage caused, or alleged to have been caused directly or indirectly, by the information contained in this book. Hence, the book should be taken as a general guide only.

The publisher has fully tried to follow the copyright law. However, if any work is found to be similar, it is unintentional and the same should not be used as defamatory or to file legal suit against the author/publisher.

If the readers find any mistakes, we shall be grateful to them to point those to us so that they can be corrected in the next edition.

All disputes are subject to the jurisdiction of Delhi court only.

Printed in India at Glorious Printers, A-13, D.S.I.D.C., Jhilmil Industrial Area, Delhi-110095

Preface

The University Grants Commission (UGC) conducts National Eligibility Test (NET) on various subjects twice every year, once each in June and December, to determine eligibility for college and university level lectureship and for award of Junior Research Fellowship (JRF), for Indian nationals in order to ensure minimum standards for the entrants in the teaching profession and research.

The book contains previous years' solved papers (objective type questions) on the subject of Political Science, from June 2005 to December 2013. It covers all three papers (Paper I, II and III). In Paper I (General Paper on Teaching and Research Aptitude), and Paper II (Elective), solved papers have been included from June 2005. In Paper III (Core and Elective), solved papers of objective type questions have been included from June 2012, conforming to the existing UGC-NET pattern. In addition, five sets of Mock Tests for Paper I, II and III have been included in the book under Practice Papers. Answers have been given at the end of each set for self-check.

It will be useful for those preparing for UGC-NET/SLET/JRF in the subject of Political Science. It will give them a feel of the type of questions asked in NET in this subject, i.e. Multiple-choice, Matching type, True/False, Assertion-Reasoning type, etc. The papers included in this book will enable the students to judge their own level of competence besides adding to their knowledge. It will also help them revise the important questions in the entire syllabus and enhance their self-confidence. Suggestions for further improvement of the book are, however, welcome.

Atlantic Research Division

Contents

DECEMBER–2013

Note: This paper contains Sixty (60) multiple-choice questions, each question carrying two (2) marks. Candidate is expected to answer any Fifty (50) questions. In case more than Fifty (50) questions are attempted, only the first Fifty (50) questions will be evaluated.

PAPER–I

1. The post-industrial society is designated as
   (a) Information society
   (b) Technology society
   (c) Mediated society
   (d) Non-agricultural society

2. The initial efforts for internet based communication was for
   (a) Commercial communication
   (b) Military purposes
   (c) Personal interaction
   (d) Political campaigns

3. Internal communication within institutions is done through
   (a) LAN (b) WAN
   (c) EBB (d) MMS

4. Virtual reality provides
   (a) Sharp pictures
   (b) Individual audio
   (c) Participatory experience
   (d) Preview of new films

5. The first virtual university of India came up in
   (a) Andhra Pradesh
   (b) Maharashtra
   (c) Uttar Pradesh
   (d) Tamil Nadu

6. Arrange the following books in chronological order in which they appeared. Use the code given below:
   (i) Limits to Growth
   (ii) Silent Spring
   (iii) Our Common Future
   (iv) Resourceful Earth
   Codes:
   (a) (i), (iii), (iv), (ii)
   (b) (ii), (iii), (i), (iv)
   (c) (ii), (i), (iii), (iv)
   (d) (i), (ii), (iii), (iv)

7. Which one of the following continents is at a greater risk of desertification?
   (a) Africa (b) Asia
   (c) South America (d) North America

8. "Women are closer to nature than men." What kind of perspective is this?
   (a) Realist (b) Essentialist
   (c) Feminist (d) Deep ecology

9. Which one of the following is not a matter a global concern in the removal of tropical forests?
   (a) Their ability to absorb the chemicals that contribute to depletion of ozone layer.
   (b) Their role in maintaining the oxygen and carbon balance of the earth.
   (c) Their ability to regulate surface and air temperatures, moisture content and reflectivity.
   (d) Their contribution to the biological diversity of the planet.

10. The most comprehensive approach to address the problems of manenvironment interaction is one of the following:

(a) Natural Resource Conservation Approach
(b) Urban-industrial Growth Oriented Approach
(c) Rural-agricultural Growth Oriented Approach
(d) Watershed Development Approach

11. The major source of the pollutant gas, carbon mono-oxide (CO), in urban areas is
(a) Thermal power sector
(b) Transport sector
(c) Industrial sector
(d) Domestic sector

12. In a fuel cell driven vehicle, the energy is obtained from the combustion of
(a) Methane (b) Hydrogen
(c) LPG (d) CNG

13. Which one of the following Councils has been disbanded in 2013?
(a) Distance Education Council (DEC)
(b) National Council for Teacher Education (NCTE)
(c) National Council of Educational Research and Training (NCERT)
(d) National Assessment and Accreditation Council (NAAC)

14. Which of the following statements are correct about the National Assessment and Accreditation Council?
1. It is an autonomous institution.
2. It is tasked with the responsibility of assessing and accrediting institutions of higher education.
3. It is located in Delhi.
4. It has regional offices.

Select the correct answer from the codes given below:

Codes:
(a) 1 and 3 (b) 1 and 2
(c) 1, 2 and 4 (d) 2, 3 and 4

15. The power of the Supreme Court of India to decide disputes between two or more States falls under its
(a) Advisory Jurisdiction
(b) Appellate Jurisdiction
(c) Original Jurisdiction
(d) Writ Jurisdiction

16. Which of the following statements are correct?
1. There are seven Union Territories in India.
2. Two Union Territories have Legislative Assemblies.
3. One Union Territory has a High Court.
4. One Union Territory is the capital of two States.

Select the correct answer from the codes given below:
(a) 1 and 3 only
(b) 2 and 4 only
(c) 2, 3 and 4 only
(d) 1, 2, 3 and 4

17. Which of the following statements are correct about the Central Information Commission?
1. The Central Information Commission is a statutory body.
2. The Chief Information Commissioner and other Information Commissioners are appointed by the President of India.
3. The Commission can impose a penalty upto a maximum of ₹ 25,000
4. It can punish an errant officer.

Select the correct answer from the codes given below:

Codes:
(a) 1 and 2 only (b) 1, 2 and 4
(c) 1, 2 and 3 (d) 2, 3 and 4

18. Who among the following conducted the CNN-IBN – The Hindu 2013 Election Tracker Survey across 267 constituencies in 18 States?
    (a) The Centre for the Study of Developing Societies (CSDS)
    (b) The Association for Democratic Reforms (ADR)
    (c) CNN and IBN
    (d) CNN, IBN and The Hindu

19. In certain code TEACHER is written as VGCEJGT. The code of CHILDREN will be
    (a) EKNJFTGP (b) EJKNFTGP
    (c) KNJFGTP (d) None of these

20. A person has to buy both apples and mangoes. The cost of one apple is ₹ 7 whereas that of a mango is ₹ 5. If the person has ₹ 38, the number of apples he can buy is
    (a) 1 (b) 2
    (c) 3 (d) 4

21. A man pointing to a lady said, "The son of her only brother is the brother of my wife". The lady is related to the man as
    (a) Mother's sister
    (b) Grandmother
    (c) Mother-in-law
    (d) Sister of father-in-law

22. In this series
    6, 4, 1, 2, 2, 8, 7, 4, 2, 1, 5, 3, 8, 6, 2, 2, 7, 1, 4, 1, 3, 5, 8, 6, how many pairs of successive numbers have a difference of 2 each?
    (a) 4 (b) 5
    (c) 6 (d) 8

23. The mean marks obtained by a class of 40 students is 65. The mean marks of half of the students is found to be 45. The mean marks of the remaining students is
    (a) 85 (b) 60
    (c) 70 (d) 65

24. Anil is twice as old as Sunita. Three years ago, he was three times as old as Sunita. The present age of Anil is
    (a) 6 years (b) 8 years
    (c) 12 years (d) 16 years

25. Which of the following is a social network?
    (a) amazon.com (b) eBay
    (c) gmail.com (d) Twitter

26. The population information is called parameter while the corresponding sample information is known as
    (a) Universe
    (b) Inference
    (c) Sampling design
    (d) Statistics

Read the following passage carefully and answer questions 27 to 32:

Heritage conservation practices improved worldwide after the International Centre for the Study of the Preservation and Restoration of Cultural Property (ICCROM) was established with UNESCO's assistance in 1959. The inter-governmental organisation with 126 member states has done a commendable job by training more than 4,000 professionals, providing practice standards, and sharing technical expertise. In this golden jubilee year, as we acknowledge its key role in global conservation, an assessment of international practices would be meaningful to the Indian conservation movement. Consistent investment, rigorous attention, and dedicated research and dissemination are some of the positive lessons to imbibe. Countries such as Italy have demonstrated that prioritising heritage with significant budget provision pays. On the other hand, India, which is no less endowed in terms of cultural capital, has a long way to go. Surveys indicate that in addition to the 6,600 protected monuments, there are over 60,000 equally valuable heritage structures that await attention. Besides the small group in the service of Archaeological Survey of India, there are only about 150 trained conservation professionals. In order to overcome this severe shortage the emphasis has been on setting up dedicated labs and training institutions. It would make much better sense for conservation to be made part of mainstream research and engineering institutes, as has been done in Europe.

Increasing funding and building institutions are the relatively easy part. The real challenge is to redefine international approaches to address local contexts. Conservation cannot limit itself to enhancing the art-historical value of the heritage structures, which international charters perhaps overemphasise. The effort has to be broad-based: It must also serve as a means to improving the quality of life in the area where the heritage structures are located. The first task therefore is to integrate conservation efforts with sound development plans that take care of people living in the heritage vicinity. Unlike in western countries, many traditional building crafts survive in India, and conservation practices offer an avenue to support them. This has been acknowledged by the Indian National Trust for Art and Cultural Heritage charter for conservation but is yet to receive substantial state support. More strength for heritage conservation can be mobilised by aligning it with the green building movement. Heritage structures are essentially eco-friendly and conservation could become a vital part of the sustainable building practices campaign in future.

27. The outlook for conservation heritage changed
    (a) after the establishment of the International Centre for the Study of the Preservation and Restoration of Cultural Property.
    (b) after training the specialists in the field.
    (c) after extending UNESCO's assistance to the educational institutions.
    (d) after ASI's measures to protect the monuments.

28. The inter-government organization was appreciated because of
    (a) increasing number of members to 126.
    (b) imparting training to professionals and sharing technical expertise.
    (c) consistent investment in conservation.
    (d) its proactive role in renovation and restoration.

29. Indian conservation movement will be successful if there would be
    (a) Financial support from the Government of India.
    (b) Non-governmental organisations role and participation in the conservation movement.
    (c) consistent investment, rigorous attention, and dedicated research and dissemination of awareness for conservation.
    (d) Archaeological Survey of India's meaningful assistance.

30. As per the surveys of historical monuments in India, there is very small number of protected monuments. As per given the total number of monuments and enlisted number of protected monuments, percentage comes to
    (a) 10 percent (b) 11 percent
    (c) 12 percent (d) 13 percent

31. What should India learn from Europe to conserve our cultural heritage?

(i) There should be significant budget provision to conserve our cultural heritage.
(ii) Establish dedicated labs and training institutions.
(iii) Force the government to provide sufficient funds.
(iv) Conservation should be made part of mainstream research and engineering institutes.

Choose correct answer from the codes given below:
(a) (i), (ii), (iii), (iv) (b) (i), (ii), (iv)
(c) (i), (ii) (d) (i), (iii), (iv)

32. INTACH is known for its contribution for conservation of our cultural heritage. The full form of INTACH is
(a) International Trust for Art and Cultural Heritage
(b) Intra-national Trust for Art and Cultural Heritage
(c) Integrated Trust for Art and Cultural Heritage
(d) Indian National Trust for Art and Cultural Heritage

33. While delivering lecture if there is some disturbance in the class, a teacher should
(a) keep quiet for a while and then continue.
(b) punish those causing disturbance.
(c) motivate to teach those causing disturbance.
(d) not bother of what is happening in the class.

34. Effective teaching is a function of
(a) Teacher's satisfaction.
(b) Teacher's honesty and commitment.
(c) Teacher's making students learn and understand.
(d) Teacher's liking for professional excellence.

35. The most appropriate meaning of learning is
(a) Acquisition of skills
(b) Modification of behaviour
(c) Personal adjustment
(d) Inculcation of knowledge

36. Arrange the following teaching process in order:
(i) Relate the present knowledge with previous one
(ii) Evaluation
(iii) Reteaching
(iv) Formulating instructional objectives
(v) Presentation of instructional materials
(a) (i), (ii), (iii), (iv), (v)
(b) (ii), (i), (iii), (iv), (v)
(c) (v), (iv), (iii), (i), (ii)
(d) (iv), (i), (v), (ii), (iii)

37. CIET stands for
(a) Centre for Integrated Education and Technology
(b) Central Institute for Engineering and Technology
(c) Central Institute for Education Technology
(d) Centre for Integrated Evaluation Techniques.

38. Teacher's role at higher education level is to
(a) provide information to students.
(b) promote self-learning in students.
(c) encourage healthy competition among students.
(d) help students to solve their problems.

39. The Verstehen School of Understanding was popularised by
(a) German Social Scientists
(b) American Philosophers
(c) British Academicians
(d) Italian Political Analysts

40. The sequential operations in scientific research are
(a) Co-variation, Elimination of Spurious Relations, Generalisation, Theorisation

(b) Generalisation, Co-variation, Theorisation, Elimination of Spurious Relations
(c) Theorisation, Generalisation, Elimination of Spurious Relations, Co-variation
(d) Elimination of Spurious Relations, Theorisation, Generalisation, Co-variation.

41. In sampling, the lottery method is used for
(a) Interpretation
(b) Theorisation
(c) Conceptualisation
(d) Randomisation

42. Which is the main objective of research?
(a) To review the literature
(b) To summarize what is already known
(c) To get an academic degree
(d) To discover new facts or to make fresh interpretation of known facts

43. Sampling error decreases with the
(a) decrease in sample size
(b) increase in sample size
(c) process of randomization
(d) process of analysis

44. The principles of fundamental research are used in
(a) action research
(b) applied research
(c) philosophical research
(d) historical research

45. Users who use media for their own ends are identified as
(a) Passive audience
(b) Active audience
(c) Positive audience
(d) Negative audience

46. Classroom communication can be described as
(a) Exploration
(b) Institutionalisation
(c) Unsignified narration
(d) Discourse

47. Ideological codes shape our collective
(a) Productions (b) Perceptions
(c) Consumptions (d) Creations

48. In communication, myths have power, but are
(a) uncultural. (b) insignificant.
(c) imprecise. (d) unpreferred.

49. The first multi-lingual news agency of India was
(a) Samachar
(b) API
(c) Hindustan Samachar
(d) Samachar Bharati

50. Organisational communication can also be equated with
(a) intra-personal communication.
(b) inter-personal communication.
(c) group communication.
(d) mass communication.

51. If two propositions having the same subject and predicate terms are such that one is the denial of the other, the relationship between them is called
(a) Contradictory (b) Contrary
(c) Sub-contrary (d) Sub-alternation

52. Ananya and Krishna can speak and follow English. Bulbul can write and speak Hindi as Archana does.

Archana talks with Ananya also in Bengali. Krishna can not follow Bengali. Bulbul talks with Ananya in Hindi. Who can speak and follow English, Hindi and Bengali?
(a) Archana (b) Bulbul
(c) Ananya (d) Krishna

53. A stipulative definition may be said to be
(a) Always true
(b) Always false

(c) Sometimes true, sometimes false
(d) Neither true nor false

54. When the conclusion of an argument follows from its premise/premises conclusively, the argument is called
(a) Circular argument
(b) Inductive argument
(c) Deductive argument
(d) Analogical argument

55. Saturn and Mars are planets like the earth. They borrow light from the Sun and moves around the Sun as the Earth does. So those planets are inhabited by various orders of creatures as the earth is. What type of argument is contained in the above passage?
(a) Deductive (b) Astrological
(c) Analogical (d) Mathematical

56. Given below are two premises. Four conclusions are drawn from those two premises in four codes. Select the code that states the conclusion validly drawn.
Premises:
(i) All saints are religious. (major)
(ii) Some honest persons are saints. (minor)
Codes:
(a) All saints are honest.
(b) Some saints are honest.
(c) Some honest persons are religious.
(d) All religious persons are honest.

Following table provides details about the Foreign Tourist Arrivals (FTAs) in India from different regions of the world in different years. Study the table carefully and answer questions from 57 to 60 based on this table.

Region	Number of Foreign Tourist Arrivals		
	2007	2008	2009
Western Europe	1686083	1799525	1610086
North America	1007276	1027297	1024469
South Asia	982428	1051846	982633
South East Asia	303475	332925	348495
East Asia	352037	355230	318292
West Asia	171661	215542	201110
Total FTAs in India	5081504	5282603	5108579

57. Find out the region that contributed around 20 percent of the total foreign tourist arrivals in India in 2009.
(a) Western Europe
(b) North America
(c) South Asia
(d) South East Asia

58. Which of the following regions has recorded the highest negative growth rate of foreign tourist arrivals in India in 2009?
(a) Western Europe
(b) North America
(c) South Asia
(d) West Asia

59. Find out the region that has been showing declining trend in terms of share of foreign tourist arrivals in India in 2008 and 2009.
(a) Western Europe
(b) South East Asia
(c) East Asia
(d) West Asia

60. Identify the region that has shown hyper growth rate of foreign tourist arrivals than the growth rate of the total FTAs in India in 2008.
(a) Western Europe
(b) North America
(c) South Asia
(d) East Asia

ANSWERS

1. (a)	2. (b)	3. (a)	4. (c)	5. (d)
6. (c)	7. (a)	8. (b)	9. (a)	10. (d)
11. (b)	12. (b)	13. (a)	14. (b)	15. (c)
16. (d)	17. (c)	18. (a)	19. (b)	20. (d)
21. (d)	22. (c)	23. (a)	24. (c)	25. (d)
26. (d)	27. (a)	28. (b)	29. (c)	30. (b)
31. (b)	32. (d)	33. (c)	34. (c)	35. (b)
36. (d)	37. (c)	38. (b)	39. (a)	40. (a)
41. (d)	42. (d)	43. (b)	44. (b)	45. (b)
46. (d)	47. (b)	48. (c)	49. (c)	50. (c)
51. (a)	52. (c)	53. (d)	54. (c)	55. (c)
56. (c)	57. (b)	58. (d)	59. (a)	60. (c)

PAPER–II

Note: This paper contains fifty (50) objective type questions, each question carrying two (2) marks. All questions are compulsory.

1. Who among the following is not a principal character in Plato's Republic?
   (a) Polemarchus (b) Adeimantus
   (c) Protagoras (d) Glaucon

2. Match List I with List II and select the correct answer from the codes given below the lists:
   List I (Authors)
   A. A. Arblaster
   B. C.B. Mac Pherson
   C. C. Pateman
   D. D. Held
   List II (Books)
   i. *Participation and Democratic Theory*
   ii. *Models of Democracy*
   iii. *The Real World of Democracy*
   iv. *Democracy*

Codes:	**A**	**B**	**C**	**D**
(a)	i	ii	iii	iv
(b)	iv	iii	i	ii
(c)	ii	i	iv	iii
(d)	iii	iv	ii	i

3. Identify the correct sequence of Marx's Writings in ascending order:
   i. Contribution to the Critique of Political Economy
   ii. Poverty of Philosophy
   iii. Thesis on Feuerbach
   iv. Communist Manifesto
   Select the correct answer from the codes given below:
   Codes:
   (a) i, ii, iii, iv (b) ii, iii, iv, i
   (c) iii, ii, iv, i (d) iv, i, ii, iii

4. Given below are two statements, one labelled as Assertion (A) and the other labelled as Reason (R):
   Assertion (A): For behaviouralists, it was better to be wrong than vague.
   Reason (R): It was better to be vague than non-relevantly precise.
   Codes:
   (a) Both (A) and (R) are true and (R) is the right explanation of (A).
   (b) Both (A) and (R) are true, but (R) is not the correct explanation of (A).
   (c) (A) is false, but (R) is true.
   (d) (A) is true, but (R) is false.

5. Who said, "Each person possesses an inviolability founded on justice that even the welfare of society as a whole cannot override"?
   (a) John Rawls
   (b) Robert Nozick
   (c) Friedrich Hayek
   (d) Habermas

6. Who was the founder of Utilitarianism?

(a) Bentham (b) James Mill
(c) David Hume (d) Priestley

7. Which one of the following writings is not written by Mao?
   (a) On New Democracy
   (b) On Coalition Government
   (c) People's War
   (d) On People's Democratic Dictatorship

8. Why did Gandhiji go to South Africa?
   (a) On invitation by the Indians in South Africa.
   (b) To study Bar-at-Law.
   (c) To fight a case of a Gujarati Businessman.
   (d) To visit South Africa with family.

9. Who founded the 'Mexican Socialist Workers' Party' which was later named as 'Mexican Communist Party'?
   (a) Jaya Prakash Narayan
   (b) B.R. Ambedkar
   (c) M.N. Roy
   (d) Lenin

10. Whom did Lord Minto describe as the most 'dangerous man'?
   (a) B.G. Tilak
   (b) Aurobindo Ghosh
   (c) Gandhiji
   (d) Sardar Patel

11. Arrange in ascending order the following stages of Political Development as enunciated by A.F.K. Organski. Select the correct answer from codes given below:
   i. Primitive National Unification
   ii. Abundance
   iii. Industrialisation
   iv. National Welfare

   Codes:
   (a) i, ii, iii, iv (b) i, iii, ii, iv
   (c) i, iii, iv, ii (d) iv, ii, iii, i

12. Who among the following talks of pseudo-pressure groups?
   (a) Jean Blondel
   (b) Almond
   (c) Maurice Duverger
   (d) V.O. Key

13. Match List I with List II and select the correct answer from the codes given below:

   List I (Thinkers)
   A. Karl Marx
   B. Chalmers Johnson
   C. Ted Gurr
   D. Barrington Moore

   List II (Ideas)
   i. State of paternalistic bond between peasantry and property owners
   ii. Aggregatepsychological perspective
   iii. Revolution as a process through which structural inequalities could be eliminated
   iv. Value co-ordinated social system model

Codes:	A	B	C	D
(a)	i	iii	ii	iv
(b)	ii	i	iii	iv
(c)	iii	iv	ii	i
(d)	iv	i	iii	ii

14. Match List I with List II and select the correct answer from the codes given below the list.

   List I (Types of Government)
   A. Military Regime
   B. Dynastic Regime
   C. Psuedo Democracy
   D. Liberal Democracy

   List II (Principal Attributes)
   i. Based on deference.
   ii. Based on coercion.
   iii. Trappings of a liberal democracy like periodic elections but power rests in the hands of oligarchy.
   iv. Voluntary participation in government process is extensive.

Codes:	A	B	C	D
(a)	i	ii	iii	iv
(b)	ii	i	iii	iv
(c)	iv	iii	ii	i
(d)	iii	i	iv	ii

15. The process of Socialisation in Modern Society is
    1. Specific 2. Universalistic
    3. Instrumental 4. Ascriptive

    Select the correct answer from the codes given below:

    Codes:
    (a) 1, 2, 3 (b) 2, 3, 4
    (c) 3, 4, 1 (d) 4, 2, 1

16. Which one of the following is not a totalitarian form of Government?
    (a) Military Government
    (b) Fascist Government
    (c) Communist Government
    (d) Parliamentary form of Government

17. Who among the following writers classified Elites into broad types?
    (i) Organising and directing elites.
    (ii) Informally organised and diffused elites
    (a) Vilfredo Pareto
    (b) Robert Michaels
    (c) Gaetano Mosca
    (d) Karl Mannheim

18. Who among the following classified parties under competitive system into two major categories?
    (i) Turnover and Hegemonic
    (ii) Ideological and Pragmatic
    (a) Myron Weiner and Lapalombara
    (b) G.A. Almond and Verba
    (c) Neil A. Mcdonald
    (d) Peter H. Merkel

19. The concept of dependency evolved in the 1960s in
    (a) Europe (b) Africa
    (c) Asia (d) Latin America

20. Match List I with List II and select the correct answer from codes given below:

    List I (Books)
    A. *Approaches to the Study of Politics*
    B. *Dynamics of Modernization*
    C. *Influencing Voters*
    D. *Studies in Political Development*

    List II (Authors)
    i. R. Young ii. C.E. Black
    iii. R. Rose iv. J.S. Coleman

Codes:	A	B	C	D
(a)	i	ii	iii	iv
(b)	ii	iii	iv	i
(c)	iv	iii	ii	i
(d)	iii	iv	ii	i

21. Given below are two statements, one labelled as Assertion (A) and the other labelled as Reason (R). Choose the correct answer from the codes:

    Assertion (A): Secularization does not necessarily imply that people have become antireligious, or that religion has disappeared from both the public domain and the domain of personal belief.

    Reason (R): Religion is not just one, and not necessarily the most important way in which people understand themselves and their relationships.

    Codes:
    (a) Both (A) and (R) are correct and (R) is the correct explanation of (A).
    (b) Both (A) and (R) are correct, but (R) is not the correct explanation of (A).
    (c) (A) is correct, but (R) is false.
    (d) (R) is correct, but (A) is false.

22. Given below are two statements, one labelled as Assertion (A) and the other labelled as Reason (R).

    Assertion (A): The 1980s, a period of great turbulence in Indian Politics, marked the appearance of several new political parties.

Reason (R): National Parties got marginalized or became adjuncts to State Parties in many States.

Codes:

(a) Both (A) and (R) are true, and (R) is the correct explanation of (A).
(b) Both (A) and (R) are true, but (R) is not the correct explanation of (A).
(c) (A) is true, but (R) is false.
(d) (R) is true, but (A) is false.

23. Arrange the following in their chronological sequence:
   i. Nehru Committee Report
   ii. Quit India Movement
   iii. Civil Disobedience Movement
   iv. Declaration of Complete Independence

   Codes:

   (a) ii, i, iv, iii (b) iii, ii, iv, i
   (c) i, iv, iii, ii (d) iv, ii, i, iii

24. In which of the following case the Supreme Court of India held that, the power of amendment belonged to the Parliament, and this power was an unlimited one?
   (a) Sankari Prasad V. Union of India
   (b) Bela Banerjee and Others V. State of West Bengal
   (c) Kesavananda Bharati V. State of Kerala
   (d) Romesh Thapar V. State of Madras

25. Which one of the following States does not have a Bicameral Legislature?
   (a) Uttar Pradesh (b) Bihar
   (c) Maharashtra (d) Kerala

26. Identify the correct chronological order of the following Prime Minister/Chief Minister of J & K:
   (a) Sheikh Abdullah, Bakshi Ghulam Mohammad, Farooq Abdullah, Omar Abdullah.
   (b) Sheikh Abdullah, G.M. Sadiq, Mir Qasim, Farooq Abdullah.
   (c) Sheikh Abdullah, G.M. Sadiq Shamsuddin, Mufti Mohammad Sayeed.
   (d) Sheikh Abdulla, Bakshi Ghulam Mohammad, Shamsuddin, G.M. Sadiq.

27. Match List I with List II and select the correct answer from the codes given below:

   List I (Conspiracy Cases)
   A. Nasik case (1909-10)
   B. Benares case (1916)
   C. Kakori case (1924)
   D. Lahore case (1929-30)

   List II (Revolutionaries Punished)
   i. Sachindranath Sanyal
   ii. Ram Prasad Bismil
   iii. Bhagat Singh
   iv. Vinayak Savarkar

Codes:	A	B	C	D
(a)	i	iii	iv	ii
(b)	i	ii	iii	iv
(c)	iv	i	ii	iii
(d)	iii	iv	i	ii

28. Which one of the following is not a sufficient ground for convening a joint sitting of both Houses of Parliament?
   (a) Rejection of a bill by one House of the Parliament when the other House has passed it.
   (b) Both Houses have finally disagreed as to the amendments to be made in a bill.
   (c) More than six months has elapsed from the date of the reception of the Bill by the other House without the Bill being passed by it.
   (d) President has refused to give his assent to the Bill.

29. Who is the author of *Federal India: A Design for Change*?
   (a) Balveer Arora
   (b) K.C. Wheare

(c) Rasheeduddin Khan
(d) Ronald Watts

30. Who among the following has made pioneering contribution in the area of subaltern studies?
(a) Ramachandra Guha
(b) Ranjit Guha
(c) Rajni Kothari
(d) James Manor

31. Who among the following questioned the claim that Public Administration is a Science?
(a) Robert Dahl (b) Luther Gulick
(c) L. Urwick (d) Frank Goodnou

32. F.W. Taylor, the founding father of Scientific Management Movement, propounded the theory which was conceived to be a scientific methodology of
(a) Careful observation
(b) Managerial techniques
(c) Generalization
(d) All of the above

33. Who among the following is not a protagonist of the managerial view of Public Administration?
(a) Simon (b) Smithburg
(c) Gulick (d) Henry Fayol

34. Match List I with List II and select the correct answer from the codes given below:
List I
A. Line Agency B. General Staff
C. Specialised Staff D. Personal Staff
List II
1. Collection of data and its analysis.
2. Maintenance of diary of different engagements of line officials.
3. Functions directly contributing to goal achievement.
4. Looking after Personnel Administration.

Codes:	**A**	**B**	**C**	**D**
(a)	3	4	1	2
(b)	2	3	4	1
(c)	1	2	3	4
(d)	4	1	2	3

35. The role of the Finance Commission in Centre-State fiscal relations has been undermined by the
(a) The State Governments
(b) The Zonal Councils
(c) The Planning Commission
(d) The Election Commission

36. To which of the following classes of job in the public service in India, merit-cum-seniority principle is adopted in promotion?
(a) Class-I (b) Class-II
(c) Class-III (d) Class-I and II

37. Which of the following, according to Kautilya, are the principles of good governance for a king?
1. Merging individuality with duties.
2. Leading a disciplined life with a code of conduct.
3. Maintaining law and order.
4. Replacing bad ministers by lekhaks (writers).

Select the correct answer from the codes given below:
Codes:
(a) 1, 2 and 4 (b) 1, 2 and 3
(c) 2, 3 and 4 (d) 1, 2, 3 and 4

38. Given below are two statements, one labelled as Assertion (A) and the other labelled as Reason (R):
Assertion (A): Position-classification is the foundation of modern personnel administration.
Reason (R): Position-classification allows rationalization in Civil Services.

Codes:
(a) Both (A) and (R) are true and (R) is the correct explanation of (A).
(b) Both (A) and (R) are true, but (R) is not the correct explanation of (A).
(c) (A) is true, but (R) is false.
(d) (A) is false, but (R) is true.

39. Given below are two statements, one labelled as Assertion (A) and the other labelled as Reason (R).
Assertion (A): The relation between a generalist and a specialist is one of a senior and a subordinate.
Reason (R): A specialist is required to assist the generalist in the formulation and implementation of public policy.
Codes:
(a) Both (A) and (R) are true and (R) is the correct explanation of (A).
(b) Both (A) and (R) are true, but (R) is not the correct explanation of (A).
(c) (A) is true, but (R) is false.
(d) (A) is false, but (R) is true.

40. Given below are two statements, one labelled as Assertion (A) and the other labelled as Reason (R).
Assertion (A): Public Administration is generally characterised by an absence of profit motive.
Reason (R): Governmental activities are not undertaken simply to maximize profit but to promote societal welfare.
Codes:
(a) Both (A) and (R) are true and (R) is the correct explanation of (A).
(b) Both (A) and (R) are true, but (R) is not the correct explanation of (A).
(c) (A) is true, but (R) is false.
(d) (A) is false, but (R) is true.

41. Given below are two statements, one labelled as Assertion (A) and the other labelled as Reason (R).
Assertion (A): In the post-Soviet era, Nuclear armed states are likely to have military run or weak civilian governments.
Reason (R): They will lack the positive constraining mechanisms of civilian control.
Codes:
(a) Both (A) and (R) are true and (R) is the correct explanation of (A).
(b) Both (A) and (R) are true, but (R) is not the correct explanation of (A).
(c) (A) is true, but (R) is false.
(d) (A) is false, but (R) is true.

42. Where is India's Hi-Tech Naval Base "Project Varsha" located?
(a) Rambilli (b) Ezhimalai
(c) Araku Valley (d) Kochi

43. "Atoms for Peace" was a disarmament plan put forward by which world leader?
(a) J. Nehru (b) Krushchev
(c) Eisenhowerü (d) Kennedy

44. Match List I with List II and select the correct answer from the codes given below:

List I (Thinkers)	List II (Concepts)
A. William Cohen	i. New Wars
B. Martin Shaw	ii. Revolution in Military Affairs
C. Raymond Aron	iii. Degenerate Wars
D. Mary Kaldor	iv. Hyperbolic Wars

Codes:	A	B	C	D
(a)	ii	iii	iv	i
(b)	i	ii	iii	iv
(c)	iii	iv	i	ii
(d)	iv	i	ii	iii

45. Who created the Global Environmental Facility (GEF) as an international mechanism specifically for funding environmental projects in developing countries?
(a) IMF (b) UNDP
(c) UNEP (d) World Bank

46. Chronologically arrange the following treaties in the correct ascending order:
    i. The Charter of the UN
    ii. The Treaty of Westphalia
    iii. Treaties of Utrecht
    iv. Treaty of Paris

    Select the correct answer from the codes given below:

    Codes:

    (a) iv, i, ii, iii (b) iii, iv, i, ii
    (c) ii, iii, iv, i (d) i, ii, iii, iv

47. What are the four defining elements of a regime?
    (a) Principles, Norms, Rules, Decision making procedures.
    (b) Principles, Rules, Regulations, Procedures.
    (c) Norms, Rules, Regulations, Precedents.
    (d) Principles, Precedents, Procedures, Practices.

48. Chronologically arrange the following milestones in the Women's movement in the correct ascending order.
    i. Mexico City – UN Conference
    ii. Copenhagen – UN Conference
    iii. Beijing
    iv. Nairobi

    Select the correct answer from the codes given below:

    Codes:

    (a) iv, i, iii, ii (b) i, ii, iv, iii
    (c) ii, iii, i, iv (d) iii, iv, ii, i

49. When did India and Nepal sign the revised Double Taxation Avoidance Agreement (DTAA)?
    (a) 2011 (b) 2012
    (c) 2010 (d) 2009

50. Which of the following countries are included in ASEAN Plus Three?
    (a) China, India, Japan
    (b) China, South Korea, Russia
    (c) China, Russia, Japan
    (d) China, Japan, South Korea

ANSWERS

1. (c)	2. (b)	3. (c)	4. (d)	5. (a)
6. (c)	7. (c)	8. (c)	9. (c)	10. (b)
11. (c)	12. (c)	13. (c)	14. (b)	15. (a)
16. (d)	17. (d)	18. (a)	19. (d)	20. (a)
21. (a)	22. (a)	23. (c)	24. (a)	25. (d)
26. (d)	27. (c)	28. (d)	29. (c)	30. (b)
31. (a)	32. (d)	33. (d)	34. (a)	35. (a)
36. (d)	37. (b)	38. (a)	39. (d)	40. (a)
41. (a)	42. (a)	43. (c)	44. (a)	45. (d)
46. (c)	47. (a)	48. (b)	49. (a)	50. (d)

PAPER–III

Note: This paper contains seventy-five (75) objective type questions of two (2) marks each. All questions are compulsory.

1. Which one of the following factors is not responsible for the decline of Political Theory?
   (a) Positivism
   (b) Historicism
   (c) Moral Relativism
   (d) Ideological Pluralism

2. Neo-liberalism does not believe in
   (a) Deregulation
   (b) Debureaucratisation
   (c) Disinvestment
   (d) Statisation

3. Who said, "Taxation equals forced labour"?
   (a) John Rawls (b) Hayek
   (c) Nozick (d) Berlin

4. Match List I with List II and select the correct answer from the codes given below:

List I (Authors)
A. Richard Lowenthal
B. Benjamin L. Schwartz
C. Edgar Snow
D. Richard H. Solomon

List II (Books)
i. *Red China Today*
ii. *Mao's Revolution and the Chinese Political Culture*
iii. *World Communism*
iv. *Communism and Chinese Ideology in Flux*

Codes:	**A**	**B**	**C**	**D**
(a)	iii	iv	i	ii
(b)	iv	iii	ii	i
(c)	ii	i	iii	iv
(d)	i	ii	iv	iii

5. Who defined an ideology as "a set of ideas by which men posit, explain and justify the ends and means of organized social action, irrespective of whether such action aims to preserve, amend, uproot or rebuild a given social order"?
(a) de Tracy (b) Martin Seliger
(c) D. McLellan (d) J. Larrain

6. Given below are two statements, one is labelled as Assertion (A) and the other labelled as Reason (R):
Assertion (A): All Political Philosophers are political theorists.
Reason (R): All Political Theorists are not necessarily Political Philosophers.
Select the correct answer from the codes given below:
Codes:
(a) Both (A) and (R) are true and (R) is the right explanation of (A).
(b) Both (A) and (R) are true, but (R) is not the correct explanation of (A).
(c) (A) is true, but (R) is false.
(d) (A) is false, but (R) is true.

7. Who said that Labour power equals the brain, muscle, and nerve of the Labourer?
(a) Lenin
(b) M.N. Roy
(c) Marx
(d) Jayaprakash Narayan

8. The reappearance of Plato is found in the
(a) Utopia of Sir Thomas More
(b) City of the Sun of Campanella
(c) New Atlantis of Bacon
(d) All of the above

9. Which one of the statements is not correct in respect of Aristotle?
(a) Men are by nature unequal.
(b) There is subordination of inferior to superior.
(c) Women are, by nature, subordinated to men.
(d) Slavery is justified because it does not secure the best conditions for the slave.

10. Who did help to humanize J.S. Mill's revised version of Utilitarianism?
(a) James Mill
(b) Mrs. Harriet Taylor
(c) Priestley
(d) Hutcheson

11. For Hobbes, 'Felicity' means
(a) Pleasure
(b) A continued success in obtaining those things which a man from time to time desires
(c) Empathy
(d) None of the above

12. 'The "natural" man will be one in whom strong conscience and stead fast reason have successfully harmonized self-love and sympathy'. Who advocated this?
(a) Hobbes (b) Rousseau
(c) Bentham (d) Locke

13. Locke's Essay Concerning Human Understanding was a refutation of
(a) Hobbes' Leviathan
(b) Priestley's Essay on Government

(c) Bentham's Fragment on Government
(d) Sir Robert Filmer's Patriarcha.

14. The Politics of Society must be based on two principles as (i) 'Treat others as self' and (ii) 'help the other persons in need'. Whose saying is this?
(a) Rammohan Roy (b) B.R. Ambedkar
(c) Aurobindo (d) Savarkar

15. Identify the correct sequence of M.N. Roy's activities/events in ascending order:
(i) Formed "The League of Radical Congressman'.
(ii) Founded "The Indian Renaissance Movement".
(iii) Expelled from "Comintern".
(iv) Founded a weekly, "The Independent India".
Select the correct answer from the codes given below:
Codes:
(a) (iii), (iv), (i), (ii) (b) (iv), (iii), (ii), (i)
(c) (ii), (i), (iii), (iv) (d) (i), (ii), (iv), (iii)

16. Who among the following was elected as U.S. President for the fourth term?
(a) George Washington
(b) Franklin D. Roosevelt
(c) Theodore Roosevelt
(d) Andrew Jackson

17. Given below are two statements, one labelled as Assertion (A) and the other labelled as Reason (R). Choose the correct answer from the codes:
Assertion (A): Democratic values command widespread acceptance within liberal democracies as an ideal, but at the same time citizens have become more critical of the working of the core institutions of representative democracy.
Reason (R): The declining faith in government represents a deflation of the political culture, reducing the capacity of the political system to achieve shared goals.
Codes:
(a) Both (A) and (R) are correct, and (R) is the correct explanation of (R).
(b) Both (A) and (R) are correct, but (R) is not the correct explanation of (A).
(c) (A) is false, but (R) is correct.
(d) (A) is correct, but (R) is false.

18. Which of the following countries has a simple constitution-amending procedure?
(a) U.S.A. (b) U.K.
(c) India (d) France

19. In reference to Presidential system which President of U.S.A. said, "for the folly of just one man may spell disaster for the whole nation."?
(a) Jimmy Carter
(b) Barrack Obama
(c) George W. Bush
(d) Woodrow Wilson

20. Which one of the following statements about the U.S. President is not correct?
(a) No U.S. President has ever been impeached.
(b) Richard Nixon's impeachment failed by one vote.
(c) The House of Representatives has the power to initiate impeachment proceedings.
(d) The case is tried by the Senate with the Chief Justice presiding.

21. Match List I with List II and select the correct answer from the codes given below:
List I (Models of Development)
A. Bourgeoisie model
B. Autocratic model
C. Technocratic model
D. Populist model
List II (Features)
i. Urban Economic growth development of Legislature and Electoral process.
ii. Suppress middle class.

iii. Low political participation and high foreign investment.
iv. Stresses high political participation as well as economic inequality.

Codes:	A	B	C	D
(a)	i	ii	iii	iv
(b)	iv	iii	ii	i
(c)	iii	ii	i	iv
(d)	ii	iii	iv	i

22. Match List I with List II and select the correct answer from the codes given below:

List I (Authors)
A. Robert Michaels
B. Samuel Huntington
C. Robert Dahll
D. Francis Fukuyama

List II (Books)
i. *Democracy and its critics*
ii. *State Building: Governance and World order in the Twenty First Century*
iii. *Political Parties*
iv. *The Third Wave: Democratization in the Late Twentieth Century*

Codes:	A	B	C	D
(a)	i	iii	iv	ii
(b)	iii	iv	i	ii
(c)	iv	ii	iii	i
(d)	ii	i	iii	iv

23. Who among the following has adopted the 'Political-conflict approach' in the analysis of revolution?
(a) Thdeda Skocpol
(b) Alexis de Tocqueville
(c) Charles Tilly
(d) Emile Durkheim

24. Match List I with List II and select the correct answer from the given codes below:

List I (Books)
A. *The Politics of Modernization*
B. *Development as Freedoms*
C. *Political order in Changing Societies*
D. *Development and Underdevelopment*

List II (Authors)
i. Amartya Sen
ii. Samuel P. Huntington
iii. Celso Furtado
iv. David E. Apter

Codes:	A	B	C	D
(a)	i	ii	iii	iv
(b)	iv	i	ii	iii
(c)	ii	iii	iv	i
(d)	iv	i	iii	ii

25. Which of the following thinkers defined modernization in terms of three conditions:
(i) An innovative social system.
(ii) Differentiated, flexible social structure
(iii) Social basis for skill and knowledge, in technologically advanced world.
(a) C.E. Black
(b) David E. Apter
(c) Samuel P. Huntington
(d) S.N. Eisenstadt

26. Which of the following statements are correct about the Swiss Political System?
1. The Centre in Switzerland is more powerful than that of the U.S.A.
2. Swiss Government has right to military intervention in case of secession.
3. The residuary powers belong to the units.
4. Swiss political system is unitary.

Codes:
(a) 1, 2, 4 (b) 2, 3, 4
(c) 1, 2, 3 (d) 1, 2, 3, 4

27. Match List I with List II and select the correct answer from the codes given below:

List I (Thinkers)	List II (Concepts)
A. M. Focault	i. Will to power
B. Steven Lukes	ii. Bio power

C. Stewart Clegg iii. Radical view of power
D. F. Nietzche iv. Circuits of power

Codes:

	A	B	C	D
(a)	iv	i	ii	iii
(b)	iii	ii	i	iv
(c)	i	iv	iii	ii
(d)	ii	iii	iv	i

28. Which one is not the attribute of one party system?
 (a) Sectarian (Exclusive, regional, class, ideological) support.
 (b) Closed, Authoritarian, Direct action, Repressive organization.
 (c) Diffused, National integration, Community building, Mobilisation.
 (d) Comprehensive, Clientele oriented, Pragmatic support.

29. Which of the following, according to Lucian Pye, are the crises of Political development?
 1. Crisis of Identity
 2. Crisis of Legitimacy
 3. Crisis of Leadership
 4. Crisis of Integrity

 Select the correct answer from the codes given below:

 Codes:
 (a) 1, 2 (b) 2, 3
 (c) 3, 4 (d) 1, 4

30. Match List I with List II. Select correct answer from the codes given below:

 List I (Elites)
 A. Current Political Elites
 B. Economic Military, Scientific, Diplomatic Elites
 C. Priest, Philosophers, Educators
 D. Artists, Writers, top Actors

 List II (Functions)
 i. Goal attainment
 ii. Adaptation
 iii. Integration
 iv. Pattern Maintenance

Codes:

	A	B	C	D
(a)	i	ii	iii	iv
(b)	iv	iii	ii	i
(c)	iii	ii	i	iv
(d)	ii	i	iv	iii

31. Who made the following statement in the Constituent Assembly in connection with the Amendment Procedure of the Constitution of India?

 "That while we want this Constitution to be solid and as permanent as a structure we can make it, nevertheless there is no permanence in Constitutions.... If you make anything rigid and permanent, you stop the Nation's growth, the growth of a living, vital organic people".
 (a) Dr. B.R. Ambedkar
 (b) Jawaharlal Nehru
 (c) Sardar Vallabhbhai Patel
 (d) Dr. Rajendra Prasad

32. Which of the following Articles cannot be suspended during National Emergency?
 (a) Articles 14 and 15
 (b) Articles 19 and 20
 (c) Articles 21 and 22
 (d) Articles 20 and 21

33. Who among the following called Jayaprakash Narain, Ram Manohar Lohia and other Socialists as Japanese agents during 1942 movement?
 (a) Communist Party of India
 (b) Akali Dal
 (c) Rashtriya Swayam Sevak Sangh
 (d) Muslim League

34. Given below are two statements, one labelled as Assertion (A) and the other labelled as Reason (R). Choose the correct answer from the codes.

 Assertion (A): Caste system was an epitome of the traditional society, a 'closed system', where generation after generation of individuals did similar kinds of work and lived more or less similar kinds of lives.

Reason (R): Caste system encapsulated within it the features of a social structure and normative religious behaviour, and even provided a fairly comprehensive idea about the personal lives of individuals living in the Hindu Caste Society.

Codes:

(a) Both (A) and (R) are correct, and (R) is the correct explanation of (A).
(b) Both (A) and (R) are correct, but (R) is not the correct explanation of (A).
(c) (A) is correct, but (R) is false.
(d) (R) is correct, but (A) is false.

35. Given below are two statements, one labelled as Assertion (A) and the other labelled as Reason (R). Choose the correct answer from the codes.

Assertion (A): Over the years, the Supreme Court of India has failed to demonstrate a commitment to preserving constitutional liberty, and expanding and protecting human rights.

Reason (R): The Supreme Court has played and continues to play a critical role in shaping India's constitutional democracy far beyond that which the drafters of the Constitution envisaged or what courts in other countries play.

Codes:

(a) Both (A) and (R) are correct and (R) is the correct explanation of (A).
(b) Both (A) and (R) are correct, but (R) is not the correct explanation of (A).
(c) (A) is correct, but (R) is false.
(d) (A) is false, but (R) is correct.

36. Which one of the following is not applicable to Public Interest Litigation?
(a) Constitutional obligation of the Judiciary towards the marginalised sections of society.
(b) Locus standi.
(c) Public spirited citizens can move the court on behalf of the poor.
(d) Judiciary overlooks a strict construction of procedural formalities in entertaining petitions.

37. Which among the following pertains to the sixty first Constitutional Amendment?
(a) Ninth Schedule
(b) Defection
(c) Amendment of Article 368
(d) Lowering of voting age

38. The Sikhs got special electorates in which of the following Acts?
(a) Indian Councils Act, 1892
(b) Indian Councils Act, 1909
(c) Government of India Act, 1919
(d) Government of India Act, 1935

39. Which of the following Committees of the Constituent Assembly was chaired by Jawaharlal Nehru?
(a) Steering Committee
(b) Union Powers Committee
(c) Committee on Fundamental Rights and Minorities
(d) Provincial Constitution Committee

40. Who among the following developed the concept, 'derivative discourse'?
(a) Ashish Nandy
(b) Partha Chatterjee
(c) Ashutosh Varshney
(d) Sudipta Kaviraj

41. MNREGA is not associated with which of the following?
(a) Providing Employment Opportunities
(b) Reduction of poverty
(c) Preventing Distress Migration
(d) Agrarian crises

42. Match List I with List II and select the correct answer from the codes given below:

List I (Commissions/Committees)
A. Mahajan Commission
B. Sri Krishna Commission
C. Punchi Commission
D. Sachar Committee

List II (Issues)
i. Maharashtra-Karnataka Boundary Dispute
ii. Muslim Minority
iii. Telengana/A.P.
iv. Centre-State Relations

Codes:	A	B	C	D
(a)	ii	iv	i	iii
(b)	i	iii	iv	ii
(c)	iii	ii	i	iv
(d)	iv	i	iii	ii

43. Who among the following first initiated the study of State Politics in India?
(a) Iqbal Narain
(b) Paul R. Brass
(c) Stanley Kochanak
(d) Myron Weiner

44. Which one of the following was the largest Opposition party in the Eighth Lok Sabha (1984)?
(a) Bhartiya Janata Party
(b) Communist Party of India
(c) Telugu Desam Party
(d) National Lok Dal

45. With which of the following States, was the Programme, Janmabhoomi associated?
(a) Kerala
(b) Karnataka
(c) Tamil Nadu
(d) Andhra Pradesh

46. Match List I with List II and select the correct answer from the codes given below:

List I (Approaches)
A. Behavioural
B. Bureaucratic
C. Ecological
D. General Systems

List II (Characteristics)
1. Agrarian-Transition Industrialization
2. Administrative system as a subsystem of the society
3. Analyses of human behaviour in administrative settings
4. Legal-Rational Authority

Codes:	A	B	C	D
(a)	2	3	4	1
(b)	3	4	1	2
(c)	1	2	3	4
(d)	4	1	2	3

47. Which of the following is concerned with the substantive functions of the Government?
(a) Staff Agency
(b) Line Agency
(c) Auxiliary Agency
(d) Staff and Auxiliary Agencies

48. Who among the following termed the four different bases of organization as four Ps?
(a) Luther Gulick
(b) L.D. White
(c) Henry Fayol
(d) Herbert Simon

49. The chief reason for delegation of authority from headquarters to field officers is to
(a) facilitate decision-making at the local level.
(b) inculcate skills in the field officers.
(c) control the field office.
(d) decongest the headquarters.

50. Which of the following are the characteristics of development administration?
1. Change-orientation
2. Client orientation
3. Citizen-participative orientation
4. Ecological perspective

Select the correct answer from the codes given below:

Codes:

(a) 1 and 2 (b) 2 and 3
(c) 1, 2 and 4 (d) 1, 2, 3 and 4

51. Domicile qualification for public services was first prescribed by
(a) The United States of America
(b) U.K.
(c) India
(d) France

52. Which one of the following is the Cadre-controlling authority for the Indian Police Service?
(a) The Ministry of Personnel, Public Grievances and Pensions
(b) The Ministry of Home Affairs
(c) Prime Minister's Office (PMO)
(d) Cabinet Secretary

53. The process of transferring funds from one budget head to another of the same department where there is a need for more expenditure is called
(a) transfer
(b) re-allocation
(c) re-appropriation
(d) sectoral allocation

54. Promotion generally means
1. Change in position
2. Change in duties
3. Change in title
4. Change in pay

Select the correct answer from the codes given below:

Codes:

(a) 1 and 2 (b) 1, 2 and 3
(c) 1, 3 and 4 (d) 1, 2, 3 and 4

55. Which of the following statements are correct?
1. Panchayati Raj is mentioned in the Constitution as a Directive Principle.
2. Sadiq Ali Committee was appointed to report on the working of the Panchayat system in India.
3. G.V.K. Rao Committee was appointed by the Planning Commission.
4. Local Government figures in State List.

Select the correct answer from the codes given below:

Codes:

(a) 1, 3 and 4 (b) 2, 3 and 4
(c) 1, 2 and 3 (d) 1, 2, 3 and 4

56. Who among the following has termed bureaucracy as "an organization that cannot correct its behaviour by learning from its errors"?
(a) R.K. Merton (b) M. Crozer
(c) Max Weber (d) C.N. Parkinson

57. Who is the Chairperson of the National Council of Joint Consultative Machinery (JCM)?
(a) Cabinet Secretary
(b) Secretary for Home Affairs
(c) Personnel Secretary
(d) Finance Secretary

58. Of all the controls over Public Administration the one which is more continuous and self-corrective is
(a) controlled by the Legislature
(b) controlled by the Executive
(c) controlled by the Judiciary
(d) controlled by the Media

59. Given below are two statements, one labelled as Assertion (A) and the other as Reason (R).

Assertion (A): A few years back, the Government of India started what is known as "filejumping experiment".

Reason (R): Hierarchical structure causes inordinate delay in the disposal of work.

Codes:
(a) Both (A) and (R) are true and (R) is the correct explanation of (A).
(b) Both (A) and (R) are true, but (R) is not the correct explanation of (A).
(c) (A) is true, but (R) is false.
(d) (A) is false, but (R) is true.

60. Given below are two statements, one labelled as Assertion (A) and the other as Reason (R).
Assertion (A): Planning Commission in India is neither a Statutory Body nor a Constitutional Body.
Reason (R): It was established by an Act of Parliament.
Codes:
(a) Both (A) and (R) are true and (R) is the correct explanation of (A).
(b) Both (A) and (R) are true, but (R) is not the correct explanation of (A).
(c) (A) is true, but (R) is false.
(d) (A) is false, but (R) is true.

61. With which liberal thinker would you associate "Democratic Peace Theory"?
(a) Michael Doyle
(b) James Rosenau
(c) Richard Falk
(d) Michael Walzer

62. Given below are two statements, one labelled as Assertion (A) and the other labelled as Reason (R).
Assertion (A): Regimes represent an important feature of globalization.
Reason (R): The onset of détente, the loss of hegemonic status by the USA and the growing awareness of environmental problems sensitized social scientists.
Codes:
(a) Both (A) and (R) are true and (R) is the right explanation of (A).
(b) Both (A) and (R) are true, but (R) is not the correct explanation of (A).
(c) (A) is true, but (R) is false.
(d) (A) is false, but (R) is true.

63. Who said, "Power in International Politics is like the weather. Everyone talks about it, but few understand it"?
(a) Hans J. Morganthau
(b) Henry Kissinger
(c) Joseph Nye
(d) Susan Strange

64. Match List I with List II and select the correct answer from the codes given below:
List I (Reasons of failure)
A. Tribal conflict
B. Endless violence for nonpolitical purposes
C. Ethnic genocide
D. Transnational war
List II (States)
i. Rwanda ii. Somalia
iii. Congo iv. Liberia

Codes:	**A**	**B**	**C**	**D**
(a)	ii	iv	i	iii
(b)	i	iii	iv	ii
(c)	iv	ii	iii	i
(d)	iii	i	ii	iv

65. Chronologically arrange the arms control and disarmament agreements in an ascending order.
1. Strategic Offensive Reduction Treaty (SORT) - 2002
2. Chemical Weapons Convention - 1993
3. Open Skies Treaty - 1992
4. Ottawa Landmine Convention - 1997
Codes:
(a) 4, 1, 3, 2 (b) 1, 4, 2, 3
(c) 3, 2, 4, 1 (d) 2, 3, 1, 4

66. Given below are two statements one labelled as Assertion (A) and the other labelled as Reason (R).

Assertion (A): The post-Cold War period is a multi polar moment in an uni polar world.

Reason (R): America remains the world's pre eminent actor, but it is also stretched militarily, in debt financially, divided domestically and unpopular internationally.

Codes:

(a) Both (A) and (R) are true and (R) is the correct explanation of (A).
(b) Both (A) and (R) are true, but (R) is not the correct explanation of (A).
(c) (A) is true, but (R) is false.
(d) (A) is false, but (R) is true.

67. With which Doctrine is "Containment" associated?
(a) Dulles Doctrine
(b) Truman Doctrine
(c) Nixon Doctrine
(d) Roosevelt Doctrine

68. Which country has the world's largest reserves of natural gas, the second largest coal reserves, and the eighth largest oil reserves?
(a) Iran (b) USA
(c) Saudi Arabia (d) Russia

69. Match List I with List II and select the correct answer from the codes given below the lists:

List I (Books)

A. *A Hundred Horizons: The Indian Ocean in the Age of Global Empire*
B. *Global Swing States: Brazil, India, Indonesia, Turkey and the Future of International Order*
C. *War in the Indian Ocean*
D. *Samundra Manthan: Sino Indian Rivalry in the Indo-Pacific*

List II (Authors)

i. C. Raja Mohan
ii. Sugato Bose
iii. David Kliman & Richard Fontaine
iv. Vice-Admiral Mihir Kumar Roy

Codes:	A	B	C	D
(a)	iv	i	ii	iii
(b)	iii	iv	i	ii
(c)	ii	iii	iv	i
(d)	i	ii	iii	iv

70. Which countries were identified as the "Axis of Evil" by President Bush in his State of Union Speech in 2002?
(a) Russia, China, Iran
(b) Iran, Iraq, Syria
(c) Cuba, Venezuela, Russia
(d) Iraq, Iran, North Korea

71. When was the UN Peace building Commission established?
(a) January 2003 (b) December 2004
(c) December 2005 (d) January 2006

72. As part of a regional initiative, India initiated the 2004 Tokyo Agreement. Name the organization which emerged as a result.
(a) BRICS (b) ARF
(c) ReCAAP (d) IOR-ARC

73. Name the military strategist who stated that all war is based on deception and praised it as the 'divine art of subtlety and secrecy.'
(a) Clausewitz (b) Kautilya
(c) Sun Tzu (d) Machiavelli

74. Name the person who headed the United Nations Monitoring, Verification and Inspection Commission (UNMOVIC) to Iraq in 2002?
(a) Kofi Annan
(b) Hans Blix
(c) David Petraeus
(d) Colin Powell

75. Which among the following States least influences India's Foreign Policy?
(a) Jammu and Kashmir
(b) West Bengal
(c) Madhya Pradesh
(d) Tamil Nadu

ANSWERS

1. (d)	2. (d)	3. (c)	4. (a)	5. (b)	41. (d)	42. (b)	43. (d)	44. (c)	45. (d)
6. (a)	7. (c)	8. (d)	9. (d)	10. (b)	46. (b)	47. (b)	48. (a)	49. (d)	50. (d)
11. (b)	12. (b)	13. (d)	14. (c)	15. (a)	51. (a)	52. (a)	53. (c)	54. (d)	55. (a)
16. (b)	17. (b)	18. (b)	19. (a)	20. (b)	56. (b)	57. (a)	58. (b)	59. (a)	60. (c)
21. (a)	22. (b)	23. (c)	24. (b)	25. (b)	61. (a)	62. (b)	63. (c)	64. (a)	65. (c)
26. (c)	27. (d)	28. (d)	29. (a)	30. (a)	66. (d)	67. (b)	68. (d)	69. (c)	70. (d)
31. (b)	32. (d)	33. (a)	34. (b)	35. (d)	71. (c)	72. (c)	73. (c)	74. (b)	75. (c)
36. (b)	37. (d)	38. (c)	39. (b)	40. (b)					

JUNE–2013

Note: This paper contains Sixty (60) multiple-choice questions, each question carrying two (2) marks. Candidate is expected to answer any Fifty (50) questions. In case more than Fifty (50) questions are attempted, only the first Fifty (50) questions will be evaluated.

PAPER–I

1. Which one of the following references is written as per Modern Language Association (MLA) format?
   (a) Hall, Donald. Fundamentals of Electronics,
   New Delhi: Prentice Hall of India, 2005
   (b) Hall, Donald, Fundamentals of Electronics,
   New Delhi: Prentice Hall of India, 2005
   (c) Hall, Donald, Fundamentals of Electronics,
   New Delhi: Prentice Hall of India, 2005
   (d) Hall, Donald. Fundamentals of Electronics.
   New Delhi: Prentice Hall of India, 2005

2. A workshop is
   (a) a conference for discussion on a topic.
   (b) a meeting for discussion on a topic.
   (c) a class at a college or a university in which a teacher and the students discuss a topic.
   (d) a brief intensive course for a small group emphasizing the development of a skill or technique for solving a specific problem.

3. A working hypothesis is
   (a) a proven hypothesis for an argument.
   (b) not required to be tested.
   (c) a provisionally accepted hypothesis for further research.
   (d) a scientific theory.

Read the following passage carefully and answer the questions (4 to 9):

The Taj Mahal has become one of the world's best known monuments. This domed white marble structure is situated on a high plinth at the southern end of a four-quartered garden, evoking the gardens of paradise, enclosed within walls measuring 305 by 549 metres. Outside the walls, in an area known as Mumtazabad, were living quarters for attendants, markets, serais and other structures built by local merchants and nobles. The tomb complex and the other imperial structures of Mumtazabad were maintained by the income of thirty villages given specifically for the tomb's support. The name Taj Mahal is unknown in Mughal chronicles, but it is used by contemporary Europeans in India, suggesting that this was the tomb's popular name. In contemporary texts, it is generally called simply the Illuminated Tomb (Rauza-i-Munavvara).

Mumtaz Mahal died shortly after delivering her fourteenth child in 1631. The Mughal court was then residing in Burhanpur. Her remains were temporarily buried by the griefstricken emperor in a spacious garden known as Zainabad on the bank of the river Tapti. Six months later her body was transported to Agra, where it was interred in land chosen for the mausoleum. This land, situated south of the Mughal city on the bank of the Jamuna, had belonged to the Kachhwaha rajas since the time of Raja Man Singh and was purchased from the then current raja, Jai Singh. Although contemporary chronicles indicate Jai Singh's willing cooperation in this exchange, extant *farmans* (imperial commands) indicate that the final price was not settled until almost two years after the mausoleum's commencement. Jai Singh's further cooperation was insured by imperial orders issued between 1632 and 1637 demanding that he provide stone masons and carts to transport marble from the mines at Makrana, within his "ancestral domain", to Agra where both the Taj Mahal and Shah Jahan's additions to the Agra fort were constructed concurrently.

Work on the mausoleum was commenced early in 1632. Inscriptional evidence indicates much of the tomb was completed by 1636. By 1643, when Shah Jahan most lavishly celebrated the 'Urs ceremony for Mumtaz Mahal', the entire complex was virtually complete.

4. Marble stone used for the construction of the Taj Mahal was brought from the ancestral domain of Raja Jai Singh. The name of the place where mines of marble is
   (a) Burhanpur (b) Makrana
   (c) Amber (d) Jaipur
5. The popular name Taj Mahal was given by
   (a) Shah Jahan
   (b) Tourists
   (c) Public
   (d) European travellers
6. Point out the true statement from the following:
   (a) Marble was not used for the construction of the Taj Mahal.
   (b) Red sand stone is non-visible in the Taj Mahal complex.
   (c) The Taj Mahal is surrounded by a four-quartered garden known as Char Bagh.
   (d) The Taj Mahal was constructed to celebrate the 'Urs ceremony for Mumtaz Mahal'.
7. In the contemporary texts the Taj Mahal is known
   (a) Mumtazabad
   (b) Mumtaz Mahal
   (c) Zainabad
   (d) Rauza-i-Munavvara
8. The construction of the Taj Mahal was completed between the period
   (a) 1632 – 1636 A.D.
   (b) 1630 – 1643 A.D.
   (c) 1632 – 1643 A.D.
   (d) 1636 – 1643 A.D.
9. The documents indicating the ownership of land, where the Taj Mahal was built, known as
   (a) Farman
   (b) Sale Deed
   (c) Sale-Purchase Deed
   (d) None of the above
10. In the process of communication, which one of the following is in the chronological order?
    (a) Communicator, Medium, Receiver, Effect, Message
    (b) Medium, Communicator, Message, Receiver, Effect
    (c) Communicator, Message, Medium, Receiver, Effect
    (d) Message, Communicator, Medium, Receiver, Effect
11. Bengal Gazette, the first Newspaper in India was started in 1780 by
    (a) Dr. Annie Besant
    (b) James Augustus Hicky
    (c) Lord Cripson
    (d) A.O. Hume

12. Press censorship in India was imposed during the tenure of the Prime Minister
(a) Rajeev Gandhi
(b) Narasimha Rao
(c) Indira Gandhi
(d) Deve Gowda

13. Communication via New media such as computers, teleshopping, internet and mobile telephony is termed as
(a) Entertainment
(b) Interactive communication
(c) Developmental communication
(d) Communitarian

14. Classroom communication of a teacher rests on the principle of
(a) Infotainment
(b) Edutainment
(c) Entertainment
(d) Enlightenment

15. ________ is important when a teacher communicates with his/her student.
(a) Sympathy (b) Empathy
(c) Apathy (d) Antipathy

16. In a certain code GALIB is represented by HBMJC. TIGER will be represented by
(a) UJHFS (b) UHJSF
(c) JHUSF (d) HUJSF

17. In a certain cricket tournament 45 matches were played. Each team played once against each of the other teams. The number of teams participated in the tournament is
(a) 8 (b) 10
(c) 12 (d) 14

18. The missing number in the series 40, 120, 60, 180, 90, ?, 135 is
(a) 110 (b) 270
(c) 105 (d) 210

19. The odd numbers from 1 to 45 which are exactly divisible by 3 are arranged in an ascending order. The number at 6th position is
(a) 18 (b) 24
(c) 33 (d) 36

20. The mean of four numbers a, b, c, d is 100. If c = 70, then the mean of the remaining numbers is
(a) 30 (b) $\frac{85}{2}$
(c) $\frac{170}{3}$ (d) 110

21. If the radius of a circle is increased by 50%, the perimeter of the circle will increase by
(a) 20% (b) 30%
(c) 40% (d) 50%

22. If the statement 'some men are honest' is false, which among the following statements will be true. Choose the correct code given below:
(i) All men are honest.
(ii) No men are honest.
(iii) Some men are not honest.
(iv) All men are dishonest.

Codes:
(a) (i), (ii) and (iii)
(b) (ii), (iii) and (iv)
(c) (i), (iii) and (iv)
(d) (ii), (i) and (iv)

23. Choose the proper alternative given in the codes to replace the question mark.
Bee – Honey, Cow – Milk, Teacher –?
(a) Intelligence (b) Marks
(c) Lessons (d) Wisdom

24. P is the father of R and S is the son of Q and T is the brother of P. If R is the sister of S, how is Q related to T?
(a) Wife
(b) Sister-in-law
(c) Brother-in-law
(d) Daughter-in-law

25. A definition put forward to resolve a dispute by influencing attitudes or stirring emotions is called
   (a) Lexical (b) Persuasive
   (c) Stipulative (d) Precisions
26. Which of the codes given below contains only the correct statements?
   Statements:
   (i) Venn diagram is a clear method of notation.
   (ii) Venn diagram is the most direct method of testing the validity of categorical syllogisms.
   (iii) In Venn diagram method the premises and the conclusion of a categorical syllogism is diagrammed.
   (iv) In Venn diagram method the three overlapping circles are drawn for testing a categorical syllogism.

   Codes:
   (a) (i), (ii) & (iii)
   (b) (i), (ii) & (iv)
   (c) (ii), (iii) & (iv)
   (d) (i), (iii) & (iv)
27. Inductive reasoning presupposes
   (a) unity in human nature
   (b) integrity in human nature
   (c) uniformity in human nature
   (d) harmony in human nature

Read the table below and based on this table answer questions from 28 to 33:

Area under Major Horticulture Crops

(in lakh hectares)

Year	Fruits	Vegetables	Flowers	Total Horti-culture Area
2005-06	53	72	1	187
2006-07	56	75	1	194
2007-08	58	78	2	202
2008-09	61	79	2	207
2009-10	63	79	2	209

28. Which of the following two years have recorded the highest rate of increase in area under the total horticulture?
   (a) 2005–06 & 2006–07
   (b) 2006–07 & 2008–09
   (c) 2007–08 & 2008–09
   (d) 2006–07 & 2007–08
29. Shares of the area under flowers, vegetables and fruits in the area under total horticulture are respectively:
   (a) 1, 38 and 30 percent
   (b) 30, 38 and 1 percent
   (c) 38, 30 and 1 percent
   (d) 35, 36 and 2 percent
30. Which of the following has recorded the highest rate of increase in area during 2005-06 to 2009-10?
   (a) Fruits
   (b) Vegetables
   (c) Flowers
   (d) Total horticulture
31. Find out the horticultural crop that has recorded an increase of area by around 10 percent from 2005-06 to 2009-10
   (a) Fruits
   (b) Vegetables
   (c) Flowers
   (d) Total horticulture
32. What has been the share of area under fruits, vegetables and flowers in the area under total horticulture in 2007-08?
   (a) 53 percent (b) 68 percent
   (c) 79 percent (d) 100 percent
33. In which year, area under fruits has recorded the highest rate of increase?
   (a) 2006-07 (b) 2007-08
   (c) 2008-09 (d) 2009-10
34. 'www' stands for
   (a) work with web
   (b) word wide web

(c) world wide web
(d) worth while web

35. A hard disk is divided into tracks which is further subdivided into
(a) Clusters (b) Sectors
(c) Vectors (d) Heads

36. A computer program that translates a program statement by statement into machine language is called a/an
(a) Compiler (b) Simulator
(c) Translator (d) Interpreter

37. A Gigabyte is equal to
(a) 1024 Megabytes
(b) 1024 Kilobytes
(c) 1024 Terabytes
(d) 1024 Bytes

38. A Compiler is a software which converts
(a) characters to bits
(b) high level language to machine language
(c) machine language to high level language
(d) words to bits

39. Virtual memory is
(a) an extremely large main memory.
(b) an extremely large secondary memory.
(c) an illusion of extremely large main memory.
(d) a type of memory used in super computers.

40. The phrase 'tragedy of commons' is in the context of
(a) tragic event related to damage caused by release of poisonous gases.
(b) tragic conditions of poor people.
(c) degradation of renewable free access resources.
(d) climate change.

41. Kyoto Protocol is related to
(a) Ozone depletion
(b) Hazardous waste
(c) Climate change
(d) Nuclear energy

42. Which of the following is a source of emissions leading to the eventual formation of surface ozone as a pollutant?
(a) Transport sector
(b) Refrigeration and Airconditioning
(c) Wetlands
(d) Fertilizers

43. The smog in cities in India mainly consists of
(a) Oxides of sulphur
(b) Oxides of nitrogen and unburnt hydrocarbons
(c) Carbon monoxide and SPM
(d) Oxides of sulphur and ozone

44. Which of the following types of natural hazards have the highest potential to cause damage to humans?
(a) Earthquakes
(b) Forest fires
(c) Volcanic eruptions
(d) Droughts and Floods

45. The percentage share of renewable energy sources in the power production in India is around
(a) 2-3% (b) 22-25%
(c) 10-12% (d) $< 1\%$

46. In which of the following categories the enrolment of students in higher education in 2010-11 was beyond the percentage of seats reserved?
(a) OBC students
(b) SC students
(c) ST students
(d) Woman students

47. Which one of the following statements is not correct about the University Grants Commission (UGC)?
(a) It was established in 1956 by an Act of Parliament.

(b) It is tasked with promoting and coordinating higher education.
(c) It receives Plan and Non-Plan funds from the Central Government.
(d) It receives funds from State Governments in respect of State Universities.

48. Consider the statement which is followed by two arguments (I) and (II):
Statement: Should India switch over to a two party system?
Arguments: (I) Yes, it will lead to stability of Government.
(II) No, it will limit the choice of voters.
(a) Only argument (I) is strong.
(b) Only argument (II) is strong.
(c) Both the arguments are strong.
(d) Neither of the arguments is strong.

49. Consider the statement which is followed by two arguments (I) and (II):
Statement: Should persons with criminal background be banned from contesting elections?
Arguments: (I) Yes, it will decriminalise politics.
(II) No, it will encourage the ruling party to file frivolous cases against their political opponents.
(a) Only argument (I) is strong.
(b) Only argument (II) is strong.
(c) Both the arguments are strong.
(d) Neither of the arguments is strong.

50. Which of the following statement(s) is/are correct about a Judge of the Supreme Court of India?
1. A Judge of the Supreme Court is appointed by the President of India.
2. He holds office during the pleasure of the President.
3. He can be suspended, pending an inquiry.
4. He can be removed for proven misbehaviour or incapacity.

Select the correct answer from the codes given below:
Codes:
(a) 1, 2 and 3 (b) 1, 3 and 4
(c) 1 and 3 (d) 1 and 4

51. In the warrant of precedence, the Speaker of the Lok Sabha comes next only to
(a) The President
(b) The Vice-President
(c) The Prime Minister
(d) The Cabinet Ministers

52. The blackboard can be utilised best by a teacher for
(a) putting the matter of teaching in black and white
(b) making the students attentive
(c) writing the important and notable points
(d) highlighting the teacher himself

53. Nowadays the most effective mode of learning is
(a) self-study
(b) face-to-face learning
(c) e-learning
(d) blended learning

54. At the primary school stage, most of the teachers should be women because they
(a) can teach children better than men.
(b) know basic content better than men.
(c) are available on lower salaries.
(d) can deal with children with love and affection.

55. Which one is the highest order of learning?
(a) Chain learning
(b) Problem-solving learning

(c) Stimulus-response learning
(d) Conditioned-reflex learning

56. A person can enjoy teaching as a profession when he
(a) has control over students.
(b) commands respect from students.
(c) is more qualified than his colleagues.
(d) is very close to higher authorities.

57. "A diagram speaks more than 1000 words." The statement means that the teacher should
(a) use diagrams in teaching.
(b) speak more and more in the class.
(c) use teaching aids in the class.
(d) not speak too much in the class.

58. A research paper
(a) is a compilation of information on a topic.
(b) contains original research as deemed by the author.
(c) contains peer-reviewed original research or evaluation of research conducted by others.
(d) can be published in more than one journal.

59. Which one of the following belongs to the category of good 'research ethics'?
(a) Publishing the same paper in two research journals without telling the editors.
(b) Conducting a review of the literature that acknowledges the contributions of other people in the relevant field or relevant prior work.
(c) Trimming outliers from a data set without discussing your reasons in a research paper.
(d) Including a colleague as an author on a research paper in return for a favour even though the colleague did not make a serious contribution to the paper.

60. Which of the following sampling methods is not based on probability?
(a) Simple Random Sampling
(b) Stratified Sampling
(c) Quota Sampling
(d) Cluster Sampling

ANSWERS

1. (d)	2. (d)	3. (c)	4. (b)	5. (d)
6. (c)	7. (d)	8. (c)	9. (a)	10. (c)
11. (b)	12. (c)	13. (b)	14. (b)	15. (b)
16. (a)	17. (b)	18. (b)	19. (c)	20. (d)
21. (d)	22. (b)	23. (d)	24. (b)	25. (b)
26. (b)	27. (c)	28. (d)	29. (a)	30. (c)
31. (b)	32. (b)	33. (a)	34. (c)	35. (b)
36. (d)	37. (a)	38. (b)	39. (c)	40. (c)
41. (c)	42. (a)	43. (b)	44. (d)	45. (c)
46. (a)	47. (d)	48. (c)	49. (a)	50. (d)
51. (c)	52. (c)	53. (d)	54. (d)	55. (d)
56. (b)	57. (c)	58. (c)	59. (b)	60. (c)

PAPER–II

Note: This paper contains fifty (50) objective type questions, each question carrying two (2) marks. All questions are compulsory.

1. What constitutes the mean in Aristotle's social structure?
(a) Wealthy class
(b) Poor citizen
(c) Middle class
(d) Artisan class

2. Whom did Machiavelli blame for the moral degradation of Italy?

(a) The Prince
(b) The Church
(c) The Aristocracy
(d) Corrupt People

3. For Hegel which one of the following is correct?
   (a) Family is the thesis, Bourgeois society is the anti-thesis and the State represents synthesis.
   (b) The rational is real and the real is rational.
   (c) Contradictions are not obstacles preventing us reaching truth.
   (d) All of the above.

4. Who among the following criticised Bentham's Philosophy as "Pig Philosophy"?
   (a) Leslie Stephen (b) Karl Marx
   (c) Carlyle (d) J.S. Mill

5. Which of the following is correct so far as John Rawls' writings are concerned?
   (a) A theory of Justice
   (b) Political Liberalism
   (c) The Law of Peoples
   (d) All of the above

6. Which one of the following Mao has not said?
   (a) Political power grows out of barrel of gun.
   (b) Three years of hard work: ten thousand years of happiness.
   (c) Atom bombs are real tigers.
   (d) A revolution is not a dinner party.

7. Which one among the following statements is true?
   (a) Behaviouralism is based on Stimulus-Response paradigm.
   (b) Post-behaviouralism consists of seven tenets.
   (c) Post-behaviouralism wholly negates behaviouralism.
   (d) There are no differences between behaviourism and behaviouralism.

8. Given below are two statements, one labelled as Assertion (A) and the other labelled as Reason (R):
   Assertion (A): Karl Marx termed early socialists as Utopian socialists.
   Reason (R): They attacked the capitalist system itself.
   Codes:
   (a) Both (A) and (R) are true and (R) is the right explanation of (A).
   (b) Both (A) and (R) are true but (R) is not the correct explanation of (A).
   (c) (A) is true but (R) is false.
   (d) (A) is false but (R) is true.

9. Identify the correct sequence of the Plato's four components of virtue:
   (i) Justice (ii) Courage
   (iii) Temperance (iv) Wisdom
   Select the correct answer from the codes given below:
   (a) (i), (ii), (iii), (iv)
   (b) (ii), (iii), (iv), (i)
   (c) (iv), (ii), (iii), (i)
   (d) (iii), (ii), (i), (iv)

10. Match List I with List II and select the correct answer from the codes given below the lists:
    List I
    A. Savarkar
    B. M.N. Roy
    C. Aurobindo Ghose
    D. Jayaprakash Narayan
    List II
    i. Associated with a secret society "Lotus and Daggers"
    ii. Author of the book *A Plea for Reconstruction of Indian Polity*
    iii. Convicted in the Kanpur conspiracy case
    iv. Hinduize all politics and militarize Hinduism

Codes:	**A**	**B**	**C**	**D**
(a)	iv	iii	i	ii
(b)	iii	ii	iv	i

(c)	ii	i	iii	iv
(d)	i	ii	iv	iii

11. Notion of uneven development was a response to the 19th century ideas of
    (a) Capitalism
    (b) Evolution and gradualism
    (c) Positivism
    (d) Anarchism

12. Match List I with List II and select the correct answer from the codes given below:

    List I (Dependency Theorists)
    A. Samir Amin
    B. A.G. Frank
    C. F. Henrique cardoso
    D. Paul Swezey

    List II (Books)
    i. *Dependency and Development*
    ii. *Accumulation on a World Scale*
    iii. *Capitalism and under Development in Latin America*
    iv. *Monopoly Capital*

Codes:	A	B	C	D
(a)	iv	i	iii	ii
(b)	iii	iv	ii	i
(c)	i	ii	iv	iii
(d)	ii	iii	i	iv

13. Who among the following is associated with Institutional Approach?
    (a) James Bryce
    (b) Merriam
    (c) Arthur Bentley
    (d) Lasswell

14. Who among the following challenged the idea of political development as an unilinear process?
    (a) Shils (b) Huntington
    (c) Almond (d) Halpren

15. Which of the following pairs are not correctly matched?

List I (Thinkers)	**List II (Concepts)**
i. Easton	Regulatory mechanisms
ii. Deutsch	Modernising oligarchy
iii. Shils	Structural differentiation
iv. Lucian Pye	Negative Feedback

Select the correct answer from the codes given below:
(a) ii and iii (b) i and ii
(c) i, iii and iv (d) ii, iii and iv

16. What is "Cultural Dualism"?
    (a) The existence of two religious cultures.
    (b) Newly emerging nations have two languages.
    (c) A small elite is modernized while the vast majority remains in rigid ascriptive patterns of tradition.
    (d) It is separation of the sacred from the secular.

17. Identify the correct sequence of the following input functions of Almond's Political System:
    (i) Interest aggregation
    (ii) Interest articulation
    (iii) Political socialisation and recruitment
    (iv) Political communication

    Select the correct answer from the codes given below:
    (a) (ii), (iii), (i) and (iv)
    (b) (iii), (ii), (i) and (iv)
    (c) (iii), (i), (ii) and (iv)
    (d) (i), (ii), (iii) and (iv)

18. The classical theory of administration is also known as
    (a) Locational theory
    (b) Historical theory
    (c) Mechanistic theory
    (d) Human Relations theory

19. Pareto's description of elites as 'speculators' and 'rentiers' resembles the characterisation of governing cliques of

(a) Plato (b) Aristotle
(c) Machiavelli (d) Marx

20. The difference between order and disorder is more important than the difference between communism and liberal democracy is advocated by
(a) Lipset (b) Lijphart
(c) Dahl (d) Huntington

21. Which of the following statements are not correct?
I. As per the provisions of the Constitution, the Council of Ministers is both collectively and individually responsible to the Lok Sabha.
II. A motion expressing lack of confidence in an individual minister is not admissible.
III. A no-confidence motion must set out the grounds on which it is based.
IV. If a no-confidence motion is passed by the Lok Sabha, the Council of Ministers is bound to resign.
Select the correct answer from the codes given below:
(a) I and II (b) I and III
(c) I, II and III (d) II and III

22. The Avadi Session of the Congress (1956) accepted the policy of
(a) Cooperative Farming
(b) Import Substitution
(c) Garibi Hatao
(d) Socialistic Pattern of Society

23. What was the main findings of the Union Government administrative committee headed by Home Secretary N.N. Vohra in 1993?
(a) Electoral reforms
(b) Minimum qualification for politicians
(c) Nexus between politicians, criminals and bureaucrats
(d) Internal security priorities

24. Partha Chatterjee has commented that the latest phase of the globalization of capital will witness an emerging opposition between
(a) Modernity and Democracy
(b) Feudalism and Democracy
(c) Inclusion and Democracy
(d) Elitism and Mass cultures

25. The President can make a proclamation of Financial Emergency under Art. 360
(a) for the whole of India or any part of India
(b) for the whole of India except Nagaland, Tripura, Manipur, Meghalaya, Mizoram and Arunachal Pradesh
(c) for the whole of India except Jammu and Kashmir
(d) for the whole of India except Andaman and Nicobar Islands

26. Given below are two statements, one labelled as Assertion (A) and the other labelled as Reason (R).
Assertion (A): The secular ideology of the Indian State appears to be paradox in view of the deeply religious orientation of the Indian society.
Reason (R): India's secularism was invented for integrating the multicultural plurality of the society into a common nationstate as well as for containing potentialities of the imperial 'divide and rule' and Muslim Leagues' 'two-nation' theory in British India.
Codes:
(a) Both (A) and (R) are true and (R) is the correct explanation of (A).
(b) Both (A) and (R) are true but (R) is not the correct explanation of (A).
(c) (A) is true but (R) is false.
(d) (R) is true but (A) is false.

27. Dharamsala model of Indian capitalism was propounded by

(a) Dandekar and Rath
(b) Arjun Sengupta
(c) Raj Krishna
(d) Amartya Sen

28. The 1963 Kamraj Plan was initiated by Nehru
(a) to revive Congress Party commitments
(b) to attract the youth to the party
(c) to plan and execute succession procedure in the party
(d) to plan gender parity in the party

29. Which of the following statements about the Central Vigilance Commissioner is not true?
(a) The Central Vigilance Commissioner is appointed by the President of India.
(b) The post of Central Vigilance Commissioner is a statutory post.
(c) He holds office for a term of five years.
(d) He is empowered to exercise superintendence over the functioning of CBI.

30. Which of the following statements are not true?
(i) The Election Commission of India has created a Special Election Expenditure Monitoring Division in the Commission.
(ii) The accounts of political parties are audited annually.
(iii) Paid news in connection with elections is an electoral offence.
(iv) Videography of the poll proceedings inside the polling stations is permissible.
Select the correct answer from the codes given below:
Codes:
(a) (i), (iii) and (iv) (b) (ii), (iii) and (iv)
(c) (i) and (iii) (d) (ii) and (iii)

31. **Assertion (A):** The arguments of C. Wright Mill's power elites are based on the classical elitist framework.
Reason (R): Elitist formulation is not possible without reference to classical elitism.
Codes:
(a) Both (A) and (R) are true and (R) is the correct explanation of (A).
(b) Both (A) and (R) are true but (R) is not the correct explanation of (A).
(c) (A) is true but (R) is false.
(d) (A) is false but (R) is true.

32. The theory of "Prismatic Society" is based on
(a) Historical studies of public administration in different societies.
(b) Study of public services in developed and developing countries.
(c) Institutional comparison of public administration in developed countries.
(d) Structural-functional analysis of public administration in developing countries.

33. Job loading means
(a) Deliberate upgrading of responsibility, scope and challenges.
(b) Shifting of an employee from one job to another.
(c) Making the job more interesting.
(d) All of the above.

34. Negative motivation is based on
(a) Anxiety (b) Threat
(c) Money (d) Fear

35. Simon was positively influenced by the ideas of
(a) L.D. White (b) Terry
(c) Barnard (d) Henry Fayol

36. **Assertion (A):** Classical theory of organisation is based on formal principles.
Reason (R): Classicists lacked behavioural analysis.

(a) (A) and (R) are true and (R) is the correct explanation of (A).
(b) (A) and (R) are true but (R) is not the correct explanation of (A).
(c) (A) is true but (R) is false.
(d) (R) is true but (A) is false.

37. What is the methodology proposed by Herbert Simon?
(a) Bounded Rationality
(b) Logical Positivism
(c) Decision Making
(d) Satisfying

38. Who among the following thinkers rejected the principles of administration as myths and proverbs?
(a) Herbert Simon
(b) W.F. Willoughby
(c) L.D. White
(d) Chester Bernard

39. The concept of the "zone of indifference" is associated with
(a) Power
(b) Decision Making
(c) Authority
(d) Leadership

40. Name the scholar who analysed leadership as "circular response".
(a) Taylor (b) Millet
(c) M.P. Follett (d) C.I. Barnard

41. Non-state dimension of warfare is also called
(a) Westphalian warfare
(b) Post-westphalian warfare
(c) New war
(d) Pre-westphalian warfare

42. Tehran Declaration of 1 December 1943 drew a plan for
(a) Trusteeship
(b) New-membership
(c) Peace-keeping
(d) Conflict resolution

43. Who coined the term "Functionalist theory of Integration"?
(a) David Mittarany
(b) Ernst Haas
(c) Joseph Nye
(d) Andrew Linklater

44. The CEPA (Comprehensive Economic Partnership Agreement) was officially endorsed in October 2010 between
(a) India and Japan
(b) India and China
(c) India and Russia
(d) India and South Korea

45. What is the correct sequence of Morton Kaplan's models of systems analysis?
(i) Balance of Power
(ii) Loose Bipolarity
(iii) Tight Bipolarity
(iv) Universal International System

Codes:
(a) (iv) (iii) (ii) (i) (b) (iii) (iv) (ii) (i)
(c) (iv) (ii) (iii) (i) (d) (i) (ii) (iii) (iv)

46. Who wrote the book *Stable Peace*?
(a) Johan Galtung
(b) Gunnar Myrdal
(c) Kenneth Boulding
(d) Peter Wallerstein

47. Security Council Resolution No. 1441 of Nov 2002 deals with
(a) U.N. involvement in Somalia.
(b) Enforced the no fly zone in Bosnia.
(c) Sanctioned intervention at the end of the Gulf War to protect the Kurds in Northern Iraq.
(d) Resolution on Iraq, which threatened serious consequences, if Saddam Hussain failed to reveal his weapons of mass destruction to team of U.N. Inspectors.

48. Who enunciated international society theory as a combination of three schools

of thought—Realism, Rationalism and Revolutionism?
(a) Martin Wight
(b) Kenneth Waltz
(c) Hedley Bull
(d) Raymond Aron

49. **Assertion (A):** The decisions of the Security Council are binding, and must only be passed by the majority of nine out of the 15 members, as well as each of the five permanent members.
Reason (R): These five permanent members have veto power over all Security Council decisions.
Codes:
(a) Both (A) and (R) are true and (R) is the correct explanation of (A).
(b) Both (A) and (R) are true but (R) is not the correct explanation of (A).
(c) (A) is true but (R) is false.
(d) (A) is false but (R) is true.

50. Which of the following are part of Morganthau's realist principles?
(i) Politics is rooted in a permanent and unchanging human nature.
(ii) Self-interest is a basic fact of the human condition.
(iii) Coercion is only part of foreign policy.
(iv) National interest defined in terms of power.
Codes:
(a) All are correct.
(b) (i), (ii) and (iv) are correct.
(c) (i), (iii) and (ii) are correct.
(d) (i), (iii) and (iv) are correct.

ANSWERS

1. (a)	2. (d)	3. (d)	4. (c)	5. (c)
6. (b)	7. (c)	8. (b)	9. (b)	10. (c)
11. (d)	12. (b)	13. (c)	14. (a)	15. (a)
16. (d)	17. (c)	18. (a)	19. (b)	20. (c)
21. (d)	22. (a)	23. (a)	24. (d)	25. (c)
26. (c)	27. (a)	28. (c)	29. (c)	30. (b)
31. (d)	32. (a)	33. (c)	34. (b)	35. (c)
36. (b)	37. (b)	38. (d)	39. (d)	40. (d)
41. (*)	42. (c)	43. (a)	44. (c)	45. (a)
46. (d)	47. (d)	48. (d)	49. (d)	50. (a)

PAPER–III

Note: This paper contains seventy-five (75) objective type questions of two (2) marks each. All questions are compulsory.

1. Who among the following said that political theory contains factors of three kinds—the factual, the causal and the valuational?
(a) Leo Strauss (b) Dunning
(c) G.H. Sabine (d) Ebenstein

2. Who among the following said that political theory is in the doghouse in the 1950s?
(a) Easton (b) Laslett
(c) R.A. Dahl (d) Riemer

3. Who among the following said, "We cannot shed our values in the way we remove our coats"?
(a) Peter Laslett
(b) David Easton
(c) Isiah Berlin
(d) Robert Dahl

4. Who among the following is associated with the resurgence of political theory?
(a) David Easton
(b) Alfred Cobban
(c) Vogelin
(d) Laslett

5. Which one of the following statements is false?

(a) The term 'liberal' has referred to a class of free men who are neither serfs nor slaves.
(b) The term 'liberalism' was first employed in Spain in 1812.
(c) Classical liberalism and modern liberalism have differences.
(d) The moral minuses of the anti-marketeers are the moral minuses of the pro-marketeers.

6. Whose ideas are sometimes referred as 'Manchester Liberalism'?
(a) Adam Smith and David Ricardo
(b) Richard Cobden and John Bright
(c) John Locke and J.S. Mill
(d) Berlin and McPherson

7. Who said, "My own existence is a social activity and activity and mind are social in their context as well as in their origin, they are social activity and social mind"?
(a) Robert Owen (b) Karl Marx
(c) Hegel (d) J.S. Mill

8. From whom did Hobbes borrow the principle of resolutive composite?
(a) Galileo (b) Euclid
(c) Descartes (d) Aristotle

9. Who said, "J.J. Rousseau is the Father of Jacobin despotism, of Caesarian dictatorship and the inspirer of the absolute doctrines of Kant and of Hegel"?
(a) H.J. Laski (b) Duguit
(c) Berlin (d) Karl Popper

10. Who among the following made the State a moral institution with a moral end?
(a) Bentham (b) Machiavelli
(c) James Mill (d) J.S. Mill

11. Who among the following formed "The League of Radical Congressmen"?
(a) M.K. Gandhi (b) M.N. Roy
(c) Aurobindo (d) B.R. Ambedkar

12. Which one among the following is not written by Aurobindo?
(a) *Life Divine*
(b) *Essays on the Gita*
(c) *Yoga: Concept and Practice*
(d) *The Ideals of Human Unity*

13. Identify the correct sequence of the events undertaken by Mahatma Gandhi.
(i) Organised the industrial workers in Ahmedabad for higher wages.
(ii) Protest against the Indigo planters at Champaran.
(iii) Satyagraha movement in Kaira against the collection of land revenue.
(iv) Protest against the Asiatic Registration Act.

Select the correct answer from the codes given below:

Codes:
(a) (iii), (iv), (ii), (i) (b) (iv), (ii), (iii), (i)
(c) (ii), (iii), (iv), (i) (d) (i), (ii), (iii), (iv)

14. Match the List I with List II and select the correct answer from the codes given below:

List I (Authors)
A. R.J. Bernstein B. M. Sandel
C. M. Waltzer D. W. Kymlicka

List II (Books)
i. *Spheres of Justice: A Defence of Pluralism and Equality*
ii. *The Restructuring of Social and Political Theory*
iii. *Contemporary Political Philosophy*
iv. *Liberalism and the Limits of Justice*

Codes:	**A**	**B**	**C**	**D**
(a)	i	ii	iii	iv
(b)	iii	iv	i	ii
(c)	ii	iv	i	iii
(d)	iv	i	iii	ii

15. Given below are two statements, one labelled as Assertion (A) and the other labelled as Reason (R).

Assertion (A): For Daniel Bell there is the 'end of ideology'.

Reason (R): This is to validate a single ideology and to discredit every other ideology.

Select the correct answer from the codes given below:

(a) Both (A) and (R) are true and (R) is the correct explanation of (A).
(b) Both (A) and (R) are true, but (R) is not the correct explanation of (A).
(c) (A) is true, but (R) is false.
(d) (A) is false, but (R) is true.

16. Structuration as a concept is a way of analyzing the relationship between structures and actors was suggested by
(a) Talcott Parsons
(b) Anthony Giddens
(c) Robert Nisbet
(d) Michael Focault

17. Match List I with List II and select the correct answer from the codes given below:

List I (Theories of Political Parties)
A. Development theory
B. Spatial theory
C. Re-alignment theory
D. Permeation theory

List II (Propounders)
i. Giovomin Sartori
ii. Joseph la Palombara
iii. Maurice Duverger
iv. Bunham and Sandquist

Codes:	A	B	C	D
(a)	i	ii	iii	iv
(b)	ii	i	iv	iii
(c)	iii	iv	ii	i
(d)	iv	ii	i	iii

18. According to Almond, which one is not a condition for political development?
(a) Availability of resources
(b) Adequate response to challenges
(c) Overlapping of stages of development
(d) Congruent development of the other social systems

19. Corporatism is an approach that is centrally concerned about
(a) Structures of the public sector
(b) Functions of the political system
(c) Class conflict is interest based
(d) Stresses the state and society interactions, especially the role of social interests influencing policy

20. Match List I with List II and select the correct answer from the codes given below:

List I (Thinkers)
A. Anthony Downs
B. Gabrial Almond and Sidney Verba
C. Stein Rokkan
D. Gosta Esping-Anderson

List II (Books)
i. *An Economic Theory of Democracy*
ii. *The Three Worlds of Welfare Capitalism*
iii. *The Civic Culture*
iv. *Citizens, Elections, Parties*

Codes:	A	B	C	D
(a)	i	iii	iv	ii
(b)	ii	i	iii	iv
(c)	iii	iv	ii	i
(d)	iv	ii	i	iii

21. The term "Cooperative Federalism" emerged after
(a) The First World War.
(b) At the time of New Deal Legislations in the USA.
(c) As part of the Soviet Constitution of 1937.
(d) After the Second World War.

22. Which one of the following is not a feature of the Bipolar Party System?
(a) Elements of both multi and two party systems
(b) Coalition government

(c) Alternation of power between parties
(d) Two large coalitions composed of several parties

23. In the electoral studies, rational choice models have been the most popular which is developed by
(a) Elinor Ostrom
(b) Hardin
(c) Karl Deutsch
(d) Anthony Downs

24. Conveyance theory between advanced capitalism and developed socialism was propounded by
(a) Huntington (b) Putman
(c) Miliband (d) Marcuge

25. Who among the following elite theorists said, "A man is effective in society as a whole, not so much because of his individual qualities as because of the social energies which have been deposited in him by the mass"?
(a) Pareto (b) Gasset
(c) Michels (d) Mosca

26. What is the correct chronological sequence of Edward Shils' categories of political system?
(i) Political Democracy
(ii) Tutelary Democracy
(iii) Modernizing Oligarchy
(iv) Totalitarian Oligarchy
(v) Traditional Oligarchy
Select the correct answer from the codes given below:
(a) (i), (ii), (iii), (iv) and (v)
(b) (i), (ii), (iv), (iii) and (v)
(c) (i), (ii), (iv), (v) and (iii)
(d) (ii), (i), (iii), (v) and (iv)

27. **Assertion (A):** Samir amin argued that Marx foresaw that no colonial power would be able to continue for long the local development of capitalism.
Reason (R): This was because of a dearth of knowledge of non-European societies.
Select the correct answer from the codes given below:
Codes:
(a) Both (A) and (R) are true and (R) is the correct explanation of (A).
(b) Both (A) and (R) are true, but (R) is not the correct explanation of (A).
(c) (A) is true, but (R) is false.
(d) (A) is false, but (R) is true.

28. Which of the following statements about the US President are true?
(i) The US President can seek reelection only once.
(ii) He can be impeached for treason, bribery and other crimes.
(iii) At the impeachment trials the Chief Justice of the Supreme Court presides.
(iv) Both the President and the Vice-President can be from the same state.
Select the correct answer from the codes given below:
Codes:
(a) (i), (ii) & (iii) (b) (i), (iii) & (iv)
(c) (ii), (iii) & (iv) (d) (i), (ii) & (iv)

29. The politics of sex is no longer on the fringe of politics, but it is a central concern for policy and law makers. Which category will this issue be placed under?
(a) Political Development
(b) Political Modernization
(c) Political Culture
(d) Political Elites

30. Who holds the view that bureaucracy as an organisation cannot correct its behaviour by learning from its errors?
(a) M. Crozier (b) H.J. Laski
(c) F.M. Marx (d) Max Weber

31. Who said the following:
"New light has been poured on us, teaching us the new lesson that Kings are

made for the people and not the people for the Kings."

(a) Mahatma Gandhi
(b) Raja Ram Mohan Roy
(c) Dadabhai Naoroji
(d) Bal Gangadhar Tilak

32. Who among the following had favoured Panchayati Raj System by giving the following statement in the Indian Constituent Assembly?
"...in the interest of democracy, the villages may be trained in the art of self-government.... We must be able to reform the villages and introduce democratic principles of government there...."

(a) Ananthasayanam Ayyangar
(b) Dr. B.R. Ambedkar
(c) B.N. Rao
(d) Jawaharlal Nehru

33. Which of the following is not within the jurisdiction of the State High Court?

(a) It can hear appeals from lower courts.
(b) It can issue writs for restoring Fundamental Rights.
(c) It can decide the river water dispute between the two states.
(d) It exercises superitendance and control over courts below it.

34. Match the List I with List II and select the correct answer from the codes given below:

List I (Lok Sabha)
A. 3rd Lok Sabha B. 5th Lok Sabha
C. 7th Lok Sabha D. 10th Lok Sabha

List II (Speakers)
i. Shivraj Patil
ii. Balram Jakhar
iii. G.S. Dhillon, Bali Ram Bhagat
iv. Hukam Singh

Codes:	**A**	**B**	**C**	**D**
(a)	iv	iii	ii	i
(b)	iv	i	ii	iii
(c)	i	ii	iii	iv
(d)	iii	iv	ii	i

35. Who characterized India as "A million mutinies" in 1990?

(a) V.S. Naipaul
(b) M.S.A. Rao
(c) Ghanshyam Shah
(d) Tedd Gurr

36. *Roses in December* is the autobiography of

(a) Maulana Abul Kalam Azad
(b) Khan Abdul Gaffar Khan
(c) Hakiṃ Ajmal Khan
(d) Mohammad Karim Chhagala

37. Match List I with List II and select the correct answer from the codes given below:

List I (Regional Political Parties)
A. Rashtriya Lok Dal
B. Indian National Lok Dal
C. Janta Dal (Secular)
D. Rashtriya Janta Dal

List II (States of Origin)
i. Bihar ii. Karnataka
iii. Uttar Pradesh iv. Haryana

Codes:	**A**	**B**	**C**	**D**
(a)	iii	iv	ii	i
(b)	i	ii	iii	iv
(c)	iv	iii	ii	i
(d)	iv	i	iii	ii

38. Who among the following is Editor/ Author of the book *The New Regional Politics of Development*.

(a) Reinhard Bendix
(b) Arie M.M. Kacowiez
(c) Anthony Payne
(d) Partha Chatterjee

39. Who among the following has described India as "weak-strong state"?

(a) Lloyd and Susan Rudolph
(b) Gunnar Myrdal

(c) Rajni Kothari
(d) K.C. Wheare

40. Who has called India a Democratic Developmental State?
(a) Paul Brass
(b) James Manor
(c) Christopher Jefferlot
(d) Atul Kohli

41. Match the List I with List II and select the correct answer from the codes given below:
List I (States)
A. Andhra Pradesh
B. Chhattisgarh
C. Jharkhand
D. Madhya Pradesh
List II (No. of Lok Sabha seats reserved for the Scheduled tribes)
i. 4 ii. 5
iii. 6 iv. 3

Codes:	A	B	C	D
(a)	i	ii	iii	iv
(b)	iv	i	ii	iii
(c)	iv	iii	ii	i
(d)	ii	iv	i	iii

42. Match the List I with List II and select the correct answer from the codes given below:
List I (Types)
A. Institutional pressure groups
B. Associational pressure groups
C. Non-Associational pressure groups
d. Anomic pressure groups
List II (Pressure groups)
i. Association of Indian Universities
ii. All India Schedule Caste Federation
iii. All India Federation of University Teachers Association
iv. Gopalgarh communal riots in Rajasthan

Codes:	A	B	C	D
(a)	i	ii	iii	iv
(b)	i	iii	ii	iv
(c)	iii	ii	iv	i
(d)	iv	i	ii	iii

43. Who has termed India as an example of "Polycentric Nationalism"?
(a) Partha Chatterji
(b) Anthony D. Smith
(c) Will Kymlicka
(d) Benedict Anderson

44. Who is the author of the book *India after Gandhi: The History of the World's Largest Democracy*?
(a) Ramchandran Guha
(b) Akhil Gupta
(c) Achin Vanaik
(d) Ashutosh Varshney

45. Which of the following was the first all Indian women's organization which came into force in 1926?
(a) All India Women's Conference
(b) National Council for Women in India
(c) National Federation of Indian Women in India
(d) Self-Employed Women's Association

46. Which one of the following Gullick has not covered under administrative functions of the Chief Executive?
(a) Staffing (b) Adjudicating
(c) Directing (d) Coordinating

47. Which of the following principles figure in the list of fourteen principles propounded by Henry Foyal?
(i) Subordination of individual interest to general interest.
(ii) Appointment on the basis of a contract.
(iii) Espirit de corps.
(iv) Equity.
Codes:
(a) (i), (ii) & (iii) (b) (i), (iii) & (iv)
(c) (ii), (iii) & (iv) (d) (i), (ii) & (iv)

48. Under the code developed by workers at the Western Electric Company, one who

passes unfavourable information about his colleagues to his superior is called
(a) A squealer (b) A puzzler
(c) A rate-buster (d) A chiseller

49. According to Herbert Simon, a decision is usually compounded of
(a) one fact statement and one value statement
(b) one value statement and several fact statements
(c) several value statements and one fact statement
(d) several value statements and several fact statements

50. Which one of the following principles of organisation has not been enunciated by Mooney and Reiley?
(a) Equity principle
(b) Scalar principle
(c) Staff/Line principle
(d) Functional principle

51. Which one of the following books contains the most comprehensive enunciation of the classical theory?
(a) *Introduction to the Study of Public Administration*
(b) *Public Administration*
(c) *Papers on the Science of Administration*
(d) *Policy and Administration*

52. According to Max Weber which one of the following is not a feature of bureaucracy?
(a) Separation of office from its incumbent
(b) Rigid adherence to rules
(c) Selection by Patronage
(d) Fix remuneration of officials

53. Which one of the following is not an element of decision making?
(a) It is an unconscious activity.
(b) It is not one time process.
(c) It is an environment linked activity.
(d) It needs studying and finding alternatives before taking final decisions.

54. Who among the following are called staff officials?
(a) Field workers.
(b) Advisory staff.
(c) Those who help the chief executive in the performance of his primary functions.
(d) Those who help the chief executive in the implementation of his functions.

55. Which of the following concepts of administration is action oriented rather than structure oriented?
(a) Democratic Administration
(b) Autocratic Administration
(c) Development Administration
(d) All of the above

56. Point out from the following the uncommon factor between public and private administrations
(a) Accounting
(b) Filling
(c) Managerial techniques
(d) Scope and complexity

57. The Fiscal Five Year Plan was started in India after independence in the year
(a) 1950 – 1951 (b) 1951 – 1952
(c) 1952 – 1953 (d) 1953 – 1954

58. **Assertion (A):** The District Collector is the most important functionary at the apex of the district administration.
Reason (R): After independence, his role has become increasingly multi-dimensional.
Codes:
(a) Both (A) and (R) are true and (R) is the correct explanation of (A).
(b) Both (A) and (R) are true, but (R) is not the correct explanation of (A).

(c) (A) is true, but (R) is false.
(d) (R) is true, but (A) is false.

59. Match List I with List II and select the correct answer from the codes given below:

List I (Authors)
A. Chester Barnard
B. Herbert Simon
C. Dwight Waldo (ed.)
D. Marshall Dimock

List II (Books)
i. *Philosophy of Administration*
ii. *Ideas and Issues in Public Administration*
iii. *Administrative Behaviour*
iv. *The Functions of the Executive*

Codes:	**A**	**B**	**C**	**D**
(a)	iii	iv	ii	i
(b)	iv	iii	ii	i
(c)	i	iv	ii	iii
(d)	ii	i	iii	iv

60. Performance Budgeting became popular in the
(a) 1950s (b) 1960s
(c) 1970s (d) 1980s

61. Who builts on Kenneth Waltz's argument concerning the stability of bipolar system as compared to multipolar system?
(a) Stanley Hoffmann
(b) Charles Kindelberger
(c) John Mearshemier
(d) John Gaddis

62. Democratic Peace Theory is placed under which theoretical approach of international relations?
(a) Structural Realism
(b) Republican Realism
(c) Neo-Realism
(d) Institutional Liberalism

63. Which of the following statements are not true?
(i) Security dilemma is an important paradox of the state system.
(ii) Arms race increases insecurity of states.
(iii) Arms control is a solution.
(iv) Standing armies contribute to security of all.

Codes:
(a) (i), (ii) & (iv) (b) (i) & (iii)
(c) (iii) & (iv) (d) (i) & (iv)

64. The "Clash of Civilizations and New World Order" predict an ideological shift in the post-Cold War period from
(a) Political ideology to economic liberalism.
(b) Geopolitics to geo-economics.
(c) Nation-state to the civilization area.
(d) Political ideology to culture and religion.

65. **Assertion (A):** Modern technology enhances the importance of war and threats of war.
Reason (R): War no longer is just a contest of strength. It is more a contest of nerve and risk taking.

Codes:
(a) Both (A) and (R) are true and (R) is the correct explanation of (A).
(b) Both (A) and (R) are true, but (R) is not the correct explanation of (A).
(c) (A) is true, but (R) is false.
(d) (A) is false, but (R) is true.

66. What is a "Quasi-State"?
(a) A State that possess juridical statehood but severely deficient in empirical statehood.
(b) A State that possesses empirical statehood.
(c) A State that possesses neither juridical statehood nor empirical statehood.
(d) A State that has divided loyalties.

67. With which approach would one associate the following statement?
Economic globalization is an uneven, hierarchical process and benefits only a tiny minority?
(a) Economic Liberalism
(b) Economic Realists
(c) Mercantilism
(d) Neo-Marxism

68. Match the List I with List II and select the correct answer from the codes given below:
List I (Foreign Policy think tank)
A. Foreign Policy Institute
B. Institute for Defense & Strategic Analysis
C. Carnegie Endowment
D. International Institute for strategic studies
List II (Country)
i. USA ii. UK
iii. Turkey iv. India

Codes:	A	B	C	D
(a)	i	ii	iii	iv
(b)	ii	iii	iv	i
(c)	iii	iv	i	ii
(d)	iv	ii	iii	i

69. Match List I with List II and select the correct answer from the codes given below:

List I (Terrorist Organisations)	List II (Countries)
A. LTTE	i. Peru
B. Hizbullah	ii. Nigeria
C. Bako Haram	iii. Iran
D. Shining Path	iv. Sri Lanka

Codes:	A	B	C	D
(a)	i	ii	iii	iv
(b)	iv	iii	ii	i
(c)	ii	i	iv	iii
(d)	iii	iv	i	ii

70. The Panel on United Nations Peace Operations was set up by the earlier Secretary General Kofi Annan. Name the report
(a) Hammarskjold Report
(b) Rajeshwar Dayal Report
(c) Brahimi Report
(d) Kofi Annan Report

71. Indian troops, military observers and civilian police personnel served in U.N.O. peace keeping operation in
(a) Western Sahara (b) Bosnia
(c) Herzegovina (d) All of the above

72. Match the List I with List II and select answer from code given below:

List I (Countries)	List II (Problems)
A. Sri Lanka	i. Kachativu
B. Pakistan	ii. Wular Barrage
C. Nepal	iii. Susta Border
D. Bangladesh	iv. New Moore Island

Codes:	A	B	C	D
(a)	i	ii	iii	iv
(b)	iv	iii	ii	i
(c)	iii	iv	i	ii
(d)	ii	iii	iv	i

73. Which one of the following is not an Indo-Pak dispute?
(a) Siachin dispute
(b) Sir Creek dispute
(c) Cross Border terrorism
(d) Dahagram dispute

74. Match List I with List II and select the correct answer from the codes given below:

List I (States)	List II (Minorities)
A. Myanmar	i. Hindus
B. Malaysia	ii. Rohingas
C. Indonesia	iii. Tamils
D. Laos	iv. Vietnamese

Codes:	A	B	C	D
(a)	iv	iii	ii	i
(b)	iii	ii	i	iv
(c)	ii	iii	i	iv
(d)	i	ii	iii	iv

75. Recently there were tensions between Cambodia and Thailand. What is the issue in conflict?
    (a) Illegal migrations
    (b) Prachvihar
    (c) Emerald Buddha
    (d) Minorities

ANSWERS

1. (d)	2. (d)	3. (d)	4. (b)	5. (a)
6. (b)	7. (d)	8. (c)	9. (d)	10. (d)
11. (b)	12. (b)	13. (c)	14. (b)	15. (a)
16. (d)	17. (a)	18. (d)	19. (b)	20. (c)
21. (c)	22. (b)	23. (a)	24. (d)	25. (a)
26. (c)	27. (b)	28. (a)	29. (d)	30. (a)
31. (b)	32. (b)	33. (b)	34. (a)	35. (a)
36. (d)	37. (d)	38. (c)	39. (b)	40. (b)
41. (c)	42. (a)	43. (c)	44. (d)	45. (d)
46. (c)	47. (d)	48. (a)	49. (b)	50. (a)
51. (a)	52. (b)	53. (b)	54. (a)	55. (c)
56. (d)	57. (b)	58. (b)	59. (b)	60. (d)
61. (d)	62. (b)	63. (a)	64. (d)	65. (b)
66. (c)	67. (a)	68. (c)	69. (d)	70. (d)
71. (d)	72. (b)	73. (c)	74. (b)	75. (a)

DECEMBER–2012

Note: This paper contains Sixty (60) multiple-choice questions, each question carrying two (2) marks. Candidate is expected to answer any Fifty (50) questions. In case more than Fifty (50) questions are attempted, only the first Fifty (50) questions will be evaluated.

PAPER–I

1. The English word 'Communication' is derived from the words
   (a) Communis and Communicare
   (b) Communist and Commune
   (c) Communism and Communalism
   (d) Communion and Common sense

2. Chinese Cultural Revolution leader Mao Zedong used a type of communication to talk to the masses is known as
   (a) Mass line communication
   (b) Group communication
   (c) Participatory communication
   (d) Dialogue communication

3. Conversing with the spirits and ancestors is termed as
   (a) Transpersonal communication
   (b) Intrapersonal communication
   (c) Interpersonal communication
   (d) Face-to-face communication

4. The largest circulated daily newspaper among the following is
   (a) *The Times of India*
   (b) *The Indian Express*
   (c) *The Hindu*
   (d) *The Deccan Herald*

5. The pioneer of the silent feature film in India was
   (a) K.A. Abbas
   (b) Satyajit Ray
   (c) B.R. Chopra
   (d) Dada Sahib Phalke

6. Classroom communication of a teacher rests on the principle of
   (a) Infotainment (b) Edutainment
   (c) Entertainment (d) Power equation

7. The missing number in the series:
   0, 6, 24, 60, 120, ?, 336, is
   (a) 240 (b) 220
   (c) 280 (d) 210

8. A group of 7 members having a majority of boys is to be formed out of 6 boys and 4 girls. The number of ways the group can be formed is
   (a) 80 (b) 100
   (c) 90 (d) 110

9. The number of observations in a group is 40. The average of the first 10 members is 4.5 and the average of the remaining 30 members is 3.5. The average of the whole group is
   (a) 4 (b) 15/2
   (c) 15/4 (d) 6

10. If MOHAN is represented by the code KMFYL, then COUNT will be represented by
    (a) AMSLR (b) MSLAR
    (c) MASRL (d) SAMLR

11. The sum of the ages of two persons A and B is 50. 5 years ago, the ratio of their

ages was 5/3. The present age of A and B are

(a) 30, 20 (b) 35, 15
(c) 38, 12 (d) 40, 10

12. Let *a* means minus (–), *b* means multiplied by (×), C means divided by (÷) and D means plus (+). The value of 90 D 9 *a* 29 C 10 *b* 2 is

(a) 8 (b) 10
(c) 12 (d) 14

13. Consider the Assertion I and Assertion II and select the right code given below:

Assertion I : Even Bank-lockers are not safe. Thieves can break them and take away your wealth. But thieves cannot go to heaven. So you should keep your wealth in heaven.

Assertion II: The difference of skin-colour of beings is because of the distance from the sun and not because of some permanent traits. Skin-colour is the result of body's reaction to the sun and its rays.

Codes:

(a) Both the assertions I and II are forms of argument.
(b) The assertion I is an argument but the assertion II is not.
(c) The assertion II is an argument but the assertion I is not.
(d) Both the assertions are explanations of facts.

14. By which of the following proposition, the proposition 'some men are not honest' is contradicted?

(a) All men are honest.
(b) Some men are honest.
(c) No men are honest.
(d) All of the above.

15. A stipulative definition is

(a) always true
(b) always false
(c) sometimes true sometimes false
(d) neither true nor false

16. Choose the appropriate alternative given in the codes to replace the question mark.

Examiner – Examinee, Pleader – Client, Preceptor – ?

(a) Customer (b) Path-finder
(c) Perceiver (d) Disciple

17. If the statement 'most of the students are obedient' is taken to be true, which one of the following pair of statements can be claimed to be true?

I. All obedient persons are students.
II. All students are obedient.
III. Some students are obedient.
IV. Some students are not disobedient.

Codes:

(a) I & II (b) II & III
(c) III & IV (d) II & IV

18. Choose the right code:

A deductive argument claims that:

I. The conclusion does not claim something more than that which is contained in the premises.
II. The conclusion is supported by the premise/premises conclusively.
III. If the conclusion is false, then premise/premises may be either true or false.
IV. If premise/combination of premises is true, then conclusion must be true.

Codes:

(a) I and II (b) I and III
(c) II and III (d) All the above

On the basis of the data given in the following table, give answers to questions from 19 to 24:

Government Expenditures on Social Services
(As percent of total expenditure)

Sl.No.	Items	2007-08	2008-09	2009-10	2010-11
	Social Services	11.06	12.94	13.06	14.02
(a)	Education, sports & youth affairs	4.02	4.04	3.96	4.46
(b)	Health & family welfare	2.05	1.91	1.90	2.03
(c)	Water supply, housing, etc.	2.02	2.31	2.20	2.27
(d)	Information & broadcasting	0.22	0.22	0.20	0.22
(e)	Welfare to SC/ST & OBC	0.36	0.35	0.41	0.63
(f)	Labour and employment	0.27	0.27	0.22	0.25
(g)	Social welfare & nutrition	0.82	0.72	0.79	1.06
(h)	North-eastern areas	0.00	1.56	1.50	1.75
(i)	Other social services	1.29	1.55	1.87	1.34
	Total Government expenditure	100.00	100.00	100.00	100.00

19. How many activities in the social services are there where the expenditure has been less than 5 percent of the total expenditures incurred on the social services in 2008-09 ?
(a) One (b) Three
(c) Five (d) All the above

20. In which year, the expenditures on the social services have increased at the highest rate?
(a) 2007-08 (b) 2008-09
(c) 2009-10 (d) 2010-11

21. Which of the following activities remains almost stagnant in terms of share of expenditures?
(a) North-eastern areas
(b) Welfare to SC/ST & OBC
(c) Information & broadcasting
(d) Social welfare and nutrition

22. Which of the following item's expenditure share is almost equal to the remaining three items in the given years?
(a) Information & broadcasting
(b) Welfare to SC/ST and OBC
(c) Labour and employment
(d) Social welfare & nutrition

23. Which of the following items of social services has registered the highest rate of increase in expenditures during 2007-08 to 2010-11?
(a) Education, sports & youth affairs
(b) Welfare to SC/ST & OBC
(c) Social welfare & nutrition
(d) Overall social services

24. Which of the following items has registered the highest rate of decline in terms of expenditure during 2007-08 to 2009-10?
(a) Labour and employment
(b) Health & family welfare
(c) Social welfare & nutrition
(d) Education, sports & youth affairs

25. ALU stands for
(a) American Logic Unit
(b) Alternate Local Unit
(c) Alternating Logic Unit
(d) Arithmetic Logic Unit

26. A Personal Computer uses a number of chips mounted on a circuit board called
(a) Microprocessor (b) System Board
(c) Daughter Board (d) Mother Board

27. Computer Virus is a
(a) Hardware (b) Bacteria
(c) Software (d) None of these

28. Which one of the following is correct?

(a) $(17)_{10} = (17)_{16}$
(b) $(17)_{10} = (17)_{8}$
(c) $(17)_{10} = (10111)_{2}$
(d) $(17)_{10} = (10001)_{2}$

29. The file extension of MS-Word document in Office 2007 is ______.
(a) .pdf (b) .doc
(c) .docx (d) .txt

30. ______ is a protocol used by e-mail clients to download e-mails to your computer.
(a) TCP (b) FTP
(c) SMTP (d) POP

31. Which of the following is a source of methane?
(a) Wetlands
(b) Foam Industry
(c) Thermal Power Plants
(d) Cement Industry

32. 'Minamata disaster' in Japan was caused by pollution due to
(a) Lead (b) Mercury
(c) Cadmium (d) Zinc

33. Biomagnification means increase in the
(a) concentration of pollutants in living organisms
(b) number of species
(c) size of living organisms
(d) biomass

34. Nagoya Protocol is related to
(a) Climate change
(b) Ozone depletion
(c) Hazardous waste
(d) Biodiversity

35. The second most important source after fossil fuels contributing to India's energy needs is
(a) Solar energy (b) Nuclear energy
(c) Hydropower (d) Wind energy

36. In case of earthquakes, an increase of magnitude 1 on Richter Scale implies
(a) a ten-fold increase in the amplitude of seismic waves.
(b) a ten-fold increase in the energy of the seismic waves.
(c) two-fold increase in the amplitude of seismic waves.
(d) two-fold increase in the energy of seismic waves.

37. Which of the following is not a measure of Human Development Index?
(a) Literacy Rate
(b) Gross Enrolment
(c) Sex Ratio
(d) Life Expectancy

38. India has the highest number of students in colleges after
(a) the U.K. (b) the U.S.A.
(c) Australia (d) Canada

39. Which of the following statement(s) is/are not correct about the Attorney General of India?
1. The President appoints a person, who is qualified to be a Judge of a High Court, to be the Attorney General of India.
2. He has the right of audience in all the Courts of the country.
3. He has the right to take part in the proceedings of the Lok Sabha and the Rajya Sabha.
4. He has a fixed tenure.
Select the correct answer from the codes given below:

Codes:
(a) 1 and 4 (b) 2, 3 and 4
(c) 3 and 4 (d) 3 only

40. Which of the following prefix President Pranab Mukherjee desires to be discontinued while interacting with Indian dignitaries as well as in official notings?
1. His Excellency 2. Mahamahim
3. Hon'ble 4. Shri/Smt.

Select the correct answer from the codes given below:

Codes:

(a) 1 and 3 (b) 2 and 3
(c) 1 and 2 (d) 1, 2 and 3

41. Which of the following can be done under conditions of financial emergency?
   1. State Legislative Assemblies can be abolished.
   2. Central Government can acquire control over the budget and expenditure of States.
   3. Salaries of the Judges of the High Courts and the Supreme Court can be reduced.
   4. Right to Constitutional Remedies can be suspended.

   Select the correct answer from the codes given below:

   Codes:

   (a) 1, 2 and 3 (b) 2, 3 and 4
   (c) 1 and 2 (d) 2 and 3

42. Match List I with List II and select the correct answer from the codes given below:

   List I
   (a) Poverty Reduction Programme
   (b) Human Development Scheme
   (c) Social Assistance Scheme
   (d) Minimum Need Scheme

   List II
   (i) Mid-day Meals
   (ii) Indira Awas Yojana (IAY)
   (iii) National Old Age Pension (NOAP)
   (iv) MNREGA

Codes:	A	B	C	D
(a)	(iv)	(i)	(iii)	(ii)
(b)	(ii)	(iii)	(iv)	(i)
(c)	(iii)	(iv)	(i)	(ii)
(d)	(iv)	(iii)	(ii)	(i)

43. For an efficient and durable learning, learner should have
   (a) ability to learn only
   (b) requisite level of motivation only
   (c) opportunities to learn only
   (d) desired level of ability and motivation

44. Classroom communication must be
   (a) Teacher centric
   (b) Student centric
   (c) General centric
   (d) Textbook centric

45. The best method of teaching is to
   (a) impart information
   (b) ask students to read books
   (c) suggest good reference material
   (d) initiate a discussion and participate in it

46. Interaction inside the classroom should generate
   (a) Argument (b) Information
   (c) Ideas (d) Controversy

47. "Spare the rod and spoil the child", gives the message that
   (a) punishment in the class should be banned.
   (b) corporal punishment is not acceptable.
   (c) undesirable behaviour must be punished.
   (d) children should be beaten with rods.

48. The type of communication that the teacher has in the classroom, is termed as
   (a) Interpersonal
   (b) Mass communication
   (c) Group communication
   (d) Face-to-face communication

49. Which one of the following is an indication of the quality of a research journal?
   (a) Impact factor (b) h-index
   (c) g-index (d) i10-index

50. Good 'research ethics' means
   (a) Not disclosing the holdings of shares/stocks in a company that sponsors your research.

(b) Assigning a particular research probiem to one Ph.D./research student only.
(c) Discussing with your colleagues confidential data from a research paper that you are reviewing for an academic journal.
(d) Submitting the same research manuscript for publishing in more than one journal.

51. Which of the following sampling methods is based on probability?
(a) Convenience sampling
(b) Quota sampling
(c) Judgement sampling
(d) Stratified sampling

52. Which one of the following references is written according to American Psychological Association (APA) format?
(a) Sharma, V. (2010). Fundamentals of Computer Science.
New Delhi: Tata McGraw Hill
(b) Sharma, V. 2010. Fundamentals of Computer Science.
New Delhi: Tata McGraw Hill
(c) Sharma. V. 2010. Fundamentals of Computer Science,
New Delhi: Tata McGraw Hill
(d) Sharma, V. (2010), Fundamentals of Computer Science,
New Delhi: Tata McGraw Hill

53. Arrange the following steps of research in correct sequence:
1. Identification of research problem
2. Listing of research objectives
3. Collection of data
4. Methodology
5. Data analysis
6. Results and discussion
(a) 1, 2, 3, 4, 5, 6 (b) 1, 2, 4, 3, 5, 6
(c) 2, 1, 3, 4, 5, 6 (d) 2, 1, 4, 3, 5, 6

54. Identify the incorrect statement:
(a) A hypothesis is made on the basis of limited evidence as a starting point for further investigations.
(b) A hypothesis is a basis for reasoning without any assumption of its truth.
(c) Hypothesis is a proposed explanation for a phenomenon.
(d) Scientific hypothesis is a scientific theory.

Read the following passage carefully and answer the questions (55 to 60):

The popular view of towns and cities in developing countries and of urbanization process is that despite the benefits and comforts it brings, the emergence of such cities connotes environmental degradation, generation of slums and squatters, urban poverty, unemployment, crimes, lawlessness, traffic chaos etc. But what is the reality? Given the unprecedental increase in urban population over the last 50 years from 300 million in 1950 to 2 billion in 2000 in developing countries, the wonder really is how well the world has coped, and not how badly.

In general, the urban quality of life has improved in terms of availability of water and sanitation, power, health and education, communication and transport. By way of illustration, a large number of urban residents have been provided with improved water in urban areas in Asia's largest countries such as China, India, Indonesia and Philippines. Despite that, the access to improved water in terms of percentage of total urban population seems to have declined during the last decade of 20th century, though in absolute numbers, millions of additional urbanites, have been provided improved services. These countries have made significant progress in the provision of sanitation services too, together, providing for an additional population of more than 293 million citizens within a decade (1990-2000). These improvements must be viewed against the backdrop of rapidly increasing urban population, fiscal crunch and strained human resources and efficient and quality-oriented public management.

55. The popular view about the process of urbanization in developing countries is
    (a) Positive (b) Negative
    (c) Neutral (d) Unspecified
56. The average annual increase in the number of urbanites in developing countries, from 1950 to 2000 A.D. was close to
    (a) 30 million (b) 40 million
    (c) 50 million (d) 60 million
57. The reality of urbanization is reflected in
    (a) How well the situation has been managed.
    (b) How badly the situation has gone out of control.
    (c) How fast has been the tempo of urbanization.
    (d) How fast the environment has degraded.
58. Which one of the following is not considered as an indicator of urban quality of life?
    (a) Tempo of urbanization
    (b) Provision of basic services
    (c) Access to social amenities
    (d) All of the above
59. The author in this passage has tried to focus on
    (a) Extension of Knowledge
    (b) Generation of Environmental Consciousness
    (c) Analytical Reasoning
    (d) Descriptive Statement
60. In the above passage, the author intends to state
    (a) The hazards of the urban life
    (b) The sufferings of the urban life
    (c) The awareness of human progress
    (d) The limits to growth

ANSWERS

1. (a)	2. (d)	3. (a)	4. (a)	5. (d)
6. (b)	7. (d)	8. (b)	9. (c)	10. (a)
11. (a)	12. (d)	13. (a)	14. (a)	15. (d)
16. (c)	17. (c)	18. (d)	19. (d)	20. (d)
21. (c)	22. (d)	23. (b)	24. (b)	25. (d)
26. (d)	27. (c)	28. (d)	29. (b)	30. (d)
31. (a)	32. (b)	33. (a)	34. (d)	35. (c)
36. (a)	37. (c)	38. (b)	39. (d)	40. (c)
41. (c)	42. (a)	43. (d)	44. (b)	45. (d)
46. (c)	47. (c)	48. (c)	49. (a)	50. (a)
51. (d)	52. (a)	53. (b)	54. (d)	55. (b)
56. (a)	57. (a)	58. (a)	59. (d)	60. (d)

PAPER–II

Note: This paper contains fifty (50) objective type questions, each question carrying two (2) marks. All questions are compulsory.

1. In Hegel's notion the highest possible achievement of Mind as expressed in social life was in
   (a) The Contemporary Prussian State
   (b) Rome
   (c) Athens
   (d) Contemporary Great Britain
2. Machiavelli advised the Prince to pursue
   (a) Moderate behaviour
   (b) Extreme generosity
   (c) Perfect strictness
   (d) Great kindness

3. Which is not a part of Rawls' well ordered society?
   (a) Stable (b) Efficient
   (c) Just (d) Equal

4. Who among the following wrote, "Laws are the rules of just and unjust; nothing being reputed unjust that is not contrary to some law"?
   (a) Bentham (b) Hegel
   (c) Hobbes (d) Rousseau

5. Arrange the following works of Rousseau chronologically, using the codes given below:
   (a) The Social Contract
   (b) A Discourse on the Arts and Sciences
   (c) Emile
   (d) A Discourse on the Origin of Inequality

   Codes:
   (a) d, c, b, a (b) a, c, d, b
   (c) c, a, b, d (d) b, d, c, a

6. Match List I with List II and select the correct answer from the codes given below:

   List I
   A. On Liberty
   B. Lectures on the Principles of Political Obligation
   C. Idea of Justice
   D. Anarchy, State and Utopia

   List II
   1. Amartya Sen
   2. T.H. Green
   3. Robert Nozick
   4. J.S. Mill

Codes:	**A**	**B**	**C**	**D**
(a)	3	1	2	4
(b)	1	3	2	4
(c)	2	4	3	1
(d)	4	2	1	3

7. Match List I with List II and select the correct answer from the codes given below:

   List I
   A. Justice as one person, one duty, one class one work
   B. Justice as fairness
   C. Justice as proportionate equality
   D. Justice as the interest of the strong

   List II
   1. Plato 2. Aristotle
   3. Rawls 4. Thrasymachas

Codes:	**A**	**B**	**C**	**D**
(a)	1	2	3	4
(b)	2	1	3	4
(c)	2	1	4	3
(d)	1	3	2	4

8. Match List I with List II and select the correct answer from the codes given below:

   List I
   A. Perpetual peace
   B. Golden Mean
   C. Analogy of the cave
   D. Fortune as a woman

   List II
   1. Plato 2. Kant
   3. Aristotle 4. Machiavelli

Codes:	**A**	**B**	**C**	**D**
(a)	1	2	3	4
(b)	2	3	1	4
(c)	2	1	4	3
(d)	4	3	2	1

Directions: Given below are two statements, one labelled as Assertion (A) and the other labelled as Reason (R). Select the correct answer from the codes given below:

9. **Assertion (A):** Marx was a revolutionary.
   Reason (R): Marx was not concerned about the processes of history.

   Codes:
   (a) Both (A) and (R) are true and (R) is the correct explanation of (A).
   (b) Both (A) and (R) are true, but (R) is not the correct explanation of (A).

(c) (A) is true, but (R) is false.
(d) (A) is false, but (R) is true.

10. **Assertion (A):** Aristotle is justifiably called the Father of Political Science.
Reason (R): His criticism of Plato's idealism justifies this claim.
Codes:
(a) Both (A) and (R) are true, and (R) is the correct explanation of (A).
(b) Both (A) and (R) are true, but (R) is not the correct explanation of (A).
(c) (A) is true, but (R) is false.
(d) (A) is false, but (R) is true.

11. The operational part of the general systems theory in social sciences has been developed first in
(a) Psychology (b) Sociology
(c) Political Science (d) Anthropology

12. Who said, "Functionalism can indeed be interpreted as a conscious alternative to Marxism"?
(a) W.G. Runciman
(b) Robert K. Merton
(c) Oran Young
(d) David Easton

13. Who among the following stated that a developing society in order to reach the goals of development would have to pass through the stages of political unification, industrialization, national welfare and abundance?
(a) Rustow (b) Organski
(c) Lucian Pye (d) David Apter

14. Which one of the following pairs is not correctly matched?
(a) Lucian Pye: Modernisation Theory
(b) Wallerstein: World System Theory
(c) Theda Skocpol: New Institutionalism
(d) Karl Deutsch: Communications Theory

15. Which one of the following pairs is not correctly matched?
(a) Pareto: The concept of residues
(b) Michels: The concept of mass mind
(c) Mills: The concept of political formula
(d) Gasset: The theory of the masses

16. The concept of civic culture developed out of a survey of
(a) Mexico, India, Pakistan, U.S.A. and U.K.
(b) U.S.A., U.K., Mexico, Germany and Italy.
(c) U.S.A., U.K., Australia, Pakistan and India.
(d) Australia, Canada, U.S.A., U.K. and France.

17. Unequal exchange is the formulation of
(a) Samir Amin
(b) Amartya Sen
(c) Paul Sweezy
(d) Andre Gunder Frank

18. Duverger's classification of the party system is derived from the experience of political parties in
(a) Western Europe
(b) All the democracies of the world
(c) Party system in the developing world
(d) Political party system in the communist world

19. Which of the following statements are correct about the President of America?
1. He is the head of the State and also the head of the Government.
2. All executive powers are vested in him.
3. He is bound by the advice of his Cabinet.
4. He has the power to dissolve the legislature.

Codes:
(a) 1 and 3 are correct.
(b) 2, 3 and 4 are correct.
(c) 1, 3 and 4 are correct.
(d) 1 and 2 are correct.

20. Which one of the following is not a feature of F.M. Marx's guardian bureaucracy?
(a) Custodian of Public interest
(b) Competent
(c) Authoritarian
(d) Corrupt

21. Which of the following Committee was appointed by the Government of India to identify the creamy layer among Backward Classes in India?
(a) Justice R.N. Mishra Committee
(b) Justice R.N. Madholkar Committee
(c) Justice Ram Nandan Committee
(d) Justice Rajender Sachar Committee

22. Who described Indian Politics as "Politics of Scarcity"?
(a) Myron Weiner (b) Paul R. Brass
(c) Atul Kohli (d) Morris-Jones

23. Which Congress President during British Raj initiated the idea of a Planning Commission?
(a) Jawaharlal Nehru
(b) Mahatma Gandhi
(c) Maulana Azad
(d) Subhas Chandra Bose

24. Which of the following statements are correct about Indian Government?
(i) Rajya Sabha represents the local interests of the States.
(ii) A member of Rajya Sabha must be a resident of the State from which he is elected.
(iii) Number of seats allotted to a State has to be proportionate to its population.
(iv) The term of a member of Rajya Sabha is same as that of Senator in the US.

Codes:
(a) (ii), (iii) and (iv) (b) (i), (ii) and (iii)
(c) (i), (iii) and (iv) (d) (i) and (ii)

25. Who of the following was the first Satyagrahi of the Individual Civil Disobedience Movement started by Gandhiji in October 1940?
(a) Dr. Rajendra Prasad
(b) J.B. Kripalani
(c) Sardar Vallabhbhai Patel
(d) Acharya Vinoba Bhave

26. Who prefers to characterize the Indian federalism as "bargaining federalism"?
(a) A.K. Chanda
(b) Morris Jones
(c) K.C.Wheare
(d) D.D. Basu

27. Who was the Chairman of Mandal Commission?
(a) B.N. Mandal
(b) B.P. Mandal
(c) D.L. Mandal
(d) R.N. Mandal

28. When was the Inter-State Council set up in India?
(a) 1987 (b) 1989
(c) 1990 (d) 1992

29. When were the Lok Sabha rules amended to provide for Department Related Parliamentary Standing Committees?
(a) 1988 (b) 1989
(c) 1991 (d) 1995

30. Which one of the following Acts/Reports created the Federal Court in India?
(a) Government of India Act, 1909
(b) Government of India Act, 1919
(c) Montague-Chelmsford Report
(d) Government of India Act, 1935

31. The book *Introduction to Public Administration* was authored by
(a) W.F. Willoughby
(b) Woodrow Wilson
(c) M.P. Follet
(d) Leonard D. White

32. The concept of 'Informal Organisation' was profounded by
(a) F.W. Taylor
(b) Herbert Simon
(c) Elton Mayo
(d) F.M. Marx

33. 'Clect' is the sub-system of Riggs' Prismatic society
(a) Social system
(b) Administrative system
(c) Economic system
(d) Political system

34. 'Jacksonian Theory' is also called
(a) Merit system
(b) Outsource theory
(c) Spoils system
(d) Contract system

35. Which of the four major issues of Public Administration were debated in the Minnowbrooke Conference, 1968?
(a) Relevance, values, equity and change.
(b) History, qualities, values and development.
(c) Text, context, relevance and status.
(d) Norms, values, context and progress.

36. Who said, "Successful Management involves Management by Objectives"?
(a) F.W. Taylor
(b) Peter F. Drucker
(c) Kothari Committee
(d) Edwin B. Flippo

37. In which book of the following, Robert Dahl explained the Theory of Decision Making?
(a) *Democracy, Liberty and Equality*
(b) *Democracy at Cross Roads*
(c) *Who Governs?*
(d) *Modern Political Analysis*

38. Which Committee recommended "Unified Grading Structure" for the British Civil Service?
(a) Masterman (b) Fulton
(c) Asheton (d) McGraw

39. Given below are two statements, one labelled as Assertion (A) and the other labelled as Reason (R). Find the correct answer using the codes given below:
Assertion (A): Adequate measures must be taken by the Government to ensure the stoppage of the practice of corruption.
Reason (R): Corruption leads to decline of democratic process.
Codes:
(a) Both (A) and (R) are true, but (R) is not correct explanation of (A).
(b) (A) is true, but (R) is false.
(c) Both (A) and (R) are true and (R) is correct explanation of (A).
(d) (A) is false, but (R) is true.

40. Match the following:
The Office of Ombudsman was set up in these countries in the following years:

(Countries)	**(Years)**
A. Sweden	1. 1967
B. Finland	2. 1809
C. New Zealand	3. 1978
D. United Kingdom	4. 1919
	5. 1962

Select the correct answer:

Codes:	**A**	**B**	**C**	**D**
(a)	2	4	5	1
(b)	1	5	3	4
(c)	3	2	1	5
(d)	4	3	5	1

41. In the post-Soviet era Russia's outlook at global level is marked by
(a) Rigid Ideological positions.
(b) Enhanced role for Soviet era legacies.
(c) Pragmatic de-ideologised worldview.
(d) Rigidities of cold war era.

42. Who of the following has coined the term under-development?

(a) Antonio Gramsci
(b) Rosa Luxemburg
(c) Emmanual Wallerstein
(d) Kenneth Waltz

43. The policy of containment formulated by the U.S. aimed at
(a) Checking globally the influence of the Soviet Union.
(b) Checking the nuclear proliferation of Iran.
(c) Containing defiant North Korea.
(d) Countering the expansionist policies of People's Republic of China.

44. The Kyoto Protocol of 1997 adopted the programme for
(a) ending global poverty
(b) the democratisation of U.N. system
(c) broadening the participation within I.M.F. and World Bank.
(d) reducing greenhouse emissions.

45. Match List I with List II and select correct answer from the codes given below:

List I
A. Morton Kaplan
B. Andre Gunder Frank
C. Hans J. Morgenthau
D. Mikhail Gorbachev

List II
1. Perestroika and Glasnost
2. Theory of Realism
3. Systems Theory
4. Dependency Theory

Codes:	A	B	C	D
(a)	3	4	2	1
(b)	4	2	3	1
(c)	2	4	1	3
(d)	2	1	3	4

46. The principle of reciprocity within WTO framework envisages
(a) lowering of trade barriers by a State to be matched in return.
(b) creation of trade barriers on uniform basis.
(c) protection of intellectual property rights.
(d) enhanced role for State controls on trade.

47. What is the correct chronological order of the events listed below?
i. U.S. Policy of Containment of the Soviet Union.
ii. Dissolution of the former Soviet Union.
iii. Iran-Iraq War.
iv. US War on terrorism in Afghanistan.

Choose the right answer from the codes given below:

Codes:
(a) iv, ii, iii, i
(b) ii, iv, i, iii
(c) iii, ii, iv, i
(d) i, iii, ii, iv

48. The dictum, 'Imperialism is the highest stage of Capitalism' was propounded by
(a) Karl Marx
(b) V.I. Lenin
(c) Andre Gunder Frank
(d) Emmanual Wallerstein

49. Hans Blix was head of U.N. body for
(a) Peace-keeping operations in Somalia.
(b) Inspecting places in Iraq for verification of Weapons of Mass Destruction.
(c) Working modalities for the creation of NIEO.
(d) Rebuilding war-torn Afghanistan.

50. Nagorno Karabakh is a disputed territory between
(a) Armenia and Azerbaizan
(b) Georgia and Ukraine
(c) Uzbekistan and Turkmenistan
(d) Russian Federation and China

ANSWERS

1. (a)	2. (a)	3. (d)	4. (c)	5. (d)
6. (d)	7. (d)	8. (b)	9. (c)	10. (a)
11. (d)	12. (a)	13. (b)	14. (a)	15. (c)
16. (b)	17. (a)	18. (a)	19. (d)	20. (d)
21. (c)	22. (a)	23. (d)	24. (*)	25. (d)
26. (b)	27. (b)	28. (c)	29. (b)	30. (d)
31. (d)	32. (c)	33. (a)	34. (c)	35. (a)
36. (b)	37. (c)	38. (b)	39. (a)	40. (a)
41. (c)	42. (c)	43. (a)	44. (d)	45. (a)
46. (a)	47. (d)	48. (b)	49. (b)	50. (a)

PAPER–III

Note: This paper contains seventy-five (75) objective type questions of two (2) marks each. All questions are compulsory.

1. The word 'theory', derived from the Greek word 'Theoria' means
   (a) A well-organized political system
   (b) A well-focused mental look
   (c) A well-articulated economic structure
   (d) A system of physical arrangement
2. Who, among the following, is not associated with decline of political theory?
   (a) Peter Laslett
   (b) David Easton
   (c) Jean Blondel
   (d) Alfred Cobban
3. Who said "negative liberty is superior to positive liberty"?
   (a) J.S. Mill (b) Isaiah Berlin
   (c) T.H. Green (d) Ernest Barker
4. Which one among the following statements is true?
   (a) Social justice violates the principles of equality.
   (b) Social justice is derived from moral reasonableness.
   (c) Social justice is a negation of justice.
   (d) Social justice is an instrument of political manipulation.
5. Which one among the following was the first mass movement Mao led?
   (a) The Cultural Revolution
   (b) The Great Leap Forward
   (c) Let hundred flowers blossom and hundred schools of thought contend
   (d) None of the above
6. The term 'Leninism' was coined by
   (a) Trotsky (b) Stalin
   (c) Marx (d) Mao
7. Who is the author of the book *The Good Boatman*?
   (a) Erikson
   (b) Rajmohan Gandhi
   (c) Romain Rolland
   (d) Noema
8. Which one among the following statements is true?
   (a) Plato's *Republic* is a book on ethics
   (b) It is a book on politics
   (c) It is both on ethics and politics
   (d) It is a book on education
9. Which one among the following is not written by M.N. Roy?
   (a) *The Future of Indian Politics*
   (b) *Gandhism, Nationalism and Socialism*
   (c) *New Humanism*
   (d) *Nationalism, Rationality and Revolution*
10. Who among the following has compared fortune with a woman?
    (a) M.N. Roy (b) Rousseau
    (c) Hobbes (d) Machiavelli
11. Which one among the following is not a work about alienation?

(a) Paris Manuscripts
(b) Theses on Feuerbach
(c) Poverty of Philosophy
(d) The German Ideology

12. General Will means
(a) Actual Will
(b) Majority Will
(c) Sum total of Wills
(d) Real Will

13. **Assertion (A):** Social Contract established a sovereign Government.
Reason (R): Citizens do have an absolute obligation to obey all laws or accept any form of Government.
In the context of the two statements, which one of the following is correct?
(a) Both (A) and (R) are true and (R) is correct explanation of (A).
(b) Both (A) and (R) are true but (R) is not the correct explanation of (A).
(c) (A) is true, but (R) is false.
(d) (A) is false, but (R) is true.

14. Match the List I with List II and select the correct answer from the codes given below with reference to Aristotle and Plato:

List I (Pure form)	List II (Degenerated form)
A. Monarchy	i. Democracy
B. Aristocracy	ii. Tyranny
C. Polity	iii. Oligarchy
D. Ideal State	iv. Timocracy (First stage)

Codes:	A	B	C	D
(a)	iv	i	ii	iii
(b)	ii	iii	i	iv
(c)	iii	ii	iv	i
(d)	i	iv	iii	ii

15. What is the chronological correct sequence of the following books?

i. Richard Attenborough	*In Search of Gandhi*
ii. Louis Fisher	*The Life of Mahatma Gandhi*
iii. E.H. Erikson	*Gandhi's Truth*
iv. J. Eaton	*Gandhi: Fighter Without a Sword*

Select the correct answer from the codes given below:
Codes:
(a) iv, ii, iii, i (b) iii, i, ii, iv
(c) ii, iv, iii, ii (d) i, ii, iv, iii

16. Match List I with List II and select the correct answer from the codes given below:
List I (System Theorists)
1. Bertallanfy
2. Hall and Fagen
3. Easton
4. Colin Cherry

List II (Systems)
A. a set of elements standing in interaction
B. a whole which is compounded of many parts
C. a set of objects together with relationships between the objects and their attributes
D. a set of interactions

Codes:	A	B	C	D
(a)	1	4	2	3
(b)	2	3	1	4
(c)	4	1	2	3
(d)	3	2	4	1

17. Who among the following presents a 'flow model' of political system?
(a) Gabriel Almond
(b) David Easton
(c) Morton Kaplan
(d) Oran Young

18. Almond borrowed most of the terminology of his approach from
(a) Robert K. Merton
(b) Talcott Parsons

(c) Malinowski
(d) Arthur Bentley

19. Who among the following attached great importance to a balance between the principles of equality and capacity in political development?
(a) Lucian Pye (b) Huntington
(c) Fred Riggs (d) Danil Lerner

20. Who among the following is associated with the "will and capacity" approach to the study of political development?
(a) Lucian Pye (b) Organski
(c) Halpern (d) David Apter

21. Who among the following has connected cultures with civilizations?
(a) Almond and Verba
(b) Huntington
(c) Lucian Pye
(d) Edward Shils

22. "We are under the Constitution but the Constitution is what the judges say it is". Which of the following countries can this be applicable to?
1. India 2. America
3. Switzerland 4. Australia
Select the correct answer from the codes given below:
Codes:
(a) 1 and 3 (b) 1 and 2
(c) 2 and 3 (d) 3 and 4

23. Who among the following has associated the origins of political parties with three theories—institutional theories, historical crisis theories and development theories?
(a) La Palombara and Myron Weiner
(b) Peter K. Merkl
(c) Harry Eckstein
(d) Jean Blondel

24. Which of the following statements are not correct?
1. The Swiss Federal Tribunal has the power to declare unconstitutional a law passed by the Federal Legislature.
2. The Communist Party is banned in the U.S.A.
3. The Constitution of India on the date of its commencement did have a provision that the advice of the Council of Ministers would be binding on the President.
4. Tories in England are known as Conservatives.

Select the correct answer from the codes given below:
Codes:
(a) 1 and 2 (b) 2 and 3
(c) 2 and 4 (d) 1 and 3

25. "There can be no comparison between the positions of number one and numbers two, three or four." Who said this about the British Prime Minister?
(a) Harold Laski
(b) Margaret Thatcher
(c) Harold Wilson
(d) Winston Churchill

26. Given below are two statements, one labelled as Assertion (A) and the other labelled as Reason (R):
Assertion (A): Once the leaders reach the pinnacle of power, nothing can bring them down.
Reason (R): The majority of human beings, according to Michels, are apathetic, indolent and slavish.
(a) Both (A) and (R) are true and (R) is the correct explanation of (A).
(b) Both (A) and (R) are true but (R) is not the correct explanation of (A).
(c) (A) is true, but (R) is false.
(d) (A) is false, but (R) is true.

27. Which of the following pairs are not correctly matched?
1. Pareto — Circulation of elites
2. Mosca — Theory of the masses
3. Michels — Concept of mass mind
4. Gasset — Political formula

Select the correct answer from the codes given below:

Codes:

(a) 2 and 4 (b) 1 and 2
(c) 3 and 4 (d) 2 and 3

28. Which of the following countries have dual citizenship—National citizenship and State citizenship?
(a) India and U.S.A.
(b) India and Switzerland
(c) Switzerland and U.S.A.
(d) U.S.A. and U.K.

29. Which of the following statements are not correct?
1. The U.S. President can seek election to the office of President for any number of times.
2. The President of India has been sending messages to Parliament.
3. Two-thirds members of Rajya Sabha retire every two years.
4. The residuary powers rest with the States in the United States of America.

Select the correct answer from the codes given below:

Codes:

(a) 1, 2 and 4 (b) 1, 2 and 3
(c) 2, 3 and 4 (d) 1, 3 and 4

30. The elite theory was first started in
(a) the United States of America
(b) the United Kingdom
(c) Central and Western European Countries
(d) Australia

31. The Preamble of the Constitution of India enshrines the ideals of liberty, equality and fraternity—ideals mainly inspired by the
(a) Russian Revolution
(b) Irish Revolution
(c) French Revolution
(d) Cultural Revolution

32. The name of a candidate for the Office of President of India is proposed by
(a) any five citizens of India
(b) any five Members of the Parliament
(c) any fifty Members of the Electoral College
(d) any ten members of the Electoral College

33. Which of the following Articles were not part of the original Constitution of India?
(i) Art. 52A (ii) Art. 51A
(iii) Art. 14 (iv) Art. 300A

Select the correct answer from the codes given below:

(a) (i) and (ii) (b) (i) and (iii)
(c) (ii) and (iii) (d) (ii) and (iv)

34. Who among the following former Presidents of India kept the 'Indian Post Office Amendment Bill' pending?
(a) Zakir Hussain
(b) V.V. Giri
(c) Zail Singh
(d) Dr. Shanker Dayal Sharma

35. Who said 'All Communalism is harmful'? The logic of minority Communalism is separatism, and majority communalism culminates in Fascism?
(a) Bhikhu Parekh
(b) T.N. Madan
(c) Bipin Chandra
(d) Ashish Nandy

36. Who wrote the book, *Democracy and Discontent*?
(a) James Manor (b) Atul Kohli
(c) Zoya Hasan (d) MSA Rao

37. Who emphasized the emergence of "a market polity" in India?
(a) Stanley A. Kochanek
(b) James Manor
(c) Morris-Jones
(d) Paul Brass

38. Who described the nature of Indian State as 'incremental democratic modernization'?
(a) Morris John
(b) Rajni Kothari
(c) Francine Frankel
(d) Susan and Lloyd Rudolph

39. "An alliance of national elites and the entrepreneurial class as a basis of development at the Centre does not preclude re-distributive concessions automatically." Who said?
(a) Partha Chatterjee
(b) Atul Kohli
(c) Yogendra Yadav
(d) Paul Brass

40. Match List I with List II and choose the correct answer from the codes given below:
List I (Books)
A. *Language, Religion and Politics*
B. *Party Building in a New Nation*
C. *The Painful Transition: Bourgeois Democracy in India*
D. *India in Transition: Freeing the Economy*
List II (Authors)
i. Jagdish Bhagwati
ii. Paul Brass
iii. Myron Weiner
iv. Achin Vanaik

Codes:	**A**	**B**	**C**	**D**
(a)	ii	iii	iv	i
(b)	iii	ii	i	iv
(c)	i	iv	iii	ii
(d)	iv	i	ii	iii

41. Identify the correct sequence in which the following Committees were appointed. Use the code given below:
i. Balwant Rai Mehta Committee
ii. L.M. Singhvi Committee
iii. G.V.K. Rao Committee
iv. Ashok Mehta Committee
Codes:
(a) i, iv, iii, ii (b) ii, iii, i, iv
(c) iii, ii, iv, i (d) iv, i, ii, iii

42. **Assertion (A):** Political parties in India have expanded their reach but their legitimacy has been deeply eroded.
Reason (R): The consolidation of the party system at the State level cannot be aggregated at the National level.
(a) Both (A) and (R) are true and (R) is the correct explanation of (A).
(b) Both (A) and (R) are true and (R) is not the correct explanation of (A).
(c) (A) is true, but (R) is false.
(d) (A) is false, but (R) is true.

43. Which among the following Articles of the Constitution of India has ensured through legislation the participation of workers in management?
(a) Article 42 (b) Article 43
(c) Article 43A (d) Article 49A

44. Who among the following termed Art. 356 as a "safety valve"?
(a) Dr. Rajendra Prasad
(b) Dr. B.R. Ambedkar
(c) Jawaharlal Nehru
(d) Sardar Vallabhbhai Patel

45. Match List I with List II and choose the correct answer from the codes given below:
List I (Books)
A. *Dalit Visions: The Anti-Caste Movement and the Construction of Indian Identity*
B. *Peasant Movements in India*
C. *Foreign Identities, Gender Communities and the State* (Ed.)
D. *Institutionalising Panchayati Raj in India*
List II (Authors)
i. Zoya Hasan ii. V. Venkatesan
iii. Gail Omvedt iv. D.N. Dhanagre

Codes:	A	B	C	D
(a)	ii	iii	iv	i
(b)	iii	iv	i	ii
(c)	i	ii	iii	iv
(d)	iv	i	ii	iii

46. Consider the following statements about Civil Service in a developing society:
   1. It should act as an instrument of change.
   2. It should have concern for social equity.
   3. It should have common concern for vested interests.
   4. It should be politically neutral.

   Select the correct statements from the codes given below:
   (a) 1, 2, 3 and 4 (b) 1, 3 and 4
   (c) 1, 2 and 4 (d) 2, 3 and 4

47. Match List I with List II and choose the correct answer from the codes given below:

   List I
   A. Span of attention
   B. Scalar process
   C. Human Relations Theory
   D. Functional Foremanship

   List II
   i. Mooney and Reiley
   ii. F.W. Taylor
   iii. V.A. Graicunas
   iv. Elton Mayo

Codes:	A	B	C	D
(a)	iii	iv	i	ii
(b)	iii	i	iv	ii
(c)	ii	i	iv	iii
(d)	i	iii	ii	iv

48. Which one of the following was not included as a principle of administration by Willoughby in his *Principles of Public Administration*?
   (a) General and overhead administration
   (b) Coordination
   (c) Finance
   (d) Personnel administration

49. The principle of unity of command mainly ensures
   (a) Accountability (b) Specialization
   (c) Acceptability (d) Coordination

50. Which one of the following is not one of the main characteristics of Taylor's scientific management?
   (a) Time and motion studies
   (b) Participation in decision making
   (c) Differential piece-rate system
   (d) Functional foremanship

51. Who among the following has called Weber's ideal type of bureaucracy as unsuitable for developing societies?
   (a) H. Simon
   (b) Chester I. Barnard
   (c) Fred W. Riggs
   (d) Dwight Waldo

52. The Committee on Assurances of the Parliament of India is an instrument of
   (a) Executive Control
   (b) Judicial Control
   (c) Civil-Society Control
   (d) Legislative Control

53. According to Herbert Simon, if a decision is directed towards individual's goal, it is
   (a) Organizationally rational
   (b) Personally rational
   (c) Objectively rational
   (d) Subjectively rational

54. The most logical criterion to distinguish a line function from staff is
   (a) the functional relationship
   (b) the authority relationship
   (c) the grouping of functions
   (d) the departmentalization

55. Central Vigilance Commission was set up on the recommendations of
   (a) First Administrative Reforms Commission
   (b) Gorwala Committee Report

(c) Kripalani Committee Report
(d) Santhanam Committee Report

56. The Lokpal and Lokayukta Bill 1968 passed by the Lok Sabha lapsed because
(a) Rajya Sabha rejected the Bill
(b) President withheld the Bill
(c) Joint Committee of the two Houses rejected the Bill
(d) of early Dissolution of Fourth Lok Sabha

57. Which one of the following committee's report said that Community Development Programme and National Extension Service had failed to evoke popular enthusiasm?
(a) Sarkaria Committee Report
(b) L.M. Singhvi Committee Report
(c) G.V.K. Rao Committee Report
(d) Balwant Rai Mehta Committee Report

58. Which one of the following was not included by C. Rajagopalachari in the list of six fundamental requirements of a good administrator?
(a) Character
(b) Capacity to judge matters
(c) Expertise in technical matters
(d) Firmness in decision making

59. Santhanam Committee on Prevention of Corruption was appointed in
(a) 1961 (b) 1962
(c) 1963 (d) 1964

60. Given below are two statements, one labelled as Assertion (A) and the other labelled as Reason (R).
Assertion (A): Practical application of unity of command is not always possible.
Reason (R): Technical and administrative tasks require different kinds of supervision.
Select the correct answer from the codes given below:
(a) Both (A) and (R) are individually true and (R) is the correct explanation of (A).
(b) Both (A) and (R) are individually true, but (R) is not the correct explanation of (A).
(c) (A) is true, but (R) is false.
(d) (A) is false, but (R) is true.

61. What is neo-realism?
(a) An attempt to ignore the unpleasant realities of the world.
(b) An attempt to restate the basic ideas of realism in a more 'scientific' form.
(c) A claim that international society is basically orderly and peaceful.
(d) A claim that individual human nature is central to an understanding of international politics.

62. Match List I with List II and select the correct answer from the codes below:
List I (Authors)
A. Hedley Bull
B. Noam Chomsky
C. Robert Kaplan
D. Kenneth Boulding
List II (Books)
i. *Failed States*
ii. *Conflict and Defense*
iii. *Anarchial Society*
iv. *Monsoon*

Codes:	**A**	**B**	**C**	**D**
(a)	iii	i	iv	ii
(b)	ii	iii	i	iv
(c)	i	iv	iii	ii
(d)	iv	ii	i	iii

63. Arrange the following international politics theorists in a chronological order from the codes given below:
(i) Reinhold Niebuhr
(ii) Immanuel Kant
(iii) Antonio Gramsci
(iv) Robert W. Cox

Codes:
(a) (iii), (iv), (i), (ii) (b) (iv), (i), (ii), (iii)
(c) (i), (ii), (iii), (iv) (d) (ii), (iii), (i), (iv)

64. What does RMA stand for?
(a) Revolution in Martial Affairs
(b) Revolution in Military Affairs
(c) Referendum in Military Affairs
(d) Raison d'etat in Mass Administration

65. What does Raison d'etat mean?
(a) The national interest.
(b) The State ought to act reasonably at all times.
(c) Citizens need to be given very good reasons for obeying the State.
(d) Citizens should consume as many raisins as possible for a good and healthy life.

66. Why is reform of the Security Council problematic?
(a) Enlarging the permanent membership could impair decision making.
(b) None of the existing permanent members are keen to give up their seats.
(c) It is difficult to make an uncontroversial case for any of the potential new permanent members.
(d) All of the above.

67. Structural adjustment programmes require that
(a) Governments of poor countries should adopt privatization and other 'liberalizing' measures.
(b) States with weak economies should redistribute more resources to the poor.
(c) Governments of poor countries should knock down all ugly or dilapidated buildings.
(d) Ministers in under-performing countries should go on diets and keep fit.

68. Bandung Conference held in 1955 had the participation of representatives from
(a) Twenty-two Asian countries
(b) Eighty Afro-Asian countries
(c) Twenty-six African countries
(d) Twenty-nine Afro-Asian countries

69. Who said, "Thus far the chief purpose of our military establishment has been to win wars. From now on its chief purpose must be to avert them."?
(a) Paul Nitze (b) George Kennan
(c) Bernard Brodie (d) Robert Jervis

70. Arrange the following treaties and agreements in a chronological order. Select the answer from the codes given below:
(i) Indo-US Nuclear Treaty
(ii) Indo-Soviet Friendship Treaty
(iii) Tashkent Agreement
(iv) Shimla Agreement
Codes:
(a) (iii), (ii), (iv), (i) (b) (ii), (iii), (i), (iv)
(c) (i), (iv), (ii), (iii) (d) (iv), (i), (iii), (ii)

71. Expand SORT.
(a) Strategic Offensive Reduction Treaty
(b) State Organization Replan Treaty
(c) Strategic Order Reorganization Treaty
(d) Security Organization Replan Treaty

72. Which of the following statements are correct?
1. India has signed the NPT.
2. China has not signed the NPT.
3. India and Pakistan have not signed the NPT.
4. NPT has been signed by Iran, North Korea.
(a) All are correct.
(b) All are false.
(c) 3 & 4 are correct.
(d) 1 & 2 are correct.

73. Identify which of the following are correct statements:

(i) India is a member of the Indian Ocean Rim Association for Regional Cooperation [IORARC].
(ii) [IORARC] helps better relations with Pakistan.
(iii) It defines the Exclusive Economic Zones.
(iv) Indian Ocean has no sea piracy.

Codes:
(a) (i) and (ii) are correct.
(b) (iii) and (iv) are correct.
(c) (i) and (iii) are correct.
(d) (ii) and (iv) are correct.

74. The Axis of evil is a phrase deliberately used by President George W. Bush in January 2002 to characterize
(a) Iran, North Korea and Iraq
(b) Taliban, Al-Queda and LeT
(c) Cuba, Venezuela, Nicaragua
(d) Pakistan, Afghanistan, Sri Lanka

75. Martin Wight emphasized three philosophical traditions of international politics, they are
(a) Realism, Liberalism, Marxism
(b) Realism, Rationalism, Revolutionism
(c) Radicalism, Realism, Religion
(d) Neo-Realism, Neo-Liberalism, Constructivism

ANSWERS

1. (b)	2. (c)	3. (b)	4. (b)	5. (c)
6. (b)	7. (b)	8. (c)	9. (d)	10. (d)
11. (c)	12. (d)	13. (c)	14. (b)	15. (a)
16. (a)	17. (b)	18. (b)	19. (c)	20. (c)
21. (b)	22. (b)	23. (a)	24. (d)	25. (d)
26. (a)	27. (a)	28. (c)	29. (b)	30. (c)
31. (c)	32. (d)	33. (d)	34. (c)	35. (c)
36. (b)	37. (c)	38. (b)	39. (b)	40. (a)
41. (a)	42. (b)	43. (c)	44. (b)	45. (b)
46. (c)	47. (b)	48. (b)	49. (a)	50. (b)
51. (c)	52. (d)	53. (b)	54. (b)	55. (d)
56. (d)	57. (d)	58. (c)	59. (b)	60. (a)
61. (b)	62. (a)	63. (d)	64. (b)	65. (a)
66. (d)	67. (a)	68. (d)	69. (c)	70. (a)
71. (a)	72. (c)	73. (c)	74. (a)	75. (b)

JUNE–2012

Note: This paper contains Sixty (60) multiple-choice questions, each question carrying two (2) marks. Candidate is expected to answer any Fifty (50) questions. In case more than Fifty (50) questions are attempted, only the first Fifty (50) questions will be evaluated.

PAPER–I

1. Video-Conferencing can be classified as one of the following types of communication:
   (a) Visual one way
   (b) Audio-Visual one way
   (c) Audio-Visual two way
   (d) Visual two way
2. MC National University of Journalism and Communication is located at
   (a) Lucknow (b) Bhopal
   (c) Chennai (d) Mumbai
3. All India Radio (A.I.R.) for broadcasting was named in the year
   (a) 1926 (b) 1936
   (c) 1946 (d) 1956
4. In India for broadcasting TV programmes which system is followed?
   (a) NTCS (b) PAL
   (c) NTSE (d) SECAM
5. The term 'DAVP' stands for
   (a) Directorate of Advertising & Vocal Publicity
   (b) Division of Audio-Visual Publicity
   (c) Department of Audio-Visual Publicity
   (d) Directorate of Advertising & Visual Publicity
6. The term "TRP" is associated with TV shows stands for
   (a) Total Rating Points
   (b) Time Rating Points
   (c) Thematic Rating Points
   (d) Television Rating Points
7. Which is the number that comes next in the following sequence?
   2, 6, 12, 20, 30, 42, 56, ______
   (a) 60 (b) 64
   (c) 72 (d) 70
8. Find the next letter for the series YVSP ....
   (a) N (b) M
   (c) O (d) L
9. Given that in a code language, '645' means 'day is warm'; '42' means 'warm spring' and '634' means 'spring is sunny'; which digit represents 'sunny'?
   (a) 3 (b) 2
   (c) 4 (d) 5
10. The basis of the following classification is:
    'first President of India' 'author of Godan' 'books in my library', 'blue things' and 'students who work hard'
    (a) Common names
    (b) Proper names
    (c) Descriptive phrases
    (d) Indefinite description
11. In the expression 'Nothing is larger than itself' the relation 'is larger than' is
    (a) antisymmetric (b) asymmetrical
    (c) intransitive (d) irreflexive
12. **Assertion (A):** There are more laws on the books today than ever before, and

more crimes being committed than ever before.

Reason (R): Because to reduce crime we must eliminate the laws.

Choose the correct answer from below:

(a) (A) is true, (R) is doubtful and (R) is not the correct explanation of (A).

(b) (A) is false, (R) is true and (R) is the correct explanation of (A).

(c) (A) is doubtful, (R) is doubtful and (R) is not the correct explanation of (A).

(d) (A) is doubtful, (R) is true and (R) is not the correct explanation of (A).

13. If the proposition "All men are not mortal" is true then which of the following inferences is correct? Choose from the code given below:

1. "All men are mortal" is true.
2. "Some men are mortal" is false.
3. "No men are mortal" is doubtful.
4. "All men are mortal" is false.

Codes:

(a) 1, 2 and 3 (b) 2, 3 and 4

(c) 1, 3 and 4 (d) 1 and 3

14. Determine the nature of the following definition: "Abortion" means the ruthless murdering of innocent beings.

(a) Lexical (b) Persuasive

(c) Stipulative (d) Theoretical

15. Which one of the following is not an argument?

(a) Devadutt does not eat in the day so he must be eating at night.

(b) If Devadutt is growing fat and if he does not eat during the day, he will be eating at night.

(c) Devadutt eats in the night so he does not eat during the day.

(d) Since Devadutt does not eat in the day, he must be eating in the night.

16. Venn diagram is a kind of diagram to

(a) represent and assess the validity of elementary inferences of syllogistic form.

(b) represent but not assess the validity of elementary inferences of syllogistic form.

(c) represent and assess the truth of elementary inferences of syllogistic form.

(d) assess but not represent the truth of elementary inferences of syllogistic form.

17. Reasoning by analogy leads to

(a) certainty

(b) definite conclusion

(c) predictive conjecture

(d) surety

18. Which of the following statements are false? Choose from the code given below:

1. Inductive arguments always proceed from the particular to the general.
2. A cogent argument must be inductively strong.
3. A valid argument may have a false premise and a false conclusion.
4. An argument may legitimately be spoken of as 'true' or 'false'.

Codes:

(a) 2, 3 and 4 (b) 1 and 3

(c) 2 and 4 (d) 1 and 2

19. Six persons A, B, C, D, E and F are standing in a circle. B is between F and C, A is between E and D, F is to the left of D. Who is between A and F?

(a) B (b) C

(c) D (d) E

20. The price of petrol increases by 25%. By what percentage must a customer reduce the consumption so that the earlier bill on the petrol does not alter?

(a) 20% (b) 25%
(c) 30% (d) 33.33%

21. If Ram knows that *y* is an integer greater than 2 and less than 7 and Hari knows that *y* is an integer greater than 5 and less than 10, then they may correctly conclude that
(a) *y* can be exactly determined
(b) *y* may be either of two values
(c) *y* may be any of three values
(d) there is no value of *y* satisfying these conditions

22. Four pipes can fill a reservoir in 15, 20, 30 and 60 hours respectively. The first one was opened at 6 AM, second at 7 AM, third at 8 AM and the fourth at 9 AM. When will the reservoir be filled?
(a) 11 AM (b) 12 Noon
(c) 1 PM (d) 1:30 PM

The total electricity generation in a country is 97 GW. The contribution of various energy sources is indicated in percentage terms in the Pie Chart given below:

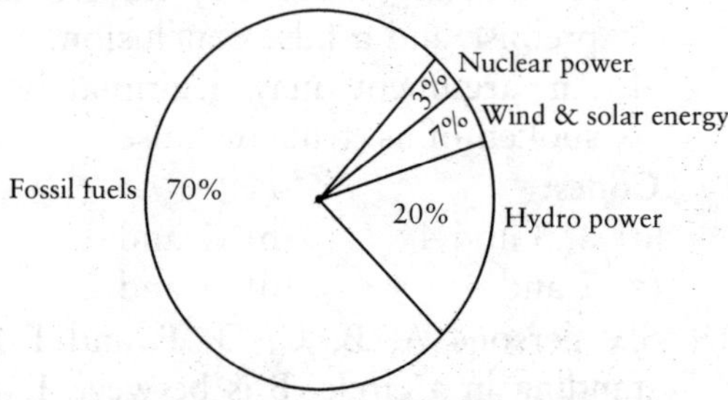

23. What is the contribution of wind and solar power in absolute terms in the electricity generation?
(a) 6.79 GW (b) 19.4 GW
(c) 9.7 GW (d) 29.1 GW

24. What is the contribution of renewable energy sources in absolute terms in the electricity generation?
(a) 29.1 GW (b) 26.19 GW
(c) 67.9 GW (d) 97 GW

25. TCP/IP is necessary if one is to connect to the
(a) Phone lines (b) LAN
(c) Internet (d) a Server

26. Each character on the keyboard of computer has an ASCII value which stands for
(a) American Stock Code for Information Interchange
(b) American Standard Code for Information Interchange
(c) African Standard Code for Information Interchange
(d) Adaptable Standard Code for Information Change

27. Which of the following is not a programming language?
(a) Pascal (b) Microsoft Office
(c) Java (d) C++

28. Minimum number of bits required to store any 3 digit decimal number is equal to
(a) 3 (b) 5
(c) 8 (d) 10

29. Internet explorer is a type of
(a) Operating System
(b) Compiler
(c) Browser
(d) IP address

30. POP3 and IMAP are e-mail accounts in which
(a) One automatically gets one's mail everyday
(b) One has to be connected to the server to read or write one's mail
(c) One only has to be connected to the server to send and receive e-mail
(d) One does not need any telephone lines

31. Irritation in eyes is caused by the pollutant
(a) Sulphur dioxide (b) Ozone
(c) PAN (d) Nitrous oxide

32. Which is the source of chlorofluorocarbons?
(a) Thermal power plants
(b) Automobiles
(c) Refrigeration and Airconditioning
(d) Fertilizers

33. Which of the following is not a renewable natural resource?
(a) Clean air (b) Fertile soil
(c) Fresh water (d) Salt

34. Which of the following parameters is not used as a pollution indicator in water?
(a) Total dissolved solids
(b) Coliform count
(c) Dissolved oxygen
(d) Density

35. S and P waves are associated with
(a) floods (b) wind energy
(c) earthquakes (d) tidal energy

36. Match List I and List II and select the correct answer from the codes given below:

List I
(A) Ozone hole
(B) Greenhouse effect
(C) Natural hazards
(D) Sustainable development

List II
(i) Tsunami (ii) UV radiations
(iii) Methane (iv) Eco-centrism

Codes:	**A**	**B**	**C**	**D**
(a)	(ii)	(iii)	(i)	(iv)
(b)	(iii)	(ii)	(i)	(iv)
(c)	(iv)	(iii)	(i)	(ii)
(d)	(iv)	(ii)	(iii)	(i)

37. Indian Institute of Advanced Study is located at
(a) Dharmshala (b) Shimla
(c) Solan (d) Chandigarh

38. Indicate the number of Regional Offices of National Council of Teacher Education.
(a) 04 (b) 05
(c) 06 (d) 08

39. Which of the following rights was considered the "Heart and Soul" of the Indian Constitution by Dr. B.R. Ambedkar?
(a) Freedom of Speech
(b) Right to Equality
(c) Right to Freedom of Religion
(d) Right to Constitutional Remedies

40. Who among the following created the office of the District Collector in India?
(a) Lord Cornwallis
(b) Warren Hastings
(c) The Royal Commission on Decentralisation
(d) Sir Charles Metcalfe

41. The Fundamental Duties of a citizen include
1. Respect for the Constitution, the National Flag and the National Anthem.
2. To develop the scientific temper.
3. Respect for the Government.
4. To protect Wildlife.

Choose the correct answer from the codes given below:

Codes:
(a) 1, 2 and 3 (b) 1, 2 and 4
(c) 2, 3 and 4 (d) 1, 3, 4 and 2

42. The President of India takes oath
(a) to uphold the sovereignty and integrity of India.
(b) to bear true faith and allegiance to the Constitution of India.
(c) to uphold the Constitution and Laws of the country.
(d) to preserve, protect and defend the Constitution and the law of the country.

43. If you get an opportunity to teach a visually challenged student along with normal students, what type of treatment would you like to give him in the class?
    (a) Not giving extra attention because majority may suffer.
    (b) Take care of him sympathetically in the classroom.
    (c) You will think that blindness is his destiny and hence you cannot do anything.
    (d) Arrange a seat in the front row and try to teach at a pace convenient to him.
44. Which of the following is not a characteristic of a good achievement test?
    (a) Reliability (b) Objectivity
    (c) Ambiguity (d) Validity
45. Which of the following does not belong to a projected aid?
    (a) Overhead projector
    (b) Blackboard
    (c) Epidiascope
    (d) Slide projector
46. For a teacher, which of the following methods would be correct for writing on the blackboard?
    (a) Writing fast and as clearly as possible.
    (b) Writing the matter first and then asking students to read it.
    (c) Asking a question to students and then writing the answer as stated by them.
    (d) Writing the important points as clearly as possible.
47. A teacher can be successful if he/she
    (a) helps students in becoming better citizens
    (b) imparts subject knowledge to students
    (c) prepares students to pass the examination
    (d) presents the subject matter in a well-organized manner
48. Dynamic approach to teaching means
    (a) Teaching should be forceful and effective
    (b) Teachers should be energetic and dynamic
    (c) The topics of teaching should not be static, but dynamic
    (d) The students should be required to learn through activities
49. The research that aims at immediate application is
    (a) Action Research
    (b) Empirical Research
    (c) Conceptual Research
    (d) Fundamental Research
50. When two or more successive footnotes refer to the same work which one of the following expressions is used?
    (a) ibid. (b) et al.
    (c) op. cit. (d) loc. cit.
51. Nine year olds are taller than seven year olds. This is an example of a reference drawn from
    (a) Vertical study
    (b) Cross-sectional study
    (c) Time series study
    (d) Experimental study
52. Conferences are meant for
    (a) Multiple target groups
    (b) Group discussions
    (c) Show-casing new Research
    (d) All of the above
53. Ex-Post Facto research means
    (a) The research is carried out after the incident.
    (b) The research is carried out prior to the incident.
    (c) The research is carried out along with the happening of an incident.
    (d) The research is carried out keeping in mind the possibilities of an incident.

54. Research ethics do not include
(a) Honesty (b) Subjectivity
(c) Integrity (d) Objectivity

Read the following passage carefully and answer the questions 55 to 60:

James Madison said, "A people who mean to be their own governors must arm themselves with power that knowledge gives." In India, the Official Secrets Act, 1923 was a convenient smokescreen to deny members of the public access to information. Public functioning has traditionally been shrouded in secrecy. But in a democracy in which people govern themselves, it is necessary to have more openness. In the maturing of our democracy, right to information is a major step forward; it enables citizens to participate fully in the decision-making process that affects their lives so profoundly. It is in this context that the address of the Prime Minister in the Lok Sabha is significant. He said, "I would only like to see that everyone, particularly our civil servants, should see the Bill in a positive spirit; not as a draconian law for paralyzing Government, but as an instrument for improving Government-Citizen interface resulting in a friendly, caring and effective Government functioning for the good of our People." He further said, "This is an innovative Bill, where there will be scope to review its functioning as we gain experience. Therefore, this is a piece of legislation, whose working will be kept under constant reviews."

The Commission, in its Report, has dealt with the application of the Right to Information in Executive, Legislature and Judiciary. The judiciary could be a pioneer in implementing the Act in letter and spirit because much of the work that the Judiciary does is open to public scrutiny, Government of India has sanctioned an e-governance project in the Judiciary for about ₹ 700 crores which would bring about systematic classification, standardization and categorization of records. This would help the judiciary to fulfil its mandate under the Act. Similar capacity building would be required in all other public authorities. The transformation from non-transparency to transparency and public accountability is the responsibility of all three organs of State.

55. A person gets power
(a) by acquiring knowledge
(b) from the Official Secrets Act, 1923
(c) through openings
(d) by denying public information

56. Right to Information is a major step forward to
(a) enable citizens to participate fully in the decision-making process
(b) to make the people aware of the Act
(c) to gain knowledge of administration
(d) to make the people Government friendly

57. The Prime Minister considered the Bill
(a) to provide power to the civil servants
(b) as an instrument for improving Government-citizen interface resulting in a friendly, caring and effective Government
(c) a draconian law against the officials
(d) to check the harassment of the people

58. The Commission made the Bill effective by
(a) extending power to the executive authorities
(b) combining the executive and legislative power
(c) recognizing Judiciary a pioneer in implementing the act in letter and spirit
(d) educating the people before its implementation

59. The Prime Minister considered the Bill innovative and hoped that

(a) It could be reviewed based on the experience gained on its functioning.
(b) The civil servants would see the Bill in a positive spirit.
(c) It would not be considered as a draconian law for paralyzing Government.
(d) All of the above.

60. The transparency and public accountability is the responsibility of three organs of the State. These three organs are
(a) Lok Sabha, Rajya Sabha and Judiciary
(b) Lok Sabha, Rajya Sabha and Executive
(c) Judiciary, Legislature and the Commission
(d) Legislature, Executive and Judiciary

ANSWERS

1. (c)	2. (b)	3. (b)	4. (b)	5. (d)
6. (a)	7. (c)	8. (b)	9. (a)	10. (c)
11. (d)	12. (a)	13. (b)	14. (b)	15. (b)
16. (a)	17. (c)	18. (c)	19. (c)	20. (a)
21. (a)	22. (c)	23. (a)	24. (b)	25. (c)
26. (b)	27. (b)	28. (d)	29. (c)	30. (c)
31. (c)	32. (c)	33. (d)	34. (d)	35. (c)
36. (a)	37. (b)	38. (a)	39. (d)	40. (b)
41. (b)	42. (d)	43. (d)	44. (c)	45. (b)
46. (d)	47. (a)	48. (d)	49. (a)	50. (a)
51. (b)	52. (d)	53. (a)	54. (b)	55. (a)
56. (a)	57. (b)	58. (c)	59. (d)	60. (d)

PAPER–II

Note: This paper contains fifty (50) objective type questions, each question carrying two (2) marks. All questions are compulsory.

1. Which of the following book is not authored by Karl Marx?
(a) *German Ideology*
(b) *Critique of the Gotha Programme*
(c) *Paris Manuscripts*
(d) *Science of Logic*

2. Who wrote "Over himself, over his own body and mind, the individual is sovereign"?
(a) J.S. Mill
(b) M.K. Gandhi
(c) Jeremy Bentham
(d) Robert Nozick

3. Rajni Kothari's book *Politics in India* is written on the basis of the methodology of:
(a) Structural functionalism
(b) Normative theory
(c) Marxism
(d) Utilitarianism

4. Who is the first modern political thinker who deliberately ignores Aristotle?
(a) Machiavelli (b) Bodin
(c) Hobbes (d) Locke

5. Match List I with List II and select the correct answer from the codes given below:

List I
(A) Dictatorship of the proletariat
(B) Communist Party
(C) Hegemony
(D) Polycentricism

List II
(i) Gramsci (ii) Marx
(iii) Lenin (iv) Togliatti

Codes:	A	B	C	D
(a)	(ii)	(iii)	(i)	(iv)
(b)	(i)	(ii)	(iii)	(iv)
(c)	(iii)	(i)	(ii)	(iv)
(d)	(ii)	(i)	(iii)	(iv)

6. Match List I with List II and select the correct answer from the codes given below:
List I
(A) Twentieth century Jacobinism
(B) Voluntary Poverty
(C) I was born a Hindu but will not die as one
(D) Integrated theory of evolution
List II
(i) Gandhi (ii) Aurobindo
(iii) Ambedkar (iv) M.N. Roy

Codes:	A	B	C	D
(a)	(i)	(ii)	(iii)	(iv)
(b)	(iv)	(i)	(iii)	(ii)
(c)	(ii)	(iii)	(i)	(iv)
(d)	(iii)	(i)	(ii)	(iv)

7. Gandhi described himself as a
(a) Liberal
(b) Socialist
(c) Social Democrat
(d) Philosophical Anarchist
8. The doctrine of overlapping consensus is advocated by
(a) Berlin (b) Barry
(c) Nozick (d) Rawls
9. Who among the following first developed the concept of general systems theory?
(a) Ludwig Von Bertallanfy
(b) Colin Cherry
(c) Robert K. Merton
(d) Talcott Parsons
10. Structural functionalism as a method was developed to study the politics of
(a) Advanced capitalism
(b) Developed socialism
(c) Modern totalitarianism
(d) Politics of developing countries
11. C. Wright Mill's "The Power Elite" is a study of the contemporary politics of
(a) China
(b) The United States of America
(c) The Soviet Union
(d) Great Britain
12. Who among the following identified the crises in political development on the basis of his study of England?
(a) A.F.K. Organski
(b) Lucian W. Pye
(c) Edward Shils
(d) David Apter
13. Which one of the following pairs is not correctly matched?

(a) C.W. Mills	The Power Elite
(b) T.B. Bottomore	Elites and Society
(c) Pareto	The Ruling Class
(d) Ortega Y Gasset	The Revolt of the Masses

14. Who among the following postulated the law "officials make work for each other"?
(a) Max Weber (b) F.M. Marx
(c) H. Finer (d) N. Parkinson
15. Which of the following pairs is not correct?

(a) U.S.A.	Double citizenship
(b) India	Procedure established by law
(c) Australia	Unitary form of Government
(d) Switzerland	Plural Executive

16. Michels' Iron law of oligarchy was formulated on the basis of the study of
(a) German Social Democratic Party
(b) British Labour Party
(c) Democratic Party of the U.S.A.
(d) Communist Party of the Soviet Union

17. Montesquieu's theory of separation of powers emphasises primarily on:
(a) Accountability (b) Efficiency
(c) Transparency (d) Liberty

Directions: (Q. 18-21) Each of the following four items consist of two statements, one labelled as Assertion (A) and the other labelled as Reason (R).
(a) Both (A) and (R) are true and (R) is the correct explanation of (A).
(b) Both (A) and (R) are true and (R) is not the correct explanation of (A).
(c) (A) is true, but (R) is false.
(d) (A) is false, but (R) is true.

18. **Assertion (A):** The Information Technology has made Staff Agency indispensable.
Reason (R): Staff Agency assists the Line Agency in decision making.

19. **Assertion (A):** While declaring war on terrorism the US asserted that the states which were not on the side of the US were against it.
Reason (R): In the wake of war on terrorism the US denied states the liberty to be neutral.

20. **Assertion (A):** Ambedkar was in favour of separate electorate for depressed classes.
Reason (R): He was in agreement with Gandhi.

21. **Assertion (A):** The presidential system is successful only in the U.S.A.
Reason (R): The United States of America is the only nation with minor contradictions that ensures the success of the presidential system.

22. Which one of the following was not associated with the Hindustan Republic Association?
(a) Chandrashekhar Azad
(b) Jogesh Chandra Chatterjee
(c) Aurobindo Ghosh
(d) Bhagat Singh

23. Who gave the Indian National Congress the Constitution and made it a mass and cadre party?
(a) Tilak (b) Gokhale
(c) Motilal Nehru (d) Gandhi

24. Who appoints the Inter-State Council?
(a) The President of India
(b) The Union Cabinet
(c) The Prime Minister
(d) The Union Home Minister

25. Identify the States whose State Assemblies also meet at places other than the State capital:
(a) Jammu-Kashmir and Madhya Pradesh
(b) Madhya Pradesh and Karnataka
(c) Maharashtra and Andhra Pradesh
(d) Jammu-Kashmir and Maharashtra

26. Which amendment of the Constitution of India limits the number of Ministers?
(a) 73rd (b) 86th
(c) 87th (d) 91st

27. Which one of the following committees is not associated with Panchayati Raj in India?
(a) Sadiq Ali Committee
(b) Dinesh Goswami Committee
(c) L.M. Singhvi Committee
(d) P.K. Thungan Committee

28. Identify the correct sequence in which the following Deputy Prime Ministers were appointed in India?
(i) Sardar Vallabhbhai Patel
(ii) Ch. Devi Lal
(iii) Ch. Charan Singh
(iv) Morarji Desai
Codes:
(a) (i), (iii), (iv), (ii)
(b) (i), (iv), (ii), (iii)

(c) (iv), (i), (ii), (iii)
(d) (i), (iv), (iii), (ii)

29. Who of the following constituted an oligrachy within the Constituent Assembly of India?
(a) Nehru, Patel, Prasad, Azad
(b) Ambedkar, B.N. Rao, K.M. Munshi, Nehru
(c) Patel, Azad, Munshi, Ambedkar
(d) Krishnamachari, Pannikar, Nehru, Patel

30. Who describes Indian economy as "Bullock Cart Capitalism"?
(a) Rajni Kothari
(b) Atul Kohli
(c) Granville Austin
(d) Lloyd and Sussane Rudolph

31. Who among the following defines Public Administration as "the activities of the Executive Branches of the National, State and Local Government"?
(a) Morstein Marx
(b) Luther Gullick
(c) Herbert A. Simon
(d) Marshal E. Dimock

32. Public Accounts Committee has the following Members. Tick the correct answer:

	Lok Sabha	Rajya Sabha	Total
(a)	10	5	15
(b)	15	7	22
(c)	11	5	16
(d)	17	10	27

33. 'Span of Control' is also known as
(a) The Repair Boss
(b) The Gang Boss
(c) Military Type of Foreman
(d) Business Frontline

34. The word 'Bureaucracy' was first coined by
(a) Max Weber
(b) Alexander Pope
(c) M. Crozier
(d) Vincent de Gournay

35. Which one of the following is the correct function of Staff Agency?
(a) Issuing orders to the subordinates
(b) Controlling the activities of the subordinates
(c) Advising the Chief Executive
(d) Providing Institutional Services

36. Which one of the following statements is not correct with regard to Riggs' Perspective of Societies?
(a) Fused societies are traditional.
(b) Developed societies are diffracted societies.
(c) Ascriptive values are found in diffracted societies.
(d) Traditional societies have ascriptive values.

37. The Informal Channel of Communication is also known as
(a) Feedback (b) Grapevine
(c) Loopline (d) Nerveline

38. Match the thinkers with the concepts:

Thinker	Concept
(a) F.W. Taylor	(i) Scalar
(b) Chester Bernard	(ii) Dissatisfier
(c) Henry Fayol	(iii) Zone of Acceptance
(d) Frederic Herzberg	(iv) Incentive system

Select the correct order:

Codes:	A	B	C	D
(a)	(ii)	(iii)	(i)	(iv)
(b)	(iii)	(ii)	(iv)	(i)
(c)	(iv)	(ii)	(iii)	(i)
(d)	(iv)	(iii)	(i)	(ii)

39. Who stated that "Budget is a series of Goals with price tags attached"?
(a) Wildavsky (b) Walpole
(c) Betram Gross (d) Allen Schick

40. Which one of the following articles of the Constitution empowers Parliament to create an All India Service?
    (a) Article 300 (b) Article 312
    (c) Article 320 (d) Article 410

41. Which of the following resulted from Bretton Woods Conference?
    (a) United Nations
    (b) League of Nations
    (c) Institutions meant for checking nuclear proliferation
    (d) World Bank and IMF

42. Which of the following is not the basic principle of Hans J. Morgenthou's realism?
    (a) Politics is rooted in the human nature
    (b) Politics is autonomous
    (c) National interest is defined in terms of power
    (d) Politics is governed by universal moral values

43. Marshall Plan was meant for
    (a) Building the economics of the third world
    (b) Rebuilding Western European economics
    (c) Rebuilding the economics of the North-American countries
    (d) Building the economics of African countries

44. Russia has been given permanent seat on the UN Security Council by virtue of its being
    (a) Second most powerful country in the world.
    (b) Successor State to the former Soviet Union.
    (c) Largest country in the world in terms of area.
    (d) One of the oldest civilisations in the world.

45. The major argument of Neo-realism of Kenneth Waltz is that
    (a) Structures are more important than actors.
    (b) Actors play more crucial role than structures.
    (c) Human nature is crucial element in politics.
    (d) The states override the constraints imposed by international structures.

46. Non-reciprocity principle of India's policy towards neighbouring countries envisages
    (a) hegemonic designs towards neighbouring countries.
    (b) efforts for improving ties with the neighbouring countries without reciprocity.
    (c) non-aligned policy posture in the South Asian context.
    (d) the disciplining of the neighbouring countries.

47. What is the correct chronological order of the developments listed below?
    (i) Indo-Soviet Treaty of Friendship
    (ii) India's first Nuclear Explosion at Pokhran
    (iii) Cuban Missile Crises
    (iv) Adoption of structural adjustment programme of India

    Select the correct answer from the following codes:
    (a) (ii), (iv), (iii), (i) (b) (iii), (i), (ii), (iv)
    (c) (iv), (ii), (i), (iii) (d) (i), (iv), (iii), (ii)

48. **Assertion (A):** WTO pleads that free trade brings prosperity for all and therefore should be promoted.
    Reason (R): Integration of the countries with global economy through the system of trade helps them to export goods abroad as also import goods which they need.

(a) (A) and (R) are true and (R) is a correct explanation of (A).
(b) Both (A) and (R) are true, but (R) is not the correct explanation of (A).
(c) (A) is true, but (R) is false.
(d) (A) is false, but (R) is true.

49. 14th SAARC Summit held in New Delhi in 2007, stressed
(a) Improving intra-regional connectivity
(b) Commitment to bilateralism within SAARC
(c) Connecting SAARC with other regional organisations
(d) Not to extend SAARC membership

50. Collective Security System of the UN is based on the principle of
(a) All for one, one for all
(b) Imposing sanctions against the belligerent state unilaterally
(c) Maintenance of security by the major powers
(d) Balance of power to be maintained by state of equilibrium

ANSWERS

1. (d)	2. (a)	3. (a)	4. (c)	5. (a)
6. (b)	7. (d)	8. (d)	9. (a)	10. (d)
11. (b)	12. (b)	13. (c)	14. (d)	15. (c)
16. (a)	17. (d)	18. (b)	19. (a)	20. (c)
21. (a)	22. (c)	23. (d)	24. (a)	25. (d)
26. (d)	27. (b)	28. (d)	29. (a)	30. (d)
31. (c)	32. (b)	33. (c)	34. (d)	35. (c)
36. (c)	37. (b)	38. (d)	39. (a)	40. (b)
41. (d)	42. (d)	43. (b)	44. (b)	45. (a)
46. (b)	47. (b)	48. (a)	49. (a)	50. (a)

PAPER–III

Note: This paper contains seventy-five (75) objective type questions of two (2) marks each. All questions are compulsory.

1. Which among the following statements is not correct?
(a) Post-behavioural political theory interrelates value and fact.
(b) Post-behavioural political theory is ethnocentric.
(c) Post-behavioural political theory is tied to action and relevancy.
(d) Post-behavioural political theory is change oriented.

2. Positive liberalism does not believe in
(a) Welfare State
(b) Nanny State
(c) State as a moral agency
(d) Minimal State

3. Marx does not believe in
(a) Human consciousness determines social existence
(b) Ideas are the reflections of the interplay of material forces
(c) The base determines the superstructure
(d) Matter is active and dynamic

4. Rawlsian concept of justice is based on
(a) Distributive principle
(b) Agreement principle
(c) Difference principle
(d) Joint method principle

5. The term 'Ideology' was first used in the year
(a) 1789 (b) 1792
(c) 1795 (d) 1797

6. Satyavir Ki Katha, translated into Gujarati by Gandhiji was from
(a) The Prince
(b) Dialogues of Plato

(c) The Social Contract
(d) War and Peace

7. Who adopted communism to Asiatic form?
(a) M.N. Roy
(b) Mao-Tse-Tung
(c) Lenin
(d) Trotsky

8. Which one among the following statements is correct?
(a) Platonic justice is a legal concept.
(b) The Greek word for Justice is dikaisune.
(c) Platonic justice meant true in word and deed and paying one's debts to Gods and men.
(d) Platonic Justice consists in conformity to the laws and institutions laid down by the Sovereign for his benefit and enforced by his power.

9. Locke's view on 'state of nature' is
(a) Pre-social
(b) Pre-political
(c) Pre-social and pre-political
(d) Social and Political

10. Which one among the following statements is true?
(a) The Prince deals with providing requirements for the maintenance of political instability in the Republics.
(b) The Discourses expound the requirements for the maintenance of political instability in principalities.
(c) The Prince is concerned with the qualities of Princes, the Discourses place a greater emphasis on the civic demands on citizens.
(d) None of the above.

11. Who said: "Human nature is an ensemble of social relations"?
(a) Gandhiji (b) M.N. Roy
(c) Aurobindo (d) Mao

12. Aurobindo is mainly famous because of his
(a) Political Ideology
(b) Revolutionary Activities
(c) Life Divine
(d) Association with Mother

13. Given below are two statements, one labelled as Assertion (A) and the other labelled as Reason (R):
Assertion (A): Platonic justice represents a disposition to do the right thing.
Reason (R): It is good to be unjust but bad to suffer injustice.
(a) Both (A) and (R) are true and (R) is the right explanation of (A).
(b) Both (A) and (R) are true but (R) is not the correct explanation of (A).
(c) (A) is true but (R) is false.
(d) (A) is false but (R) is true.

14. Match the List I with List II and select the correct answer from the codes given below:
List I (Authors)
(A) Friedrich Hayek (B) John Rawls
(C) Amartya Sen (D) Plato
List II (Books)
(i) *The Politics*
(ii) *Idea of Justice*
(iii) *The Road to Serfdom*
(iv) *A Theory of Justice*

Codes:	**A**	**B**	**C**	**D**
(a)	(iv)	(i)	(iii)	(ii)
(b)	(iii)	(iv)	(ii)	(i)
(c)	(i)	(ii)	(iv)	(iii)
(d)	(ii)	(iii)	(i)	(iv)

15. What is the correct sequence of the following in the Aristotle's Theory of Causation?
(i) Material cause (ii) Formal cause
(iii) Final cause (iv) Efficient cause
Select the correct answer from the codes given below:

(a) (ii) (iv) (iii) (i) (b) (iv) (iii) (i) (ii)
(c) (iii) (i) (ii) (iv) (d) (i) (iv) (ii) (iii)

16. Who said that the structural-functional approach was weak in change, the social process approach was weak in politics and the comparative history approach was weak in theory?
(a) Huntington (b) Paul F. Kress
(c) Jean Blondel (d) Samir Amin

17. Who among the following interpreted functionalism as an alternative approach to Marxism?
(a) Paul F. Kress
(b) Nicholson and Reynolds
(c) W.G. Runciman
(d) Morton Kaplan

18. Which one of the following has tried to give an essentially engineering orientation to human behaviour?
(a) Input-output analysis
(b) Structural-functional approach
(c) Communications theory
(d) Behavioural approach

19. The characteristics of Almond's political system mostly resemble those of the political system(s) of
(a) United States of America
(b) Scandinavian countries
(c) Developing countries
(d) Latin American countries

20. Who among the following identifies political development with the "institutionalisation of political organisations and procedures"?
(a) Huntington (b) Lucian Pye
(c) Organski (d) Almond

21. Which one of the following approaches/theories was first started as a critique of democracy and socialism?
(a) Elite theory
(b) Structural-functional approach
(c) Communications theory
(d) Game theory

22. Who among the following divided the non-competitive party system into one-party authoritarian, one-party pluralistic and one-party totalitarian?
(a) Alan Ball
(b) La Palombara and Myron Weiner
(c) Harry Eckstein
(d) James Jupp

23. In which of the following forms of Government is the second chamber as indispensable part of legislature?
(a) Presidential (b) Parliamentary
(c) Unitary (d) Federal

24. Which one of the following books has a chapter on 'Politics in India'?
(a) *The Civic Culture Revisited*
(b) *Politics and Government*
(c) *Political Development and Social Change*
(d) *Comparative Politics Today*

25. Match List I with List II and select the correct answer from the codes given below the lists:

List I (Form of Government)
(A) Parliamentary, Federal, Republican
(B) Presidential, Federal, Republican
(C) Parliamentary, Unitary, Monarchical
(D) Parliamentary-cum-Presidential, Unitary, Republican

List II (Name of the Country)
(i) The United Kingdom
(ii) India
(iii) France
(iv) The United States of America

Codes:	**A**	**B**	**C**	**D**
(a)	(i)	(ii)	(iii)	(iv)
(b)	(ii)	(iii)	(iv)	(i)
(c)	(iii)	(ii)	(i)	(iv)
(d)	(ii)	(iv)	(i)	(iii)

26. In which country all courts including all levels of the State Courts have the power of Judicial review?
   (a) India (b) Switzerland
   (c) America (d) Australia

27. The Indian Federal System differs from the American Federal System in respect of the following:
   (1) Representation of the States in the Upper House of the Federal Legislature.
   (2) Existence of a Written Constitution.
   (3) Vesting of Residuary Powers.
   (4) Dual Citizenship.

   Select the correct answer from the codes given below:

   Codes:
   (a) (1) and (2) (b) (3) and (4)
   (c) (1), (2) and (3) (d) (4) only

28. Which one of the following is the most important characteristic of a Parliamentary Government?
   (a) Majority Rule
   (b) Rule of Law
   (c) Direct election of Member of Parliament
   (d) Collective responsibility of the Executive to the Legislature

29. Which one of the following federal systems was taken as a model by K.C. Wheare for judging other federal systems?
   (a) Australian federal system
   (b) American federal system
   (c) Swiss federal system
   (d) Canadian federal system

30. Given below are two statements, one labelled as Assertion (A) and the other labelled as Reason (R). Choose the correct answer from the codes.

   Assertion (A): Presidential system is suitable for meeting crises.

   Reason (R): The President has a fixed tenure.

   (a) Both (A) and (R) are true and (R) is the correct explanation of (A).
   (b) Both (A) and (R) are correct but (R) is not the correct explanation of (A).
   (c) (A) is true but (R) is false.
   (d) (A) is false but (R) is true.

31. The Constituent Assembly was setup under the
   (a) Cripp Mission
   (b) Cabinet Mission Plan
   (c) Wavell Plan
   (d) Nehru Report

32. Who said the following? "India's Constitution was born more in fear and trepidation than in hope and inspiration"
   (a) Paul Brass (b) Myron Weiner
   (c) K.C. Wheare (d) Jennings

33. Which of the following Articles of the Constitution shields legislation from being declared unconstitutional and void?
   (a) Art. 15B (b) Art. 51A
   (c) Art. 31B (d) Art. 29A

34. Which of the following Amendments to the Indian Constitution has made Right to Education a Fundamental Right?
   (a) 92nd (b) 94th
   (c) 93rd (d) 91st

35. Which of the following statements is not correct?
   (a) First Proclamation of Emergency was declared in 1962.
   (b) Second Proclamation of Emergency was declared in 1971.
   (c) Third Proclamation of Emergency was declared in 1975.
   (d) Second and Third Proclamations of Emergency were revoked in 1978.

36. The power of Supreme Court of India to decide the dispute between the Centre and the States falls under its
   (a) Advisory Jurisdiction
   (b) Appellate Jurisdiction

(c) Original Jurisdiction
(d) Advisory and Appellate Jurisdiction

37. Who tried to period Indian politics in terms of the tussle between a "demand polity" and a "command polity"?
(a) Rajni Kothari
(b) Partha Chatterjee
(c) Lloyd and Susanne Rudolph
(d) Myron Weiner

38. Caste-based reservations are labelled as
(a) Affirmative Action
(b) Positive Discrimination
(c) State Intervention
(d) Society Egalitarianism

39. Which of the following was headed by Raja Dhale and Nam Devdhasal?
(a) Dalit Tiger (b) Bheem Shakti
(c) Dalit Panther (d) Dalit Elephant

40. Lloyd and Susanne Rudolf saw the State in India as 'Polymorphous'. What does it mean?
(a) Creature of manifold forms and orientation
(b) Creature of multiple layers
(c) Hybrid creature
(d) Constantly changing creature

41. Who is the author of *Political Economy of Development in India*?
(a) Amartya Sen (b) Subipta Kaviraj
(c) Pranab Bardhan (d) Hanza Allavi

42. In order to ensure free and fair elections and to conduct all elections to the Panchayats, the power is vested with
(a) Chief Election Commissioner of India
(b) Chief Minister of the State
(c) State Election Commission
(d) Chief Secretary of the State

43. **Assertion (A):** The President of India is the Constitutional Head of the State.
Reason (R): All powers are vested in the Council of Ministers headed by the Prime Minister.
Select the correct answer from the codes given below:
Codes:
(a) Both (A) and (R) are true and (R) is the correct explanation of (A).
(b) Both (A) and (R) are true, but (R) is not the correct explanation of (A).
(c) (A) is true, but (R) is false.
(d) (A) is false, but (R) is true.

44. Match List I with List II and select the correct answer from the codes given below:
List I
(A) Emergence of Muslim League
(B) Lucknow Pact
(C) Motilal Nehru Report
(D) Two-Nation Theory
List II
(i) 1940 (ii) 1906
(iii) 1916 (iv) 1928

Codes:	A	B	C	D
(a)	(iii)	(ii)	(iv)	(i)
(b)	(ii)	(iii)	(iv)	(i)
(c)	(iv)	(iii)	(i)	(ii)
(d)	(i)	(iii)	(iv)	(ii)

45. What is the correct sequence of the following Presidents of India? Use the code given below:
(i) Dr. Zakir Hussain
(ii) Dr. Rajendra Prasad
(iii) Dr. Shankar Dayal Sharma
(iv) R. Venkataraman
(a) (i) (ii) (iv) (iii) (b) (ii) (i) (iv) (iii)
(c) (iv) (iii) (i) (ii) (d) (iii) (iv) (ii) (i)

46. Consider the following statements: In the area of organizational principles
(1) In working out organizational principles, Gulick was influenced by Fayol's fourteen principles.
(2) Urwick warns against the 'use of committees for the purpose of administration'.

(3) Gulick gives no regard to the bases on which work may be divided.
(4) Fayol believed in the principle of 'unity of command'.

Which of these statements are correct?
(a) 1, 2, 3 and 4 (b) 1, 2 and 3
(c) 1 and 4 (d) 1, 2 and 4

47. Match List I with List II and select the correct answer from the codes given below:

List I
(A) Frederick Herzberg
(B) Abraham Maslow
(C) Fred W. Riggs
(D) M.P. Follett

List II
(i) The Need Hierarchy
(ii) The existence of 'Clects'
(iii) Motivator-Hygiene Approach
(iv) Concept of Partnership

Codes:	A	B	C	D
(a)	(iii)	(i)	(ii)	(iv)
(b)	(ii)	(iii)	(iv)	(i)
(c)	(i)	(iv)	(ii)	(iii)
(d)	(iv)	(iii)	(ii)	(i)

48. According to Chester I. Barnard which one of the following is not correct about an order to be authoritative?
(a) It should conform to the purpose of the organization.
(b) It should be intelligible.
(c) It should be motivating monetarily.
(d) It should be feasible.

49. According to Mooney, conferring of specified authority by a higher authority is
(a) Decentralization (b) Delegation
(c) Deconcentration (d) Disintegration

50. Who defined development administration as "Action-oriented, goal-oriented administrative system"?
(a) Fred W. Riggs
(b) Dwight Waldo
(c) Robert Dahl
(d) Edward Weidner

51. According to David Nachmias and D.H. Rosenbloom, which one of the following is not a feature of participatory bureaucracy?
(a) Civil Service Associations to protect them from political tyranny.
(b) High level of social representativeness in a national bureaucracy.
(c) Participation of bureaucratic employees in decisions.
(d) Citizen participation in bureaucratic policy making.

52. Who among the following introduced the concept of 'Zone of Indifference' in an organization?
(a) Herbert Simon
(b) Douglas McGregor
(c) Chester I. Barnard
(d) Chris Argyris

53. Taylor's concept of Mental Revolution stands for
(a) Cooperation, Harmony and Restricted output
(b) Restricted output and Cooperation
(c) Harmony and Cooperation
(d) Economy, Cooperation and restricted output

54. Which of the following committees recommended two-tier Panchayatiraj institutions?
(a) Ashok Mehta Committee
(b) G.V.K. Rao Committee
(c) R.R. Diwakar Committee
(d) L.M. Singhvi Committee

55. When was the Central Vigilance Commission set up by the Government of India?

(a) 1961 (b) 1964
(c) 1967 (d) 1971

56. Arrange the following committees in chronological order and choose the correct answer from the codes given below:
(i) Kripalani Committee
(ii) Santhanam Committee
(iii) Tek Chand Committee
(iv) Vivian Bose Committee
Codes:
(a) (iii), (iv), (i), (ii) (b) (i), (iv), (iii), (ii)
(c) (iv), (i), (iii), (ii) (d) (iii), (i), (iv), (ii)

57. Which of the following committees recommended Block Level Planning?
(a) Hanumantha Rao Committee
(b) G.V.K. Rao Committee
(c) L.M. Singhvi Committee
(d) Dantwala Committee

58. Which among the following is not a feature of Liberalisation?
(a) Deregulation
(b) Debureaucratisation
(c) Disinvestment
(d) Statisation

59. The institution of 'Ombudsman' was first introduced in
(a) Denmark (b) UK
(c) Sweden (d) Switzerland

60. Given below are two statements, one labelled as Assertion (A) and the other labelled as Reason (R).
Assertion (A): Talking about responsibility, Follett maintains that "the distinction between those who manage and those who are managed is somewhat fading."
Reason (R): "Each individual function must be seen in terms of its interdependence with other functions" in the organization.
Select the correct answer from the codes given below:
Codes:
(a) Both (A) and (R) are individually true and (R) is the correct explanation of (A).
(b) Both (A) and (R) are individually true, but (R) is not the correct explanation of (A).
(c) (A) is true, but (R) is false.
(d) (A) is false, but (R) is true.

61. Which of the following was an important figure in the development of liberal perspectives on international politics?
(a) Thomas Hobbes
(b) Woodrow Wilson
(c) Hans J. Morganthan
(d) Henry Kissinger

62. Match List I with List II and select the correct answer from the codes given below:
List I
(A) Samuel P. Huntington
(B) Joseph Nye
(C) Susan Strange
(D) Immanuel Wallerstein
List II
(i) Retreat of the State
(ii) World Systems
(iii) Clash of Civilizations
(iv) Soft Power

Codes:	**A**	**B**	**C**	**D**
(a)	(iii)	(iv)	(i)	(ii)
(b)	(ii)	(iii)	(iv)	(i)
(c)	(iv)	(ii)	(iii)	(i)
(d)	(iii)	(i)	(ii)	(iv)

63. The Bretton Woods Agreement
(a) led to a campaign to save the rainforest
(b) argues that the Soviet Union was a success of the unmixed economy

(c) led to the establishment of the International Monetary Fund (IMF)
(d) led to the establishment of the World Wildlife Fund (WWF)

64. According to many realists, how is international peace best secured?
(a) Concessions by peaceful States to powerful ones.
(b) A balance of power between States.
(c) Trying to spread democratic values throughout the world.
(d) A worldwide federation of States.

65. In the field of nuclear strategy what does MAD stand for?
(a) Missiles Are Dangerous
(b) Mammals Are Doomed
(c) Make America Die
(d) Mutually Assured Destruction

66. Who said the following, "War is Foreign Policy by other means"?
(a) Carl von Clausewitz
(b) Napoleon Bonaparte
(c) Quincy Wright
(d) Hugo Clausewitz

67. Non-alignment as India's foreign policy meant
(a) neutrality.
(b) equidistance between the three blocs during the cold war.
(c) independence and judging each issue on its relevance to our national interest.
(d) interference into the internal affairs of other States.

68. Given below are two statements, one labelled as Assertion (A) and the other labelled as Reason (R):

Assertion (A): India is for nuclear disarmament at the global level and for a credible minimum deterrence at the regional level.

Reason (R): India's nuclear policy has dual objectives.

Codes:
(a) Both (A) and (R) are true and (R) is the correct explanation of (A).
(b) Both (A) and (R) are true, but (R) is not the correct explanation of (A).
(c) (A) is true but (R) is false
(d) Both (A) and (R) are false.

69. What is the correct sequence of the following Ministers of External Affairs of India?
(i) S.M. Krishna
(ii) Atal. B. Vajpayee
(iii) Pranab Mukherjee
(iv) Swarna Singh

Arrange the following chronologically from who came first:
(a) (iv) (ii) (iii) (i)   (b) (ii) (iv) (i) (iii)
(c) (iv) (iii) (ii) (i)   (d) (i) (iii) (iv) (ii)

70. "Indira Doctrine" is considered an important aspect of India's foreign policy for it defines
(a) The objectives of India's foreign policy.
(b) It equates India's security with that of the region and the predominance of India.
(c) India's security is coterminous with the region and any interference of external powers is taken as a threat to India's security.
(d) Doctrine enunciated by Prime Minister Indira Gandhi which was for the neighbours.

71. The United Nations Charter is mainly
(a) largely concerned with individual human rights.
(b) wholly concerned with the relationship between States.
(c) devoted to a wide range of subjects including peace, justice, freedom and economic and social rights.
(d) devoted to duties and rights of great, medium and small powers.

72. International society tradition is also known as the
    (a) Anglo-American School of International Relations.
    (b) English School of International Relations.
    (c) European School of International Relations
    (d) Alternative School of International Relations

73. The main purpose of the Indo-Sri Lanka Accord was
    (a) India's war against Tamils.
    (b) India's intention to partition Sri Lanka.
    (c) To end the ethnic strife between the Sinhalese and Tamils.
    (d) To legalise Tamil Militant groups.

74. The Asia-Pacific Economic Cooperation (APEC) forum
    (a) is part of a more general trend towards regional blocs.
    (b) accounts for over half the world's GDP
    (c) has member states which include authoritarian regimes as well as democracies.
    (d) All of the above are true.

75. The US approach to the Cold War was originally set out in
    (a) The Nixon Doctrine
    (b) The Marshall Plan
    (c) The Monroe Doctrine
    (d) The Truman Doctrine

ANSWERS

1. (b)	2. (d)	3. (a)	4. (c)	5. (d)
6. (b)	7. (b)	8. (b)	9. (b)	10. (c)
11. (b)	12. (c)	13. (c)	14. (b)	15. (d)
16. (a)	17. (c)	18. (c)	19. (a)	20. (a)
21. (a)	22. (b)	23. (d)	24. (d)	25. (d)
26. (c)	27. (b)	28. (d)	29. (b)	30. (b)
31. (b)	32. (a)	33. (c)	34. (c)	35. (d)
36. (c)	37. (c)	38. (b)	39. (c)	40. (a)
41. (c)	42. (c)	43. (a)	44. (b)	45. (b)
46. (d)	47. (a)	48. (c)	49. (b)	50. (d)
51. (a)	52. (c)	53. (c)	54. (a)	55. (b)
56. (d)	57. (d)	58. (d)	59. (c)	60. (b)
61. (b)	62. (a)	63. (c)	64. (b)	65. (d)
66. (a)	67. (c)	68. (a)	69. (a)	70. (c)
71. (c)	72. (b)	73. (c)	74. (d)	75. (d)

DECEMBER–2011

Note: This paper contains Sixty (60) multiple-choice questions, each question carrying two (2) marks. Candidate is expected to answer any Fifty (50) questions. In case more than Fifty (50) questions are attempted, only the first Fifty (50) questions will be evaluated.

PAPER–I

1. Photo bleeding means
   (a) Photo cropping
   (b) Photo placement
   (c) Photo cutting
   (d) Photo colour adjustment

2. While designing communication strategy feed-forward studies are conducted by
   (a) Audience (b) Communicator
   (c) Satellite (d) Media

3. In which language the newspapers have highest circulation?
   (a) English (b) Hindi
   (c) Bengali (d) Tamil

4. Aspect ratio of TV screen is
   (a) 4 : 3 (b) 3 : 4
   (c) 2 : 3 (d) 2 : 4

5. Communication with oneself is known as
   (a) Organisational Communication
   (b) Grapevine Communication
   (c) Interpersonal Communication
   (d) Intrapersonal Communication

6. The term 'SITE' stands for
   (a) Satellite Indian Television Experiment
   (b) Satellite International Television Experiment
   (c) Satellite Instructional Television Experiment
   (d) Satellite Instructional Teachers Education

7. What is the number that comes next in the sequence?
   2, 5, 9, 19, 37, ___
   (a) 76 (b) 74
   (c) 75 (d) 50

8. Find the next letter for the series MPSV.....
   (a) X (b) Y
   (c) Z (d) A

9. If '367' means 'I am happy'; '748' means 'you are sad' and '469' means 'happy and sad' in a given code, then which of the following represents 'and' in that code?
   (a) 3 (b) 6
   (c) 9 (d) 4

10. The basis of the following classification is 'animal', 'man', 'house', 'book', and 'student':
    (a) Definite descriptions
    (b) Proper names
    (c) Descriptive phrases
    (d) Common names

11. **Assertion (A):** The coin when flipped next time will come up tails.
    Reason (R): Because the coin was flipped five times in a row, and each time it came up heads.
    Choose the correct answer from below:
    (a) Both (A) and (R) are true, and (R) is the correct explanation of (A).
    (b) Both (A) and (R) are false, and (R) is the correct explanation of (A).

(c) (A) is doubtful, (R) is true, and (R) is not the correct explanation of (A).
(d) (A) is doubtful, (R) is false, and (R) is the correct explanation of (A).

12. The relation 'is a sister of' is
(a) non-symmetrical (b) symmetrical
(c) asymmetrical (d) transitive

13. If the proposition "Vegetarians are not meat eaters" is false, then which of the following inferences is correct? Choose from the codes given below:
1. "Some vegetarians are meat eaters" is true.
2. "All vegetarians are meat eaters" is doubtful.
3. "Some vegetarians are not meat eaters" is true.
4. "Some vegetarians are not meat eaters" is doubtful.

Codes:
(a) 1, 2 and 3 (b) 2, 3 and 4
(c) 1, 3 and 4 (d) 1, 2 and 4

14. Determine the nature of the following definition:
'Poor' means having an annual income of ₹ 10,000.
(a) persuasive (b) precising
(c) lexical (d) stipulative

15. Which one of the following is not an argument?
(a) If today is Tuesday, tomorrow will be Wednesday.
(b) Since today is Tuesday, tomorrow will be Wednesday.
(c) Ram insulted me so I punched him in the nose.
(d) Ram is not at home, so he must have gone to town.

16. Venn diagram is a kind of diagram to
(a) represent and assess the truth of elementary inferences with the help of Boolean Algebra of classes.
(b) represent and assess the validity of elementary inferences with the help of Boolean Algebra of classes.
(c) represent but not assess the validity of elementary inferences with the help of Boolean Algebra of classes.
(d) assess but not represent the validity of elementary inferences with the help of Boolean Algebra of classes.

17. Inductive logic studies the way in which a premise may
(a) support and entail a conclusion
(b) not support but entail a conclusion
(c) neither support nor entail a conclusion
(d) support a conclusion without entailing it

18. Which of the following statements are true? Choose from the codes given below.
1. Some arguments, while not completely valid, are almost valid.
2. A sound argument may be invalid.
3. A cogent argument may have a probably false conclusion.
4. A statement may be true or false.

Codes:
(a) 1 and 2 (b) 1, 3 and 4
(c) Only 4 (d) 3 and 4

19. If the side of the square increases by 40%, then the area of the square increases by
(a) 60% (b) 40%
(c) 196% (d) 96%

20. There are 10 lamps in a hall. Each one of them can be switched on independently. The number of ways in which hall can be illuminated is
(a) 10^2 (b) 1023
(c) 2^{10} (d) 10!

21. How many numbers between 100 and 300 begin or end with 2?
(a) 100 (b) 110
(c) 120 (d) 180

22. In a college having 300 students, every student reads 5 newspapers and every newspaper is read by 60 students. The number of newspapers required is
(a) at least 30 (b) at most 20
(c) exactly 25 (d) exactly 5

The total CO_2 emissions from various sectors are 5 mmt. In the Pie Chart given below, the percentage contribution to CO_2 emissions from various sectors is indicated.

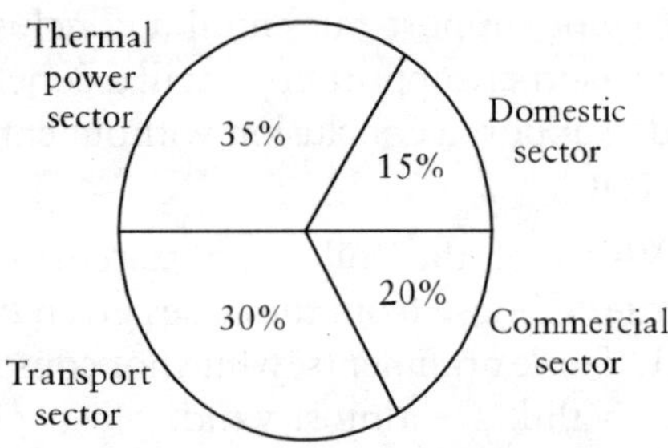

23. What is the absolute CO_2 emission from domestic sector?
(a) 1.5 mmt (b) 2.5 mmt
(c) 1.75 mmt (d) 0.75 mmt

24. What is the absolute CO_2 emission for combined thermal power and transport sectors?
(a) 3.25 mmt (b) 1.5 mmt
(c) 2.5 mmt (d) 4 mmt

25. Which of the following operating systemms is used on mobile phones?
(a) Windows Vista
(b) Android
(c) Windows XP
(d) All of the above

26. If $(y)_x$ represents a number y in base x, then which of the following numbers is smallest of all?
(a) $(1111)_2$ (b) $(1111)_8$
(c) $(1111)_{10}$ (d) $(1111)_{16}$

27. High level programming language can be converted to machine language using which of the following?
(a) Oracle (b) Compiler
(c) Mat lab (d) Assembler

28. HTML is used to create
(a) machine language program
(b) high level program
(c) web page
(d) web server

29. The term DNS stands for
(a) Domain Name System
(b) Defense Nuclear System
(c) Downloadable New Software
(d) Dependent Name Server

30. IPv4 and IPv6 are addresses used to identify computers on the Internet. Find the correct statement out of the following:
(a) Number of bits required for IPv4 address is more than number of bits required for IPv6 address.
(b) Number of bits required for IPv4 address is same as number of bits required for IPv6 address.
(c) Number of bits required for IPv4 address is less than number of bits required for IPv6 address.
(d) Number of bits required for IPv4 address is 64.

31. Which of the following pollutants affects the respiratory tract in humans?
(a) Carbon monoxide
(b) Nitric oxide
(c) Sulphur dioxide
(d) Aerosols

32. Which of the following pollutants is not emitted from the transport sector?
(a) Oxides of nitrogen
(b) Chlorofluorocarbons
(c) Carbon monoxide
(d) Poly aromatic hydrocarbons

33. Which of the following sources of energy has the maximum potential in India?
(a) Solar energy
(b) Wind energy
(c) Ocean thermal energy
(d) Tidal energy

34. Which of the following is not a source of pollution in soil?
(a) Transport sector
(b) Agriculture sector
(c) Thermal power plants
(d) Hydropower plants

35. Which of the following is not a natural hazard?
(a) Earthquake (b) Tsunami
(c) Flash floods (d) Nuclear accident

36. Ecological footprint represents
(a) area of productive land and water to meet the resources requirement
(b) energy consumption
(c) CO_2 emissions per person
(d) forest cover

37. The aim of value education to inculcate in students is
(a) the moral values
(b) the social values
(c) the political values
(d) the economic values

38. Indicate the number of Regional Offices of University Grants Commission of India.
(a) 10 (b) 07
(c) 08 (d) 09

39. One-rupee currency note in India bears the signature of
(a) The President of India
(b) Finance Minister of India
(c) Governor, Reserve Bank of India
(d) Finance Secretary of Government of India

40. Match the List I with the List II and select the correct answer from the codes given below:

List I (Commissions and Committees)
A. First Administrative Reforms Commission
B. Paul H. Appleby Committee I
C. K. Santhanam Committee
D. Second Administrative Reforms Commission

List II (Years)
1. 2005 2. 1962
3. 1966 4. 1953

Codes:	A	B	C	D
(a)	1	3	2	4
(b)	3	4	2	1
(c)	4	2	3	1
(d)	2	1	4	3

41. Constitutionally the registration and recognition of political parties is the function performed by
(a) The State Election Commission of respective States
(b) The Law Ministry of Government of India
(c) The Election Commission of India
(d) Election Department of the State Governments

42. The members of Gram Sabha are
(a) Sarpanch, Upsarpanch and all elected Panchas
(b) Sarpanch, Upsarpanch and Village level worker
(c) Sarpanch, Gram Sevak and elected Panchas
(d) Registered voters of Village Panchayat

43. By which of the following methods the true evaluation of the students is possible?
(a) Evaluation at the end of the course
(b) Evaluation twice in a year
(c) Continuous evaluation
(d) Formative evaluation

44. Suppose a student wants to share his problems with his teacher and he visits the teacher's house for the purpose, the teacher should

(a) contact the student's parents and solve his problem
(b) suggest him that he should never visit his house
(c) suggest him to meet the principal and solve the problem
(d) extend reasonable help and boost his morale

45. When some students are deliberately attempting to disturb the discipline of the class by making mischief, what will be your role as a teacher?
(a) Expelling those students
(b) Isolate those students
(c) Reform the group with your authority
(d) Giving them an opportunity for introspection and improve their behaviour

46. Which of the following belongs to a projected aid?
(a) Blackboard (b) Diorama
(c) Epidiascope (d) Globe

47. A teacher is said to be fluent in asking questions, if he can ask
(a) meaningful questions
(b) as many questions as possible
(c) maximum number of questions in a fixed time
(d) many meaningful questions in a fixed time

48. Which of the following qualities is most essential for a teacher?
(a) He should be a learned person
(b) He should be a well-dressed person
(c) He should have patience
(d) He should be an expert in his subject

49. A hypothesis is a
(a) law (b) canon
(c) postulate (d) supposition

50. Suppose you want to investigate the working efficiency of nationalised bank in India, which one of the following would you follow?
(a) Area Sampling
(b) Multi-stage Sampling
(c) Sequential Sampling
(d) Quota Sampling

51. Controlled group condition is applied in
(a) Survey Research
(b) Historical Research
(c) Experimental Research
(d) Descriptive Research

52. Workshops are meant for
(a) giving lectures
(b) multiple target groups
(c) showcase new theories
(d) hands on training/experience

53. Which one of the following is a research tool?
(a) Graph (b) Illustration
(c) Questionnaire (d) Diagram

54. Research is not considered ethical if it
(a) tries to prove a particular point.
(b) does not ensure privacy and anonymity of the respondent.
(c) does not investigate the data scientifically.
(d) is not of a very high standard.

Read the following passage carefully and answer the questions (55 to 60):

The catalytic fact of the twentieth century is uncontrollable development, consumerist society, political materialism, and spiritual devaluation. This inordinate development has led to the transcendental 'second reality' of sacred perception that biologically transcendence is a part of human life. As the century closes, it dawns with imperative vigour that the 'first reality' of enlightened rationalism and the 'second reality' of the Beyond have to be harmonised in a worthy state of man. The *de facto* values describe what we are, they portray the 'is' of our ethic, they are *est* values

(Latin *est* means is). The ideal values tell us what we ought to be, they are *esto* values (Latin *esto* 'ought to be'). Both have to be in the ebb and flow of consciousness. The ever new science and technology and the ever-perennial faith are two modes of one certainty, that is the wholeness of man, his courage to be, his share in Being.

The materialistic foundations of science have crumbled down. Science itself has proved that matter is energy, processes are as valid as facts, and affirmed the non-materiality of the universe. The encounter of the 'two cultures', the scientific and the humane, will restore the normal vision, and will be the bedrock of a 'science of understanding' in the new century. It will give new meaning to the ancient perception that quantity (measure) and quality (value) coexist at the root of nature. Human endeavours cannot afford to be humanistically irresponsible.

55. The problem raised in the passage reflects overall on
    (a) Consumerism
    (b) Materialism
    (c) Spiritual devaluation
    (d) Inordinate development

56. The *de facto* values in the passage means
    (a) What is
    (b) What ought to be
    (c) What can be
    (d) Where it is

57. According to the passage, the 'first reality' constitutes
    (a) Economic prosperity
    (b) Political development
    (c) Sacred perception of life
    (d) Enlightened rationalism

58. Encounter of the 'two cultures', the scientific and the human implies
    (a) Restoration of normal vision
    (b) Universe is both material and non-material
    (c) Man is superior to nature
    (d) Co-existence of quantity and quality in nature

59. The contents of the passage are
    (a) Descriptive (b) Prescriptive
    (c) Axiomatic (d) Optional

60. The passage indicates that science has proved that
    (a) universe is material
    (b) matter is energy
    (c) nature has abundance
    (d) humans are irresponsible

ANSWERS

1. (a)	2. (b)	3. (b)	4. (a)	5. (d)
6. (c)	7. (c)	8. (b)	9. (c)	10. (d)
11. (c)	12. (b)	13. (a)	14. (b)	15. (a)
16. (b)	17. (d)	18. (d)	19. (d)	20. (b)
21. (b)	22. (c)	23. (d)	24. (a)	25. (b)
26. (a)	27. (b)	28. (c)	29. (a)	30. (c)
31. (a)	32. (b)	33. (b)	34. (d)	35. (d)
36. (a)	37. (a)	38. (b)	39. (d)	40. (b)
41. (c)	42. (d)	43. (d)	44. (d)	45. (d)
46. (c)	47. (d)	48. (c)	49. (d)	50. (b)
51. (c)	52. (d)	53. (c)	54. (b)	55. (c)
56. (a)	57. (d)	58. (a)	59. (a)	60. (b)

PAPER–II

Note: This paper contains fifty (50) objective type questions, each question carrying two (2) marks. All questions are compulsory.

1. The thinker who synthesized German and English Liberalism was
    (a) Bosanquet (b) Hobhouse
    (c) G.D.H. Cole (d) T.H. Green

2. Which one of the following is not a theorist of Political Realism?
(a) Kenneth Waltz
(b) Norman Angell
(c) Morgenthau
(d) Joseph Grecho

3. Which one of the following is not a supporter of Deontological view?
(a) John Locke (b) John Rawls
(c) Machiavelli (d) Isaiah Berlin

4. 'Hind Swaraj' depends
(a) Mazzini's Italy
(b) Disraeli's England
(c) Lincoln's USA
(d) Bismarck's Germany

5. Which one of the following is not one of the indicators of political development?
(a) Capacity (b) Equality
(c) Fraternity (d) Differentiation

6. The ideal type of federalism is
(a) Dual federalism
(b) Bargaining federalism
(c) New federalism
(d) Co-operative federalism

7. Independence of executive is the principle of
(a) Indian Constitution
(b) British Constitution
(c) American Constitution
(d) Swiss Constitution

8. Who says that a proper revolution should be restricted to the political and should not extend to the social?
(a) Che Guevara (b) Regis Debray
(c) Crane Brinton (d) Hannah Arendt

9. Which of the following Commissions does not have the constitutional status?
(a) Finance Commission
(b) Union Public Service Commission
(c) National Commission for Scheduled Castes
(d) Planning Commission

10. Which of the following cases propounded the concept of basic structure of the Indian Constitution?
(a) Golak Nath case
(b) Minerva Mills case
(c) Keshvananda Bharti case
(d) Maneka Gandhi case

11. "Swaraj will not be a free gift of the British Parliament, it will be a declaration of India's full expression."—Among the following who made this statement?
(a) Jawaharlal Nehru
(b) Radhakrishnan
(c) Mahatma Gandhi
(d) Maulana Abul Kalam Azad

12. A political party is recognised as a regional party if
(a) It gets 4 per cent votes in the state either in the Lok Sabha or the Assembly elections.
(b) It gets 5 per cent votes in the state either in the Lok Sabha or the Assembly elections.
(c) It gets 6 per cent votes in the state either in the Lok Sabha or the Assembly elections.
(d) It gets 7 per cent votes in the state either in the Lok Sabha or in the Assembly elections.

13. The foremost pioneer of contemporary world-system theory is
(a) Paul Sweezy
(b) Immanuel Wallerstein
(c) Tariq Ali
(d) Andre G. Frank

14. The doctrine of 'limited sovereignty' was propounded by
(a) Stalin (b) Khrushchev
(c) Brezhnev (d) Andropov

15. After the break-up of USSR, some of its Republics have constituted themselves into

(a) Commonwealth of Independent States (CIS)
(b) Commonwealth of Independent Nations (CIN)
(c) Commonwealth of Independent Countries (CIC)
(d) Commonwealth of Independent Republics (CIR)

16. India has not signed the NPT because it
(a) gives undue advantage to advanced countries.
(b) is immoral.
(c) is discriminatory.
(d) is inimical to the interests of post colonial countries.

17. Which one of the following is not correct about New Public Administration?
(a) It is more public-oriented than generic.
(b) It is more analytical than descriptive.
(c) It is more customer-oriented than institution-oriented.
(d) It is more value-laden than being neutral.

18. According to Fayol, an administrator or a manager must possess six types of abilities. Which of the following is not one of those suggested by him?
(a) Appearance
(b) Technical Knowledge
(c) Academic Qualifications
(d) Tactfulness

19. Which of the following is not one of the 'functional foremen' who sit in the 'planning room', as suggested by F.W. Taylor?
(a) Speed Boss
(b) Route Clerk
(c) Instruction Card Clerk
(d) Shop Disciplinarian

20. The scholar who after finding Max Weber's model of bureaucracy irrelevant and inappropriate for explaining the administrative ecology of developing and transitional societies, developed Prismatic and Sala Models for the study of such societies, was
(a) Hebert Simon
(b) Waldo
(c) Fred W. Riggs
(d) Alfred Diamond

21. Given below are two statements, one labelled as Assertion (A) and the other as Reason (R):
Assertion (A): According to Herbert Simon, 'maximising decision is not possible'.
Reason (R): He believes that rationality is possible in administrative behaviour.
Select the correct answer from the codes below:
Codes:
(a) Both (A) and (R) are true and (R) is the correct explanation of (A).
(b) Both (A) and (R) are true, but (R) is not the correct explanation of (A).
(c) (A) is true, but (R) is false.
(d) (A) is false, but (R) is true.

22. Given below are two statements, one labelled as Assertion (A) and the other labelled as Reason (R):
Assertion (A): Gandhi's critique of determinism is revealed in his belief in relative truth.
Reason (R): Because of this he believed in the theory of one step at a time.
Choose the correct answer from the codes below:
Codes:
(a) Both (A) and (R) are true and (R) is the correct explanation of (A).
(b) Both (A) and (R) are true, but (R) is not the correct explanation of (A).
(c) (A) is true, but (R) is false.
(d) (A) is false, but (R) is true.

23. Given below are two statements, one labelled as Assertion (A) and the other labelled as Reason (R):
    Assertion (A): The Indian citizens need patience and determination to preserve the gains made so far by the social and economic reforms.
    Reason (R): Indian society is involved in democratic churning.
    Choose the correct answer from the codes given below:
    Codes:
    (a) Both (A) and (R) are individually correct and (R) is the correct explanation of (A).
    (b) Both (A) and (R) are individually correct and (R) is not the correct explanation of (A).
    (c) (A) is true, but (R) is false.
    (d) (A) is false, but (R) is true.

24. Given below are two statements, one labelled as Assertion (A) and the other labelled as Reason (R):
    Assertion (A): Preferential policies need not always violate the principle of fairness.
    Reason (R): Treating citizens as equals may require treating them differently.
    Choose the correct answer from the codes given below:
    Codes:
    (a) Both (A) and (R) are individually true and (R) is the correct explanation of (A).
    (b) Both (A) and (R) are individually true but (R) is not the correct explanation of (A).
    (c) (A) is true, but (R) is false.
    (d) (A) is false, but (R) is true.

25. Given below are two statements, Assertion (A) and Reason (R):
    Assertion (A): The Westphalian state system created in 1648 is not valid in the post-Communist world.
    Reason (R): Because the sanctity of territorial sovereignty can be done away with UN sanctions.
    Choose the correct answer from the codes below:
    Codes:
    (a) Both (A) and (R) are true and (R) is the correct explanation of (A).
    (b) Both (A) and (R) are true, but (R) is not the correct explanation of (A).
    (c) (A) is true, but (R) is false.
    (d) (A) is false, but (R) is true.

26. Given below are two statements, one labelled as Assertion (A) and the other labelled as Reason (R):
    Assertion (A): The Administrative Science should study facts about human behaviour without getting involved in the question of values.
    Reason (R): It is not necessary for science to possess concepts before it develops principles.
    Select the correct answer from the codes below:
    Codes:
    (a) Both (A) and (R) are true and (R) is the correct explanation of (A).
    (b) Both (A) and (R) are true, but (R) is not the correct explanation of (A).
    (c) (A) is true, but (R) is false.
    (d) (A) is false, but (R) is true.

27. Arrange the following in chronological order and choose correct answer from the codes given below:
    (i) The Statesman – Plato
    (ii) Emile – Rousseau
    (iii) A Fragment of Government – Bentham
    (iv) Art of War – Machiavelli
    Codes:
    (a) (ii), (i), (iv), (iii) (b) (iv), (ii), (iii), (i)
    (c) (i), (iv), (ii), (iii) (d) (iii), (ii), (iv), (i)

28. Arrange the following books in chronological order as per codes given below:

(i) *An Essay Concerning Toleration*
(ii) *De Cive*
(iii) *Confessions*
(iv) *Political Liberalism*

Codes:
(a) (iii), (iv), (ii), (i) (b) (i), (ii), (iv), (iii)
(c) (ii), (i), (iii), (iv) (d) (iv), (iii), (i), (ii)

29. Arrange the following in chronological order and choose the correct answer from the codes given below:
(i) Fulton Committee Report
(ii) Brownlow Committee Report
(iii) First Hoover Commission Report
(iv) Assheton Committee Report

Codes:
(a) (iv), (i), (iii), (ii) (b) (iii), (ii), (iv), (i)
(c) (i), (iv), (ii), (iii) (d) (ii), (i), (iv), (iii)

30. Arrange the following Earth Summits held so far in chronological order:
(i) Rio-de-Jeneiro Summit
(ii) Kyoto Summit
(iii) Bali Summit
(iv) Copenhagen Summit

Codes:
(a) (ii), (iii), (i), (iv) (b) (i), (ii), (iii), (iv)
(c) (iii), (ii), (i), (iv) (d) (iii), (iv), (i), (ii)

31. Identify the correct chronological order in which the following approaches emerged in comparative politics.
(i) New Institutional Approach
(ii) Marxist Approach
(iii) Philosophical Approach
(iv) Behavioural Approach

Codes:
(a) (ii), (i), (iv), (iii) (b) (iv), (ii), (i), (iii)
(c) (iii), (ii), (iv), (i) (d) (i), (iii), (ii), (iv)

32. Identify the correct chronological order of the following from the codes given below:
(i) Arthur F. Bentley
(ii) H.D. Lasswell
(iii) James Bryce
(iv) A.V. Dicey

Codes:
(a) (ii), (iv), (i), (iii) (b) (iv), (iii), (i), (ii)
(c) (iii), (ii), (iv), (i) (d) (i), (iii), (iv), (ii)

33. Identify the correct chronological order of the following:
(i) Cabinet Mission Plan
(ii) Cripps Mission
(iii) Simon Commission
(iv) Communal Award

Codes:
(a) (ii), (i), (iii), (iv) (b) (iv), (iii), (ii), (i)
(c) (i), (iii), (iv), (ii) (d) (iii), (iv), (ii), (i)

34. Identify the correct chronological order in which the following states were created. Use the codes given below:
(i) Goa
(ii) Himachal Pradesh
(iii) Haryana
(iv) Sikkim

Codes:
(a) (iv), (ii), (iii), (i) (b) (i), (iii), (iv), (ii)
(c) (i), (ii), (iv), (iii) (d) (iii), (ii), (iv), (i)

35. Arrange the following in correct chronological order and give answer from the codes given below:
(i) Ostpolitic
(ii) Warsaw Pact
(iii) NATO
(iv) Helsinki Agreement

Codes:
(a) (iv), (i), (iii), (ii) (b) (ii), (iv), (i), (iii)
(c) (iii), (ii), (i), (iv) (d) (i), (iii), (iv), (ii)

36. Arrange the following in chronological order and choose the correct answer from the codes given below:
(i) Fall of Berlin Wall
(ii) Cuban Missile Crisis
(iii) Korean War
(iv) Berlin Blockade

Codes:
(a) (i), (ii), (iii), (iv) (b) (iv), (iii), (i), (ii)
(c) (i), (iv), (iii), (ii) (d) (iv), (iii), (ii), (i)

37. Arrange the following in chronological order and choose correct answer from the codes given below:
   (i) Bal Gangadhar Tilak
   (ii) Sir Syed Ahmad Khan
   (iii) Rabindranath Tagore
   (iv) Raja Ram Mohan Roy

   Codes:

   (a) (ii), (iii), (iv), (i) (b) (i), (ii), (iv), (iii)
   (c) (iv), (ii), (i), (iii) (d) (iii), (iv), (ii), (i)

38. Arrange the following books in order in which they appeared. Use the codes given below:
   (i) *India Wins Freedom*
   (ii) *My Experiments with Truth*
   (iii) *Idea of Justice*
   (iv) *The Indian Struggle*

   Codes:

   (a) (iv), (ii), (i), (iii) (b) (iii), (i), (iv), (ii)
   (c) (ii), (iv), (i), (iii) (d) (i), (iii), (iv), (ii)

39. Match List I with List II and choose the correct answer from the codes given below:

   List I

   (A) Habeas Corpus (B) Certiorari
   (C) Mandamus (D) Quo Warranto

   List II

   (i) Command to public authority to do its duty.
   (ii) Command to produce the body in person.
   (iii) A proceeding to enquire into the legality of a claim of a person to public office.
   (iv) Directive to lower court or judicial body not to exceed its limits.

Codes:	A	B	C	D
(a)	(i)	(iii)	(iv)	(ii)
(b)	(ii)	(iii)	(iv)	(i)
(c)	(iii)	(iv)	(ii)	(i)
(d)	(ii)	(iv)	(i)	(iii)

40. Match List I with List II and choose the correct answer from the codes given below:

   List I (School of Thought)

   (A) Cambridge School
   (B) Marxist School
   (C) Imperialist School
   (D) Nationalist School

   List II (Concepts)

   (i) Indian nationalist movement is an outcome of a sordid fight among the elites for spoils and benefits in the government.
   (ii) Structured Bourgeois movement.
   (iii) Nationalist movement reflected the needs and interests of the elite.
   (iv) Indian national movement was not anti-imperialist.

Codes:	A	B	C	D
(a)	(ii)	(iv)	(i)	(iii)
(b)	(i)	(ii)	(iii)	(iv)
(c)	(iv)	(i)	(ii)	(iii)
(d)	(iii)	(ii)	(iv)	(i)

41. Match List I with List II and choose the correct answer from the codes given below:

   List I

   (a) Alfred Cobban (b) S.M. Lipset
   (c) Dante Germino (d) David Eason

   List II

   (i) Because of the overwhelming control by bureaucracy and the creation of huge military machines inimical to political thinking, political theory has ceased to be relevant.
   (ii) Since centuries, old quest for a good society has come to an end and appropriate values for contemporary society have already been settled, political theory has lost its relevance.
   (iii) Political theory has declined because of the emergence of positivism and dominance of ideologies.
   (iv) Since there have been no thinkers since the last one hundred years who could match Hobbes and Hegel and

also Marx and Mill, political theory has declined.

Codes:	A	B	C	D
(a)	(ii)	(i)	(iii)	(iv)
(b)	(i)	(ii)	(iv)	(iii)
(c)	(i)	(ii)	(iii)	(iv)
(d)	(iv)	(iii)	(i)	(ii)

42. Match List I with List II and choose the correct answer from the codes given below:

List I
(A) Agenda for Peace
(B) Responsibility to protect
(C) Millennium Development Goals
(D) Af-Pak Policy

List II
(i) Obama
(ii) Boutros Boutros Ghali
(iii) Government of Canada
(iv) Kofi Annan

Codes:	A	B	C	D
(a)	(ii)	(iii)	(iv)	(i)
(b)	(iv)	(ii)	(iii)	(i)
(c)	(i)	(ii)	(iii)	(iv)
(d)	(ii)	(iv)	(i)	(iii)

43. Match List I with List II and choose the correct answer from the codes given below:

List I	List II
(A) Rule of Law	(i) Montesquieue
(B) Separation of Powers	(ii) John Austin
(C) Natural Rights	(iii) Dicey
(D) Monism	(iv) John Locke

Codes:	A	B	C	D
(a)	(iii)	(i)	(iv)	(ii)
(b)	(i)	(iii)	(ii)	(iv)
(c)	(iv)	(ii)	(i)	(iii)
(d)	(iii)	(i)	(ii)	(iv)

44. Match List I with List II and choose the correct answer from the codes given below:

List I
(A) Chagla Commission
(B) Administrative Reforms Commission
(C) Gore Committee
(D) Sarkaria Commission

List II
(i) Strengthening of Indian Foreign Service
(ii) Ministerial Responsibility
(iii) Training of IPS
(iv) Functional fields of IAS

Codes:	A	B	C	D
(a)	(i)	(iv)	(ii)	(iii)
(b)	(ii)	(iv)	(iii)	(i)
(c)	(iii)	(ii)	(iv)	(i)
(d)	(iv)	(iii)	(i)	(ii)

45. Match List I with List II and choose the correct answer from the codes given below:

List I	List II
(A) Staff agencies	(i) Gullick
(B) Supervision	(ii) Barnard
(C) Authority	(iii) Mooney
(D) Coordination	(iv) Millet

Codes:	A	B	C	D
(a)	(ii)	(iv)	(iii)	(i)
(b)	(iv)	(ii)	(i)	(iii)
(c)	(iii)	(iv)	(ii)	(i)
(d)	(i)	(iii)	(iv)	(ii)

46. Match List I with List II and choose the correct answer from the codes given below:

List I
(A) Govt. of India Act, 1919
(B) Govt. of India Act, 1935
(C) Minto-Morley Reforms, 1909
(D) Indian Councils Act, 1861

List II
(i) Provincial Autonomy
(ii) Dyarchy in Provinces
(iii) Legislative Councils for the Provinces
(iv) Introduction of Communal Electorates

Codes:	A	B	C	D
(a)	(iv)	(iii)	(i)	(ii)
(b)	(iii)	(ii)	(iv)	(i)
(c)	(ii)	(i)	(iv)	(iii)
(d)	(i)	(ii)	(iv)	(iii)

47. Match List I with List II and choose the correct answer from the codes given below:

List I

(A) Formation of BJP
(B) Acceptance of Mandal Commission Report by the Government
(C) Formation of the first Communist Party Government in an Indian State
(D) Passage of the 42nd Amendment

List II

(i) 1990 (ii) 1976
(iii) 1980 (iv) 1957

Codes:	A	B	C	D
(a)	(ii)	(iii)	(i)	(iv)
(b)	(iii)	(iv)	(ii)	(i)
(c)	(iv)	(i)	(iii)	(ii)
(d)	(iii)	(i)	(iv)	(ii)

48. Match List I with List II and choose the correct answer from the codes given below:

List I

(A) Father of Normative Political Theory
(B) Father of Science of Politics
(C) Father of Positivism
(D) Father of Modern Political Thought

List II

(i) Aristotle (ii) Plato
(iii) August Comte (iv) Machiavelli

Codes:	A	B	C	D
(a)	(iv)	(iii)	(i)	(ii)
(b)	(i)	(ii)	(iv)	(iii)
(c)	(i)	(iii)	(iv)	(ii)
(d)	(ii)	(i)	(iii)	(iv)

49. Match List I with List II and choose the correct answer from the codes given below:

List I

(A) Marxian Theory
(B) Realist Theory
(C) Decision-Making Theory
(D) Game Theory

List II

(i) Pay off (ii) Environment
(iii) Power (iv) Class struggle

Codes:	A	B	C	D
(a)	(iii)	(iv)	(ii)	(i)
(b)	(iv)	(iii)	(ii)	(i)
(c)	(iii)	(iv)	(i)	(ii)
(d)	(iv)	(iii)	(i)	(ii)

50. Match List I with List II and choose the correct answer from the codes given below:

List I	List II
(A) The neoliberal	(i) John Rawls
(B) The liberal	(ii) Edward Said
(C) The Marxist	(iii) Robert Nozik
(D) The Third World	(iv) Rosa Luxumburg

Codes:	A	B	C	D
(a)	(iv)	(ii)	(iii)	(i)
(b)	(iii)	(i)	(iv)	(ii)
(c)	(iv)	(i)	(iii)	(ii)
(d)	(iii)	(ii)	(iv)	(i)

ANSWERS

1. (b)	2. (d)	3. (d)	4. (c)	5. (d)
6. (a)	7. (c)	8. (b)	9. (d)	10. (a)
11. (c)	12. (c)	13. (b)	14. (b)	15. (a)
16. (c)	17. (c)	18. (a)	19. (a)	20. (c)
21. (a)	22. (a)	23. (b)	24. (b)	25. (a)
26. (b)	27. (c)	28. (c)	29. (b)	30. (b)
31. (c)	32. (b)	33. (d)	34. (d)	35. (c)
36. (d)	37. (c)	38. (c)	39. (d)	40. (d)
41. (c)	42. (c)	43. (a)	44. (b)	45. (a)
46. (c)	47. (d)	48. (d)	49. (b)	50. (b)

JUNE–2011

Note: This paper contains Sixty (60) multiple-choice questions, each question carrying two (2) marks. Candidate is expected to answer any Fifty (50) questions. In case more than Fifty (50) questions are attempted, only the first Fifty (50) questions will be evaluated.

PAPER–I

1. A research paper is a brief report of research work based on
   (a) Primary Data only
   (b) Secondary Data only
   (c) Both Primary and Secondary Data
   (d) None of the above

2. Newton gave three basic laws of motion. This research is categorised as
   (a) Descriptive Research
   (b) Sample Survey
   (c) Fundamental Research
   (d) Applied Research

3. A group of experts in a specific area of knowledge assembled at a place and prepared a syllabus for a new course. The process may be termed as
   (a) Seminar (b) Workshop
   (c) Conference (d) Symposium

4. In the process of conducting research "Formulation of Hypothesis" is followed by
   (a) Statement of Objectives
   (b) Analysis of Data
   (c) Selection of Research Tools
   (d) Collection of Data

Read the following passage carefully and answer questions 5 to 10:

All historians are interpreters of text if they be private letters, Government records or parish birthlists or whatever. For most kinds of historians, these are only the necessary means to understanding something other than the texts themselves, such as a political action or a historical trend, whereas for the intellectual historian, a full understanding of his chosen texts is itself the aim of his enquiries. Of course, the intellectual history is particularly prone to draw on the focus of other disciplines that are habitually interpreting texts for purposes of their own, probing the reasoning that ostensibly connects premises and conclusions. Furthermore, the boundaries with adjacent subdisciplines are shifting and indistinct: the history of art and the history of science both claim a certain autonomy, partly just because they require specialised technical skills, but both can also be seen as part of a wider intellectual history, as is evident when one considers, for example, the common stock of knowledge about cosmological beliefs or moral ideals of a period.

Like all historians, the intellectual historian is a consumer rather than a producer of 'methods'. His distinctiveness lies in which aspect of the past he is trying to illuminate, not in having exclusive possession of either a corpus of evidence or a body of techniques. That being said, it does seem that the label 'intellectual history' attracts a disproportionate share of misunderstanding.

It is alleged that intellectual history is the history of something that never really mattered. The long dominance of the historical profession by political historians bred a kind of philistinism, an unspoken belief that power and its exercise was 'what mattered'. The prejudice was reinforced by the assertion that political action was never really the outcome of principles or ideas that were 'more flapdoodle'. The legacy of this precept is still discernible in the tendency to require ideas to have 'licensed' the political class before they can be deemed worthy of intellectual attention, as if there were some reasons why the history of art or science, of philosophy or literature, were somehow of interest and significance than the history of Parties or Parliaments. Perhaps in recent years the mirror-image of this philistinism has been more common in the claim that ideas of any one is of systematic expression or sophistication do not matter, as if they were only held by a minority.

Answer the following questions:

5. An intellectual historian aims to fully understand
   (a) the chosen texts of his own
   (b) political actions
   (c) historical trends
   (d) his enquiries

6. Intellectual historians do not claim exclusive possession of
   (a) conclusions
   (b) any corpus of evidence
   (c) distinctiveness
   (d) habitual interpretation

7. The misconceptions about intellectual history stem from
   (a) a body of techniques
   (b) the common stock of knowledge
   (c) the dominance of political historians
   (d) cosmological beliefs

8. What is philistinism?
   (a) Reinforcement of prejudice
   (b) Fabrication of reasons
   (c) The hold of land-owning classes
   (d) Belief that power and its exercise matter

9. Knowledge of cosmological beliefs or moral ideas of a period can be drawn as part of
   (a) literary criticism
   (b) history of science
   (c) history of philosophy
   (d) intellectual history

10. The claim that ideas of any one is of systematic expression do not matter, as if they were held by a minority, is
    (a) to have a licensed political class
    (b) a political action
    (c) a philosophy of literature
    (d) the mirror-image of philistinism

11. Public communication tends to occur within a more
    (a) complex structure
    (b) political structure
    (c) convenient structure
    (d) formal structure

12. Transforming thoughts, ideas and messages into verbal and non-verbal signs is referred to as
    (a) Channelisation (b) Mediation
    (c) Encoding (d) Decoding

13. Effective communication needs a supportive
    (a) economic environment
    (b) political environment
    (c) social environment
    (d) multi-cultural environment

14. A major barrier in the transmission of cognitive data in the process of communication is an individual's
    (a) personality (b) expectation
    (c) social status (d) coding ability

15. When communicated, institutionalised stereotypes become
    (a) Myths (b) Reasons
    (c) Experiences (d) Convictions

16. In mass communication, selective perception is dependent on the receiver's

(a) Competence
(b) Pre-disposition
(c) Receptivity
(d) Ethnicity

17. Determine the relationship between the pair of words NUMERATOR: DENOMINATOR and then select the pair of words from the following which have a similar relationship:
(a) fraction : decimal
(b) divisor : quotient
(c) top : bottom
(d) dividend : divisor

18. Find the wrong number in the sequence 125, 127, 130, 135, 142, 153, 165.
(a) 130 (b) 142
(c) 153 (d) 165

19. If HOBBY is coded as IOBY and LOBBY is coded as MOBY; then BOBBY is coded as
(a) BOBY (b) COBY
(c) DOBY (d) OOBY

20. The letters in the first set have certain relationship. On the basis of this relationship, make the right choice for the second set
K/T : 11/20 :: J/R : ?
(a) 10/8 (b) 10/18
(c) 11/19 (d) 10/19

21. If A = 5, B = 6, C = 7, D = 8 and so on, what do the following numbers stand for?
17, 19, 20, 9, 8
(a) Plane (b) Moped
(c) Motor (d) Tonga

22. The price of oil is increased by 25%. If the expenditure is not allowed to increase, the ratio between the reduction in consumption and the original consumption is
(a) 1:3 (b) 1:4
(c) 1:5 (d) 1:6

23. How many 8s are there in the following sequence which are preceded by 5 but not immediately followed by 3?
5 8 3 7 5 8 6 3 8 5 4 5 8 4 7 6
5 5 8 3 5 8 7 5 8 2 8 5
(a) 4 (b) 5
(c) 7 (d) 3

24. If a rectangle were called a circle, a circle a point, a point a triangle and a triangle a square, the shape of a wheel is
(a) Rectangle (b) Circle
(c) Point (d) Triangle

25. Which one of the following methods is best suited for mapping the distribution of different crops as provided in the standard classification of crops in India?
(a) Pie diagram
(b) Chorochromatic technique
(c) Isopleth technique
(d) Dot method

26. Which one of the following does not come under the methods of data classification?
(a) Qualitative (b) Normative
(c) Spatial (d) Quantitative

27. Which one of the following is not a source of data?
(a) Administrative records
(b) Population census
(c) GIS
(d) Sample survey

28. If the statement 'some men are cruel' is false, which of the following statements/ statement are/is true?
(i) All men are cruel.
(ii) No men are cruel.
(iii) Some men are not cruel.
(a) (i) and (iii) (b) (i) and (ii)
(c) (ii) and (iii) (d) Only (iii)

29. The octal number system consists of the following symbols

(a) 0 – 7 (b) 0 – 9
(c) 0 – 9, A – F (d) None of these

30. The binary equivalent of $(-19)_{10}$ in signed magnitude system is
(a) 11101100 (b) 11101101
(c) 10010011 (d) None of these

31. DNS in internet technology stands for
(a) Dynamic Name System
(b) Domain Name System
(c) Distributed Name System
(d) None of these

32. HTML stands for
(a) Hyper Text Markup Language
(b) Hyper Text Manipulation Language
(c) Hyper Text Managing Links
(d) Hyper Text Manipulating Links

33. Which of the following is type of LAN?
(a) Ethernet (b) Token Ring
(c) FDDI (d) All of the above

34. Which of the following statements is true?
(a) Smart cards do not require an operating system.
(b) Smart cards and PCs use some operating system.
(c) COS is smart card operating system.
(d) The communication between reader and card is in full duplex mode.

35. The Ganga Action Plan was initiated during the year
(a) 1986 (b) 1988
(c) 1990 (d) 1992

36. Identify the correct sequence of energy sources in order of their share in the power sector in India.
(a) Thermal > nuclear > hydro > wind
(b) Thermal > hydro > nuclear > wind
(c) Hydro > nuclear > thermal > wind
(d) Nuclear > hydro > wind > thermal

37. Chromium as a contaminant in drinking water in excess of permissible levels, causes
(a) Skeletal damage
(b) Gastrointestinal problem
(c) Dermal and nervous problems
(d) Liver/Kidney problems

38. The main precursors of winter smog are
(a) N_2O and hydrocarbons
(b) NO_x and hydrocarbons
(c) SO_2 and hydrocarbons
(d) SO_2 and ozone

39. Flash floods are caused when
(a) the atmosphere is convectively unstable and there is considerable vertical wind shear
(b) the atmosphere is stable
(c) the atmosphere is convectively unstable with no vertical windshear
(d) winds are catabatic

40. In mega cities of India, the dominant source of air pollution is
(a) transport sector
(b) thermal power
(c) municipal waste
(d) commercial sector

41. The first Open University in India was set up in the State of
(a) Andhra Pradesh
(b) Delhi
(c) Himachal Pradesh
(d) Tamil Nadu

42. Most of the Universities in India are funded by
(a) the Central Government
(b) the State Governments
(c) the University Grants Commission
(d) Private bodies and Individuals

43. Which of the following organisations looks after the quality of Technical and Management education in India?
(a) NCTE (b) MCI
(c) AICTE (d) CSIR

44. Consider the following statements: Identify the statement which implies natural justice.

(a) The principle of natural justice is followed by the Courts.
(b) Justice delayed is justice denied.
(c) Natural justice is an inalienable right of a citizen.
(d) A reasonable opportunity of being heard must be given.

45. The President of India is
(a) the Head of State
(b) the Head of Government
(c) both Head of the State and the Head of the Government
(d) None of the above

46. Who among the following holds office during the pleasure of the President of India?
(a) Chief Election Commissioner
(b) Comptroller and Auditor General of India
(c) Chairman of the Union Public Service Commission
(d) Governor of a State

Questions 47 to 49 are based upon the following diagram in which there are three interlocking circles A, P and S where A stands for Artists, circle P for Professors and circle S for Sportspersons. Different regions in the figure are lettered from a to f:

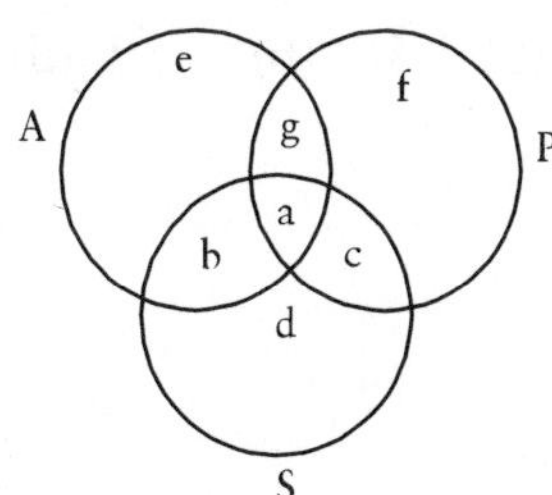

47. The region which represents artists who are neither sportsmen nor professors.
(a) d (b) e
(c) b (d) g

48. The region which represents professors, who are both artists and sportspersons.
(a) a (b) c
(c) d (d) g

49. The region which represents professors, who are also sportspersons, but not artists.
(a) e (b) f
(c) c (d) g

Questions 50 to 52 are based on the following data:

Measurements of some variable X were made at an interval of 1 minute from 10 A.M. to 10:20 A.M. The data, thus, obtained is as follows:

X: 60, 62, 65, 64, 63, 61, 66, 65, 70, 68
63, 62, 64, 69, 65, 64, 66, 67, 66, 64

50. The value of X, which is exceeded 10% of the time in the duration of measurement, is
(a) 69 (b) 68
(c) 67 (d) 66

51. The value of X, which is exceeded 90% of the time in the duration of measurement, is
(a) 63 (b) 62
(c) 61 (d) 60

52. The value of X, which is exceeded 50% of the time in the duration of measurement, is
(a) 66 (b) 65
(c) 64 (d) 63

53. For maintaining an effective discipline in the class, the teacher should
(a) Allow students to do what they like.
(b) Deal with the students strictly.
(c) Give the students some problem to solve.
(d) Deal with them politely and firmly.

54. An effective teaching aid is one which
(a) is colourful and good looking
(b) activates all faculties
(c) is visible to all students
(d) easy to prepare and use

55. Those teachers are popular among students who
    (a) develop intimacy with them
    (b) help them solve their problems
    (c) award good grades
    (d) take classes on extra tuition fee

56. The essence of an effective classroom environment is
    (a) a variety of teaching aids
    (b) lively student-teacher interaction
    (c) pin-drop silence
    (d) strict discipline

57. On the first day of his class, if a teacher is asked by the students to introduce himself, he should
    (a) ask them to meet after the class
    (b) tell them about himself in brief
    (c) ignore the demand and start teaching
    (d) scold the students for this unwanted demand

58. Moral values can be effectively inculcated among the students when the teacher
    (a) frequently talks about values
    (b) himself practises them
    (c) tells stories of great persons
    (d) talks of Gods and Goddesses

59. The essential qualities of a researcher are
    (a) spirit of free enquiry
    (b) reliance on observation and evidence
    (c) systematisation or theorising of knowledge
    (d) All of the above

60. Research is conducted to
    1. Generate new knowledge
    2. Not to develop a theory
    3. Obtain research degree
    4. Reinterpret existing knowledge

    Which of the above are correct?
    (a) 1, 3 & 2 (b) 3, 2 & 4
    (c) 2, 1 & 3 (d) 1, 3 & 4

ANSWERS

1. (c)	2. (c)	3. (b)	4. (c)	5. (a)
6. (b)	7. (c)	8. (d)	9. (d)	10. (d)
11. (d)	12. (c)	13. (d)	14. (c)	15. (d)
16. (b)	17. (d)	18. (d)	19. (b)	20. (b)
21. (b)	22. (c)	23. (a)	24. (c)	25. (b)
26. (b)	27. (a)	28. (b)	29. (a)	30. (d)
31. (b)	32. (a)	33. (d)	34. (c)	35. (a)
36. (b)	37. (d)	38. (c)	39. (a)	40. (a)
41. (a)	42. (c)	43. (c)	44. (d)	45. (b)
46. (d)	47. (b)	48. (a)	49. (c)	50. (c)
51. (b)	52. (d)	53. (d)	54. (b)	55. (b)
56. (b)	57. (b)	58. (b)	59. (d)	60. (d)

DECEMBER–2010

Note: This paper contains Sixty (60) multiple-choice questions, each question carrying two (2) marks. Candidate is expected to answer any Fifty (50) questions. In case more than Fifty (50) questions are attempted, only the first Fifty (50) questions will be evaluated.

PAPER–I

1. Which of the following variables cannot be expressed in quantitative terms?
   (a) Socio-economic Status
   (b) Marital Status
   (c) Numerical Aptitude
   (d) Professional Attitude
2. A doctor studies the relative effectiveness of two drugs of dengue fever. His research would be classified as
   (a) Descriptive Survey
   (b) Experimental Research
   (c) Case Study
   (d) Ethnography
3. The term 'phenomenology' is associated with the process of
   (a) Qualitative Research
   (b) Analysis of Variance
   (c) Correlational Study
   (d) Probability Sampling
4. The 'Sociogram' technique is used to study
   (a) Vocational Interest
   (b) Professional Competence
   (c) Human Relations
   (d) Achievement Motivation

Read the following passage carefully and answer questions from 5 to 10.

It should be remembered that the nationalist movement in India, like all nationalist movements, was essentially a bourgeois movement. It represented the natural historical stage of development, and to consider it or to criticise it as a working-class movement is wrong. Gandhi represented that movement and the Indian masses in relation to that movement to a supreme degree, and he became the voice of Indian people to that extent. The main contribution of Gandhi to India and the Indian masses has been through the powerful movements which he launched through the National Congress. Through nation-wide action he sought to mould the millions, and largely succeeded in doing so, and changing them from a demoralised, timid and hopeless mass, bullied and crushed by every dominant interest, and incapable of resistance, into a people with self-respect and self-reliance, resisting tyranny, and capable of united action and sacrifice for a larger cause.

Gandhi made people think of political and economic issues and every village and every bazaar hummed with argument and debate on the new ideas and hopes that filled the people. That was an amazing psychological change. The time was ripe for it, of course, and circumstances and world conditions worked for this change. But a great leader is necessary to take advantage of circumstances and conditions. Gandhi was that leader, and he released many of the bonds that imprisoned and disabled our minds, and none of us who experienced it can ever forget that great feeling of release and exhilaration that came over the Indian people.

Gandhi has played a revolutionary role in India of the greatest importance because he knew how to make the most of the objective conditions and could reach the heart of the masses, while groups with a more advanced ideology functioned largely in the air because they did not fit in with those conditions and could therefore not evoke any substantial response from the masses.

It is perfectly true that Gandhi, functioning in the nationalist plane, does not think in terms of the conflict of classes, and tries to compose their differences. But the action he has indulged and taught the people has inevitably raised mass consciousness tremendously and made social issues vital. Gandhi and the Congress must be judged by the policies they pursue and the action they indulge in. But behind this, personality counts and colours those policies and activities. In the case of very exceptional person like Gandhi the question of personality becomes especially important in order to understand and appraise him. To us he has represented the spirit and honour of India, the yearning of her sorrowing millions to be rid of their innumerable burdens, and an insult to him by the British Government or others has been an insult to India and her people.

5. Which one of the following is true of the given passage?
   (a) The passage is a critique of Gandhi's role in Indian movement for independence
   (b) The passage hails the role of Gandhi in India's freedom movement
   (c) The author is neutral on Gandhi's role in India's freedom movement
   (d) It is an account of Indian National Congress's support to the working-class movement
6. The change that the Gandhian movement brought among the Indian masses was
   (a) Physical (b) Cultural
   (c) Technological (d) Psychological
7. To consider the nationalist movement or to criticise it as a working-class movement was wrong because it was a
   (a) historical movement
   (b) voice of the Indian people
   (c) bourgeois movement
   (d) movement represented by Gandhi
8. Gandhi played a revolutionary role in India because he could
   (a) preach morality
   (b) reach the heart of Indians
   (c) see the conflict of classes
   (d) lead the Indian National Congress
9. Groups with advanced ideology functioned in the air as they did not fit in with
   (a) objective conditions of masses
   (b) the Gandhian ideology
   (c) the class consciousness of the people
   (d) the differences among masses
10. The author concludes the passage by
    (a) criticising the Indian masses
    (b) the Gandhian movement
    (c) pointing out the importance of the personality of Gandhi
    (d) identifying the sorrows of millions of Indians
11. Media that exist in an interconnected series of communication—points are referred to as
    (a) Networked media
    (b) Connective media
    (c) Nodal media
    (d) Multimedia
12. The information function of mass communication is described as
    (a) Diffusion (b) Publicity
    (c) Surveillance (d) Diversion
13. An example of asynchronous medium is

(a) Radio (b) Television
(c) Film (d) Newspaper

14. In communication, connotative words are
(a) explicit (b) simple
(c) abstract (d) cultural

15. A message beneath a message is labelled as
(a) embedded text (b) internal text
(c) inter-text (d) sub-text

16. In analogue mass communication, stories are
(a) Static (b) Dynamic
(c) Interactive (d) Exploratory

17. Determine the relationship between the pair of words ALWAYS : NEVER and then select from the following pair of words which have a similar relationship
(a) often : rarely
(b) frequently : occasionally
(c) constantly : frequently
(d) intermittently : casually

18. Find the wrong number in the sequence 52, 51, 48, 43, 34, 27, 16.
(a) 27 (b) 34
(c) 43 (d) 48

19. In a certain code, PAN is written as 31 and PAR as 35, then PAT is written in the same code as
(a) 30 (b) 37
(c) 39 (d) 41

20. The letters in the first set have certain relationship. On the basis of this relationship, make the right choice for the second set:
AF : IK : : LQ : ?
(a) MO (b) NP
(c) OR (d) TV

21. If 5472 = 9, 6342 = 6, 7584 = 6, what is 9236?
(a) 2 (b) 3
(c) 4 (d) 5

22. In an examination, 35% of the total students failed in Hindi, 45% failed in English and 20% in both. The percentage of those who passed in both subjects is
(a) 10 (b) 20
(c) 30 (d) 40

23. Two statements I and II given below are followed by two conclusions (A) and (B). Supposing the statements are true, which of the following conclusions can logically follow?

Statements:

I. Some flowers are red.
II. Some flowers are blue.

Conclusions:

(A) Some flowers are neither red nor blue.
(B) Some flowers are both red and blue.
(a) Only (A) follows
(b) Only (B) follows
(c) Both (A) and (B) follows
(d) Neither (A) nor (B) follows

24. If the statement 'all students are intelligent' is true, which of the following statements are false?
(i) No students are intelligent.
(ii) Some students are intelligent.
(iii) Some students are not intelligent.
(a) (i) and (ii) (b) (i) and (iii)
(c) (ii) and (iii) (d) Only (i)

25. A reasoning where we start with certain particular statements and conclude with a universal statement is called
(a) Deductive Reasoning
(b) Inductive Reasoning
(c) Abnormal Reasoning
(d) Transcendental Reasoning

26. What is the smallest number of ducks that could swim in this formation—two ducks in front of a duck, two ducks behind a duck and a duck between two ducks?

(a) 5 (b) 7
(c) 4 (d) 3

27. Mr. A, Miss B, Mr. C and Miss D are sitting around a table and discussing their trades.
(i) Mr. A sits opposite to the cook.
(ii) Miss B sits right to the barber.
(iii) The washerman sits right to the barber.
(iv) Miss D sits opposite to Mr. C.
What are the trades of A and B?
(a) Tailor and barber
(b) Barber and cook
(c) Tailor and cook
(d) Tailor and washerman

28. Which one of the following methods serve to measure correlation between two variables?
(a) Scatter Diagram
(b) Frequency Distrubution
(c) Two-way table
(d) Coefficient of Rank Correlation

29. Which one of the following is not an Internet Service Provider (ISP)?
(a) MTNL
(b) BSNL
(c) ERNET India
(d) Infotech India Ltd.

30. The hexadecimal number system consists of the symbols
(a) 0 - 7 (b) 0 - 9, A - F
(c) 0 - 7, A - F (d) None of these

31. The binary equivalent of $(-15)_{10}$ is (2's complement system is used)
(a) 11110001 (b) 11110000
(c) 10001111 (d) None of these

32. 1 GB is equal to
(a) 2^{30} bits (b) 2^{30} bytes
(c) 2^{20} bits (d) 2^{20} bytes

33. The set of computer programs that manage the hardware/software of a computer is called
(a) Compiler system
(b) Operation system
(c) Operating system
(d) None of these

34. SMIME in Internet Technology stands for
(a) Secure Multipurpose Internet Mail Extension
(b) Secure Multimedia Internet Mail Extension
(c) Simple Multipurpose Internet Mail Extension
(d) Simple Multimedia Internet Mail Extension

35. Which of the following is not covered in 8 missions under the Climate Action Plan of Government of India?
(a) Solar power
(b) Waste to energy conversion
(c) Afforestation
(d) Nuclear energy

36. The concentration of Total Dissolved Solids (TDS) in drinking water should not exceed
(a) 500 mg/L (b) 400 mg/L
(c) 300 mg/L (d) 200 mg/L

37. 'Chipko' movement was first started by
(a) Arundhati Roy
(b) Medha Patkar
(c) Ila Bhatt
(d) Sunderlal Bahuguna

38. The constituents of photochemical smog responsible for eye irritation are
(a) SO_2 and O_3
(b) SO_2 and NO_2
(c) HCHO and PAN
(d) SO_2 and SPM

39. **Assertion (A):** Some carbonaceous aerosols may be carcinogenic.
Reason (R): They may contain polycyclic aromatic hydrocarbons (PAHs).
(a) Both (A) and (R) are correct and (R) is the correct explanation of (A).

(b) Both (A) and (R) are correct but (R) is not the correct explanation of (A).
(c) (A) is correct, but (R) is false.
(d) (A) is false, but (R) is correct.

40. Volcanic eruptions affect
(a) atmosphere and hydrosphere
(b) hydrosphere and biosphere
(c) lithosphere, biosphere and atmosphere
(d) lithosphere, hydrosphere and atmosphere

41. India's first Defence University is in the State of
(a) Haryana
(b) Andhra Pradesh
(c) Uttar Pradesh
(d) Punjab

42. Most of the Universities in India
(a) conduct teaching and research only
(b) affiliate colleges and conduct examinations
(c) conduct teaching/research and examinations
(d) promote research only

43. Which one of the following is not a Constitutional Body?
(a) Election Commission
(b) Finance Commission
(c) Union Public Service Commission
(d) Planning Commission

44. Which one of the following statements is not correct?
(a) Indian Parliament is supreme.
(b) The Supreme Court of India has the power of judicial review.
(c) There is a division of powers between the Centre and the States.
(d) There is a Council of Ministers to aid and advise the President.

45. Which one of the following statements reflects the republic character of Indian democracy?
(a) Written constitution
(b) No State religion
(c) Devolution of power to local Government institutions
(d) Elected President and directly or indirectly elected Parliament

46. Who among the following appointed by the Governor can be removed by only the President of India?
(a) Chief Minister of a State
(b) A member of the State Public Service Commission
(c) Advocate-General
(d) Vice Chancellor of a State University

47. If two small circles represent the class of the 'men' and the class of the 'plants' and the big circle represents 'mortality', which one of the following figures represent the proposition 'All men are mortal?.'

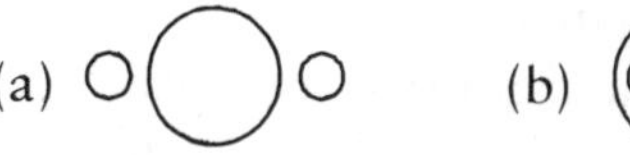

The following table presents the production of electronic items (TVs and LCDs) in a factory during the period from 2006 to 2010. Study the table carefully and answer the questions from 48 to 52:

Year	2006	2007	2008	2009	2010
TVs	6000	9000	13000	11000	8000
LCDs	7000	9400	9000	10000	12000

48. In which year, the total production of electronic items is maximum?
(a) 2006 (b) 2007
(c) 2008 (d) 2010

49. What is the difference between averages of production of LCDs and TVs from 2006 to 2008?

(a) 3000 (b) 2867
(c) 3015 (d) None of these

50. What is the year in which production of TVs is half the production of LCDs in the year 2010?
(a) 2007 (b) 2006
(c) 2009 (d) 2008

51. What is the ratio of production of LCDs in the years 2008 and 2010?
(a) 4:3 (b) 3:4
(c) 1:3 (d) 2:3

52. What is the ratio of production of TVs in the years 2006 and 2007?
(a) 6:7 (b) 7:6
(c) 2:3 (d) 3:2

53. Some students in a class exhibit great curiosity for learning. It may be because such children
(a) Are gifted
(b) Come from rich families
(c) Show artificial behaviour
(d) Create indiscipline in the class

54. The most important quality of a good teacher is
(a) Sound knowledge of subject matter
(b) Good communication skills
(c) Concern for students' welfare
(d) Effective leadership qualities

55. Which one of the following is appropriate in respect of teacher-student relationship?
(a) Very informal and intimate
(b) Limited to classroom only
(c) Cordial and respectful
(d) Indifferent

56. The academic performance of students can be improved if parents are encouraged to
(a) supervise the work of their wards
(b) arrange for extra tuition
(c) remain unconcerned about it
(d) interact with teachers frequently

57. In a lively classroom situation, there is likely to be
(a) occasional roars of laughter
(b) complete silence
(c) frequent teacher-student dialogue
(d) loud discussion among students

58. If a parent approaches the teacher to do some favour to his/her ward in the examination, the teacher should
(a) try to help him
(b) ask him not to talk in those terms
(c) refuse politely and firmly
(d) ask him rudely to go away

59. Which of the following phrases is not relevant to describe the meaning of research as a process?
(a) Systematic Activity
(b) Objective Observation
(c) Trial and Error
(d) Problem Solving

60. Which of the following is not an example of a continuous variable?
(a) Family size (b) Intelligence
(c) Height (d) Attitude

ANSWERS

1. (d)	2. (b)	3. (a)	4. (c)	5. (b)
6. (d)	7. (c)	8. (b)	9. (a)	10. (c)
11. (a)	12. (c)	13. (d)	14. (d)	15. (d)
16. (a)	17. (a)	18. (b)	19. (b)	20. (d)
21. (a)	22. (b)	23. (c)	24. (d)	25. (b)
26. (a)	27. (c)	28. (d)	29. (d)	30. (b)
31. (d)	32. (b)	33. (c)	34. (a)	35. (d)
36. (a)	37. (d)	38. (b)	39. (a)	40. (d)
41. (a)	42. (c)	43. (d)	44. (b)	45. (d)
46. (b)	47. (c)	48. (c)	49. (d)	50. (b)
51. (b)	52. (c)	53. (a)	54. (b)	55. (c)
56. (d)	57. (c)	58. (c)	59. (c)	60. (c)

PAPER–II

Note: This paper contains fifty (50) objective type questions, each question carrying two (2) marks. All questions are compulsory.

1. During the Radical Humanist Phase M.N. Roy advocated
   (a) Bi-Party System
   (b) Single Party System
   (c) Partyless System
   (d) Multi Party System

2. In his book *The Untouchable* Ambedkar gave the following theory for the origin of the untouchable.
   (a) Radical Theory
   (b) Occupational Theory
   (c) Buddhist Origin of Untouchables
   (d) Ethnic Theory

3. Saint Augustine's *The City of God* was considered as the first book on the
   (a) Philosophy of Religion
   (b) Comparative Philosophy
   (c) Philosophy of History
   (d) Philosophy of Christianity

4. Who condemned Natural Rights as an invention of Fantasy?
   (a) Locke (b) Bentham
   (c) Rousseau (d) J.S. Mill

5. Which theory suggests the minor adjustments within the capitalist system to save the individual's liberty?
   (a) Functionalism
   (b) System's Theory
   (c) Liberal-Individual Theory
   (d) Social Contract Theory

6. Who insisted that type of Government depended on economic and geographic factors?
   (a) Jean Bodin (b) Plato
   (c) Cicero (d) Machiavelli

7. "With Satyagraha combined with Ahimsa, you will bring the world to your feet." Who said this?
   (a) Vinoba Bhave
   (b) Mahatma Gandhi
   (c) Jayaprakash Narayan
   (d) Baba Amte

8. Dialectic method was first introduced by
   (a) Aristotle (b) Hegel
   (c) Marx (d) Tolstoy

9. Given below are two statements, one labelled as Assertion (A) and the other labelled as Reason (R).
   Assertion (A): The State is neither the handiwork of God, nor the result of superior physical force, nor the creation of resolution or convention, nor a mere expansion of the family.
   Reason (R): The State is an institution of natural growth.
   In the context of the above two statements, which one of the following is correct?
   (a) Both (A) and (R) are true and (R) is the correct explanation of (A).
   (b) Both (A) and (R) are correct, but (R) is not the correct explanation of (A).
   (c) (A) is true, but (R) is false.
   (d) (A) is false, but (R) is true.

10. Given below are two statements, one labelled as Assertion (A) and the other labelled as Reason (R):
   Assertion (A): Human consciousness postulates Liberty; Liberty demands Rights and Rights demand State.
   Reason (R): Constitution of a State is the safest guarantee of Rights.
   In the context of the above two statements, which one of the following is correct?
   (a) Both (A) and (R) are true, and (R) is the correct explanation of (A).

(b) Both (A) and (R) are true but (R) is not the correct explanation of (A).
(c) (A) is true, but (R) is false.
(d) (A) is false, but (R) is true.

11. Who among the following has given the concept of capabilities of a political system?
(a) Lucian Pye
(b) David Easton
(c) Samuel P. Huntington
(d) Gabriel Almond

12. 'World System Analysis' was first presented by
(a) David Easton
(b) Gabriel Almond
(c) Raul Prebisch
(d) Immanuel Wallerstein

13. The role of pressure groups is limited to the welfare of
(a) Marginalised sections of the society
(b) All sections of the society
(c) Its members only
(d) Humanity as a whole

14. Who wrote the work *Political Order in Changing Societies*?
(a) Thomas L. Friedman
(b) Gabriel Almond
(c) Samuel P. Huntington
(d) Vilfredo Pareto

15. Match List I with List II and select the correct answer from codes given below:
List I
(A) Samuel P. Huntington
(B) John Rawls
(C) Samir Amin
(D) Ronald H. Chilcotte
List II
(i) Political Economy
(ii) Dependency
(iii) Fault lines of Civilization
(iv) Theory of Justice

Codes:	**A**	**B**	**C**	**D**
(a)	(iv)	(iii)	(ii)	(i)
(b)	(ii)	(iv)	(iii)	(i)
(c)	(i)	(iii)	(iv)	(ii)
(d)	(iii)	(iv)	(ii)	(i)

16. Match List I with List II and select the correct answer from the codes given below:
List I
(A) Vilfredo Pareto (B) Karl Deutsch
(C) Max Weber (D) David Apter
List II
(i) Bureaucracy
(ii) Politics of Modernisation
(iii) Circulation of Elites
(iv) Political Communication

Codes:	**A**	**B**	**C**	**D**
(a)	(iv)	(i)	(ii)	(iii)
(b)	(ii)	(iv)	(i)	(iii)
(c)	(i)	(iv)	(iii)	(ii)
(d)	(iii)	(iv)	(i)	(ii)

17. What is the correct sequence of the following?
(i) Commonwealth of Independent States
(ii) Civil Rights Movement in U.S.A.
(iii) First General Election of India
(iv) Glorious Revolution in the United Kingdom
Select the correct answer from the codes given below:
(a) (ii), (iii), (i), (iv) (b) (i), (iv), (ii), (iii)
(c) (iv), (ii), (iii), (i) (d) (iii), (iv), (ii), (i)

18. What is the correct sequence of the former Prime Ministers of the United Kingdom?
(i) Mrs. Margaret Thatcher
(ii) Disraeli
(iii) Tony Blair
(iv) Winston Churchill
Select the correct answer from the codes given below:

(a) (iv), (iii), (i), (ii) (b) (iii), (iv), (i), (ii)
(c) (ii), (iii), (iv), (i) (d) (ii), (iv), (i), (iii)

Directions: The following questions consist of two statements, one labelled as 'Assertion' (A) and the other labelled as 'Reason' (R). You are to examine these two statements carefully and decide if the Assertion (A) and the Reason (R) are individually true and if so, whether the Reason is a correct explanation of the Assertion. Select your answers to these questions using the codes given below:

(a) Both (A) and (R) are true and (R) is the correct explanation of (A).
(b) Both (A) and (R) are true, but (R) is not the correct explanation of (A).
(c) (A) is true, but (R) is false.
(d) (A) is false, but (R) is true.

19. **Assertion (A):** The existence of an hereditary Second Chamber of Parliament is against the principle of equality.
Reason (R): Equality means the absence of special privileges.

20. **Assertion (A):** In a democratic country, the Government ignores the distinctions of class and property.
Reason (R): In a democratic country, the right to vote and participate in politics is determined by the fact that he or she is an adult citizen.

21. The Communist Party of India (Marxist) was established in
(a) 1964 (b) 1962
(c) 1961 (d) 1960

22. Who authored *Annihilation of Caste*?
(a) M.N. Roy (b) C.R. Das
(c) B.R. Ambedkar (d) M.K. Gandhi

23. Under which Article of the Indian Constitution is there the provision for having the Election Commission?
(a) Article 320 (b) Article 324
(c) Article 326 (d) Article 330

24. Who authored *The Indian Constitution: Cornerstone of a Nation*?
(a) Donald Smith (b) Rajni Kothari
(c) Granville Austin (d) K.N. Panikkar

Given below are two statements, one labelled as Assertion (A) and the other labelled as Reason (R):

25. **Assertion (A):** The Governor of a State cannot be dismissed by the Chief Minister.
Reason (R): The Governor is not elected.
In the context of the two statements above, which is correct?
(a) Both (A) and (R) are true and (R) is the correct explanation of (A).
(b) Both (A) and (R) are true, but (R) is not the correct explanation of (A).
(c) (A) is true, but (R) is false.
(d) (A) is false, but (R) is true.

26. **Assertion (A):** Article 352 of the Indian Constitution deals with the declaration of an emergency.
Reason (R): An emergency may take place at any time.
In the context of the two statements above, which is correct?
(a) Both (A) and (R) are true and (R) is the correct explanation of (A).
(b) Both (A) and (R) are true, but (R) is not the correct explanation of (A).
(c) (A) is true, but (R) is false.
(d) (A) is false, but (R) is true.

27. Match List I with List II and select the correct answer from codes given below:
List I
(A) Syed Ahmed Khan
(B) Jayaprakash Narayan
(C) Bal Gangadhar Tilak
(D) M.K. Gandhi
List II
(i) Total Revolution
(ii) Aligarh Movement
(iii) Kesari
(iv) Young India

Codes:	A	B	C	D
(a)	(i)	(ii)	(iii)	(iv)
(b)	(ii)	(i)	(iii)	(iv)
(c)	(iii)	(iv)	(i)	(ii)
(d)	(iv)	(i)	(ii)	(iii)

28. Match List I with List II and select the correct answer from codes given below:

List I

(A) Cripps Proposals
(B) Government of India Act
(C) Cabinet Mission Plan
(D) Civil Disobedience Movement

List II

(i) 1946 (ii) 1930
(iii) 1942 (iv) 1935

Codes:	A	B	C	D
(a)	(i)	(ii)	(iii)	(iv)
(b)	(ii)	(i)	(iii)	(iv)
(c)	(iii)	(iv)	(i)	(ii)
(d)	(iv)	(i)	(ii)	(iii)

29. Identify the correct chronological sequence of the following:
(i) Round Table Conferences
(ii) Quit India Movement
(iii) Formation of Indian National Congress
(iv) Simon Commission

Select the correct answer from the codes given below:
(a) (iv), (ii), (iii), (i) (b) (iii), (iv), (i), (ii)
(c) (ii), (iii), (iv), (i) (d) (i), (iv), (ii), (iii)

30. Identify the correct chronological sequence of the following:
(i) Shankari Prasad Vs. Union of India
(ii) Mandal Commission
(iii) Formation of Bangladesh
(iv) Lal Bahadur Shastri as Prime Minister

Select the correct answer from the codes given below:

Codes:
(a) (iv), (ii), (iii), (i) (b) (i), (iv), (iii), (ii)
(c) (iii), (iv), (ii), (i) (d) (iii), (ii), (i), (iv)

31. The book *Administration in Developing Countries: The Theory of Prismatic Society* was written by
(a) Mayo (b) Wilson
(c) Waldo (d) Riggs

32. The theories of 'X' and 'Y' were propounded by
(a) Abraham Maslow
(b) M.C. Gregor
(c) Herzberg
(d) Simon

33. The concept of 'New Public Administration' is associated with
(a) Berkeley Conference
(b) Prenceton School of Public Administration
(c) Frankfurt School
(d) Minnowbrook Conference

34. 'Grapevine' refers to
(a) Formal Communication
(b) Written Communication
(c) Informal Communication
(d) Downward Communication

35. The Whitley Councils first originated in
(a) India (b) USA
(c) England (d) Switzerland

36. Which one of the following pairs is not correctly matched?
(a) H. Simon: Administrative Behaviour
(b) A. Etzioni: The Practice of Management
(c) Dwight Waldo: Ideas and Issues in Public Administration
(d) Rennis Likert: The Human Organization

37. Vote on account means
(a) A proposal passed by Rajya Sabha on account.
(b) A proposal submitted by the Finance Minister before presenting the Budget.
(c) To bring a proposal related to the speech of the President before the joint session of the Parliament.

(d) If the Budget is not passed before 1st April, the Parliament is authorised to sanction any grant in advance to meet the expenses.

38. Identify the correct sequence in which the following theories/approaches appeared:
(i) Human Relations Theory
(ii) Max Weber's Bureaucratic Theory
(iii) New Public Management
(iv) Decision-Making Theory
(a) (i), (ii), (iii), (iv) (b) (iv), (iii), (ii), (i)
(c) (iii), (iv), (i), (ii) (d) (ii), (i), (iv), (iii)

39. Match List I with List II and select the correct answer from the codes given below:
List I
(A) F.W. Taylor (B) H. Simon
(C) Elton Mayo (D) F.W. Riggs
List II
(i) Scientific Management
(ii) Ecological Approach
(iii) Hawthorn Experiments
(iv) Decision-Making

Codes:	A	B	C	D
(a)	(i)	(iv)	(iii)	(ii)
(b)	(ii)	(iii)	(i)	(iv)
(c)	(iii)	(ii)	(iv)	(i)
(d)	(iv)	(i)	(ii)	(iii)

40. Given below are two statements, one labelled as Assertion (A) and the other labelled as Reason (R): Choose the correct answer from the codes given below:
Assertion (A): In his "Administrative Theory" Herbert Simon followed Positivist Approach.
Reason (R): It is based on the assumption that administration can be reduced to a science by considering facts and not dealing with the values.
Codes:
(a) Both (A) and (R) are true and (R) is the correct explanation of (A).
(b) Both (A) and (R) are true, but (R) is not the correct explanation of (A).
(c) (A) is true, but (R) is false.
(d) (A) is false, but (R) is true.

41. Panchsheel which became guiding principle in the relationship between India and China was signed in the year
(a) 1954 (b) 1955
(c) 1956 (d) 1957

42. Which one among the following is not a member of G-8 countries?
(a) Italy (b) France
(c) Japan (d) China

43. Decisions of International Court of Justice are binding force
(a) for the Parties only.
(b) for all the States of World.
(c) for all members of U.N.O.
(d) for all States Parties to the Statute of the International Court of Justice.

44. Who among the following authors is not associated with realist school?
(a) Max Weber
(b) Edward H. Carr
(c) Hans J. Morgenthau
(d) Aldous Huxley

45. **Assertion (A):** Collective security rests on the rock bottom principle that a attack on any one State would be considered as an attack on all States.
Reason (R): Wars are likely to occur and that they have to be prevented.
Codes:
(a) Both (A) and (R) are true and (R) is the correct explanation of (A).
(b) Both (A) and (R) are true, but (R) is not the correct explanation of (A).
(c) (A) is true, but (R) is false.
(d) (A) is false, but (R) is true.

46. **Assertion (A):** For Realist the master key is the concept of National Interest defined in term of National Power.

Reason (R): Political Realism takes a fixed meaning of National Interest.

(a) Both (A) and (R) are true and (R) is the correct explanation of (A).
(b) Both (A) and (R) are true, but (R) is not the correct explanation of (A).
(c) (A) is true, but (R) is false.
(d) (A) is false, but (R) is true.

47. Match the List I with List II and select the correct answer from the codes given below:

List I
(A) Morton Kaplan
(B) Karl Duetch
(C) Richard C. Synder, H.W. Bruck and Burton Sapine
(D) Hans J. Morgenthau

List II
(i) Realist Approach
(ii) Decision Making Approach
(iii) Communication Approach
(iv) System Approach

Codes:	**A**	**B**	**C**	**D**
(a)	(iv)	(iii)	(ii)	(i)
(b)	(iv)	(ii)	(iii)	(i)
(c)	(iv)	(i)	(ii)	(iii)
(d)	(iv)	(iii)	(i)	(ii)

48. Match the List I with List II and select the correct answer from the codes given below:

List I	**List II**
(A) SEATO	(i) 1955
(B) SAARC	(ii) 1949
(C) NATO	(iii) 1985
(D) WARSAW PACT	(iv) 1954

Codes:	**A**	**B**	**C**	**D**
(a)	(iv)	(iii)	(ii)	(i)
(b)	(iii)	(ii)	(i)	(iv)
(c)	(ii)	(iv)	(iii)	(i)
(d)	(i)	(ii)	(iv)	(iii)

49. Identify following events in correct chronological order:
(i) China's Invasion on India.
(ii) Bangladesh Liberation War.
(iii) Rajeev-Jayawardene Accord.
(iv) Kargil War.
(a) (i), (ii), (iii), (iv) (b) (iv), (iii), (ii), (i)
(c) (iii), (iv), (i), (ii) (d) (ii), (iii), (i), (iv)

50. Identify the following events in correct chronological order:
(i) P.T.B.T. (Partial Test Ban Treaty)
(ii) Pokhran Nuclear Explosion – I
(iii) N.P.T. (Non Proliferation Treaty)
(iv) C.T.B.T. (Comprehensive Test Ban Treaty)
(a) (i), (ii), (iii), (iv)
(b) (i), (iii), (ii), (iv)
(c) (iv), (ii), (iii), (i)
(d) (iii), (ii), (iv), (i)

ANSWERS

1. (c)	2. (c)	3. (c)	4. (b)	5. (c)
6. (a)	7. (b)	8. (b)	9. (a)	10. (a)
11. (a)	12. (d)	13. (c)	14. (c)	15. (d)
16. (d)	17. (c)	18. (d)	19. (a)	20. (a)
21. (a)	22. (c)	23. (b)	24. (c)	25. (b)
26. (c)	27. (b)	28. (c)	29. (b)	30. (b)
31. (d)	32. (b)	33. (d)	34. (c)	35. (c)
36. (b)	37. (d)	38. (d)	39. (a)	40. (d)
41. (a)	42. (d)	43. (d)	44. (d)	45. (a)
46. (b)	47. (a)	48. (a)	49. (a)	50. (b)

JUNE–2010

Note: This paper contains Sixty (60) multiple-choice questions, each question carrying two (2) marks. Candidate is expected to answer any Fifty (50) questions. In case more than Fifty (50) questions are attempted, only the first Fifty (50) questions will be evaluated.

PAPER–I

1. Which one of the following is the most important quality of a good teacher?
   (a) Punctuality and sincerity
   (b) Content mastery
   (c) Content mastery and reactive
   (d) Content mastery and sociable

2. The primary responsibility for the teacher's adjustment lies with
   (a) The children
   (b) The principal
   (c) The teacher himself
   (d) The community

3. As per the NCTE norms, what should be the staff strength for a unit of 100 students at B.Ed. level?
   (a) 1 + 7 (b) 1 + 9
   (c) 1 + 10 (d) 1 + 5

4. Research has shown that the most frequent symptom of nervous instability among teachers is
   (a) Digestive upsets
   (b) Explosive behaviour
   (c) Fatigue
   (d) Worry

5. Which one of the following statements is correct?
   (a) Syllabus is an annexure to the curriculum.
   (b) Curriculum is the same in all educational institutions.
   (c) Curriculum includes both formal and informal education.
   (d) Curriculum does not include methods of evaluation.

6. A successful teacher is one who is
   (a) Compassionate and disciplinarian
   (b) Quite and reactive
   (c) Tolerant and dominating
   (d) Passive and active

Read the following passage carefully and answer the questions 7 to 12.

The phrase "What is it like?" stands for a fundamental thought process. How does one go about observing and reporting on things and events that occupy segments of earth space? Of all the infinite variety of phenomena on the face of the earth, how does one decide what phenomena to observe? There is no such thing as a complete description of the earth or any part of it, for every microscopic point on the earth's surface differs from every other such point. Experience shows that the things observed are already familiar, because they are like phenomena that occur at home or because they resemble the abstract images and models developed in the human mind.

How are abstract images formed? Humans alone among the animals possess language; their words symbolise not only specific things but also mental images of classes of things. People can remember what they have seen or experienced because they attach a word symbol to them.

During the long record of our efforts to gain more and more knowledge about the face of the earth as the human habitat, there has been a continuing interplay between things and events. The direct observation through the senses is described as a percept; the mental image is described as a concept. Percepts are what some people describe as reality, in contrast to mental images, which are theoretical, implying that they are not real.

The relation of Percept to Concept is not as simple as the definition implies. It is now quite clear that people of different cultures or even individuals in the same culture develop different mental images of reality and what they perceive is a reflection of these preconceptions. The direct observation of things and events on the face of the earth is so clearly a function of the mental images of the mind of the observer that the whole idea of reality must be reconsidered.

Concepts determine what the observer perceives, yet concepts are derived from the generalisations of previous percepts. What happens is that the educated observer is taught to accept a set of concepts and then sharpens or changes these concepts during a professional career. In any one field of scholarship, professional opinion at one time determines what concepts and procedures are acceptable, and these form a kind of model of scholarly behaviour.

7. The problem raised in the passage reflects on
   (a) thought process
   (b) human behaviour
   (c) cultural perceptions
   (d) professional opinion

8. According to the passage, human beings have mostly in mind
   (a) Observation of things
   (b) Preparation of mental images
   (c) Expression through language
   (d) To gain knowledge

9. Concept means
   (a) A mental image
   (b) A reality
   (c) An idea expressed in language form
   (d) All the above

10. The relation of Percept to Concept is
   (a) Positive (b) Negative
   (c) Reflective (d) Absolute

11. In the passage, the earth is taken as
   (a) The Globe
   (b) The Human Habitat
   (c) A Celestial Body
   (d) A Planet

12. Percept means
   (a) Direct observation through the senses
   (b) A conceived idea
   (c) Ends of a spectrum
   (d) An abstract image

13. Action research means
   (a) A longitudinal research
   (b) An applied research
   (c) A research initiated to solve an immediate problem
   (d) A research with socio-economic objective

14. Research is
   (a) Searching again and again
   (b) Finding solution to any problem
   (c) Working in a scientific way to search for truth of any problem
   (d) None of the above

15. A common test in research demands much priority on
   (a) Reliability (b) Usability
   (c) Objectivity (d) All of the above

16. Which of the following is the first step in starting the research process?
   (a) Searching sources of information to locate problem
   (b) Survey of related literature
   (c) Identification of problem
   (d) Searching for solutions to the problem

17. If a researcher conducts a research on finding out which administrative style

contributes more to institutional effectiveness? This will be an example of
(a) Basic Research
(b) Action Research
(c) Applied Research
(d) None of the above

18. Normal Probability Curve should be
(a) Positively skewed
(b) Negatively skewed
(c) Leptokurtic skewed
(d) Zero skewed

19. In communication, a major barrier to reception of messages is
(a) audience attitude
(b) audience knowledge
(c) audience education
(d) audience income

20. Post-modernism is associated with
(a) Newspapers (b) Magazines
(c) Radio (d) Television

21. Didactic communication is
(a) Intra-porsonal (b) Inter-personal
(c) Organisational (d) Relational

22. In communication, the language is
(a) the non-verbal code
(b) the verbal code
(c) the symbolic code
(d) the iconic code

23. Identify the correct sequence of the following:
(a) Source, channel, message, receiver
(b) Source, receiver, channel, message
(c) Source, message, receiver, channel
(d) Source, message, channel, receiver

24. **Assertion (A):** Mass media promote a culture of violence in the society.
Reason (R): Because violence sells in the market as people themselves are violent in character.
(a) Both (A) and (R) are true and (R) is the correct explanation of (A).
(b) Both (A) and (R) are true, but (R) is not the correct explanation of (A).
(c) (A) is true, but (R) is false.
(d) Both (A) and (R) are false.

25. When an error of 1% is made in the length of a square, the percentage error in the area of a square will be
(a) 0 (b) 1/2
(c) 1 (d) 2

26. On January 12, 1980, it was a Saturday. The day of the week on January 12, 1979 was
(a) Thursday (b) Friday
(c) Saturday (d) Sunday

27. If water is called food, food is called tree, tree is called earth, earth is called world, which of the following grows a fruit?
(a) Water (b) Tree
(c) World (d) Earth

28. E is the son of A, D is the son of B, E is married to C, C is the daughter of E. How is D related to E?
(a) Brother (b) Uncle
(c) Father-in-law (d) Brother-in-law

29. If INSURANCE is coded as ECNARUSNI, how HINDRANCE will be coded?
(a) CADNIHWCE (b) HANODEINR
(c) AENIRHDCN (d) ECNARDNIH

30. Find the next number in the following series: 2, 5, 10, 17, 26, 37, 50, ?
(a) 63 (b) 65
(c) 67 (d) 69

31. Which of the following is an example of circular argument?
(a) God created man in his image and man created God in his own image.
(b) God is the source of a scripture and the scripture is the source of our knowledge of God.
(c) Some of the Indians are great because India is great.
(d) Rama is great because he is Rama.

32. Lakshmana is a morally good person because
    (a) he is religious (b) he is educated
    (c) he is rich (d) he is rational

33. Two statements I and II given below are followed by two conclusions (A) and (B). Supposing the statements are true, which of the following conclusions can logically follow?
    Statements:
    I. Some religious people are morally good.
    II. Some religious people are rational.
    Conclusion:
    (A) Rationally religious people are good morally.
    (B) Non-rational religious persons are not morally good.
    (a) Only (A) follows
    (b) Only (B) follows
    (c) Both (A) and (B) follow
    (d) Neither (A) nor (B) follows

34. Certainty is
    (a) an objective fact
    (b) emotionally satisfying
    (c) logical
    (d) ontological

Questions from 35 to 36 are based on the following diagram in which there are three intersecting circles I, S and P where circle I stands for Indians, circle S stands for Scientists and circle P for Politicians. Different regions of the figure are lettered from a to g.

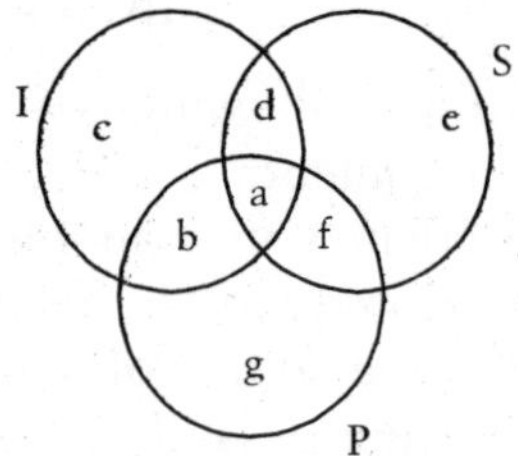

35. The region which represents non-indian scientists who are politicians.
    (a) f (b) d
    (c) a (d) c

36. The region which represents politicians who are Indians as well as scientists.
    (a) b (b) c
    (c) a (d) d

37. The population of a city is plotted as a function of time (years) in graphic form below:

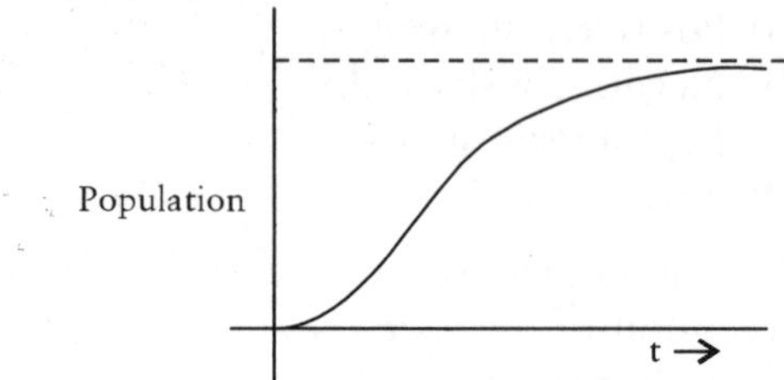

Which of the following inference can be drawn from above plot?
    (a) The population increases exponentially.
    (b) The population increases in parabolic fashion.
    (c) The population initially increases in a linear fashion and then stabilises.
    (d) The population initially increases exponentially and then stabilises.

In the following chart, the price of logs is shown in per cubic metre and that of Plywood and Saw Timber in per tonnes. Study the chart and answer the following questions 38, 39 and 40.

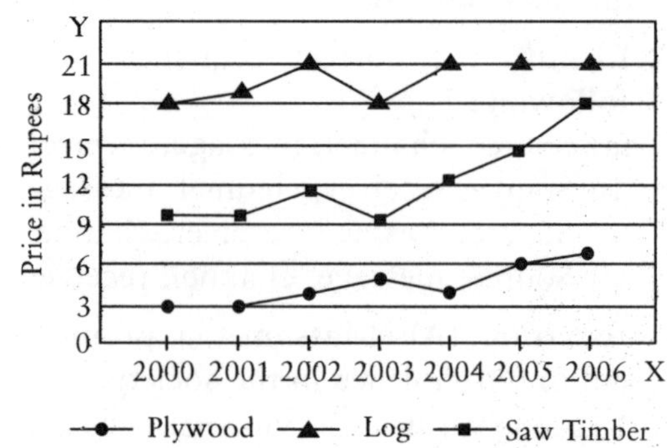

38. Which product shows the maximum percentage increase in price over the period?

(a) Saw timber (b) Plywood
(c) Log (d) None of these

39. What is the maximum percentage increase in price per cubic metre of log?
(a) 6 (b) 12
(c) 18 (d) None of these

40. In which year the prices of two products deceased and that of the third increased?
(a) 2000 (b) 2002
(c) 2003 (d) 2006

41. Which one of the following is the oldest Archival source of data in India?
(a) National Sample Surveys
(b) Agricultural Statistics
(c) Census
(d) Vital Statistics

42. In a large random data set following normal distribution, the ratio (%) of number of data points which are in the range of (mean ± standard deviation) to the total number of data points, is
(a) ~ 50% (b) ~ 67%
(c) ~ 97% (d) ~ 47%

43. Which number system is usually followed in a typical 32-bit computer?
(a) 2 (b) 8
(c) 10 (d) 16

44. Which one of the following is an example of Operating System?
(a) Microsoft Word
(b) Microsoft Excel
(c) Microsoft Access
(d) Microsoft Windows

45. Which one of the following represents the binary equivalent of the decimal number 23?
(a) 01011 (b) 10111
(c) 10011 (d) None of these

46. Which one of the following is different from other members?
(a) Google (b) Windows
(c) Linux (d) Mac

47. Where does a computer add and compare its data?
(a) CPU (b) Memory
(c) Hard disk (d) Floppy disk

48. Computers on an Internet are identified by
(a) e-mail address
(b) street address
(c) IP address
(d) None of the above

49. The Right to Information Act, 2005 makes the provision of
(a) Dissemination of all types of information by all Public authorities to any person
(b) Establishment of Central, State and District Level Information Commissions as an appellate body
(c) Transparency and accountability in Public authorities
(d) All of the above

50. Which type of natural hazards cause maximum damage to property and lives?
(a) Hydrological
(b) Hydro-meteorological
(c) Geological
(d) Geo-chemical

51. Dioxins are produced from
(a) Wastelands
(b) Power plants
(c) Sugar factories
(d) Combustion of plastics

52. The slogan "A tree for each child" was coined for
(a) Social forestry program
(b) Clean Air program
(c) Soil conservation program
(d) Environmental protection program

53. The main constituents of biogas are

(a) Methane and Carbon dioxide
(b) Methane and Nitric oxide
(c) Methane, Hydrogen and Nitric oxide
(d) Methane and Sulphur dioxide

54. **Assertion (A):** In the world as a whole, the environment has degraded during past several decades.
Reason (R): The population of the world has been growing significantly.
(a) (A) is correct, (R) is correct and (R) is the correct explanation of (A).
(b) (A) is correct, (R) is correct and (R) is not the correct explanation of (A).
(c) (A) is correct, but (R) is false.
(d) (A) is false, but (R) is correct.

55. Climate change has implications for
1. soil moisture 2. forest fires
3. biodiversity 4. groundwater
Identify the correct combination according to the code:
Codes:
(a) 1 and 3 (b) 1, 2 and 3
(c) 1, 3 and 4 (d) 1, 2, 3 and 4

56. The accreditation process by National Assessment and Accreditation Council (NAAC) differs from that of National Board of Accreditation (NBA) in terms of
(a) Disciplines covered by both being the same, there is duplication of efforts.
(b) One has institutional grading approach and the other has program grading approach.
(c) Once get accredited by NBA or NAAC, the institution is free from renewal of grading, which is not a progressive decision.
(d) This accreditation amounts to approval of minimum standards in the quality of education in the institution concerned.

57. Which option is not correct?
(a) Most of the educational institutions of National repute in scientific and technical sphere fall under 64th entry of Union list.
(b) Education, in general, is the subject of concurrent list since 42nd Constitutional Amendment Act 1976.
(c) Central Advisory Board on Education (CABE) was first established in 1920.
(d) India had implemented the right to Free and Compulsory Primary Education in 2002 through 86th Constitutional Amendment.

58. Which statement is not correct about the "National Education Day" of India?
(a) It is celebrated on 5th September every year.
(b) It is celebrated on 11th November every year.
(c) It is celebrated in the memory of India's first Union Minister of Education, Dr. Abul Kalam Azad.
(d) It is being celebrated since 2008.

59. Match List I with List II and select the correct answer from the codes given below:
List I (Articles of the Constitution)
A. Article 280 B. Article 324
C. Article 323 D. Article 315
List II (Institutions)
1. Administrative Tribunals
2. Election Commission of India
3. Finance Commission at Union level
4. Union Public Service Commission

Codes:	**A**	**B**	**C**	**D**
(a)	1	2	3	4
(b)	3	2	1	4
(c)	2	3	4	1
(d)	2	4	3	1

60. Deemed Universities declared by UGC under Section 3 of the UGC Act 1956, are not permitted to

(a) offer programs in higher education and issue degrees
(b) give affiliation to any institute of higher education
(c) open off-campus and off-shore campus anywhere in the country and overseas respectively without the permission of the UGC
(d) offer distance education programs without the approval of the Distance Education Council

ANSWERS

1. (b)	2. (c)	3. (c)	4. (b)	5. (c)
6. (a)	7. (c)	8. (a)	9. (a)	10. (c)
11. (b)	12. (a)	13. (c)	14. (c)	15. (d)
16. (c)	17. (c)	18. (d)	19. (c)	20. (d)
21. (b)	22. (b)	23. (d)	24. (d)	25. (d)
26. (b)	27. (c)	28. (d)	29. (d)	30. (b)
31. (b)	32. (a)	33. (d)	34. (c)	35. (a)
36. (c)	37. (d)	38. (c)	39. (d)	40. (b)
41. (c)	42. (b)	43. (a)	44. (d)	45. (b)
46. (b)	47. (a)	48. (c)	49. (d)	50. (c)
51. (d)	52. (d)	53. (a)	54. (b)	55. (d)
56. (c)	57. (a)	58. (a)	59. (b)	60. (b)

PAPER–II

Note: This paper contains fifty (50) objective type questions, each question carrying two (2) marks. All questions are compulsory.

1. Which theory of the State is expounded in Santhi Parva?
   (a) Divine Right Theory
   (b) Social Contract Theory
   (c) Theory of Consent
   (d) Both Divine Right and Social Contract Theory
2. According to Gandhi,
   (a) There is no relation between Ends and Means.
   (b) Ends justify the Means.
   (c) Means are not important.
   (d) Ends and Means are interrelated.
3. "The public good ought to be the object of the Legislator."—Who said it?
   (a) Hobbes (b) Plato
   (c) Marx (d) Bentham
4. Who said, "Men are equal by nature; society, through the institution of property, has made them unequal"?
   (a) Marx (b) Rousseau
   (c) Locke (d) Hegel
5. The method of proceeding from general to the particular is
   (a) Deductive Method
   (b) Inductive Method
   (c) Formal Logic
   (d) Traditional Logic
6. Who said that "the world at every stage is both a product and a prophecy"?
   (a) Plato (b) Socrates
   (c) Hegel (d) Marx
7. One of the criticism for the theory of Natural Rights is that it
   (a) places societal interests over individual interests
   (b) assumes that rights exist prior to society
   (c) believes that rights are the creations of the sovereign
   (d) puts too much emphasis on social recognition of rights
8. The Entitlement Theory of Property has been propounded by
   (a) John Locke (b) John Rawls
   (c) Nozick (d) Rousseau

9. The State is a necessary evil. This statement refers to
   (a) Anarchist Theory of State
   (b) Individualist Theory of State
   (c) Marxian Theory of State
   (d) Neo-Liberal Theory of State

10. Given below are two statements, one labelled as Assertion (A) and the other labelled as Reason (R).
   Assertion (A): Democratic socialism values unity in diversity.
   Reason (R): Cultural Pluralism hinders the functioning of democratic institutions.
   In the context of the above two statements, which one of the following is correct?
   (a) Both (A) and (R) are true and (R) is the correct explanation of (A).
   (b) Both (A) and (R) are true but (R) is not the correct explanation of (A).
   (c) (A) is true but (R) is false.
   (d) (A) is false but (R) is true.

11. Robert Merton's concept of 'Political Machine' in a large city is associated with
   (a) Decentralisation of Power
   (b) Behaviouralism
   (c) Functionalism
   (d) Bureaucracy

12. Who among the following is a proponent of the Theory of Underdevelopment?
   (a) Max Weber (b) David Apter
   (c) Samir Amin (d) Amartya Sen

13. In which one of the following systems of Government is Bicameralism an essential feature?
   (a) Parliamentary system
   (b) Presidential system
   (c) Unitary system
   (d) Federal system

14. According to Max Weber, which one of the following types of authority is the basis of modern bureaucracy?
   (a) Traditional (b) Charismatic
   (c) Legal-Rational (d) Popular

15. Match List I with List II and select the correct answer from the codes given below:
   List I
   (A) Collective Responsibility
   (B) Multiparty System
   (C) Referendum
   (D) Due process of law
   List II
   (i) India
   (ii) United States of America
   (iii) United Kingdom
   (iv) Switzerland

Codes:	A	B	C	D
(a)	(iv)	(iii)	(i)	(ii)
(b)	(ii)	(iv)	(iii)	(i)
(c)	(iii)	(i)	(iv)	(ii)
(d)	(i)	(iv)	(iii)	(ii)

16. Match List I with List II and select the correct answer from the codes given below:
   List I
   (A) Robert A. Dahl
   (B) Putnam
   (C) Francis Fukuyama
   (D) Almond and Powell
   List II
   (i) End of History and the Last Man
   (ii) Civic Culture
   (iii) Civic Traditions in Modern Italy
   (iv) Democracy and its critics

Codes:	A	B	C	D
(a)	(iii)	(i)	(iv)	(ii)
(b)	(iv)	(iii)	(i)	(ii)
(c)	(i)	(iv)	(iii)	(ii)
(d)	(ii)	(i)	(iii)	(iv)

Directions: The following two questions consists of two statements, one labelled as 'Assertion' (A) and the other labelled as 'Reason' (R). You are to examine these two statements carefully and decide if the Assertion (A) and the Reason (R) are individually true and if so, whether the Reason is a correct explanation of the Assertion. Select your answers to these questions using the codes given below:

(a) Both (A) and (R) are true and (R) is the correct explanation of (A).
(b) Both (A) and (R) are true but (R) is not the correct explanation of (A).
(c) (A) is true but (R) is false.
(d) (A) is false but (R) is true.

17. **Assertion (A):** The Senate of U.S.A. is the most powerful second chamber in the world.
Reason (R): All States in U.S.A. enjoy equal representation in the Senate.

18. **Assertion (A):** Interest Groups compete for making their voice heard and interests protected by the decision makers in political systems.
Reason (R): Interest Groups extend support to political parties in a consistent manner.

19. What is the correct sequence of the following Presidents of the U.S.A.
(i) Franklin D. Roosevelt
(ii) George Bush (Sr.)
(iii) Bill Clinton
(iv) John F. Kennedy
Select the correct answer from the codes given below:
(a) (i), (iv), (iii), (ii) (b) (i), (iv), (ii), (iii)
(c) (ii), (iv), (iii), (i) (d) (iv), (i), (ii), (iii)

20. Write the following in the correct sequence:
(i) The first meeting of the Constituent Assembly of India.
(ii) New Deal Legislation in U.S.A.
(iii) The Maastritch Treaty in Europe.
(iv) Merger of Baltic States into Soviet Union.
Choose the correct code:
(a) (iii), (ii), (i), (iv) (b) (iv), (ii), (i), (iii)
(c) (i), (iv), (iii), (ii) (d) (ii), (i), (iv), (iii)

21. Which of the following statements is correct about the Vice-President of India?
(a) Elected by the Rajya Sabha
(b) Ex-officio Chairman of Rajya Sabha
(c) Elected for a four year term
(d) Presides over the Joint Sessions of the two Houses of Parliament

22. The Dalit Panther Movement was launched in
(a) West Bengal (b) Bihar
(c) Orissa (d) Maharashtra

23. The First Backward Classes Commission emphasized which of the following as a condition identifying social and educational backwardness?
(a) Religion (b) Language
(c) Class (d) Caste

24. When the UPA Government was formed in 2004 at the Centre, the CPI (M) was
(a) neither supporting nor opposing it.
(b) not part of the alliance, but was supporting the Government from outside.
(c) part of the alliance.
(d) opposed to the Government.

25. Match List I and List II and select the correct answer from codes given below:
List I
(A) Finance Commission
(B) Financial Emergency
(C) Rajya Sabha
(D) Constitutional Amendment
List II
(i) Article 360 (ii) Article 312
(iii) Article 368 (iv) Article 280

Codes:	**A**	**B**	**C**	**D**
(a)	(i)	(ii)	(iii)	(iv)
(b)	(ii)	(i)	(iii)	(iv)
(c)	(iii)	(iv)	(i)	(ii)
(d)	(iv)	(i)	(ii)	(iii)

26. Match List I and List II and select the correct answer from codes given below:
List I
(A) Morley Minto Reforms
(B) Montford Reforms

(C) Swadeshi and Boycott Movement
(D) Home-Rule Movement

List II

(i) 1919 (ii) 1909
(iii) 1905 (iv) 1916

Codes:	A	B	C	D
(a)	(i)	(ii)	(iii)	(iv)
(b)	(ii)	(i)	(iii)	(iv)
(c)	(iii)	(iv)	(i)	(ii)
(d)	(iv)	(i)	(ii)	(iii)

27. Identify the correct chronological sequence of the following:
    (i) 42nd Constitution Amendment Act
    (ii) A.K. Gopalan Vs. State of Madras Case
    (iii) Declaration of Internal Emergency
    (iv) Kesavananda Bharti Vs. State of Kerala Case

    Select the correct answer from the codes given below:
    (a) (ii), (i), (iv), (iii) (b) (i), (ii), (iii), (iv)
    (c) (ii), (iv), (iii), (i) (d) (iii), (iv), (ii), (i)

28. Identify the correct chronological sequence in which the following became Prime Ministers of India:
    (i) Charan Singh
    (ii) V.P. Singh
    (iii) Lal Bahadur Shastri
    (iv) Morarji Desai

    Select the correct answer from the codes given below:
    (a) (ii), (i), (iv), (iii) (b) (iii), (iv), (i), (ii)
    (c) (ii), (iv), (iii), (i) (d) (ii), (iv), (i), (iii)

29. **Assertion (A):** Fundamental Rights are enshrined in the Constitution for the people.
    Reason (R): People can move Court for violation of Fundamental Rights.
    In the context of the above two statements which is correct?
    (a) Both (A) and (R) are true and (R) is the correct explanation of (A).
    (b) Both (A) and (R) are true, but (R) is not the correct explanation of (A).
    (c) (A) is true, but (R) is false.
    (d) (A) is false, but (R) is true.

30. **Assertion (A):** There are three lists dividing legislative authority between the Union and the States in India.
    Reason (R): India has a federal system.
    In the context of the two statements above, which is correct?
    (a) Both (A) and (R) are true and (R) is the correct explanation of (A).
    (b) Both (A) and (R) are true, but (R) is not the correct explanation of (A).
    (c) (A) is true, but (R) is false.
    (d) (A) is false, but (R) is true.

31. Development Administration was defined as a 'goal oriented' and 'change oriented' Administration by
    (a) Milton Essman
    (b) Fred Riggs
    (c) Nicholas Henry
    (d) Edward Weidner

32. The concept of 'Line and Staff' Agencies in Public Administration is borrowed from
    (a) Revenue Administration
    (b) Police Administration
    (c) Military Administration
    (d) International Administration

33. F.W. Taylor's concept of 'Scientific Management' was criticised by
    (a) Trade Unions
    (b) Managers
    (c) Classical Scholars of Public Administration
    (d) Human Relations Theorists

34. In India the Planning Commission was set up in the yeaı
    (a) 1949 (b) 1950
    (c) 1951 (d) 1952

35. Recruitment to Civil Service in India is based on the recommendation of
    (a) Montague-Chelmsford
    (b) Minto-Morley

(c) Paul H. Appleby
(d) Lord Macaulay

36. The communication that passes across different departments refers to
(a) Upward Communication
(b) Downward Communication
(c) Lateral Communication
(d) Oral Communication

37. The Contingency Fund in India has been placed at the disposal of
(a) Prime Minister (b) President
(c) Finance Minister (d) Home Minister

38. Identify the correct sequence in which the following theories appeared?
I. Decision-Making Theory
II. Human Relations Theory
III. Classical Theory
IV. Public Choice Theory

Codes:
(a) I, II, III, IV (b) III, II, I, IV
(c) IV, III, II, I (d) II, IV, I, III

39. Match List I with the List II and select correct answer from the codes given below:

List I
(A) Charismatic Authority
(B) Administrative Behaviour
(C) Development Administration
(D) Prismatic Society

List II
(i) Riggs (ii) Weidner
(iii) Simon (iv) Weber

Select the answer from the codes:

Codes:	**A**	**B**	**C**	**D**
(a)	(iv)	(iii)	(ii)	(i)
(b)	(iii)	(ii)	(i)	(iv)
(c)	(ii)	(iii)	(iv)	(i)
(d)	(i)	(iv)	(ii)	(iii)

40. **Assertion (A):** The institution of Lok Pal has not been established to this day in India in spite of the best efforts of the Government.

Reason (R): The Political Parties in the Indian Parliament have not been able to arrive at a consensus.
(a) Both (A) and (R) are true and (R) is the correct explanation of (A).
(b) Both (A) and (R) are true but (R) is not the correct explanation of (A).
(c) (A) is true but (R) is false.
(d) (A) is false but (R) is true.

41. Who used first time the word "Cold War"?
(a) Bernard Brouch
(b) Hans J. Morgenthau
(c) C.K. Webster
(d) Karl Duetch

42. The General Assembly of U.N.O. passed the Declaration of Human Rights on
(a) 10 December, 1949
(b) 10 December, 1948
(c) 10 December, 1947
(d) 10 December, 1946

43. The Headquarter of Economic Commission for Asia and Far East is situated at
(a) Bangkok (b) Tokyo
(c) Kuala Lumpur (d) Jakarta

44. "One for all and all for one" is statement given by one of the following authors in regard to collective security.
(a) Palmer and Perkins
(b) Hans. J. Morgenthau
(c) Morton Kaplan
(d) Karl Duetch

45. What is the correct chronological sequence of the below? Choose the right answers from codes:
(i) The Atlantic Charter
(ii) Bretton Woods Conference
(iii) Casablance Conference
(iv) Yalta Conference
(a) (i), (iii), (ii), (iv) (b) (iv), (ii), (iii), (i)
(c) (ii), (iv), (i), (iii) (d) (iii), (i), (iv), (ii)

46. What is the correct chronological sequence of the models given by Morton Kaplan? Choose the right answers from codes:
(i) Balance of Power
(ii) Universal International System
(iii) Tight Bi-polar system
(iv) Loose Bi-polar system
(a) (i), (iv), (iii), (ii) (b) (iv), (iii), (ii), (i)
(c) (iii), (ii), (i), (iv) (d) (ii), (i), (iv), (iii)

47. Match List I with List II and select the correct answer from the codes given below:
List I
(A) Farrakha barrage
(B) 1, 2, 3 Nuclear Agreement
(C) Srimao – Shastri Pact
(D) Treaty of Peace and Friendship 1950
List II
(i) India-Bangladesh (ii) India-Sri Lanka
(iii) India-Nepal (iv) India-U.S.A.

Codes:	**A**	**B**	**C**	**D**
(a)	(i)	(ii)	(iii)	(iv)
(b)	(i)	(iv)	(ii)	(iii)
(c)	(iii)	(ii)	(i)	(iv)
(d)	(ii)	(iii)	(iv)	(i)

48. Match List I with List II and select the correct answer from the codes given below:
List I
(A) Inis Claude
(B) K.J. Holsti
(C) A LeRoy Bernett
(D) K. Knorr & J.N. Rosenau
List II
(i) Power and International Relations
(ii) International Organization Principle and Issues
(iii) Contending Approaches to International Politics
(iv) International Politics

Codes:	**A**	**B**	**C**	**D**
(a)	(i)	(iv)	(ii)	(iii)
(b)	(iv)	(iii)	(ii)	(i)
(c)	(iii)	(ii)	(i)	(iv)
(d)	(ii)	(iii)	(iv)	(i)

49. **Assertion (A):** For the realist the ruthless quest of power to promote National Interest is in the law of nature.
Reason (R): They firmly believe that moral and legal prescription are irrelevant at best convinces that may be discarded at will.
(a) Both (A) and (R) are true and (R) is the correct explanation of (A).
(b) Both (A) and (R) are true but (R) is not correct explanation of (A).
(c) (A) is true but (R) is false.
(d) (A) is false but (R) is true

50. **Assertion (A):** The members of U.N.O. have committed to promote the respect for observance of Human Rights.
Reason (R): The Human Rights are inalienable, natural interdependent and indivisible. They are means to achieve human dignity.
(a) Both (A) and (R) are true and (R) is the correct explanation of (A).
(b) Both (A) and (R) are true and (R) is not the correct explanation of (A).
(c) (A) is true but (R) is false.
(d) (A) is false but (R) is true.

ANSWERS

1. (a)	2. (d)	3. (d)	4. (b)	5. (d)
6. (a)	7. (c)	8. (c)	9. (c)	10. (b)
11. (c)	12. (d)	13. (a)	14. (c)	15. (c)
16. (b)	17. (b)	18. (b)	19. (c)	20. (b)
21. (b)	22. (d)	23. (d)	24. (b)	25. (d)
26. (b)	27. (c)	28. (b)	29. (b)	30. (b)
31. (d)	32. (c)	33. (d)	34. (b)	35. (b)
36. (c)	37. (b)	38. (b)	39. (a)	40. (a)
41. (a)	42. (a)	43. (d)	44. (c)	45. (a)
46. (a)	47. (b)	48. (a)	49. (a)	50. (a)

DECEMBER–2009

Note: This paper contains Sixty (60) multiple-choice questions, each question carrying two (2) marks. Candidate is expected to answer any Fifty (50) questions. In case more than Fifty (50) questions are attempted, only the first Fifty (50) questions will be evaluated.

PAPER–I

1. The University which telecasts interaction educational programs through its own channel is
   (a) Osmania University
   (b) University of Pune
   (c) Annamalai University
   (d) Indira Gandhi National University (IGNOU)

2. Which of the following skills are needed for present-day teacher to adjust effectively with the classroom teaching?
   1. Knowledge of technology
   2. Use of technology in teaching learning
   3. Knowledge of students' needs
   4. Content mastery

   (a) 1 and 3 (b) 2 and 3
   (c) 2, 3 and 4 (d) 2 and 4

3. Who has signed as MoU for Accreditation of Teacher Education Institutions in India?
   (a) NAAC and UGC
   (b) NCTE and NAAC
   (c) UGC and NCTE
   (d) NCTE and IGNOU

4. The primary duty of the teacher is to
   (a) raise the intellectual standard of the students
   (b) improve the physical standard of the students
   (c) help all-round development of the students
   (d) imbibe value system in the students

5. Micro teaching is more effective
   (a) during the preparation for teaching-practice
   (b) during the teaching-practice
   (c) after the teaching-practice
   (d) always

6. What quality the students like the most in a teacher?
   (a) Idealist philosophy
   (b) Compassion
   (c) Discipline
   (d) Entertaining

7. A null hypothesis is
   (a) when there is no difference between the variables
   (b) the same as research hypothesis
   (c) subjective in nature
   (d) when there is difference between the variables

8. The research which is exploring new facts through the study of the past is called
   (a) Philosophical research
   (b) Historical research
   (c) Mythological research
   (d) Content analysis

9. Action research is
   (a) An applied research
   (b) A research carried out to solve immediate problems
   (c) A longitudinal research
   (d) Simulative research

10. The process not needed in Experimental Researches is
    (a) Observation (b) Manipulation
    (c) Controlling (d) Content Analysis

11. Manipulation is always a part of
    (a) Historical research
    (b) Fundamental research
    (c) Descriptive research
    (d) Experimental research

12. Which correlation co-efficient best explains the relationship between creativity and intelligence?
    (a) 1.00 (b) 0.6
    (c) 0.5 (d) 0.3

Read the following passage and answer the Question Nos. 13 to 18:

The decisive shift in British Policy really came about under mass pressure in the autumn and winter of 1945 to 46—the months which Penderel Moon while editing Wavell's Journal has perceptively described as 'The Edge of a Volcano'. Very foolishly, the British initially decided to hold public trials of several hundreds of the 20,000 I.N.A. prisoners (as well as dismissing from service and detaining without trial no less than 7,000). They compounded the folly by holding the first trial in the Red Fort, Delhi in November 1945, and putting on the dock together a Hindu, a Muslim and a Sikh (P.K. Sehgal, Shah Nawaz, Gurbaksh Singh Dhillon). Bhulabhai Desai, Tejbahadur Sapru and Nehru appeared for the defence (the latter putting on his barrister's gown after 25 years), and the Muslim League also joined the countrywide protest. On 20 November, an Intelligence Bureau note admitted that "there has seldom been a matter which has attracted so much Indian public interest and, it is safe to say, sympathy...this particular brand of sympathy cuts across communal barriers". A journalist (B. Shiva Rao) visiting the Red Fort prisoners on the same day reported that "There is not the slightest feeling among them of Hindu and Muslim.... A majority of the men now awaiting trial in the Red Fort is Muslim. Some of these men are bitter that Mr. Jinnah is keeping alive a controversy about Pakistan." The British became extremely nervous about the I.N.A. spirit spreading to the Indian Army, and in January the Punjab Governor reported that a Lahore reception for released I.N.A. prisoners had been attended by Indian soldiers in uniform.

13. Which heading is more appropriate to assign to the above passage?
    (a) Wavell's Journal
    (b) Role of Muslim League
    (c) I.N.A. Trials
    (d) Red Fort Prisoners

14. The trial of P.K. Sehgal, Shah Nawaz and Gurbaksh Singh Dhillon symbolises
    (a) communal harmony
    (b) threat to all religious persons
    (c) threat to persons fighting for the freedom
    (d) British reaction against the natives

15. I.N.A. stands for
    (a) Indian National Assembly
    (b) Indian National Association
    (c) Inter-national Association
    (d) Indian National Army

16. "There has seldom been a matter which has attracted so much Indian Public Interest and, it is safe to say, sympathy... this particular brand of sympathy cuts across communal barriers." Who sympathises to whom and against whom?
    (a) Muslims sympathised with Shah Nawaz against the British
    (b) Hindus sympathised with P.K. Sehgal against the British
    (c) Sikhs sympathised with Gurbaksh Singh Dhillon against the British
    (d) Indians sympathised with the persons who were to be trialled

17. The majority of people waiting for trial outside the Red Fort and criticising Jinnah were the
(a) Hindus
(b) Muslims
(c) Sikhs
(d) Hindus and Muslims both

18. The sympathy of Indian soldiers in uniform with the released I.N.A. prisoners at Lahore indicates
(a) Feeling of Nationalism and Fraternity
(b) Rebellion nature of Indian soldiers
(c) Simply to participate in the reception party
(d) None of the above

19. The country which has the distinction of having the two largest circulated newspapers in the world is
(a) Great Britain
(b) The United States
(c) Japan
(d) China

20. The chronological order of non-verbal communication is
(a) Signs, symbols, codes, colours
(b) Symbols, codes, signs, colours
(c) Colours, signs, codes, symbols
(d) Codes, colours, symbols, signs

21. Which of the following statements is not connected with communication?
(a) Medium is the message.
(b) The world is an electronic cocoon.
(c) Information is power.
(d) Telepathy is technological.

22. Communication becomes circular when
(a) the decoder becomes an encoder
(b) the feedback is absent
(c) the source is credible
(d) the channel is clear

23. The site that played a major role during the terrorist attack on Mumbai (26/11) in 2008 was
(a) Orkut (b) Facebook
(c) Amazon.com (d) Twitter

24. **Assertion (A):** For an effective classroom communication at times it is desirable to use the projection technology.
Reason (R): Using the projection technology facilitates extensive coverage of course contents.
(a) Both (A) and (R) are true, and (R) is the correct explanation.
(b) Both (A) and (R) are true, but (R) is not the correct explanation.
(c) (A) is true, but (R) is false.
(d) (A) is false, but (R) is true.

25. January 1, 1995 was a Sunday. What day of the week lies on January 1, 1996?
(a) Sunday (b) Monday
(c) Wednesday (d) Saturday

26. When an error of 1% is made in the length and breadth of a rectangle, the percentage error (%) in the area of a rectangle will be
(a) 0 (b) 1
(c) 2 (d) 4

27. The next number in the series 2, 5, 9, 19, 37, ? will be
(a) 74 (b) 75
(c) 76 (d) None of these

28. There are 10 true-false questions in an examination. Then these questions can be answered in
(a) 20 ways (b) 100 ways
(c) 240 ways (d) 1024 ways

29. What will be the next term in the following?
DCXW, FEVU, HGTS, ?
(a) AKPO (b) ABYZ
(c) JIRQ (d) LMRS

30. Three individuals X, Y, Z hired a car on a sharing basis and paid ₹ 1,040. They used it for 7, 8, 11 hours, respectively. What are the charges paid by Y?

(a) ₹ 290 (b) ₹ 320
(c) ₹ 360 (d) ₹ 440

31. Deductive argument involves
(a) sufficient evidence
(b) critical thinking
(c) seeing logical relations
(d) repeated observation

32. Inductive reasoning is based on or presupposes
(a) uniformity of nature
(b) God created the world
(c) unity of nature
(d) laws of nature

33. To be critical, thinking must be
(a) practical
(b) socially relevant
(c) individually satisfying
(d) analytical

34. Which of the following is an analogous statement?
(a) Man is like God
(b) God is great
(c) Gandhiji is the Father of the Nation
(d) Man is a rational being

Questions from 35-36 are based on the following diagram in which there are three intersecting circles. H representing The Hindu, I representing Indian Express and T representing The Times of India. A total of 50 persons were surveyed and the number in the Venn diagram indicates the number of persons reading the newspapers.

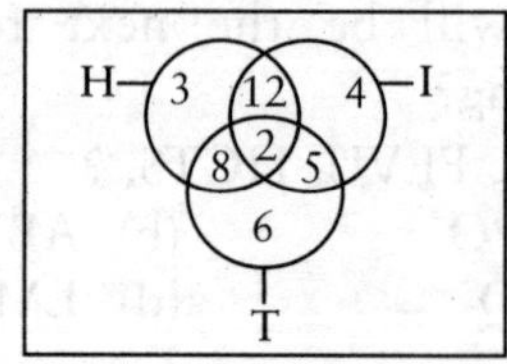

35. How many persons would be reading at least two newspapers?
(a) 23 (b) 25
(c) 27 (d) 29

36. How many persons would be reading almost two newspapers?
(a) 23 (b) 25
(c) 27 (d) 48

37. Which of the following graphs does not represent regular (periodic) behaviour of the variable f(t)?

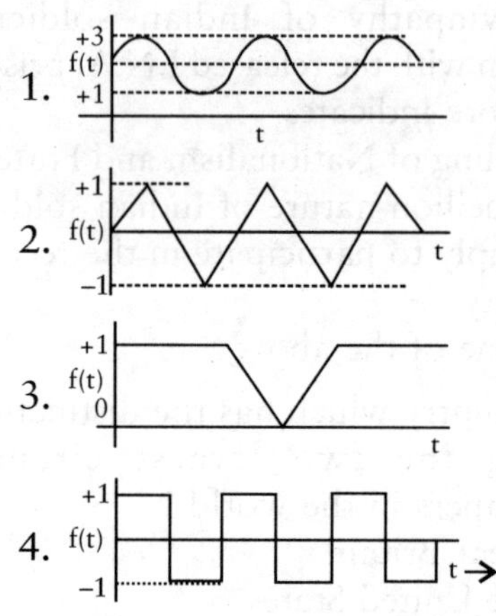

(a) 1 (b) 2
(c) 3 (d) 4

Study the following graph and answer the questions 38 to 40.

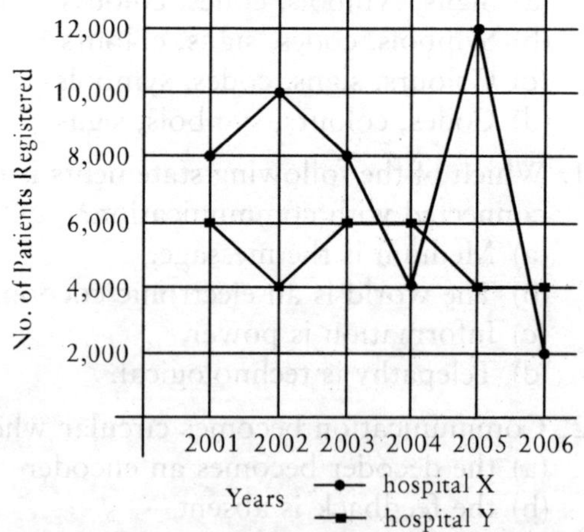

38. In which year total number of patients registered in hospital X and hospital Y was the maximum?
(a) 2003 (b) 2004
(c) 2005 (d) 2006

39. What is the maximum dispersion in the registration of patients in the two hospitals in a year?
(a) 8000 (b) 6000
(c) 4000 (d) 2000

40. In which year there was maximum decrease in registration of patients in hospital X?
(a) 2003 (b) 2004
(c) 2005 (d) 2006

41. Which of the following sources of data is not based on primary data collection?
(a) Census of India
(b) National Sample Survey
(c) Statistical Abstracts of India
(d) National Family Health Survey

42. Which of the four data sets have more dispersion?

(a)	88	91	90	92	89	91
(b)	0	1	1	0	–1	–2
(c)	3	5	2	4	1	5
(d)	0	5	8	10	–2	–8

43. Which of the following is not related to information security on the Internet?
(a) Data Encryption
(b) Water Marking
(c) Data Hiding
(d) Information Retrieval

44. Which is the largest unit of storage among the following?
(a) Terabyte (b) Megabyte
(c) Kilobyte (d) Gigabyte

45. Bit stands for
(a) binary information term
(b) binary digit
(c) binary tree
(d) Bivariate Theory

46. Which one of the following is not a linear data structure?
(a) Array (b) Binary Tree
(c) Queue (d) Stack

47. Which one of the following is not a network device?
(a) Router (b) Switch
(c) Hub (d) CPU

48. A compiler is used to convert the following to object code which can be executed
(a) High-level language
(b) Low-level language
(c) Assembly language
(d) Natural language

49. The great Indian Bustard bird is found in
(a) Thar Desert of Rajasthan
(b) Malabar Coast
(c) Coastal regions of India
(d) Delta regions

50. The Sagarmanthan National Park has been established to preserve the eco-system of which mountain peak?
(a) Kanchenjunga (b) Mount Everest
(c) Annapurna (d) Dhaulavira

51. Maximum soot is released from
(a) Petrol vehicles
(b) CNG vehicles
(c) Diesel vehicles
(d) Thermal Power Plants

52. Surface Ozone is produced from
(a) Transport sector
(b) Cement plants
(c) Textile industry
(d) Chemical industry

53. Which one of the following non-conventional energy sources can be exploited most economically?
(a) Solar
(b) Wind
(c) Geo-thermal
(d) Ocean Thermal Energy Conversion (OTEC)

54. The most recurring natural hazard in India is

(a) Earthquakes (b) Floods
(c) Landslides (d) Volcanoes

55. The recommendation of National Knowledge Commission for the establishment of 1500 Universities is to
(a) create more teaching jobs
(b) ensure increase in student enrolment in higher education
(c) replace or substitute the privately managed higher education institutions by public institutions
(d) enable increased movement of students from rural areas to urban areas

56. According to Article 120 of the Constitution of India, the business in Parliament shall be transacted in
(a) Only English
(b) Only Hindi
(c) Both English and Hindi
(d) All the languages included in Eighth Schedule of the Constitution

57. Which of the following is more interactive and student centric?
(a) Seminar
(b) Workshop
(c) Lecture
(d) Group Discussion

58. The Parliament in India is composed of
(a) Lok Sabha and Rajya Sabha
(b) Lok Sabha, Rajya Sabha and Vice-President
(c) Lok Sabha, Rajya Sabha and President
(d) Lok Sabha, Rajya Sabha with their Secretariats

59. The enrolment in higher education in India is contributed both by Formal System of Education and by System of Distance Education. Distance education contributes
(a) 50% of formal system
(b) 25% of formal system
(c) 10% of the formal system
(d) Distance education system's contribution is not taken into account while considering the figures of enrolment in higher education

60. **Assertion (A):** The UGC Academic Staff Colleges came into existence to improve the quality of teachers.
Reason (R): University and college teachers have to undergo both orientation and refresher courses.
(a) Both (A) and (R) are true and (R) is the correct explanation.
(b) Both (A) and (R) are correct but (R) is not the correct explanation of (A).
(c) (A) is correct and (R) is false.
(d) (A) is false and (R) is correct.

ANSWERS

1. (d)	2. (c)	3. (b)	4. (c)	5. (b)
6. (c)	7. (a)	8. (b)	9. (b)	10. (b)
11. (c)	12. (b)	13. (c)	14. (a)	15. (d)
16. (d)	17. (b)	18. (a)	19. (c)	20. (a)
21. (d)	22. (a)	23. (a)	24. (a)	25. (b)
26. (c)	27. (b)	28. (d)	29. (c)	30. (b)
31. (c)	32. (a)	33. (b)	34. (a)	35. (c)
36. (d)	37. (c)	38. (c)	39. (a)	40. (d)
41. (c)	42. (d)	43. (d)	44. (a)	45. (b)
46. (b)	47. (d)	48. (a)	49. (a)	50. (b)
51. (d)	52. (a)	53. (a)	54. (b)	55. (b)
56. (c)	57. (d)	58. (c)	59. (b)	60. (a)

PAPER–II

Note: This paper contains fifty (50) objective type questions, each question carrying two (2) marks. All questions are compulsory.

1. Gandhi wrote *Hind Swaraj* in the year
   (a) 1907 (b) 1908
   (c) 1919 (d) 1920
2. "They (Moderates) lick the dust of the feet that kick." Who said this?
   (a) M.N. Roy
   (b) B.G. Tilak
   (c) Aurobindo Ghosh
   (d) Veer Savarkar
3. The core idea of ancient Greek political philosophy is
   (a) Social equality
   (b) Liberty of the individual
   (c) Good life
   (d) State sovereignty
4. Which one of the following pairs is not correctly matched?
   (a) Sovereignty of Truth – M.K. Gandhi
   (b) New Humanism – Aurobindo Ghosh
   (c) Dictatorship of the Proletariat – V.I. Lenin
   (d) New Democracy – Mao Zedong
5. Who, among the following philosophers, is famous for adopting the "golden mean"?
   (a) Plato
   (b) Aristotle
   (c) St. Thomas Aquinas
   (d) Machiavelli
6. The study of the Political System of a country at one time, in all its contexts, is known as the
   (a) Configurative approach
   (b) Comparative approach
   (c) Structural approach
   (d) Behavioural approach
7. Limited Government has a close affinity to
   (a) Separation of powers
   (b) Judicial supremacy
   (c) Two-party system
   (d) Rule of Law
8. The Residuary Powers rest with the States/ Units in the political systems of
   (a) U.S.A. and India
   (b) U.S.A. and Switzerland
   (c) Switzerland and India
   (d) India and U.K.
9. Who, among the following, is not a dependency theorist?
   (a) Gunder Frank (b) S.E. Finer
   (c) Wallerstein (d) Cardoso
10. Which of the following is not a feature of the Parliamentary System?
    (a) Collective responsibility
    (b) Close relationship between the legislature and the executive
    (c) Leadership of the Prime Minister
    (d) Fixed Tenure of the Government
11. Who, of the following, was not an extremist?
    (a) Lala Lajpat Rai
    (b) Bipin Chandra Pal
    (c) Bal Gangadhar Tilak
    (d) Gopal Krishna Gokhale
12. Which one of the following is not a part of Fundamental Duties under Indian Constitution?
    (a) To uphold and protect the sovereignty, unity and integrity of India.
    (b) To safeguard public property and to abjure violence.
    (c) To provide opportunities for education to his child or, as the case may be, ward between the age of six and fourteen years.
    (d) To help in organising village panchayats.

13. Which one of the following writs is issued by the Courts for the release of a person unlawfully detained?
    (a) Quo Warranto (b) Prohibition
    (c) Habeas Corpus (d) Certiorari
14. Which of the following was not associated with electoral reforms in India?
    (a) Dinesh Goswami Committee
    (b) Inderjit Gupta Committee
    (c) G.V.K. Rao Committee
    (d) Tarkunde Committee
15. Who described India as a "Soft State"?
    (a) Gunnar Myrdal (b) Myron Weiner
    (c) Rajni Kothari (d) K.C. Wheare
16. Who, among the following, scrutinises the report of the Comptroller and Auditor General of India?
    (a) Cabinet Secretariat
    (b) Public Accounts Committee
    (c) Union Finance Minister
    (d) Department of Expenditure, Union Ministry of Finance
17. To Ronald Reagan, the "Evil Empire" was
    (a) People's Republic of China
    (b) Soviet Union
    (c) Iran
    (d) Libya
18. The Fundamental Principle of the League of Nations was
    (a) Collective defence
    (b) International peace
    (c) Collective security
    (d) International brotherhood
19. A State which dominates and subordinates neighbouring States without taking them over is
    (a) Colonial power (b) Garrison State
    (c) Dominion State (d) Suzerain State
20. 'Prisoner's dilemma' is a phenomenon that fuels
    (a) Arms race (b) Arms control
    (c) Disarmament (d) Peace
21. The 'tragedy of commons' explained by Garett Hardison is related to
    (a) War (b) Peace
    (c) Human Rights (d) Environment
22. When did Minnowbrook-I Conference take place?
    (a) 1966 (b) 1967
    (c) 1968 (d) 1969
23. Who, among the following, has been considered as "the St. Paul of the concept of bureaucracy and capitalist nationality"?
    (a) Woodrow Wilson
    (b) F.W. Taylor
    (c) Max Weber
    (d) H. Simon
24. Who, among the following, is considered as the high priest of development administration?
    (a) Woodrow Wilson
    (b) Chester Barnard
    (c) Paul Appleby
    (d) Fred Riggs
25. Right to Information Act (2005) primarily helps the cause of
    (a) Legal reforms
    (b) Political reforms
    (c) Social integrity
    (d) Transparent administration
26. Which one of the following recommended the establishment of Ombudsman for Local Governments in India?
    (a) Balwant Rai Mehta Committee
    (b) Administrative Reforms Commission I
    (c) Administrative Reforms Commission II
    (d) Santhanam Committee
27. Match List I with List II and select the correct answer with the help of the codes given below:

List I	List II
(A) Plato	(i) Utilitarianism
(B) Rawls	(ii) Surplus value
(C) Bentham	(iii) Philosopher-king
(D) Marx	(iv) Justice as fairness

Codes:	A	B	C	D
(a)	(iv)	(iii)	(ii)	(i)
(b)	(iii)	(iv)	(i)	(ii)
(c)	(i)	(ii)	(iv)	(iii)
(d)	(ii)	(i)	(iii)	(iv)

28. Match List I with List II and select the correct answer from the codes given below:

List I
(A) Critical Community Studies
(B) Security Community
(C) Security Regime
(D) Security Complex

List II
(i) Barry Buzon (ii) Robert Jervis
(iii) Karl Deutsch (iv) Kenneth Booth

Codes:	A	B	C	D
(a)	(i)	(iv)	(iii)	(ii)
(b)	(ii)	(i)	(iv)	(iii)
(c)	(iv)	(iii)	(ii)	(i)
(d)	(iii)	(ii)	(i)	(iv)

29. Match List I with List II and select the correct answer from the codes given below:

List I
(A) Classical Realism
(B) Structural Realism
(C) Neo-classical Realism
(D) Rational choice

List II
(i) Krasner (ii) Kenneth Waltz
(iii) Morgenthau (iv) Schwaller

Codes:	A	B	C	D
(a)	(iii)	(ii)	(iv)	(i)
(b)	(iv)	(i)	(ii)	(iii)
(c)	(iv)	(ii)	(iii)	(i)
(d)	(i)	(ii)	(iii)	(iv)

30. Which one of the following pairs is not properly matched?

(A) David Easton (i) Post-modernism
(B) C. Wright Mills (ii) Guild Socialism
(C) G.D.H. Cole (iii) Power Elite
(D) Derrida (iv) Political system

Select the correct answer from the codes given below:

Codes:	A	B	C	D
(a)	(i)	(ii)	(iii)	(iv)
(b)	(iv)	(iii)	(ii)	(i)
(c)	(i)	(iii)	(iv)	(ii)
(d)	(ii)	(i)	(iv)	(iii)

31. Identify the correct chronological order of following Prime Ministers of India:

(i) V.P. Singh
(ii) Chandrashekhar
(iii) Morarji Desai
(iv) Rajiv Gandhi

Select the correct answer from the codes given below:

Codes:
(a) (iii) (iv) (i) (ii) (b) (i) (iv) (iii) (ii)
(c) (iii) (i) (iv) (ii) (d) (iv) (iii) (ii) (i)

32. Identify the correct chronological order in which the following events occurred.

(i) Death of Fakharuddin Ali Ahmed.
(ii) First split in the Congress after Independence.
(iii) Arrest of Shaikh Md. Abdullah as the Prime Minister of Jammu and Kashmir.
(iv) Signing of Indo-Soviet Treaty.

Select the correct answer from the codes given below:

Codes:
(a) (iv) (iii) (ii) (i) (b) (iii) (ii) (iv) (i)
(c) (ii) (i) (iii) (iv) (d) (iii) (iv) (ii) (i)

33. According to Organski, the stages of political development are

(1) Unification
(2) Industrialization

(3) Abundance
(4) National Welfare

Identify the correct chronological sequence of the above from the codes given below:

(a) 1, 2, 3 and 4 (b) 1, 2, 4 and 3
(c) 1, 3, 4 and 2 (d) 2, 1, 3 and 4

34. Arrange the chronological order of the following treaties in the evolution of European Union:
(i) Amsterdam Treaty
(ii) Maastricht Treaty
(iii) Nice Treaty
(iv) Constitutional Treaty

Select the correct answer with the help of the codes given below:

Codes:

(a) (i) (ii) (iii) (iv) (b) (iv) (ii) (i) (iii)
(c) (ii) (i) (iii) (iv) (d) (iii) (iv) (i) (ii)

35. Give the chronological order of the following events in the evolution of the modern State system.
(i) Vienna Congress
(ii) Paris Peace Treaties
(iii) Treaty of Westphalia
(iv) The Treaty of Utrect

Codes:

(a) (iii) (iv) (i) (ii) (b) (i) (ii) (iii) (iv)
(c) (ii) (i) (iv) (iii) (d) (iv) (ii) (i) (iii)

Directions (Q. 36 to 45): Each of the following items consists of two statements, one labelled as Assertion (A) and other labelled as Reason (R). You are to examine these two statements carefully and decide if the (A) and the (R) are individually true and if so, whether (R) is the correct explanation of (A).

Select your answers to these items using the codes given below:

(a) Both (A) and (R) true, and (R) is the correct explanation of (A).
(b) Both (A) and (R) are true, and (R) is not the correct explanation of (A).
(c) (A) is true but (R) is false.
(d) (A) is false but (R) is true.

36. **Assertion (A):** To J.S. Mill, the scope of liberty includes that of conscience, thought and feeling, so long as it is voluntary, informal and without harmful intent.

Reason (R): A liberal social order can be justified on utilitarian grounds, without appeal to doctrines of natural rights.

37. **Assertion (A):** Gandhi's Satyagraha is the vindication of truth through self-inflicted suffering.

Reason (R): The purpose Satyagraha is to show moral superiority of the Satyagrahi.

38. **Assertion (A):** The President of India can return back a recommendation of the Cabinet for reconsideration.

Reason (R): He has been given this power because he is not expected to be a mere figure head.

39. **Assertion (A):** Fundamental Rights are considered fundamental in the governance of the polity and hence they have been made justiciable under Article 32.

Reason (R): Civil Rights, even when important, cannot be considered as Fundamental Rights because they are not justiciable under Article 32.

40. **Assertion (A):** The method of systems analysis adopted by Almond is more representative than that of David Easton.

Reason (R): Almond is the first major political scientist who has developed the systems analysis approach for the study of politics.

41. **Assertion (A):** Bureaucracy has contributed to the growth of democracy but it has also stood in the way of democratisation.

Reason (R): Democracy does not need bureaucracy.

42. **Assertion (A):** Whitley type councils have been set up in India.
Reason (R): The councils have the powers to take up the grievances of individual employees on priority basis.

43. **Assertion (A):** Lokayuktas have been appointed in all the States.
Reason (R): The National Commission to review the working of the Constitution has recommended the establishment of Lokayuktas.

44. **Assertion (A):** Balance of power results in Status quo in world politics.
Reason (R): States are primary actors in international relations.

45. **Assertion (A):** India seeks permanent membership of Security Council.
Reason (R): India wants to legitimise its nuclear weapon state status through India-US Civilian Nuclear Agreement.

Read the passage given below and answer the questions on the basis of your understanding of the passage:

In every country some regions are richer than others, and some (not necessarily the richest) are developing more rapidly than others. To make a plan which gives equal emphasis to every square mile, or spent an equal sum on every inhabitant, would be quite uneconomic. In the first place different areas have different growth potential; some have minerals, or water, or good natural harbours, while others are poorly favoured. And secondly, even if all areas started with equal resources, it would pay to concentrate development in relatively few places, because of the economies of geographical concentration. Hence, as soon as one area got ahead for any reason, however accidental (e.g. the birth there of some entrepreneurial genius, which explains the growth of motor manufacture near Singur), it would grow much faster than the rest. It could offer many services and commodities more cheaply, because produced on a large scale; it would possess an interlocking network of markets, banks, transport facilities, engineering repair services and the like; its schools, hospitals and research institutes would offer more specialized services, and so on. That some parts of the country will develop faster than the rest is a natural economic phenomenon; and so is its corollary, that some areas will contract, relatively, or even absolutely.

If the country is fully integrated, it is in the general interest that resources be invested where they are likely to prove most productive. Full integration means a right to participate equally in economic activities in any part of one's country. If the savings of citizens of county B are to be used to develop county C, on the ground that will be most productive there, the citizens of B must be allowed to enjoy the new opportunities which their savings will be creating in C: to seek work there, to trade without customs barriers and to enjoy any facilities (schools, hospitals, etc.) which are going to be financed out of taxes collected as a result of such development. Resistance to the proposition that resources be invested where they are most productive derives from the expectation that those who live where the resources are invested are going to benefit most. Such resistance cannot be eliminated altogether, since it is true that residents have an advantage, but it can be minimized by furthering the country's integration: by building transport facilities, and by using some of the wealth produced in the richer areas to finance improved public facilities in the poorer areas, thus buying their consent to concentration of development policies in the areas with the best prospects.

46. The author is primarily concerned with
   (a) Differing potentials of the State.
   (b) Allocation of development funds.
   (c) Promoting regional balance.
   (d) Wealth generation.

47. According to the author some states develop faster than other as they are
   (I) Rich in natural resources.
   (II) Due to faulty economic policy.
   (III) Accidental growth due to various factors.
   (IV) Concentrated development.
   (a) I and II only (b) III only
   (c) II and III only (d) II, III, IV only

48. Development funds should be allocated
   (a) Haphazardly to States based on geographical location.
   (b) Judiciously to States rich in natural resources.
   (c) Unevenly based on the potentiality of the States.
   (d) Evenly to all States.

49. According to the author the country is fully integrated when
   (a) Resources are invested in the States where productivity is more.
   (b) Equal participation in economic activities in all parts of the country.
   (c) More concession and opportunities for productive States.
   (d) Advantage to enjoy the benefits of the investments by the residents.

50. The material in the passage can best be used in an argument for
   (I) Investing in uneven development funds.
   (II) Protecting the rights of poorer States.
   (III) To understand the uneven development of States.
   (IV) To minimize the regional imbalance.
   (a) I and II only (b) II only
   (c) I and III only (d) II and IV only

ANSWERS

1. (b)	2. (d)	3. (b)	4. (b)	5. (b)
6. (b)	7. (d)	8. (a)	9. (b)	10. (a)
11. (d)	12. (d)	13. (c)	14. (c)	15. (d)
16. (b)	17. (b)	18. (b)	19. (c)	20. (a)
21. (d)	22. (c)	23. (c)	24. (c)	25. (d)
26. (d)	27. (b)	28. (c)	29. (d)	30. (c)
31. (a)	32. (b)	33. (a)	34. (c)	35. (d)
36. (a)	37. (c)	38. (c)	39. (a)	40. (a)
41. (b)	42. (c)	43. (b)	44. (b)	45. (a)
46. (b)	47. (d)	48. (d)	49. (b)	50. (d)

JUNE–2009

Note: This paper contains Fifty (50) multiple-choice questions, each question carrying two (2) marks. Attempt all of them.

PAPER–I

1. Good evaluation of written material should not be based on
   (a) Linguistic expression
   (b) Logical presentation
   (c) Ability to reproduce whatever is read
   (d) Comprehension of subject

2. Why do teachers use teaching aid?
   (a) To make teaching fun-filled
   (b) To teach within understanding level of students
   (c) For students' attention
   (d) To make students attentive

3. Attitudes, concepts, skills and knowledge are products of
   (a) Learning (b) Research
   (c) Heredity (d) Explanation

4. Which among the following gives more freedom to the learner to interact?
   (a) Use of film
   (b) Small group discussion
   (c) Lectures by experts
   (d) Viewing country-wide classroom program on TV

5. Which of the following is not a product of learning?
   (a) Attitudes (b) Concepts
   (c) Knowledge (d) Maturation

6. How can the objectivity of the research be enhanced?
   (a) Through its impartiality
   (b) Through its reliability
   (c) Through its validity
   (d) All of these

7. Action-research is
   (a) An applied research
   (b) A research carried out to solve immediate problems
   (c) A longitudinal research
   (d) All the above

8. The basis on which assumptions are formulated
   (a) Cultural background of the country
   (b) Universities
   (c) Specific characteristics of the castes
   (d) All of these

9. Which of the following is classified in the category of the developmental research?
   (a) Philosophical research
   (b) Action research
   (c) Descriptive research
   (d) All the above

10. We use Factorial Analysis
   (a) To know the relationship between two variables
   (b) To test the Hypothesis
   (c) To know the difference between two variables
   (d) To know the difference among the many variables

Read the following passage and answer the questions 11 to 15:

While the British rule in India was detrimental to the economic development of the country, it did help in starting of the process of modernising Indian society and formed several progressive institutions during that process. One of the most beneficial institutions, which were initiated by the British, was democracy. Nobody can dispute that despite its many shortcomings, democracy was and is far better alternative to the arbitrary rule of the rajas and nawabs, which prevailed in India in the pre-British days.

However, one of the harmful traditions of British democracy inherited by India was that of conflict instead of cooperation between elected members. This was its essential feature. The party, which got the support of the majority of elected members, formed the Government while the others constituted a standing opposition. The existence of the opposition to those in power was and is regarded as a hallmark of democracy.

In principle, democracy consists of rule by the people; but where direct rule is not possible, it's rule by persons elected by the people. It is natural that there would be some differences of opinion among the elected members as in the rest of the society.

Normally, members of any organisations have differences of opinion between themselves on different issues but they manage to work on the basis of a consensus and they do not normally form a division between some who are in majority and are placed in power, while treating the others as in opposition.

The members of an organisation usually work on consensus. Consensus simply means that after an adequate discussion, members agree that the majority opinion may prevail for the time being. Thus persons who form a majority on one issue and whose opinion is allowed to prevail may not be on the same side if there is a difference on some other issue.

It was largely by accident that instead of this normal procedure, a two-party system came to prevail in Britain and that is now being generally taken as the best method of democratic rule.

Many democratically inclined persons in India regret that such a two-party system was not brought about in the country. It appears that to have two parties in India—of more or less equal strength—is a virtual impossibility. Those who regret the absence of a two-party system should take the reasons into consideration.

When the two-party system got established in Britain, there were two groups among the rulers (consisting of a limited electorate) who had the same economic interests among themselves and who therefore formed two groups within the selected members of Parliament.

There were members of the British aristocracy (which landed interests and consisting of lord, barons, etc.) and members of the new commercial class consisting of merchants and artisans. These groups were more or less of equal strength and they were able to establish their separate rule at different times.

Answer the following questions:

11. In pre-British period, when India was ruled by the independent rulers
    (a) Peace and prosperity prevailed in the society
    (b) People were isolated from political affairs
    (c) Public opinion was inevitable for policy making
    (d) Law was equal for one and all
12. What is the distinguishing feature of the democracy practised in Britain?
    (a) End to the rule of might is right.
    (b) Rule of the people, by the people and for the people.
    (c) It has stood the test of time.
    (d) Cooperation between elected members.

13. Democracy is practiced where
    (a) Elected members form a uniform opinion regarding policy matter.
    (b) Opposition is more powerful than the ruling combine.
    (c) Representatives of masses.
    (d) None of these.

14. Which of the following is true about the British rule in India?
    (a) It was behind the modernisation of the Indian society.
    (b) India gained economically during that period.
    (c) Various establishments were formed for the purpose of progress.
    (d) None of these.

15. Who became the members of the new commercial class during that time?
    (a) British Aristocrats
    (b) Lords and Barons
    (c) Political Persons
    (d) Merchants and Artisans

16. Which one of the following Telephonic Conferencing with a radio link is very popular throughout the world?
    (a) TPS (b) Telepresence
    (c) Video conference (d) Video teletext

17. Which is not 24 hours news channel?
    (a) NDTV 24×7
    (b) ZEE News
    (c) Aajtak
    (d) Lok Sabha Channel

18. The main objective of FM station in radio is
    (a) Information, Entertainment and Tourism
    (b) Entertainment, Information and Interaction
    (c) Tourism, Interaction and Entertainment
    (d) Entertainment only

19. In communication chatting on internet is
    (a) Verbal communication
    (b) Non-verbal communication
    (c) Parallel communication
    (d) Grapevine communication

20. Match List I with List II and select the correct answer using the codes given below:

List I (Artists)
A. Pandit Jasraj B. Kishan Maharaj
C. Ravi Shankar D. Udai Shankar

List II (Art)
1. Hindustani vocalist
2. Sitar
3. Tabla
4. Dance

Codes:	A	B	C	D
(a)	1	2	3	4
(b)	1	3	4	2
(c)	1	3	2	4
(d)	3	2	1	4

21. Insert the missing number in the following.
    3, 8, 18, 23, 33, ?, 48
    (a) 37 (b) 40
    (c) 38 (d) 45

22. In a certain code, CLOCK is written as KCOLC. How would STEPS be written in that code?
    (a) SPEST (b) SPSET
    (c) SPETS (d) SEPTS

23. The letters in the first set have a certain relationship. On the basis of this relationship mark the right choice for the second set
    BDFH : OMKI :: GHIK : ?
    (a) FHJL (b) RPNL
    (c) LNPR (d) LJHF

24. What was the day of the week on 1st January 2001?
    (a) Friday (b) Monday
    (c) Sunday (d) Wednesday

25. Find out the wrong number in the sequence.
    52, 51, 48, 43, 34, 27, 16
    (a) 27 (b) 34
    (c) 43 (d) 48
26. In a deductive argument conclusion is
    (a) Summing up of the premises
    (b) Not necessarily based on premises
    (c) Entailed by the premises
    (d) Additional to the premises
27. 'No man are mortal' is contradictory of
    (a) Some man are mortal
    (b) Some man are not mortal
    (c) All men are mortal
    (d) No mortal is man
28. A deductive argument is valid if
    (a) premises are false and conclusion is true
    (b) premises are false and conclusion is also false
    (c) premises are true and conclusion is false
    (d) premises are true and conclusion is true
29. Structure of logical argument is based on
    (a) Formal validity
    (b) Material truth
    (c) Linguistic expression
    (d) Aptness of examples
30. Two ladies and two men are playing bridge and seated at North, East, South and West of a table. No lady is facing East. Persons sitting opposite to each other are not of the same sex. One man is facing South. Which direction are the ladies facing to?
    (a) East and West
    (b) North and West
    (c) South and East
    (d) None of these

Questions 31 and 32 are based on the following Venn diagram in which there are three intersecting circles representing Hindi knowing persons, English knowing persons and persons who are working as teachers. Different regions so obtained in the figure are marked as a, b, c, d, e, f and g.

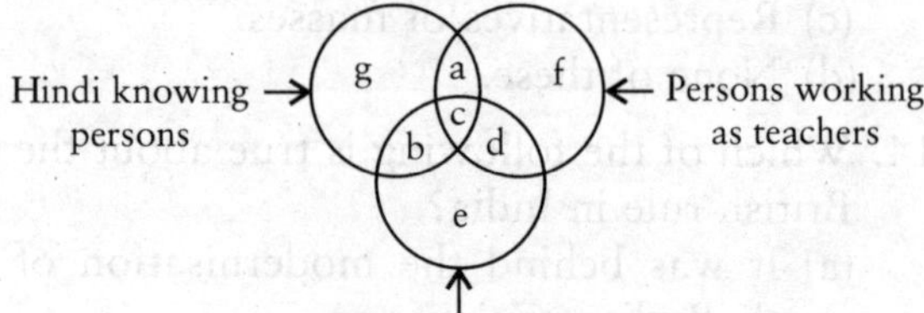

31. If you want to select Hindi and English knowing teachers, which of the following is to be selected?
    (a) g (b) b
    (c) c (d) e
32. If you want to select persons, who do not know English and are not teachers, which of the region is to be selected?
    (a) e (b) g
    (c) b (d) a

Study the following graph carefully and answer questions 33 to 35.

Export of Engineering Goods

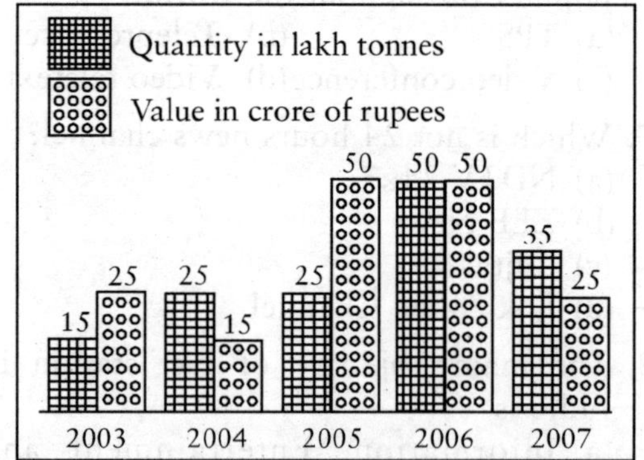

33. In which year the quantity of engineering goods' exports was maximum?
    (a) 2005 (b) 2006
    (c) 2004 (d) 2007
34. In which year the value of engineering goods decreased by 50 percent compared to the previous year?

(a) 2004 (b) 2007
(c) 2005 (d) 2006

35. In which year the quantity of exports was 100 percent higher than the quantity of previous year?
(a) 2004 (b) 2005
(c) 2006 (d) 2007

36. What do you need to put your web pages on the www?
(a) a connection to internet
(b) a web browser
(c) a web server
(d) All of the above

37. Which was the first company to launch mobile phone services in India?
(a) Essar (b) BPL
(c) Hutchison (d) Airtel

38. Chandrayan I was launched on 22nd October, 2008 in India from
(a) Bangalore (b) Sri Harikota
(c) Chennai (d) Ahmedabad

39. What is blog?
(a) Online music
(b) Intranet
(c) A personal or corporate website in the form of an online journal
(d) A personal or corporate Google search

40. Which is not online Indian Matrimonial website?
(a) www.jeevansathi.com
(b) www.bharatmatrimony.com
(c) www.shaadi.com
(d) www.u.k.singlemuslim.com

41. Environmental impact assessment is an objective analysis of the probable changes in
(a) physical characteristics of the environment
(b) biophysical characteristics of the environment
(c) socio-economic characteristics of the environment
(d) All of the above

42. Bog is a wetland that receives water from
(a) nearby water bodies
(b) melting
(c) Only rainfall
(d) Only sea

43. Which of the following region is in the very high risk zone of earthquakes?
(a) Central Indian Highland
(b) Coastal region
(c) Himalayan region
(d) Indian desert

44. Match List I with List II and select the correct answer using the codes given below.

List I (Institutes)
A. Central Arid Zone Institute
B. Space Application Centre
C. Indian Institute of Public Administration
D. Headquarters of Indian Science Congress

List II (Cities)
1. Kolkata 2. New Delhi
3. Ahmedabad 4. Jodhpur

Codes:	A	B	C	D
(a)	4	3	2	1
(b)	4	2	1	3
(c)	3	1	2	4
(d)	1	2	4	3

45. Indian coastal areas experienced Tsunami disaster in the year
(a) 2005 (b) 2004
(c) 2006 (d) 2007

46. The Kothari Commission's report was entitled on
(a) Education and National Development
(b) Learning to be adventure
(c) Diversification of Education
(d) Education and socialisation in democracy

47. Which of the following is not a Dual mode University?
(a) Delhi University
(b) Bangalore University

(c) Madras University
(d) Indira Gandhi National Open University

48. Which part of the Constitution of India is known as "Code of Administrators"?
(a) Part I (b) Part II
(c) Part III (d) Part IV

49. Which article of the constitution provides safeguards to Naga Customary and their social practices against any act of Parliament?
(a) Article 371A (b) Article 371B
(c) Article 371C (d) Article 263

50. Which one of the following is not the tool of good governance?
(a) Right to Information
(b) Citizens' Charter
(c) Social Auditing
(d) Judicial Activism

ANSWERS

1. (a)	2. (a)	3. (a)	4. (b)	5. (d)
6. (d)	7. (b)	8. (a)	9. (d)	10. (d)
11. (b)	12. (d)	13. (a)	14. (c)	15. (a)
16. (b)	17. (d)	18. (b)	19. (b)	20. (c)
21. (c)	22. (c)	23. (b)	24. (b)	25. (b)
26. (c)	27. (c)	28. (d)	29. (b)	30. (b)
31. (c)	32. (b)	33. (b)	34. (b)	35. (c)
36. (d)	37. (d)	38. (b)	39. (c)	40. (d)
41. (d)	42. (a)	43. (b)	44. (a)	45. (b)
46. (a)	47. (d)	48. (d)	49. (a)	50. (d)

DECEMBER–2008

Note: This paper contains Fifty (50) multiple-choice questions, each question carrying two (2) marks. Attempt all of them.

PAPER–I

1. According to Swami Vivekananda, teacher's success depends on
   (a) His renunciation of personal gain and service to others
   (b) His professional training and creativity
   (c) His concentration on his work and duties with a spirit of obedience to God
   (d) His mastery on the subject and capacity in controlling the students
2. Which of the following teacher will be liked most?
   (a) A teacher of high idealistic attitude
   (b) A loving teacher
   (c) A teacher who is disciplined
   (d) A teacher who often amuses his students
3. A teacher's most important challenge is
   (a) To make students do their home work
   (b) To make teaching-learning process enjoyable
   (c) To maintain discipline in the classroom
   (d) To prepare the question paper
4. Value-education stands for
   (a) making a student healthy
   (b) making a student to get a job
   (c) inculcation of virtues
   (d) all-round development of personality
5. When a normal student behaves in an erratic manner in the class, you would
   (a) pull up the student then and there
   (b) talk to the student after the class
   (c) ask the student to leave the class
   (d) ignore the student
6. The research is always
   (a) verifying the old knowledge
   (b) exploring new knowledge
   (c) filling the gap between knowledge
   (d) All of these
7. The research that applies the laws at the time of field study to draw more and more clear ideas about the problem is
   (a) Applied research
   (b) Action research
   (c) Experimental research
   (d) None of these
8. When a research problem is related to heterogeneous population, the most suitable sampling method is
   (a) Cluster Sampling
   (b) Stratified Sampling
   (c) Convenient Sampling
   (d) Lottery Method
9. The process not needed in experimental research is:
   (a) Observation
   (b) Manipulation and replication
   (c) Controlling
   (d) Reference collection
10. A research problem is not feasible only when

(a) it is researchable
(b) it is new and adds something to knowledge
(c) it consists of independent and dependent variables
(d) it has utility and relevance

Read the following passage carefully and answer the questions 11 to 15:

Radically changing monsoon patterns, reduction in the winter rice harvest and a quantum increase in respiratory diseases all part of the environmental doomsday scenario which is reportedly playing out in South Asia. According to a United Nations Environment Program report, a deadly three-kilometer deep blanket of pollution comprising a fearsome, cocktail of ash, acids, aerosols and other particles has enveloped in this region. For India, already struggling to cope with a drought, the implication of this are devastating and further crop failure will amount to a life and death question for many Indians. The increase in premature deaths will have adverse social and economic consequences and a rise in morbidities will place an unbearable burden on our crumbling health system. And there is no one to blame but ourselves. Both official and corporate India has always been allergic to any mention of clean technology. Most mechanical two wheelers roll of the assembly line without proper pollution control system. Little effort is made for R&D on simple technologies, which could make a vital difference to people's lives and the environment.

However, while there is no denying that South Asia must clean up its act, skeptics might question the timing of the haze report. The Kyoto meet on climate change is just two weeks away and the stage is set for the usual battle between the developing world and the West, particularly the Unites States of America. President Mr. Bush has adamantly refused to sign any protocol, which would mean a change in American consumption level. U.N. environment report will likely find a place in the U.S. arsenal as it plants an accusing finger towards controls like India and China. Yet the U.S.A. can hardly deny its own dubious role in the matter of erasing trading quotas.

Richer countries can simply buy up excess credits from poorer countries and continue to pollute. Rather than try to get the better of developing countries, who undoubtedly have taken up environmental shortcuts in their bid to catch up with the West, the USA should take a look at the environmental profigacy, which is going on within. From opening up virgin territories for oil exploration to relaxing the standards for drinking water, Mr. Bush's policies are not exactly beneficial, not even to America's interests. We realise that we are all in this together and that pollution anywhere should be a global concern otherwise there will only be more tunnels at the end of the tunnel.

11. Both official and corporate India is allergic to
(a) Failure of Monsoon
(b) Poverty and Inequality
(c) Slowdown in Industrial Production
(d) Mention of Clean Technology

12. If the rate of premature death increases it will
(a) Exert added burden on the crumbling economy
(b) Have adverse social and economic consequences
(c) Make positive effect on our effort to control population
(d) Have less job aspirants in the society

13. According to the passage, the two-wheeler industry is not adequately concerned about
(a) Passenger safety on the roads
(b) Life cover insurance of the vehicle owner

(c) Pollution control system in the vehicle
(d) Rising cost of the two wheelers

14. What could be the reason behind timing of the haze report just before the Kyoto meet?
(a) United Nations is working hand-in-glove with U.S.A.
(b) Organisers of the forthcoming meet to teach a lesson to the U.S.A.
(c) Drawing attention of the world towards devastating effects of environment degradation.
(d) U.S.A. wants to use it as a handle against the developing countries in the forthcoming meet.

15. Which of the following is the indication of environmental degradation in South Asia?
(a) Social and economic inequality
(b) Crumbling health care system
(c) Inadequate pollution control system
(d) Radically changing monsoon pattern

16. Community Radio is a type of radio service that caters to the interest of
(a) Local audience (b) Education
(c) Entertainment (d) News

17. Orkut is a part of
(a) Intrapersonal Communication
(b) Mass Communication
(c) Group Communication
(d) Interpersonal Communication

18. Match List I with List II and select the correct answer using the codes given below.

List I (Artists)
A. Amrita Shergill
B. T. Swaminathan Pillai
C. Bhimsen Joshi
D. Padma Subramaniyam

List II (Art)
1. Flute 2. Classical Song
3. Painting 4. Bharat Natyam

Codes:	A	B	C	D
(a)	3	1	2	4
(b)	2	3	1	4
(c)	4	2	3	1
(d)	1	4	2	3

19. Which is not correct in latest communication award?
(a) Salman Rushdie - Booker's Prize—July 20, 2008
(b) Dilip Sanghavi - Business Standard CEO Award, July 22, 2008
(c) Tapan Sinha - Dada Saheb Falke Award, July 21, 2008
(d) Gautam Ghosh - Osians Lifetime Achievement Award, July 11, 2008

20. Firewalls are used to protect a communication network system against
(a) Unauthorised attacks
(b) Virus attacks
(c) Data-driven attacks
(d) Fire-attacks

21. Insert the missing number in the following

$\frac{2}{7}, \frac{4}{7}, ?, \frac{11}{21}, \frac{16}{31}$

(a) $\frac{10}{8}$ (b) $\frac{6}{10}$
(c) $\frac{5}{10}$ (d) $\frac{7}{13}$

22. In a certain code, GAMESMAN is written as AGMEMSAN. How would DISCLOSE be written in that code?
(a) IDSCOLSE (b) IDCSOLES
(c) IDSCOLES (d) IDSCLOSE

23. The letters in the first set have a certain relationship. On the basis of this

relationship mark the right choice for the second set : AST : BRU :: NQV: ?
(a) ORW (b) MPU
(c) MRW (d) OPW

24. On what dates of April, 1994 did Sunday fall?
(a) 2, 9, 16, 23, 30
(b) 3, 10, 17, 24
(c) 4, 11, 18, 25
(d) 1, 8, 15, 22, 29

25. Find out the wrong number in the sequence.
125, 127, 130, 135, 142, 153, 165
(a) 130 (b) 142
(c) 153 (d) 165

26. There are five books A, B, C, D and E. The book C lies above D, the book E is below A and B is below E. Which is at the bottom?
(a) E (b) B
(c) A (d) C

27. Logical reasoning is based on
(a) Truth of involved propositions
(b) Valid relation among the involved propositions
(c) Employment of symbolic language
(d) Employment of ordinary language

28. Two propositions with the same subject and predicate terms but different in quality are
(a) Contradictory (b) Contrary
(c) Subaltern (d) Identical

29. The premises of a valid deductive argument
(a) Provide some evidence for its conclusion
(b) Provide no evidence for its conclusion
(c) Are irrelevant for its conclusion
(d) Provide conclusive evidence for its conclusion

30. Syllogistic reasoning is
(a) Deductive (b) Inductive
(c) Experimental (d) Hypothetical

Study the following Venn diagram and answer questions nos. 31 to 33.

Three circles representing Graduates, Clerks and Government employees are intersecting. The intersections are marked A, B, C, e, f, g and h. Which part best represents the statements in questions 31 to 33?

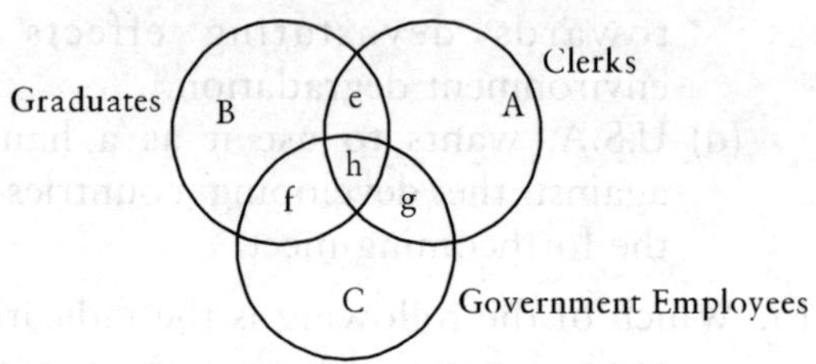

31. Some Graduates are Government employees but not Clerks.
(a) h (b) g
(c) f (d) e

32. Clerks who are Graduates as well as Government employees.
(a) e (b) f
(c) g (d) h

33. Some Graduates are Clerks but not Government employees.
(a) f (b) g
(c) h (d) e

Study the following graph and answer questions numbers from 34 to 35

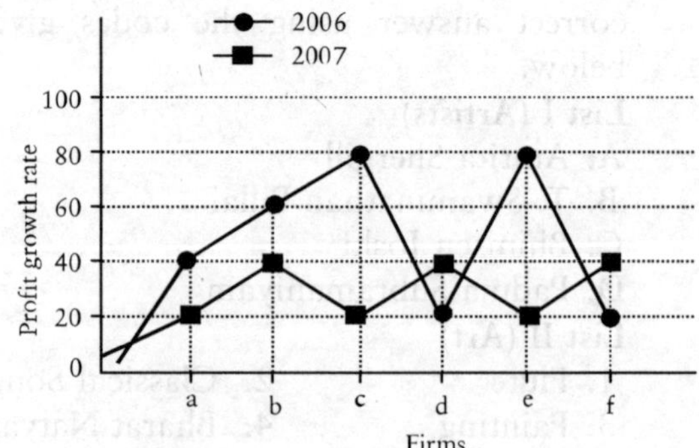

34. Which of the firms got maximum profit growth rate in the year 2006?
(a) ab (b) ce
(c) cd (d) ef

35. Which of the firms got maximum profit growth rate in the year 2007?
(a) bdf (b) acf
(c) bed (d) ace

36. The accounting software 'Tally' was developed by
(a) HCL (b) TCS
(c) Infosys (d) Wipro

37. Errors in computer programs are called
(a) Follies (b) Mistakes
(c) Bugs (d) Spam

38. HTML is basically used to design
(a) Webpage
(b) Website
(c) Graphics
(d) Tables and Frames

39. 'Micro Processing' is made for
(a) Computer
(b) Digital System
(c) Calculator
(d) Electronic Goods

40. Information, a combination of graphics, text, sound, video and animation is called
(a) Multiprogram (b) Multifacet
(c) Multimedia (d) Multiprocess

41. Which of the following pairs regarding typical composition of hospital wastes is incorrect?
(a) Plastic - 9-12%
(b) Metals - 1-2%
(c) Ceramic - 8-10%
(d) Biodegradable - 35-40%

42. Freshwater achieves its greatest density at
(a) –4°C (b) 0°C
(c) 4°C (d) –2.5°C

43. Which one of the following is not associated with earthquakes?
(a) Focus (b) Epicenter
(c) Seismograph (d) Swells

44. The tallest trees in the world are found in the region
(a) Equatorial region
(b) Temperate region
(c) Monsoon region
(d) Mediterranean region

45. Match List I with List II and select the correct answer from the codes given below.

List I (National Parks)
A. Periyar
B. Nandan Kanan
C. Corbett National Park
D. Sariska Tiger Reserve

List II (States)
1. Odisha
2. Kerala
3. Rajasthan
4. Uttarakhand

Codes:	A	B	C	D
(a)	2	1	4	3
(b)	1	2	4	3
(c)	3	2	1	4
(d)	1	2	3	4

46. According to Radhakrishnan Commission, the aim of Higher Education is
(a) To develop the democratic values, peace and harmony
(b) To develop great personalities who can give their contributions in politics, administration, industry and commerce
(c) Both (a) and (b)
(d) None of these

47. The National Museum at New Delhi is attached to

(a) Delhi University
(b) a Deemed University
(c) a Subordinate Office of the JNU
(d) Part of Ministry of Tourism and Culture

48. Match List I with List II and select the correct answer from the code given below.

List I (Institutions)
A. National Law Institute
B. Indian Institute of Advanced Studies
C. National Judicial Academy
D. National Savings Institute

List II (Locations)
1. Shimla
2. Bhopal
3. Hyderabad
4. Nagpur

Codes:	A	B	C	D
(a)	3	2	4	1
(b)	1	2	3	4
(c)	4	3	1	2
(d)	3	1	2	4

49. Election of Rural and Urban local bodies are conducted and ultimately supervised by
(a) Election Commission of India
(b) State Election Commission
(c) District Collector and District Magistrate
(d) Concerned Returning Officer

50. Which opinion is not correct?
(a) Education is a subject of concurrent list of VII schedule of Constitution of India
(b) University Grants Commission is a statutory body
(c) Patent, inventions, design, copyright and trade marks are the subject of concurrent list
(d) Indian Council of Social Science Research is a statutory body related to research in social sciences

ANSWERS

1. (d)	2. (c)	3. (b)	4. (c)	5. (b)
6. (d)	7. (a)	8. (b)	9. (d)	10. (b)
11. (d)	12. (b)	13. (c)	14. (c)	15. (d)
16. (a)	17. (d)	18. (a)	19. (b)	20. (a)
21. (d)	22. (a)	23. (d)	24. (b)	25. (d)
26. (b)	27. (b)	28. (a)	29. (d)	30. (a)
31. (c)	32. (d)	33. (d)	34. (b)	35. (a)
36. (b)	37. (c)	38. (a)	39. (a)	40. (c)
41. (d)	42. (c)	43. (d)	44. (b)	45. (a)
46. (c)	47. (d)	48. (d)	49. (b)	50. (c)

PAPER–II

Note: This paper contains fifty (50) objective type questions, each question carrying two (2) marks. All questions are compulsory.

1. The first systematic Indian political theory can be found in:
(a) The Vedas
(b) The Arthashastra
(c) The Sukra Niti Sara
(d) The Bhagavad Gita

2. The idea of the cave and shadows is associated with:
(a) Socrates
(b) Democrates
(c) Plato
(d) Aristotle

3. Who said that some men are ruled by force and some others by law?
(a) Marx
(b) Lenin
(c) Hegel
(d) Machiavelli

4. Who propounded the idea of 'felicific calculus'?

(a) Machiavelli (b) Hobbes
(c) Bentham (d) Marx

5. The theory of contradictions was propounded by:
(a) Mao (b) Hobbes
(c) Mill (d) Locke

6. The problem of 'minority opinion' was tackled by:
(a) Hobbes (b) Locke
(c) Marx (d) Rousseau

7. Given below are two statements, one labelled as Assertion (A) and the other as Reason (R).
Assertion (A): Nozic was a libertarian.
Reason (R): Nozic stood for individual liberty and just property.
Which one of the following is correct?
(a) Both (A) and (R) are true and (R) is the correct explanation of (A).
(b) Both (A) and (R) are true but (R) is not the correct explanation of (A).
(c) (A) is true but (R) is false.
(d) (A) is false but (R) is true.

8. **Assertion (A):** Post behavioralism consisted of normative element.
Reason (R): Easton conceded relevance of values in political analysis.
Which one of the following is correct?
(a) Both (A) and (R) are true and (R) is the correct explanation of (A).
(b) Both (A) and (R) are true but (R) is not the correct explanation of (A).
(c) (A) is true and (R) is false.
(d) (A) is false and (R) is true.

9. Identify the order in which the following occured:
(i) The Russian Revolution
(ii) The American Revolution
(iii) The French Revolution
(iv) The Glorious Revolution
(a) (iv), (iii), (i), (ii) (b) (iv), (ii), (iii), (i)
(c) (i), (iii), (ii), (iv) (d) (i), (iv), (ii), (iii)

10. Match the List I with the List II:

List I	List II
(A) Libertarianism	(i) Bentham
(B) Utilitarianism	(ii) Gandhi
(C) Civil Society	(iii) Nozick
(D) Swaraj	(iv) Hegel

Codes:	A	B	C	D
(a)	(iii)	(i)	(iv)	(ii)
(b)	(i)	(iii)	(ii)	(iv)
(c)	(ii)	(i)	(iii)	(iv)
(d)	(iv)	(i)	(ii)	(iii)

11. Who among the following liberated political development from socio-economic modernisation?
(a) Gabriel Almond
(b) Lucian Pye
(c) W.W. Rostow
(d) Samuel Huntington

12. Who among the following described elites as "speculators" and "rentiers"?
(a) Pareto (b) Mosca
(c) Michels (d) Gasset

13. In communications theory, the ability to act in response to forecasts of future consequences is called:
(a) Gain (b) Lead
(c) Load (d) Lag

14. Who among the following talks of pseudo pressure groups?
(a) Duverger (b) Jean Blondel
(c) Almond (d) James Jupp

15. Which one of the following books was authored by David Easton?
(a) *A Systems Analysis of Political Life*
(b) *The Politics of the Developing Areas*
(c) *Modern Political Analysis*
(d) *The Nerves of Government*

16. The behavioural critics of Max Weber's model of bureaucracy are:
(i) Robert Merton (ii) M.Crozier
(iii) Fred Riggs (iv) Karl Deutsch

Select the correct answer from the codes given below:

(a) (i), (ii), (iv) (b) (ii), (iii), (iv)
(c) (ii), (iv) (d) (i), (ii), (iii)

17. Which of the following statements are true about the British Parliamentary System?
   (i) The Queen always acts on the advice of the Cabinet.
   (ii) The Cabinet functions on the principle of collective responsiblity.
   (iii) The Parliament can make laws on any subject.
   (iv) The Courts can declare a law unconstitutional.

   Select the correct answer from the code below:

   (a) (i), (ii) and (iv) (b) (ii), (iii) and (iv)
   (c) (i), (ii) and (iii) (d) (i), (iii) and (iv)

18. Given below are the two statements one labelled as Assertion (A) and the other as Reason (R):

   Assertion (A): Political socialisation is the process by which political cultures are maintained and changed.

   Reason (R): Family, School, Peer groups, experiences during employment, mass media and direct contact with political system are the main agents of the process of socialisation.

   Codes:
   (a) Both (A) and (R) are true and (R) is the correct explanation of (A)
   (b) Both (A) and (R) are true but (R) is not the correct explanation of (A)
   (c) (A) is true but (R) is false
   (d) (A) is false but (R) is true

19. Given below are two statements, one labelled as Assertion (A) and the other labelled as Reason (R):

   Assertion (A): The U.S. Supreme Court is more powerfull than the Supreme Court of India in the exercise of power of judicial review.

   Reason (R): The U.S. Supreme Court follows the principle of 'due process of law'.

   Codes:
   (a) Both (A) and (R) are true and (R) is the correct explanation of (A)
   (b) Both (A) and (R) are true but (R) is not the correct explanation of (A)
   (c) (A) is true but (R) is false
   (d) (A) is false but (R) is true

20. Match List I with List II and select the correct answer from the code given below:

   List I
   (A) Deutsch (B) Riggs
   (C) Pareto (D) Huntington

   List II
   (i) Development Trap
   (ii) Modernisation—A multi-faceted process
   (iii) Receptors or reception centres
   (iv) Identifying democracy with corruption, machine politics and gangsterism

Codes:	**A**	**B**	**C**	**D**
(a)	(iii)	(i)	(iv)	(ii)
(b)	(i)	(ii)	(iii)	(iv)
(c)	(ii)	(iii)	(i)	(iv)
(d)	(iv)	(ii)	(i)	(iii)

21. Anti-defection law was placed in:
   (a) the Preamble
   (b) the fundamental rights chapter in the Constitution
   (c) 6th Schedule of the Constitution
   (d) 10th Schedule of the Constitution

22. Who votes in the election of the Vice-President? Choose the correct answer from the following.
   (a) Members of the Legislative Assemblies
   (b) Members of the Legislative Councils
   (c) Elected Members of the Parliament
   (d) Elected and Nominated Members of Parliament

23. Which of the following terms is not incorporated in the Constitution?
(a) Secular (b) Federal
(c) Democratic (d) Socialist

24. The Supreme Court of India:
(i) has original but not appellate jurisdictions
(ii) appoints the Attorney General of India
(iii) has exclusive jurisdiction in disputes between Union and the States
(iv) enforces fundamental rights
Choose the correct answer from the codes given below:
Codes:
(a) (i) and (iii) (b) (iii) and (iv)
(c) (iii) and (ii) (d) (iv) and (i)

25. National Commission to Review the Constitution was formed during the Prime Ministership of:
(a) Morarji Desai
(b) V.P. Singh
(c) Atal Bihari Vajpayee
(d) Manmohan Singh

26. Given below are two statements. One is labelled as Assertion (A) and the other is labelled as Reason (R).
Assertion (A): Nehru said that it is crime against man and God to submit to anybody's rule.
Reason (R): Individuals are not born equal.
Choose the correct answer from the following:
(a) Both (A) and (R) are true and (R) is the correct explanation of (A)
(b) Both (A) and (R) are true but (R) is not the correct explanation of (A)
(c) (A) is true but (R) is false
(d) (A) is false but (R) is true

27. Given below are two statements, one labelled as Assertion (A) and the other is labelled as Reason (R).
Assertion (A): Economic Development reduces the significance of parochial ties by the creation of non-parochial economic loyalties.
Reason (R): Sectarian strifes have increasingly got aggravated.
Choose the correct answer from the following:
(a) Both (A) and (R) are true and (R) is the correct explanation of (A)
(b) Both (A) and (R) are true but (R) is not the correct explanation of (A)
(c) (A) is true but (R) is false
(d) (A) is false but (R) is true

28. Arrange the following in chronological order and use the codes given below:
(i) Kesavananda Bharati case
(ii) Golak Nath case
(iii) Minerva Mills case
(iv) Sajjan Singh case
Codes:
(a) (iii), (ii), (iv), (i) (b) (i), (iv), (iii), (ii)
(c) (iv), (ii), (i), (iii) (d) (ii), (iv), (iii), (i)

29. Match List I with List II and select the correct answer from the codes given below:
List I
(A) Emergence of All India Muslim League
(B) Lucknow Pact
(C) Motilal Nehru Report
(D) Komagatamaru Incident
List II
(i) 1914 (ii) 1906
(iii) 1916 (iv) 1928

Codes:	**A**	**B**	**C**	**D**
(a)	(iii)	(ii)	(iv)	(i)
(b)	(ii)	(iii)	(iv)	(i)
(c)	(iv)	(iii)	(i)	(ii)
(d)	(i)	(iii)	(iv)	(ii)

30. Match List I with List II and select the correct answer from the codes given below:

List I (State)

(A) Maharashtra (B) Punjab
(C) Goa (D) Sikkim

List II (No. of Members in the 14th Lok Sabha)

(i) 13 (ii) 48
(iii) 1 (iv) 2

Codes:	**A**	**B**	**C**	**D**
(a)	(ii)	(i)	(iv)	(iii)
(b)	(i)	(ii)	(iv)	(iii)
(c)	(iii)	(ii)	(iv)	(i)
(d)	(iv)	(iii)	(i)	(ii)

31. Which is the correct sequential order of the following stages in the appointment of Civil Servants?
    (i) Induction (ii) Advertisement
    (iii) Viva-Voce (iv) Written Examination
    Codes:
    (a) (ii), (iv), (iii), (i) (b) (i), (ii), (iii), (iv)
    (c) (ii), (iii), (i), (iv) (d) (iv), (i), (ii), (iii)

32. The word "Bureaucracy" was first coined by:
    (a) Max Weber
    (b) Karl Marx
    (c) Vincent de Gaurnay
    (d) Spencer

33. Who represents the Government while presenting the budget to Parliament?
    (a) Prime Minister
    (b) The Finance Minister
    (c) The Speaker of Lok Sabha
    (d) The Chairman of Rajya Sabha

34. In India, the Office of the Lokpal was suggested in 1966 on the basis of the recommendations of the:
    (a) Administrative Reforms Commission
    (b) Planning Commission
    (c) Law Commission
    (d) Finance Commission

35. Which one of the following functions is performed by the Comptroller and Auditor General of India?
    (a) Presentation and sanction of the Budget
    (b) Execution of the Budget
    (c) National Accounting
    (d) Audit

36. The emoluments and allowances of the President of India are charged on the:
    (a) Consolidated Fund of India
    (b) Contingency Fund of India
    (c) Public Accounts Fund
    (d) Treasury

37. Given below are two statements, one labelled as Assertion (A) and the other labelled as Reason (R).
    Assertion (A): State Governments are obliged to appoint a State Finance Commission under the Constitution.
    Reason (R): The quantum of money to be paid annually by the State Governments to the local bodies is determined by the State Finance Commission.
    In the context of the above two statements which one of the following is correct?
    (a) Both (A) and (R) are true and (R) is the correct explanation of (A)
    (b) Both (A) and (R) are true but (R) is not a correct explanation of (A)
    (c) (A) is true but (R) is false
    (d) (A) is false but (R) is true

38. Given below are two statements, one labelled as Assertion (A) and the other labelled as Reason (R).
    Assertion (A): Delegation is a functional imperative for all types of Organisations.
    Reason (R): The Chief Executive cannot provide effective leadership without sufficient powers.
    In the context of the above two statements which one of the following is correct?
    (a) Both (A) and (R) are true and (R) is the correct explanation of (A)

(b) Both (A) and (R) are true but (R) is not a correct explanation of (A)
(c) (A) is true but (R) is false
(d) (A) is false but (R) is true

39. Match List I with List II and give the answer by using the codes given below:

List I
(A) Santhanam Committee
(B) Ashok Mehta Committee
(C) Kothari Committee
(D) Fulcon Committee

List II
(i) Recruitment policy and selection methods
(ii) Reorganisation of the British Civil Service
(iii) Prevention of corruption
(iv) Two-tier system of Panchayati Raj

Codes:	**A**	**B**	**C**	**D**
(a)	(iii)	(iv)	(i)	(ii)
(b)	(iv)	(iii)	(ii)	(i)
(c)	(iii)	(ii)	(i)	(iv)
(d)	(ii)	(iii)	(iv)	(i)

40. What is Herbert A. Simon's approach to the study of Public Administration?
(a) Behavioural approach
(b) Structural approach
(c) Institutional approach
(d) Philosophical approach

41. Which one of the following chapters of the United Nations Charter is a counterpart to Article 16 of the Covenant of the League of Nation?
(a) Chapter V (b) Chapter VI
(c) Chapter VII (d) Chapter VIII

42. According to Hans Margenthau, the patterns of balance of power are:
(i) the pattern of direct opposition
(ii) the pattern of competition
(iii) the pattern of support
(iv) the pattern of mutual trust

Choose the correct answer from the code given below:
(a) (i) and (ii) are correct
(b) (i) and (iii) are correct
(c) (iii) and (iv) are correct
(d) (i), (ii), (iv) are correct

43. Arrange the following in chronological order as these emerged:
(i) NAM
(ii) WTO
(iii) New International Economic Order
(iv) SAPTA

Codes:
(a) (iv), (iii), (i), (ii) (b) (i), (iii), (iv), (ii)
(c) (iii), (ii), (iv), (i) (d) (ii), (iv), (iii), (i)

44. Which one of the following is not considered an instrument for promotion of National Interest?
(a) Propaganda
(b) War
(c) International Law
(d) Diplomacy

45. Which one of the following countries is not signatory to the NPT?
(a) U.K. (b) U.S.A.
(c) France (d) India

46. SAARC Secretariat is located at:
(a) New Delhi (b) Islamabad
(c) Dhaka (d) Kathmandu

47. Which is the largest trade partner of India?
(a) ASEAN (b) APEC
(c) OIC (d) EU

48. Given below are two statements, one labelled as Assertion (A) and the other labelled as Reason (R).

Assertion (A): Peacekeeping freezes hostilities rather than resolves them.

Reason (R): Peacekeeping is not even mentioned in the U.N. charter.

Choose the correct answer from the following:

(a) Both (A) and (R) are true and (R) is the correct explanation of (A)
(b) Both (A) and (R) are true but (R) is not the correct explanation of (A)
(c) (A) is true and (R) is false
(d) (A) is false and (R) is true

49. Given below are two statements, one is labelled as Assertion (A) and the other is labelled as Reason (R).

Assertion (A): It is not the idealism but national interests that shape the foreign policy of a country.

Reason (R): USA has often been supporting dictatorial regimes.

In the context of the above two statements which one of the following is correct?

(a) Both (A) and (R) are true and (R) is the correct explanation of (A)
(b) Both (A) and (R) are true but (R) is not the correct explanation of (A)
(c) (A) is true but (R) is false
(d) (A) is false but (R) is true

50. Match List I with List II in context of the events and regimes of the Prime Ministers. Select correct answer from the codes given below:

List I
(A) Indo-US Nuclear Cooperation Agreement
(B) Tashkant Summit
(C) Shimla Accord
(D) Panchsheel

List II
(i) Jawaharlal Nehru
(ii) Indira Gandhi
(iii) Lal Bahadur Shastri
(iv) Manmohan Singh

Codes:	A	B	C	D
(a)	(i)	(iii)	(ii)	(iv)
(b)	(ii)	(i)	(iv)	(iii)
(c)	(iv)	(iii)	(ii)	(i)
(d)	(iii)	(i)	(ii)	(iv)

ANSWERS

1. (a)	2. (c)	3. (b)	4. (c)	5. (a)
6. (b)	7. (b)	8. (b)	9. (b)	10. (a)
11. (d)	12. (a)	13. (b)	14. (a)	15. (a)
16. (c)	17. (b)	18. (b)	19. (c)	20. (a)
21. (d)	22. (c)	23. (b)	24. (b)	25. (c)
26. (b)	27. (b)	28. (c)	29. (b)	30. (a)
31. (a)	32. (a)	33. (b)	34. (d)	35. (d)
36. (d)	37. (b)	38. (a)	39. (a)	40. (d)
41. (c)	42. (c)	43. (b)	44. (b)	45. (d)
46. (d)	47. (c)	48. (c)	49. (c)	50. (c)

JUNE–2008

Note: This paper contains Fifty (50) multiple-choice questions, each question carrying two (2) marks. Attempt all of them.

PAPER–I

1. The teacher has been glorified by the phrase "Friend, philosopher and guide" because
   (a) He has to play all vital roles in the context of society
   (b) He transmits the high value of humanity to students
   (c) He is the great reformer of the society
   (d) He is a great patriot
2. The most important cause of failure for teacher lies in the area of
   (a) interpersonal relationship
   (b) lack of command over the knowledge of the subject
   (c) verbal ability
   (d) strict handling of the students
3. A teacher can establish rapport with his students by
   (a) becoming a figure of authority
   (b) impressing students with knowledge and skill
   (c) playing the role of a guide
   (d) becoming a friend to the students
4. Education is a powerful instrument of
   (a) Social transformation
   (b) Personal transformation
   (c) Cultural transformation
   (d) All of the above
5. A teacher's major contribution towards the maximum self-realisation of the student is affected through
   (a) Constant fulfilment of the students' needs
   (b) Strict control of classroom activities
   (c) Sensitivity to students' needs, goals and purposes
   (d) Strict reinforcement of academic standards
6. Research problem is selected from the stand point of
   (a) Researcher's interest
   (b) Financial support
   (c) Social relevance
   (d) Availability of relevant literature
7. Which one is called non-probability sampling?
   (a) Cluster sampling
   (b) Quota sampling
   (c) Systematic sampling
   (d) Stratified random sampling
8. Formulation of hypothesis may not be required in
   (a) Survey method
   (b) Historical studies
   (c) Experimental studies
   (d) Normative studies
9. Field-work based research is classified as
   (a) Empirical (b) Historical
   (c) Experimental (d) Biographical
10. Which of the following sampling method is appropriate to study the prevalence of AIDS amongst male and female in India in 1976, 1986, 1996 and 2006?

(a) Cluster sampling
(b) Systematic sampling
(c) Quota sampling
(d) Stratified random sampling

Read the following passage and answer the questions 11 to 15:

The fundamental principle is that Article 14 forbids class legislation but permits reasonable classification for the purpose of legislation which classification must satisfy the twin tests of classification being founded on an intelligible differentia which distinguishes persons or things that are grouped together from those that are left out of the group and that differentia must have a rational nexus to the object sought to be achieved by the Statute in question. The thrust of Article 14 is that the citizen is entitled to equality before law and equal protection of laws. In the very nature of things the society being composed of unequals a welfare State will have to strive by both executive and legislative action to help the less fortunate in society to ameliorate their condition so that the social and economic inequality in the society may be bridged. This would necessitate a legislative application to a group of citizens otherwise unequal and amelioration of whose lot is the object of state affirmative action. In the absence of the doctrine of classification such legislation is likely to flounder on the bedrock of equality enshrined in Article 14. The Court realistically appraising the social and economic inequality and keeping in view the guidelines on which the State action must move as constitutionally laid down in Part IV of the Constitution evolved the doctrine of classification. The doctrine was evolved to sustain a legislation or State action designed to help weaker sections of the society or some such segments of the society in need of succour. Legislative and executive action may accordingly be sustained if it satisfies the twin tests of reasonable classification and the rational principle correlated to the object sought to be achieved.

The concept of equality before the law does not involve the idea of absolute equality among human beings which is a physical impossibility. All that Article 14 guarantees is a similarity of treatment contra-distinguished from identical treatment. Equality before law means that among equals the law should be equal and should be equally administered and that the likes should be treated alike. Equality before the law does not mean that things which are different shall be as though they are the same. It of course means denial of any special privilege by reason of birth, creed or the like. The legislation as well as the executive government, while dealing with diverse problems arising out of an infinite variety of human relations must of necessity have the power of making special laws, to attain any particular object and to achieve that object it must have the power of selection or classification of persons and things upon which such laws are to operate.

11. Right to equality, one of the fundamental rights, is enunciated in the Constitution under Part III, Article
(a) 12 (b) 13
(c) 14 (d) 15

12. The main thrust of Right to equality is that it permits
(a) class legislation
(b) equality before law and equal protection under the law
(c) absolute equality
(d) special privilege by reason of birth

13. The social and economic inequality in the society can be bridged by
(a) executive and legislative action
(b) universal suffrage
(c) identical treatment
(d) None of the above

14. The doctrine of classification is evolved to
    (a) Help weaker sections of the society
    (b) Provide absolute equality
    (c) Provide identical treatment
    (d) None of the above

15. While dealing with diverse problems arising out of an infinite variety of human relations, the government
    (a) must have the power of making special laws
    (b) must not have any power to make special laws
    (c) must have power to withdraw equal rights
    (d) None of the above

16. Communication with oneself is known as
    (a) Group communication
    (b) Grapevine communication
    (c) Interpersonal communication
    (d) Intrapersonal communication

17. Which broadcasting system for TV is followed in India?
    (a) NTSE (b) PAL
    (c) SECAM (d) NTCS

18. All India Radio before 1936 was known as
    (a) Indian Radio Broadcasting
    (b) Broadcasting Service of India
    (c) Indian State Broadcasting Service
    (d) All India Broadcasting Service

19. The biggest news agency of India is
    (a) PTI
    (b) UNI
    (c) NANAP
    (d) Samachar Bharati

20. Prasar Bharati was launched in the year
    (a) 1995 (b) 1997
    (c) 1999 (d) 2001

21. A statistical measure based upon the entire population is called parameter while measure based upon a sample is known as
    (a) Sample parameter
    (b) Inference
    (c) Statistics
    (d) None of these

22. The importance of the correlation coefficient lies in the fact that
    (a) There is a linear relationship between the correlated variables
    (b) It is one of the most valid measures of statistics
    (c) It allows one to determine the degree or strength of the association between two variables
    (d) It is a non-parametric method of statistical analysis

23. The F-test
    (a) is essentially a two-tailed test
    (b) is essentially a one-tailed test
    (c) can be one tailed as well as two tailed depending on the hypothesis
    (d) can never be a one-tailed test

24. What will be the next letter in the following series
    DCXW, FEVU, HGTS, _____
    (a) AKPO (b) JBYZ
    (c) JIRQ (d) LMRS

25. The following question is based on the diagram given below. If the two small circles represent formal classroom education and distance education and the big circle stands for university system of education, which figure represents the university systems.
    (a) (b)
    (c) 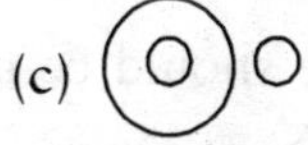 (d) 

26. The statement, 'To be non-violent is good' is a

(a) Moral judgement
(b) Factual judgement
(c) Religious judgement
(d) Value judgement

27. **Assertion (A):** Man is a rational being.
Reason (R): Man is a social being.
(a) Both (A) and (R) are true and (R) is the correct explanation of (A)
(b) Both (A) and (R) are true but (R) is not the correct explanation of (A)
(c) (A) is true but (R) is false
(d) (A) is false but (R) is true

28. Value Judgements are
(a) Factual Judgements
(b) Ordinary Judgements
(c) Normative Judgements
(d) Expression of public opinion

29. Deductive reasoning proceeds from
(a) general to particular
(b) particular to general
(c) one general conclusion to another general conclusion
(d) one particular conclusion to another particular conclusion

30. AGARTALA is written in code as 14168171, the code for AGRA is
(a) 1641 (b) 1416
(c) 1441 (d) 1461

31. Which one of the following is the most comprehensive source of population data?
(a) National Family Health Surveys
(b) National Sample Surveys
(c) Census
(d) Demographic Health Surveys

32. Which one of the following principles is not applicable to sampling?
(a) Sample units must be clearly defined
(b) Sample units must be dependent on each other
(c) Same units of sample should be used throughout the study
(d) Sample units must be chosen in a systematic and objective manner

33. If January 1st, 2007 is Monday, what was the day on 1st January 1995?
(a) Sunday (b) Monday
(c) Friday (d) Saturday

34. Insert the missing number in the following series
4 16 8 64 ? 256
(a) 16 (b) 24
(c) 32 (d) 20

35. If an article is sold for ₹ 178 at a loss of 11%; what would be its selling price in order to earn a profit of 11%?
(a) ₹ 222.50 (b) ₹ 267
(c) ₹ 222 (d) ₹ 220

36. WYSIWYG—describes the display of a document on screen as it will actually print
(a) What you state is what you get
(b) What you see is what you get
(c) What you save is what you get
(d) What you suggest is what you get

37. Which of the following is not a computer language?
(a) PASCAL (b) UNIX
(c) FORTRAN (d) COBOL

38. A keyboard has at least
(a) 91 keys (b) 101 keys
(c) 111 keys (d) 121 keys

39. An e-mail address is composed of
(a) two parts (b) three parts
(c) four parts (d) five parts

40. Corel Draw is a popular
(a) Illustration program
(b) Programming language
(c) Text program
(d) None of the above

41. Human ear is most sensitive to noise in which of the following ranges
(a) 1-2 kHz (b) 100-500 Hz
(c) 10-12 kHz (d) 13-16 kHz

42. Which one of the following units is used to measure intensity of noise?
(a) Decible (b) Hz
(c) Phon (d) Watts/m^2

43. If the population growth follows a logistic curve, the maximum sustainable yield
(a) is equal to half the carrying capacity
(b) is equal to the carrying capacity
(c) depends on growth rates
(d) depends on the initial population

44. Chemical weathering of rocks is largely dependent upon
(a) high temperature
(b) strong wind action
(c) heavy rainfall
(d) glaciation

45. Structure of earth's system consists of the following: Match List I with List II and give the correct answer.
List I (Zone)
A. Atmosphere B. Biosphere
C. Hydrosphere D. Lithosphere
List II (Chemical Character)
1. Inert gases
2. Salt, freshwater, snow and ice
3. Organic substances, skeleton matter
4. Light silicates

Codes:	A	B	C	D
(a)	2	3	1	4
(b)	1	3	2	4
(c)	2	1	3	4
(d)	3	1	2	4

46. NAAC is an autonomous institution under the aegis of
(a) ICSSR (b) CSIR
(c) AICTE (d) UGC

47. National Council for Women's Education was established in
(a) 1958 (b) 1976
(c) 1989 (d) 2000

48. Which one of the following is not situated in New Delhi?
(a) Indian Council of Cultural Relations
(b) Indian Council of Scientific Research
(c) National Council of Educational Research and Training
(d) Indian Institute of Advanced Studies

49. Autonomy in higher education implies freedom in
(a) Administration
(b) Policy-making
(c) Finance
(d) Curriculum development

50. Match List I with List II and select the correct answer from the code given below
List I (Institutions)
A. Dr. Hari Singh Gour University
B. S.N.D.T. University
C. M.S. University
D. J.N. Vyas University
List II (Locations)
1. Mumbai 2. Baroda
3. Jodhpur 4. Sagar

Codes:	A	B	C	D
(a)	4	1	2	3
(b)	1	2	3	4
(c)	3	1	2	4
(d)	2	4	1	3

ANSWERS

1. (b)	2. (b)	3. (b)	4. (d)	5. (c)
6. (c)	7. (b)	8. (b)	9. (a)	10. (d)
11. (c)	12. (b)	13. (a)	14. (a)	15. (a)
16. (d)	17. (b)	18. (c)	19. (a)	20. (b)
21. (a)	22. (c)	23. (c)	24. (c)	25. (b)
26. (a)	27. (b)	28. (c)	29. (a)	30. (d)
31. (c)	32. (b)	33. (d)	34. (a)	35. (c)
36. (b)	37. (b)	38. (b)	39. (a)	40. (a)
41. (b)	42. (a)	43. (a)	44. (c)	45. (b)
46. (d)	47. (a)	48. (d)	49. (c)	50. (a)

PAPER–II

Note: This paper contains fifty (50) objective type questions, each question carrying two (2) marks. All questions are compulsory.

1. Which part of the Mahabharata deals with the theory of Government?
   (a) Adi Parva (b) Sabha Parva
   (c) Yuddha Parva (d) Shanti Parva
2. Aristotle is called the 'father of Political Science' because of his idea of:
   (a) Revolution (b) Slavery
   (c) Classification (d) Citizenship
3. Who propounded the principle that the political ruler should be amoral?
   (a) Machiavelli (b) Hobbes
   (c) Locke (d) Rousseau
4. The theory of 'political obligation' was propounded by:
   (a) J.S. Mill (b) Hegel
   (c) Marx (d) T.H. Green
5. The concept of 'hegemony' is associated with:
   (a) Lenin (b) Mao
   (c) Gramsci (d) Marx
6. For propounding their theories the 'social contract theory' was used by:
   (i) Marx (ii) Rawls
   (iii) Lenin (iv) Nozick
   (a) (i) and (ii) are correct
   (b) (ii) and (iv) are correct
   (c) (i) and (iii) are correct
   (d) (iii) and (iv) are correct
7. Given below are two statements, one labelled as Assertion (A) and the other as Reason (R):
   Assertion (A): People and the state are of the same status.
   Reason (R): People create the state.
   In the context of the above two statements which one of the following is correct?
   (a) Both (A) and (R) are true and (R) is the correct explanation of (A)
   (b) Both (A) and (R) are true but (R) is not the correct explanation of (A)
   (c) (A) is true but (R) is false
   (d) (A) is false but (R) is true
8. Identify the correct order in which the political thinkers propounded their respective theories:
   (a) Machiavelli, Hobbes, Rousseau, Mill
   (b) Machiavelli, Rousseau, Hobbes, Mill
   (c) Hobbes, Machiavelli, Rousseau, Mill
   (d) Hobbes, Rousseau, Mill, Machiavelli
9. Match the List I with the List II and select the correct answer from the codes given below:
   List I
   (A) Radical Humanism
   (B) Death of political theory
   (C) Decline of political theory
   (D) Entitlement theory
   List II
   (i) Nozick (ii) Laslett
   (iii) M.N. Roy (iv) Easton

Codes:	A	B	C	D
(a)	(iii)	(ii)	(iv)	(i)
(b)	(i)	(iii)	(ii)	(iv)
(c)	(ii)	(i)	(iv)	(iii)
(d)	(iii)	(ii)	(i)	(iv)

10. Match the List I with the List II:
   List I
   (A) Annihilation of Caste
   (B) The Cunning Reason
   (C) The Human Cycle
   (D) Hind Swaraj
   List II
   (i) Gandhi (ii) Aurobindo
   (iii) Ambedkar (iv) Hegel
   Select the correct answer from the code given below:

Codes:	A	B	C	D
(a)	(iii)	(iv)	(ii)	(i)
(b)	(i)	(ii)	(iii)	(iv)
(c)	(ii)	(i)	(iv)	(iii)
(d)	(iv)	(iii)	(ii)	(i)

11. According to David Easton, which of the following are the regulatory mechanisms in a political system?
   (i) Socio-cultural norms
   (ii) Communication channels
   (iii) Extractive capabilities
   (iv) Distributive capabilities
   Select the correct answer from the code given below.
   Codes:
   (a) (ii), (iii) and (iv) (b) (i) and (ii)
   (c) (iii) and (iv) (d) (i), (iii) and (iv)

12. Who among the following has categorised political systems into political democracy, tutelary democracy, modernizing oligarchy totalitarian oligarchy and traditional oligarchy?
   (a) Edward Shils (b) Lucian Pye
   (c) A.F.K. Organski (d) David Apter

13. The residuary powers rest with the states in the federal system of:
   (i) USA (ii) India
   (iii) Switzerland (iv) Canada
   Codes:
   (a) (i) and (ii) are correct
   (b) (ii) and (iii) are correct
   (c) (iii) and (iv) are correct
   (d) (i) and (iii) are correct

14. Which one of the following has a close affinity to the rule of law?
   (a) Written Constitution
   (b) Judicial Supremacy
   (c) Separation of Powers
   (d) Limited Government

15. Which one of the following political parties is described as a pioneer of the socialist parties in the world?
   (a) Indian National Congress
   (b) Democratic Party of USA
   (c) British Labour Party
   (d) Christian Democratic Party of France

16. Given below are two statements one labelled as Assertion (A) and the other labelled as Reason (R):
   Assertion (A): Elite theory is based on the idea that every society consists of two broad categories—the selected few and the vast masses of people.
   Reason (R): The elite theory first started as a critique of democracy and Socialism.
   Select the correct answer from the codes given below.
   (a) Both (A) and (R) are true and (R) is the correct explanation of (A)
   (b) Both (A) and (R) are true but (R) is not the correct explanation of (A)
   (c) (A) is true but (R) is false
   (d) (A) is false but (R) is true

17. Given below are two statements one labelled as Assertion (A) and the other labelled as Reason (R).
   Assertion (A): A political system receives a more or less continuous support from society if the process of political socialization is homogeneous.
   Reason (R): The individuals cooperate with each other and there is an atmosphere of trust in the political culture.
   Select the correct answer from the codes given below.
   (a) Both (A) and (R) are true and (R) is the correct explanation of (A)
   (b) Both (A) and (R) are true but (R) is not the correct explanation of (A)
   (c) (A) is true but (R) is false
   (d) (A) is false but (R) is true

18. Match List I with List II and select the correct answer from the codes given below.

List I

(A) Almond (B) Easton
(C) Lucian Pye (D) Huntington

List II

(i) Authoritative allocation of values for a society
(ii) Capabilities of a political system
(iii) Institutions decay dissolution as well as growth
(iv) Equality, capacity and differentiation

Codes:	A	B	C	D
(a)	(ii)	(i)	(iv)	(iii)
(b)	(i)	(ii)	(iii)	(iv)
(c)	(ii)	(i)	(iii)	(iv)
(d)	(iii)	(i)	(iv)	(ii)

19. Match List I with List II and select the correct answer from the code given below.

List I

(A) France (B) U.K.
(C) USA (D) India

List II

(i) Judicial Review
(ii) Procedure Established by Law
(iii) Two Sets of Courts
(iv) Sovereign Parliament

Codes:	A	B	C	D
(a)	(iii)	(iv)	(i)	(ii)
(b)	(ii)	(iii)	(i)	(iv)
(c)	(i)	(ii)	(iii)	(iv)
(d)	(iv)	(iii)	(i)	(ii)

20. Put the following concepts in sequence in which they were used by Karl Deutsch in his conceptual frame work. Use the code given below:
(i) Lead (ii) Load
(iii) Lag (iv) Gain Code
(a) (ii), (iii), (iv), (i) (b) (i), (iv), (ii), (iii)
(c) (ii), (i), (iii), (iv) (d) (i), (ii), (iii), (iv)

21. Who is the author of *Igniting Minds*?
(a) J.N. Dixit
(b) Joginder Singh
(c) Bipin Chandra
(d) A.P.J. Abdul Kalam

22. 93rd Amendment of the Constitution deals with:
(a) Panchayati Raj Institutions
(b) Reservation of Women in Legislatures
(c) Reservation of OBCs in Educational Institutions
(d) Fundamental Duties

23. Who was the first Dalit President of India?
(a) Giani Zail Singh
(b) A.P.J. Abdul Kalam
(c) K.R. Narayanan
(d) Fakhruddin Ali Ahmed

24. Which of the following regional political parties did not join the UNPA at the time of its formation?
(a) AIADMK
(b) Shiromani Akali Dal
(c) Telugu Desam
(d) Samajwadi Party

25. Which of the following Prime Ministers was not member of the Lok Sabha?
(a) Pt. Jawaharlal Nehru
(b) Lal Bahadur Shastri
(c) P.V. Narsimha Rao
(d) H.D. Deve Gowda

26. Given below are two statements one labelled as Assertion (A) and the other labelled as Reason (R):
Assertion (A): Public Interest Litigation is the strategic arm of the legal aid movement.
Reason (R): Public Interest Litigation is meant to bring justice to the doorstep of the weak.
In the context of these two statements, which one of the following is correct?
(a) Both (A) and (R) are true and (R) is the correct explanation of (A)
(b) Both (A) and (R) are true and (R) is not the correct explanation of (A)
(c) (A) is true but (R) is false
(d) (A) is false but (R) is true

27. Given below are two statements, one is labelled as Assertion (A) and the other is labelled as Reason (R):

Assertion (A): The purpose of fundamental rights is to create an egalitarian society.

Reason (R): There is an inherent tendency among the individuals to dominate others.

Select the correct answer from below:

(a) Both (A) and (R) are true and (R) is the correct explanation of (A)
(b) Both (A) and (R) are true but (R) is not the correct explanation of (A)
(c) (A) is true but (R) is false
(d) (A) is false but (R) is true

28. What is the correct chronological sequence of the below. Choose the write answer from the codes.

(i) Subhash as President of the Indian National Congress
(ii) Formation of Congress Socialist Party
(iii) Formation of Satyagraha Sabha by Gandhi
(iv) Communal Award

Codes:

(a) (iv) (ii) (iii) (i) (b) (iii) (iv) (ii) (i)
(c) (ii) (iii) (iv) (i) (d) (i) (iii) (ii) (iv)

29. Arrange the following in the order in which these appeared. Use the codes given below:

(i) Knowledge Commission
(ii) Sarkaria Commission
(iii) States Reorganization Commission
(iv) National Commission to Review the Constitution

Codes:

(a) (iv) (iii) (i) (ii) (b) (iii) (ii) (iv) (i)
(c) (ii) (iii) (i) (iv) (d) (i) (iv) (iii) (ii)

30. In context of Articles of the Constitution given below match List I with List II and select the correct answer from the codes given below:

List I

(A) Article 148 (B) Article 280
(C) Article 315 (D) Article 324

List II

(i) Election Commission of India
(ii) Comptroller and Auditor General of India
(iii) Finance Commission
(iv) Union Public Service Commission

Codes:	A	B	C	D
(a)	(ii)	(iii)	(iv)	(i)
(b)	(i)	(ii)	(iv)	(iii)
(c)	(ii)	(iv)	(i)	(iii)
(d)	(iii)	(iv)	(ii)	(i)

31. Which one of the following is not considered an element of National Power?

(a) Leadership
(b) National Character
(c) National Resources
(d) Party System

32. Which one of the following countries has been recently made member of the SAARC?

(a) Bhutan (b) Maldives
(c) Afghanistan (d) Nepal

33. Which one of the following is not a part of the European Union?

(a) European Commission
(b) European Territorial Commission
(c) European Parliament
(d) European Central Bank

34. The author of *American Foreign Policy: Three Essays.*

(a) Karl W. Deutsch
(b) S. Hoffe man
(c) Henry Kissinger
(d) Woodrow Wilson

35. "Promotion of International Peace and Security" has been enshrined in the constitution of:

(a) People's Republic of China
(b) France

(c) India
(d) U.S.A.

36. Given below are two statements, one labelled as Assertion (A) and the other labelled as Reason (R):
Choose the correct answer from the given codes.
Assertion (A): After the collapse of the Soviet Union, USA has emerged as the only superpower.
Reason (R): Globalization as a trend of International Economic System has come to stay.
(a) Both (A) and (R) are true and (R) is the correct explanation of (A)
(b) Both (A) and (R) are true but (R) is not the correct explanation of (A)
(c) (A) is true but (R) is false
(d) (A) is false but (R) is true

37. Given below are two statements one is labelled as Assertion (A) and the other is labelled as Reason (R):
Assertion (A): In the changed world scenario, non-alignment in its traditional form is not relevant.
Reason (R): India can be considered as an upcoming economic power.
In the context of these two statements which one of the following is correct?
(a) Both (A) and (R) are true and (R) is the correct explanation of (A)
(b) Both (A) and (R) are true but (R) is not the correct explanation of (A)
(c) (A) is true but (R) is false
(d) (A) is false but (R) is true

38. Match List I with List II and choose the correct answer from the code given below:
List I
(A) NAM Summit at Havana
(B) Agra Summit
(C) Kargil Conflict
(D) Nuclear Tests

List II
(i) 1998 (ii) 1999
(iv) 2006 (iii) 2001

Codes:	**A**	**B**	**C**	**D**
(a)	(iv)	(ii)	(iii)	(i)
(b)	(i)	(ii)	(iv)	(iii)
(c)	(iv)	(iii)	(ii)	(i)
(d)	(iii)	(iv)	(ii)	(i)

39. Match List I with List II and select the correct answer from the code given below:
List I
(A) India-US Nuclear Cooperation Agreement
(B) Terrorist Attack on Indian Parliament
(C) Vajpayee's Bus Diplomacy
(D) Establishment of SAARC

List II
(i) 1999 (ii) 2007
(iii) 2001 (iv) 1985

Codes:	**A**	**B**	**C**	**D**
(a)	(ii)	(iii)	(i)	(iv)
(b)	(iv)	(iii)	(ii)	(i)
(c)	(iii)	(iv)	(ii)	(i)
(d)	(i)	(iv)	(iii)	(ii)

40. Identify the correct chronological sequence of the following events:
(a) Formation of the league of Nations, World War I, Birth of Bangladesh, Disintegration of U.S.S.R.
(b) World War I, Birth of Bangladesh, Disintegration of U.S.S.R., Formation of the League of Nations
(c) World War I, Formation of the League of Nations, Birth of Bangladesh, Disintegration of U.S.S.R.
(d) Disintegration of U.S.S.R., World War I, Formation of the League of Nations, Birth of Bangladesh

41. The emergence of "New Public Administration" was initially associated with:

(a) American Society of Public Administration
(b) Comparative Administration Group
(c) Minnowbrook Conference
(d) Indian Institute of Public Administration

42. Which one of the following is not a function of the District Collector?
(a) Realisation of taquavi loans
(b) Maintenance of land records
(c) Hearing of appeals against the decisions of Nyaya Panchayats
(d) Collection of revenue

43. The states that first implemented the Panchayati Raj in 1959 were:
(a) Rajasthan and Andhra Pradesh
(b) Rajasthan and Karnataka
(c) Andhra Pradesh and Gujarat
(d) Tamil Nadu and Rajasthan

44. Given below are two statements, one labelled as Assertion (A) and the other labelled as Reason (R):
Assertion (A): Public Administration is more comprehensive than private administration.
Reason (R): Public Administration regulates private administration.
In the context of the above two statements which one of the following is correct?
(a) Both (A) and (R) are true and (R) is the correct explanation of (A)
(b) Both (A) and (R) are true but (R) is not the correct explanation of (A)
(c) (A) is true but (R) is false
(d) (A) is false but (R) is true

45. Given below are two statements, one labelled as Assertion (A) and the other labelled as Reason (R):
Assertion (A): Promotion should be made on the basis of performance evaluation.
Reason (R): There is a need to recognise the potentialities and qualities of efficient civil servants.
In the context of the above two statements which one of the following is correct?
(a) Both (A) and (R) are true and (R) is the correct explanation of (A)
(b) Both (A) and (R) are true but (R) is not correct explanation of (A)
(c) (A) is true but (R) is false
(d) (A) is false but (R) is true

46. Match List I with List II and select the correct answer using the codes given below:
List I
(A) Estimates Committee
(B) Public Accounts Committee
(C) Committee on Subordinate Legislation
(D) Committee on Public Undertakings
List II
(i) Examination of Appropriated Accounts
(ii) Suggestion of Economy in Expenditure
(iii) Examination of rules made by the executive departments under Acts passed by the Legislature
(iv) Review of working of Public Sector Undertakings

Codes:	A	B	C	D
(a)	(i)	(ii)	(iii)	(iv)
(b)	(ii)	(i)	(iii)	(iv)
(c)	(iii)	(iv)	(i)	(ii)
(d)	(iv)	(i)	(ii)	(iii)

47. Consider the following 'Hierarchy of needs'
(i) Safety needs
(ii) Esteem needs
(iii) Social needs
(iv) Self-actualization needs
(v) Physiological needs
According to Maslow, the correct sequence of the above is:
(a) (iii), (iv), (ii), (v), (i)
(b) (v), (i), (iii), (ii), (iv)
(c) (v), (iv), (ii), (i), (iii)
(d) (iii), (ii), (i), (v), (iv)

48. Which one of the following types of training seeks to prepare future recruits for the public service?
    (a) Formal training
    (b) Pre-entry training
    (c) Informal training
    (d) Post-entry training
49. Which one of the following tests was advocated by Macaulay:
    (a) Written Examination
    (b) Evaluation of education and experience
    (c) Demonstration of performance
    (d) None of the above
50. Below are given some functions:
    (i) To review the working of the National Plan from time to time
    (ii) To consider important questions of social and economic policy
    (iii) To recommend measures for the achievement of the aims and targets set out in the National Plan

    These above functions are performed by the:
    (a) Planning Commission
    (b) Council of Ministers
    (c) National Development Council
    (d) Finance Commission

ANSWERS

1. (b)	2. (a)	3. (d)	4. (d)	5. (c)
6. (b)	7. (a)	8. (d)	9. (d)	10. (a)
11. (c)	12. (b)	13. (a)	14. (b)	15. (c)
16. (b)	17. (b)	18. (b)	19. (a)	20. (a)
21. (d)	22. (c)	23. (c)	24. (b)	25. (b)
26. (b)	27. (b)	28. (b)	29. (b)	30. (a)
31. (d)	32. (c)	33. (c)	34. (c)	35. (c)
36. (b)	37. (b)	38. (a)	39. (a)	40. (c)
41. (c)	42. (d)	43. (a)	44. (c)	45. (b)
46. (b)	47. (b)	48. (b)	49. (d)	50. (c)

DECEMBER–2007

Note: This paper contains Fifty (50) multiple-choice questions, each question carrying two (2) marks. Attempt all of them.

PAPER–I

1. Verbal guidance is least effective in the learning of
   (a) Aptitudes (b) Skills
   (c) Attitudes (d) Relationship

2. Which is the most important aspect of the teacher's role in learning?
   (a) The development of insight into what constitutes an adequate performance
   (b) The development of insight into what constitutes the pitfalls and dangers to be avoided
   (c) The provision of encouragement and moral support
   (d) The provision of continuous diagnostic and remedial help

3. The most appropriate purpose of learning is
   (a) personal adjustment
   (b) modification of behaviour
   (c) social and political awareness
   (d) preparing oneself for employment

4. The students who keep on asking questions in the class should be
   (a) encouraged to find answer independently
   (b) advised to meet the teacher after the class
   (c) encouraged to continue questioning
   (d) advised not to disturb during the lecture

5. Maximum participation of students is possible in teaching through
   (a) discussion method
   (b) lecture method
   (c) audio-visual aids
   (d) textbook method

6. Generalised conclusion on the basis of a sample is technically known as
   (a) Data analysis and interpretation
   (b) Parameter inference
   (c) Statistical inference
   (d) All of the above

7. The experimental study is based on
   (a) The manipulation of variables
   (b) Conceptual parameters
   (c) Replication of research
   (d) Survey of literature

8. The main characteristic of scientific research is
   (a) Empirical (b) Theoretical
   (c) Experimental (d) All of the above

9. Authenticity of a research finding is its
   (a) Originality (b) Validity
   (c) Objectivity (d) All of the above

10. Which technique is generally followed when the population is finite?
   (a) Area Sampling Technique
   (b) Purposive Sampling Technique
   (c) Systematic Sampling Technique
   (d) None of the above

Read the following passage and answer the questions 11 to 15:

Gandhi's overall social and environmental philosophy is based on what human beings need rather than what they want. His early introduction to the teachings of Jains, Theosophists, Christian sermons, Ruskin and Tolstoy, and most significantly the *Bhagavad Gita*, were to have profound impact on the development of Gandhi's holistic thinking on humanity, nature and their ecological interrelation. His deep concern for the disadvantaged, the poor and rural population created an ambience for an alternative social thinking that was at once far-sighted, local and immediate. For Gandhi was acutely aware that the demands generated by the need to feed and sustain human life, compounded by the growing industrialisation of India, far outstripped the finite resources of nature. This might nowadays appear naive or commonplace, but such pronouncements were as rare as they were heretical a century ago. Gandhi was also concerned about the destruction, under colonial and modernist designs, of the existing infrastructures which had more potential for keeping a community flourishing within ecologically-sensitive traditional patterns of subsistence, especially in the rural areas, than did the incoming Western alternatives based on nature-blind technology and the enslavement of human spirit and energies.

Perhaps the moral principle for which Gandhi is best known is that of active non-violence, derived from the traditional moral restraint of not injuring another being. The most refined expression of this value is in the great epic of the *Mahabharata* (c. 100 BCE to 200 CE), where moral development proceeds through placing constraints on the liberties, desires and acquisitiveness endemic to human life. One's action is judged in terms of consequences and the impact it is likely to have on another. Jainas had generalised this principle to include all sentient creatures and biocommunities alike. Advanced Jaina monks and nuns will sweep their path to avoid harming insects and even bacteria. Non-injury is a non-negotiable universal prescription.

11. Which one of the following have a profound impact on the development of Gandhi's holistic thinking on humanity, nature and their ecological interrelations?
    (a) Jain teachings
    (b) Christian sermons
    (c) *Bhagavad Gita*
    (d) Ruskin and Tolstoy

12. Gandhi's overall social and environmental philosophy is based on human beings'
    (a) Need (b) Desire
    (c) Wealth (d) Welfare

13. Gandhiji's deep concern for the disadvantaged, the poor and rural population created an ambience for an alternative
    (a) rural policy
    (b) social thinking
    (c) urban policy
    (d) economic thinking

14. Colonial policy and modernisation led to the destruction of
    (a) major industrial infrastructure
    (b) irrigation infrastructure
    (c) urban infrastructure
    (d) rural infrastructure

15. Gandhi's active non-violence is derived from
    (a) Moral restraint of not injuring another being
    (b) Having liberties, desires and acquisitiveness
    (c) Freedom of action
    (d) Nature-blind technology and enslavement of human spirit and energies

16. DTH service was started in the year
    (a) 2000 (b) 2002
    (c) 2004 (d) 2006

17. National Press day is celebrated on
    (a) 16th November (b) 19th November
    (c) 21st November (d) 30th November

18. The total number of members in the Press Council of India are
(a) 28 (b) 14
(c) 17 (d) 20

19. The right to impart and receive information is guaranteed in the Constitution of India by Article
(a) 19(2)(a) (b) 19(16)
(c) 19(2) (d) 19(1)(a)

20. Use of radio for higher education is based on the presumption of
(a) Enriching curriculum based instruction
(b) Replacing teacher in the long run
(c) Everybody having access to a radio set
(d) Other means of instruction getting outdated

21. Find out the number which should come at the place of question mark which will complete the following series.
5, 4, 9, 17, 35, ? = 139
(a) 149 (b) 79
(c) 49 (d) 69

Questions 22 to 24 are based on the following diagram in which there are three interlocking circles I, S and P, where circle I stands for Indians, circle S for Scientists and circle P for Politicians. Different regions in the figure are lettered from a to f.

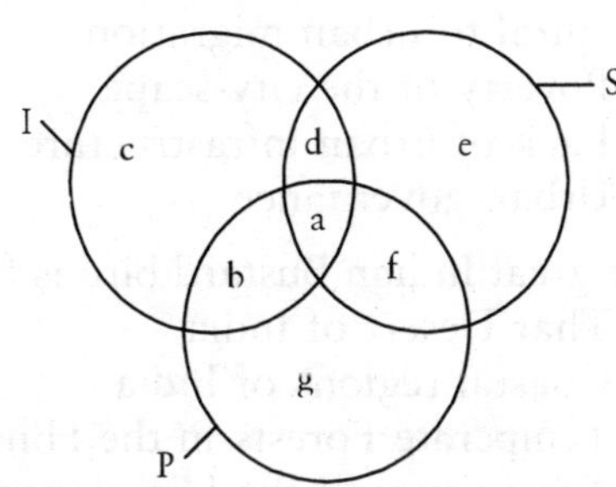

22. The region which represents Non-Indian Scientists who are Politicians.
(a) f (b) d
(c) a (d) c

23. The region which represents Indians who are neither Scientists nor Politicians.
(a) g (b) c
(c) f (d) a

24. The region which represents Politicians who are Indians as well as Scientists.
(a) b (b) c
(c) a (d) d

25. Which number is missing in the following series?
2, 5, 10, 17, 26, 37, 50, ?
(a) 63 (b) 65
(c) 67 (d) 69

26. The function of measurement includes
(a) Prognosis (b) Diagnosis
(c) Prediction (d) All of the above

27. Logical arguments are based on
(a) Scientific reasoning
(b) Customary reasoning
(c) Mathematical reasoning
(d) Syllogistic reasoning

28. Insert the missing number 4 : 17 : : 7 : ?
(a) 48 (b) 49
(c) 50 (d) 51

29. Choose the odd word.
(a) Nun (b) Knight
(c) Monk (d) Priest

30. Choose the number which is different from others in the group.
(a) 49 (b) 63
(c) 77 (d) 81

31. Probability sampling implies
(a) Stratified Random Sampling
(b) Systematic Random Sampling
(c) Simple Random Sampling
(d) All of the above

32. Insert the missing number.
$\frac{36}{62}, \frac{39}{63}, \frac{43}{61}, \frac{48}{64}, ?$

(a) $\frac{51}{65}$ (b) $\frac{56}{60}$

(c) $\frac{54}{65}$ (d) $\frac{33}{60}$

33. At what time between 3 and 4 O'clock will the hands of a watch point in opposite directions?
    (a) 40 minutes past three
    (b) 45 minutes past three
    (c) 50 minutes past three
    (d) 55 minutes past three

34. Mary has three children. What is the probability that none of the three children is a boy?
    (a) $\frac{1}{2}$ (b) $\frac{1}{3}$
    (c) $\frac{3}{4}$ (d) 1

35. If the radius of a circle is increased by 50 percent. Its area is increased by
    (a) 125 percent (b) 100 percent
    (c) 75 percent (d) 50 percent

36. CD ROM stands for
    (a) Computer Disk Read Only Memory
    (b) Compact Disk Read Over Memory
    (c) Compact Disk Read Only Memory
    (d) Computer Disk Read Over Memory

37. The 'brain' of a computer which keeps peripherals under its control is called
    (a) Common Power Unit
    (b) Common Processing Unit
    (c) Central Power Unit
    (d) Central Processing Unit

38. Data can be saved on backing storage medium known as
    (a) Compact Disk Recordable
    (b) Computer Disk Rewritable
    (c) Compact Disk Rewritable
    (d) Computer Data Rewritable

39. RAM means
    (a) Random Access Memory
    (b) Rigid Access Memory
    (c) Rapid Access Memory
    (d) Revolving Access Memory

40. www represents
    (a) who what and where
    (b) weird wide web
    (c) word wide web
    (d) world wide web

41. Deforestation during the recent decades has led to
    (a) Soil erosion
    (b) Landslides
    (c) Loss of bio-diversity
    (d) All of the above

42. Which one of the following natural hazards is responsible for causing highest human disaster?
    (a) Earthquakes
    (b) Volcanic eruptions
    (c) Snowstorms
    (d) Tsunami

43. Which one of the following is appropriate for natural hazard mitigation?
    (a) International AID
    (b) Timely Warning System
    (c) Rehabilitation
    (d) Community Participation

44. Slums in metro city are the result of
    (a) Rural to urban migration
    (b) Poverty of the city-scape
    (c) Lack of urban infrastructure
    (d) Urban-governance

45. The great Indian Bustard bird is found in
    (a) Thar Desert of India
    (b) Coastal regions of India
    (c) Temperate Forests in the Himalaya
    (d) Tarai zones of the Himalayan Foot

46. The first Indian Satellite for serving the educational sector is known as
    (a) SATEDU (b) INSAT-B
    (c) EDUSAT (d) INSAT-C

47. Exclusive educational channel of IGNOU is known as
(a) Gyan Darshan (b) Gyan Vani
(c) Door Darshan (d) Prasar Bharati

48. The headquarter of Mahatma Gandhi Antarrashtriya Hindi Vishwavidyalaya is situated in
(a) Sevagram (b) New Delhi
(c) Wardha (d) Ahmedabad

49. Match List I with List II and select the correct answer using the codes given below.

List I (Institutes)
A. Central Institute of English and Foreign Languages
B. Gramodaya Vishwavidyalaya
C. Central Institute of Higher Tibetan Studies
D. IGNOU

List II (Locations)
1. Chitrakoot 2. Hyderabad
3. New Delhi 4. Dharmasala

Codes:	A	B	C	D
(a)	2	1	4	3
(b)	4	3	2	1
(c)	3	4	1	2
(d)	1	2	4	3

50. The aim of vocationalisation of education is
(a) preparing students for a vocation along with knowledge
(b) converting liberal education into vocational education
(c) giving more importance to vocational than general education
(d) making liberal education job-oriented

ANSWERS

1. (b)	2. (a)	3. (b)	4. (a)	5. (a)
6. (c)	7. (c)	8. (c)	9. (d)	10. (c)
11. (c)	12. (a)	13. (b)	14. (c)	15. (a)
16. (d)	17. (a)	18. (a)	19. (d)	20. (b)
21. (d)	22. (a)	23. (b)	24. (d)	25. (b)
26. (d)	27. (d)	28. (c)	29. (b)	30. (c)
31. (d)	32. (c)	33. (c)	34. (d)	35. (a)
36. (c)	37. (d)	38. (c)	39. (a)	40. (d)
41. (d)	42. (a)	43. (b)	44. (a)	45. (a)
46. (c)	47. (a)	48. (c)	49. (a)	50. (d)

PAPER–II

Note: This paper contains fifty (50) objective type questions, each question carrying two (2) marks. All questions are compulsory.

1. Who, among the following is the author of *The Laws*?
(a) Aristotle (b) Plato
(c) St. Augustine (d) Dicey

2. Whose name is associated with the concept 'Relative Autonomy of State'?
(a) Lenin (b) Stalin
(c) Gramsci (d) Mao

3. Who, among the following, had introduced 'Christian Humanitarian Values' in an otherwise hedonistic philosophy?
(a) Bentham (b) James Mill
(c) John Stuart Mill (d) Spencer

4. Which one of the following statements is correct?
(a) 'Comparative Politics' as a sub-discipline of Political Science had emerged due to some gaps in 'Comparative Government'.
(b) 'Comparative Politics' was born in the United States because of the

emphasis the American scholars had placed on a scientific study of politics in the last century.

(c) 'Comparative Politics' was born of Behavioural movement in Political Science.

(d) 'Comparative Politics' was born in the fifties of the last century.

5. Which one of the following statements is correct?
   (a) The British Constitutional tradition requires separation of membership between Parliament and Cabinet.
   (b) The West Minister model of government insists on informal status of the cabinet.
   (c) The British Cabinet as a collective body is responsible for formulating the policy to be placed before the Parliament and is also the supreme controlling and directing body of the entire executive branch.
   (d) The Cabinet Minister in Britain need not be a member of the legislature.

6. Which one of the following statements is correct?
   (a) In Political Socialisation there is need to observe degree of political participation.
   (b) Non-Political experiences do not contribute to the Political Socialisation.
   (c) Political Socialisation is the establishment and development of attitudes to and beliefs about the Political System.
   (d) Political Socialisation ignores the links between authoritarian family structure and values.

7. Political parties are registered as per the provision of:
   (a) Article 324 of the Constitution
   (b) The Election Commission
   (c) The Election Commission in consultation with the Government
   (d) Representation of People's Act 1951

8. Which one of the following is the partner in the UPA Government?
   (a) AIADMK
   (b) Asom Gana Parishad
   (c) INLD
   (d) DMK

9. Which one of the following State Assemblies has six years term?
   (a) Punjab
   (b) Jammu and Kashmir
   (c) Himachal Pradesh
   (d) Kerala

10. Who called Hierarchy the 'scalar process'?
    (a) Mooney and Reiley
    (b) Felix A. Nigro
    (c) Henri Fayol
    (d) L.D. White

11. Which one of the following theories focusses on what is called informal organization?
    (a) Systems Theory
    (b) Bureaucratic Theory
    (c) Classical Theory
    (d) Human Relations Theory

12. Who among the following argues that public administration is different from private administration?
    (a) Paul H. Appleby
    (b) Henri Fayol
    (c) L. Urwick
    (d) Mary P. Follett

13. Who said the following?
    "The world must be made safe for democracy. We have no selfish ends to serve...we are but one of the champions of the right of mankind".
    (a) Mahatma Gandhi
    (b) Henry Kissinger

(c) Morgenthau
(d) Woodrow Wilson

14. With the end of Cold War, and the disintegration of the erstwhile Soviet Union, we are in:
(a) Bipolar World
(b) Multipolar World Order
(c) Unipolar System
(d) Anarchy

15. "Human nature was at the base of International Relations. And humans were Self-interested and power-seeking ...." Who said this?
(a) Woodrow Wilson
(b) Evans and Newham
(c) Hans J. Morgenthau
(d) Kenneth Waltz

Directions: Each of the following ten items consist of two statements, one labelled as Assertion (A) and the other labelled as Reason (R). You are to examine these two statements carefully and decide if the Assertion (A) and the Reason (R) are individually true and if so, whether Reason (R) is the correct explanation of Assertion (A). Select your answers to these items using the codes given below:
(a) Both (A) and (R) are true and (R) is the correct explanation of (A)
(b) Both (A) and (R) are true but (R) is not the correct explanation of (A)
(c) (A) is true but (R) is false
(d) (A) is false but (R) is true

16. **Assertion (A):** For Sri Aurobindo history is spiritually determined.
Reason (R): Culture and Civilization both act and interact in history.

17. **Assertion (A):** According to Kautilya four wings of the army—elephants, cavalry, chariots and infantry—should be placed under different officers.
Reason (R): The officers do not fall prey to the enemy's intrigues.

18. **Assertion (A):** There is no society today which can claim a single uniform political culture.
Reason (R): Patterns of cultural change differ from country to country.

19. **Assertion (A):** States and the State system are basic and permanent features of the modern Political life.
Reason (R): The State system and Modernity are not closely related historically.

20. **Assertion (A):** Exaggerated emphasis on bureaucratic and technocratic structures of management has done a great deal of harm to democratic polity in India.
Reason (R): Initiative from below has become the main victim.

21. **Assertion (A):** Politicisation of criminals is more dangerous than criminalisation of politics.
Reason (R): Political parties have lost governing capacities.

22. **Assertion (A):** Control over public administration is shifting from legislature to executive.
Reason (R): Parliament does not have sufficient time for detailed examination and scrutiny of governmental activities.

23. **Assertion (A):** The government imparts various types of training to its employees.
Reason (R): Training enhances the efficiency of the employees by improving their work skills.

24. **Assertion (A):** The underdeveloped countries suffer from the profound inequalities in contemporary world.
Reason (R): International system should address issues of security, freedom and progress.

25. **Assertion (A):** The central issue in International Politics is the inability of

our present global political system to adequately meet the problems created by globalization.

Reason (R): Westphalia system has failed to satisfy the long-term conditions for sustainability.

26. Identify the correct chronological order in which the following were published:
    (i) Leviathan
    (ii) Modern Political Analysis
    (iii) A Theory of Justice
    (iv) The calculus of Consent

    Codes:
    (a) (i), (iv), (iii), (ii) (b) (i), (ii), (iv), (iii)
    (c) (i), (iii), (ii), (iv) (d) (i), (iv), (ii), (iii)

27. Identify the correct chronological order in which the following concepts/theories were born:
    (i) 'General Will'
    (ii) 'Authority as Federal'
    (iii) 'Satyagraha'
    (iv) 'Gram Swaraj'

    Codes:
    (a) (i), (iii), (iv), (ii) (b) (i), (ii), (iii), (iv)
    (c) (i), (iv), (ii), (iii) (d) (i), (ii), (iv), (iii)

28. Identify the correct chronological order in which the following approaches emerged:
    (i) Philosophical Approach
    (ii) Behavioural Approach
    (iii) Marxist Approach
    (iv) Systems Approach

    Codes:
    (a) (iii), (ii), (iv), (i) (b) (iv), (i), (iii), (ii)
    (c) (ii), (i), (iv), (iii) (d) (i), (iii), (ii), (iv)

29. Identify the correct chronological order in which the following books were published:
    (i) *Political Man*
    (ii) *The Power Elite*
    (iii) *Theory and Practice of Modern Governments*
    (iv) *Comparative Politics: A Developmental Approach*

    Codes:
    (a) (i), (iv), (ii), (iii) (b) (iv), (i), (iii), (ii)
    (c) (iii), (ii), (i), (iv) (d) (ii), (iv), (i), (iii)

30. Identify the correct chronological order in which the following events occurred:
    (i) Unseating of Indira Gandhi according to Allahabad High Court verdict.
    (ii) First split in the Congress after Independence.
    (iii) "Garibi Hatao" slogan used by Congress in Parliamentary Elections.
    (iv) First Non-Congress Government at the centre.

    Codes:
    (a) (iii), (iv), (ii), (i) (b) (iv), (ii), (iii), (i)
    (c) (ii), (iii), (i), (iv) (d) (ii), (iv), (i), (iii)

31. Identify the correct chronological order of the following landmark judgements by the Supreme Court:
    (i) Minerva Mills Case
    (ii) Golak Nath Case
    (iii) A.K. Gopalan Case
    (iv) Ninth Schedule of the Constitution Case

    Codes:
    (a) (iv), (ii), (iii), (i) (b) (iii), (iv), (i), (ii)
    (c) (iii), (i), (ii), (iv) (d) (iii), (ii), (i), (iv)

32. Consider the following landmarks in the emergence and growth of New Public Administration:
    (i) Honey Report
    (ii) Philadelphia Conference
    (iii) Publication of "Towards a New Public Administration"
    (iv) Minnowbrook Conference

    What is the correct sequence of the above? Select the correct answer from the codes given below:

    Codes:
    (a) (ii), (i), (iv) and (iii)
    (b) (i), (ii), (iii) and (iv)
    (c) (ii), (iv), (iii) and (i)
    (d) (ii), (i), (iii) and (iv)

33. What is the correct sequence in which the following theories/approaches appeared?
    (i) Human Relations Theory
    (ii) Max Weber's Bureaucratic Theory
    (iii) New Public Management
    (iv) Decision-making Theory
    Select the correct answer from the codes given below:
    Codes:
    (a) (ii), (i) (iv) and (iii)
    (b) (i), (ii), (iii) and (iv)
    (c) (ii), (iii), (iv) and (i)
    (d) (i), (iii) (ii) and (iv)

34. Identify the correct chronological sequence of the following:
    (i) Dismemberment of Soviet Union
    (ii) NAM
    (iii) NATO
    (iv) Indian Ocean Rim
    Codes:
    (a) (ii), (iv), (i), (iii) (b) (iv), (iii), (i), (ii)
    (c) (i), (iv), (iii), (ii) (d) (iii), (ii), (i), (iv)

35. Identify the correct chronological order of the following events:
    (i) Camp David
    (ii) My-lai Massacre
    (iii) Iraq's invasion of Kuwait
    (iv) G-8 summit in St. Petersburg
    Codes:
    (a) (iii), (iv), (ii), (i) (b) (ii), (iii), (iv), (i)
    (c) (ii), (i), (iii), (iv) (d) (i), (iii), (iv), (ii)

36. Match List I with List II and select the correct answer from the codes given below:
    List I
    (A) Plato (B) Machiavelli
    (C) Hegel (D) Aurobindo
    List II
    (i) Private and Public Morality
    (ii) Savitri
    (iii) Time-Spirit
    (iv) Philosopher King

Codes:	**A**	**B**	**C**	**D**
(a)	(iv)	(i)	(iii)	(ii)
(b)	(i)	(ii)	(iv)	(iii)
(c)	(ii)	(i)	(iii)	(iv)
(d)	(iii)	(ii)	(i)	(iv)

37. Match List I with List II and select the correct answer from the codes given below:
    List I
    (A) 'The gate-keepers'
    (B) 'Better to be a Socrates dissatisfied than a pig satisfied'
    (C) 'Total revolution'
    (D) 'Encoding and decoding'
    List II
    (i) Deutsch
    (ii) Jaya Prakash Narayan
    (iii) David Easton
    (iv) J.S. Mill

Codes:	**A**	**B**	**C**	**D**
(a)	(i)	(iii)	(iv)	(ii)
(b)	(iii)	(iv)	(ii)	(i)
(c)	(ii)	(iii)	(iv)	(i)
(d)	(i)	(ii)	(iv)	(iii)

38. Which one of the following pairs is not correctly matched?
    (a) Pareto : Circulation of elites
    (b) Political Socialisation : Process of induction into the political culture
    (c) Lucian Pye : Structural differentiation
    (d) Organski : Political decay

39. Which one of the following pairs is not correctly matched?
    (a) Robert Michels : Iron Law of Oligarchy
    (b) Huntington : Modernisation—a multifaceted process
    (c) Karl Deutsch : Receptors
    (d) Almond : Elitist theory of democracy

40. Match List I with List II and select the correct answer from the codes given below:

List I

(A) Communal Award
(B) JP's Bihar Movement
(C) Giani Zail Singh's accession to Presidency
(D) Vajpayee's first Prime Ministership

List II

(i) 1996 (ii) 1982
(iii) 1932 (iv) 1974

Codes:	A	B	C	D
(a)	(i)	(ii)	(iv)	(iii)
(b)	(iii)	(ii)	(iv)	(i)
(c)	(iii)	(iv)	(ii)	(i)
(d)	(iv)	(ii)	(iii)	(i)

41. Match List I with List II and select the correct answer from the codes given below:

List I

(A) Rajni Kothari
(B) Lloyd and Susanne Rudolph
(C) Jawaharlal Nehru
(D) Mahatma Gandhi

List II

(i) *In Pursuit of Lakshmi: The political Economy of the Indian State*
(ii) *Discovery of India*
(iii) *An Autobiography: The Story of My Experiments with Truth*
(iv) *State against Democracy: In Search of Humane Governance*

Codes:	A	B	C	D
(a)	(ii)	(i)	(iii)	(iv)
(b)	(iv)	(i)	(ii)	(iii)
(c)	(iii)	(iv)	(ii)	(i)
(d)	(i)	(iii)	(iv)	(ii)

42. Match List I with List II and select the correct answer from the codes given below:

List I

(A) Span of control
(B) Scalar process
(C) Hereditary authority
(D) Fourteen principles of organisation

List II

(i) J.D. Mooney (ii) V.A. Graicunas
(iii) Henri Fayol (iv) Max Weber

Codes:	A	B	C	D
(a)	(i)	(ii)	(iv)	(iii)
(b)	(ii)	(i)	(iv)	(iii)
(c)	(iv)	(iii)	(ii)	(i)
(d)	(i)	(iii)	(ii)	(iv)

43. Match List I with List II and select the correct answer from the codes given below:

List I

(A) Bureaucratic (B) Behavioural
(C) General system (D) Ecological

List II

(i) Administrative system as a sub-system of social system
(ii) Agraria-industria
(iii) Legal rational authority
(iv) Analysis of human behaviour

Codes:	A	B	C	D
(a)	(iii)	(iv)	(ii)	(i)
(b)	(iv)	(iii)	(i)	(ii)
(c)	(iii)	(iv)	(i)	(ii)
(d)	(ii)	(i)	(iv)	(iii)

44. Match List I with List II and select the correct answer from the codes given below:

List I

(A) Architect of India's Foreign Policy
(B) Russia
(C) Panchsheel
(D) INA

List II

(i) S.C. Bose
(ii) China
(iii) Putin
(iv) Jawaharlal Nehru

Codes:	A	B	C	D
(a)	(iv)	(iii)	(i)	(ii)
(b)	(ii)	(i)	(iv)	(iii)
(c)	(iv)	(iii)	(ii)	(i)
(d)	(iii)	(ii)	(iv)	(i)

45. Match List I with List II and select the correct answer from the codes given below:

List I

(A) Bull, H. (B) Kaplan, M.
(C) Fukuyam, F. (D) Karl Marx

List II

(i) Revolutionary System
(ii) The End of History
(iii) Systems Theory
(iv) Evolutionary System

Codes:	A	B	C	D
(a)	(ii)	(iv)	(i)	(iii)
(b)	(i)	(iv)	(ii)	(iii)
(c)	(iii)	(ii)	(iv)	(i)
(d)	(iv)	(iii)	(ii)	(i)

Read the passage below, and answer the questions on the basis of your understanding of the passage:

It is this impatience with the inability of the 'critical' theorists to provide an alternative model of society, as distinct from suggesting an alternative method of analysis of the present one, which is in part at the root of the criticisms which have been levelled against the 'critical' philosophers and political theorists in the course of the second half of the 1970s, but another reason for this (often strident) criticisms is the increasing feeling of 'inauthenticity'—or 'hypocrisy'—which seems to surround the 'critical' approach. For instance, Rousseau felt disgusted by Voltaire's double standard, which led Voltaire to become the protege of the King of Prussia and yet to continue to be engaged in virulent attacks on absolutist regimes. The so-called 'new philosophers' who emerged in the 1970s in France in particular, have increasingly felt that the rarefied, hypersophisticated and complex critiques of Western Capitalist society under the banner of neo-Marxism acted as a huge smokescreen to cover-up the even more unacceptable modes of behaviour of Eastern totalitarian communist governments, the aim of the 'new' philosophers is to 'unmask', once more, but in the name of commonsense, because, to borrow the title of one of the works written in this vein, 'Barbary' has now 'a human face'. (B.H. Levy, 1977)

Much of the 'critique of the critics' has an emotional base, but much of the critical analysis itself—and that of Marx to begin with—had or has an emotional base—namely that capitalism was unacceptable because of the sufferings it was imposing on human beings and that it is still imposing, in the eyes of the neo-Marxists, on the human race. The anti-Marxist critics also start from the emotional standpoint that, under the cover of Marxism, a totalitarian lead casket is imposed already on part of mankind and is gradually being imposed on an increasingly larger part. Thus, the new critics of Marxism write in the same vein as and emulate some of the older political theorists. The contemporary world is in many ways as Hobbesian as the state of nature described by the seventeenth-century English writer; the excesses of dictatorship have to be stigmatized and alternatives have to be elaborated and presented to mankind as, otherwise the dominance of the ruthless will be assured. Political theory started from a disgust with the state of things as they were as well as out of a desire to understand what was going on. Blueprints presented by Plato, Hobbes, Locke and Rousseau were means of getting out of the human predicament; political theory must continue to fulfil this function because if it does not, mankind will once more, fall into a barbaric state.

46. The author is primarily concerned with the criticism of:
(a) Critical Theorists
(b) Traditional Theorists
(c) Western Philosophers
(d) Gaps in a few Political Theories

47. The author finds fault with Voltaire because of:
    (a) his attacks on democracy
    (b) his criticism of Prussian regime
    (c) his criticism of absolutism and support to absolutist Prussian state system
    (d) his ideas on human freedom

48. The 'new philosophers' use the expression 'smokescreen' for:
    (a) Analysing the views of the socialists
    (b) Exposing the dictatorial regimes
    (c) Supporting the western capitalist society
    (d) Camouflaging the unacceptable behaviour of Eastern totalitarian regimes

49. The contemporary world, according to the author, is:
    (a) basically democratic
    (b) full of sufferings of the people
    (c) largely totalitarian
    (d) full of human rights violations

50. The basic objective of political theory, according to the author is:
    (a) to steer clear of all the cover-ups
    (b) to criticize capitalist society
    (c) to expose totalitarian regimes
    (d) to help human beings in their predicament

ANSWERS

1. (b)	2. (a)	3. (a)	4. (a)	5. (b)
6. (c)	7. (b)	8. (d)	9. (b)	10. (a)
11. (d)	12. (c)	13. (d)	14. (d)	15. (d)
16. (b)	17. (b)	18. (a)	19. (b)	20. (b)
21. (b)	22. (a)	23. (a)	24. (b)	25. (b)
26. (c)	27. (c)	28. (a)	29. (c)	30. (d)
31. (b)	32. (c)	33. (c)	34. (d)	35. (d)
36. (a)	37. (b)	38. (c)	39. (c)	40. (c)
41. (b)	42. (b)	43. (c)	44. (c)	45. (d)
46. (a)	47. (c)	48. (d)	49. (d)	50. (d)

JUNE–2007

Note: This paper contains Fifty (50) multiple-choice questions, each question carrying two (2) marks. Attempt all of them.

PAPER–I

1. Teacher uses visual-aids to make learning
   (a) simple
   (b) more knowledgeable
   (c) quicker
   (d) interesting
2. The teacher's role at the higher educational level is to
   (a) provide information to students
   (b) promote self-learning in students
   (c) encourage healthy competition among students
   (d) help students to solve their personal problems
3. Which one of the following teachers would you like the most?
   (a) Punctual
   (b) Having research aptitude
   (c) Loving and having high idealistic philosophy
   (d) Who often amuses his students
4. Micro teaching is most effective for the student-teacher
   (a) during the practice-teaching
   (b) after the practice-teaching
   (c) before the practice-teaching
   (d) None of the above
5. Which is the least important factor in teaching?
   (a) Punishing the students
   (b) Maintaining discipline in the class
   (c) Lecturing in impressive way
   (d) Drawing sketches and diagrams on the blackboard
6. To test null hypothesis, a researcher uses
   (a) t test
   (b) ANOVA
   (c) χ^2
   (d) factorial analysis
7. A research problem is feasible only when
   (a) it has utility and relevance
   (b) it is researchable
   (c) it is new and adds something to knowledge
   (d) All of the above
8. Bibliography given in a research report
   (a) shows vast knowledge of the researcher
   (b) helps those interested in further research
   (c) has no relevance to research
   (d) All of the above
9. Fundamental research reflects the ability to
   (a) Synthesise new ideals
   (b) Expound new principles
   (c) Evaluate the existing material concerning research
   (d) Study the existing literature regarding various topics
10. The study in which the investigators attempt to trace an effect is known as
    (a) Survey Research
    (b) *Ex-post Facto* Research

(c) Historical Research
(d) Summative Research

Read the following passage and answer the questions 11 to 15:

All political systems need to mediate the relationship between private wealth and public power. Those that fail risk a dysfunctional government captured by wealthy interests. Corruption is one symptom of such failure with private willingness-to-pay trumping public goals. Private individuals and business firms pay to get routine services and to get to the head of the bureaucratic queue. They pay to limit their taxes, avoid costly regulations, obtain contracts at inflated prices and get concessions and privatised firms at low prices. If corruption is endemic, public officials—both bureaucrats and elected officials—may redesign programs and propose public projects with few public benefits and many opportunities for private profit. Of course, corruption, in the sense of bribes, pay-offs and kickbacks, is only one type of government failure. Efforts to promote "good governance' must be broader than anti-corruption campaigns. Governments may be honest but inefficient because no one has an incentive to work productively, and narrow elites may capture the state and exert excess influence on policy. Bribery may induce the lazy to work hard and permit those not in the inner circle of cronies to obtain benefits. However, even in such cases, corruption cannot be confined to 'functional' areas. It will be a temptation whenever private benefits are positive. It may be a reasonable response to a harsh reality but, over time, it can facilitate a spiral into an even worse situation.

11. The governments which fail to focus on the relationship between private wealth and public power are likely to become
(a) Functional
(b) Dysfunctional
(c) Normal functioning
(d) Good governance

12. One important symptom of bad governance is
(a) Corruption
(b) High taxes
(c) Complicated rules and regulations
(d) High prices

13. When corruption is rampant, public officials always aim at many opportunities for:
(a) Public benefits (b) Public profit
(c) Private profit (d) Corporate gains

14. Productivity linked incentives to public/private officials is one of the indicatives for
(a) Efficient government
(b) Bad governance
(c) Inefficient government
(d) Corruption

15. The spiralling corruption can only be contained by promoting
(a) Private profit
(b) Anti-corruption campaign
(c) Good governance
(d) Pay-offs and kickbacks

16. Press Council of India is located at
(a) Chennai (b) Mumbai
(c) Kolkata (d) Delhi

17. Adjusting the photo for publication by cutting is technically known as
(a) Photo cutting
(b) Photo bleeding
(c) Photo cropping
(d) Photo adjustment

18. Feedback of a message comes from
(a) Satellite (b) Media
(c) Audience (d) Communicator

19. Collection of information in advance before designing communication strategy is known as

(a) Feedback (b) Feed-forward
(c) Research study (d) Opinion poll

20. The aspect ratio of TV screen is
(a) 4:3 (b) 4:2
(c) 3:5 (d) 2:3

21. Which is the number that comes next in the sequence?
9, 8, 8, 8, 7, 8, 6, __
(a) 5 (b) 6
(c) 8 (d) 4

22. If in a certain language PUNCTUAL is coded as 16598623, how would ACTUPULN be coded?
(a) 834536 (b) 29861635
(c) 834530 (d) 834539

23. The question to be answered by factorial analysis of the quantitative data does not explain one of the following
(a) Is 'X' related to 'Y'?
(b) How is 'X' related to 'Y'?
(c) How does 'X' affect the dependent variable 'Y' at different levels of another independent variable 'K' or 'M'?
(d) How is 'X' by 'K' related to 'M'?

24. January 12, 1980 was Saturday, what day was January 12, 1979?
(a) Saturday (b) Friday
(c) Sunday (d) Thursday

25. How many Mondays are there in a particular month of a particular year, if the month ends on Wednesday?
(a) 5 (b) 4
(c) 3 (d) None of these

26. From the given four statements, select the two which cannot be true but yet both can be false. Choose the right pair.
1. All men are mortal
2. Some men are mortal
3. No man is mortal
4. Some men are not mortal
(a) 1 and 2 (b) 3 and 4
(c) 1 and 3 (d) 2 and 4

27. A Syllogism must have
(a) Three terms (b) Four terms
(c) Six terms (d) Five terms

28. Copula is that part of proposition which denotes the relationship between
(a) Subject and predicate
(b) Known and unknown
(c) Major premise and minor premise
(d) Subject and object

29. "E" denotes
(a) Universal Negative Proposition
(b) Particular Affirmative Proposition
(c) Universal Affirmative Proposition
(d) Particular Negative Proposition

30. 'A' is the father of 'C' and 'D' is the son of 'B'. 'E' is the brother of 'A'. If 'C' is the sister of 'D' how is 'B' related to 'E'?
(a) Daughter (b) Husband
(c) Sister-in-law (d) Brother-in-law

31. Which of the following methods will you choose to prepare choropleth map of India showing urban density of population?
(a) Quartiles (b) Quintiles
(c) Mean and SD (d) Break-point

32. Which of the following methods is best suited to show on a map the types of crops being grown in a region?
(a) Choropleth (b) Chorochromatic
(c) Choroschematic (d) Isopleth

33. A ratio represents the relation between
(a) Part and Part
(b) Part and Whole
(c) Whole and Whole
(d) All of the above

34. Out of four numbers, the average of the first three numbers is thrice the fourth number. If the average of the four numbers is 5, the fourth number is

(a) 4.5 (b) 5
(c) 2 (d) 4

35. Circle graphs are used to show
(a) How various sections share in the whole
(b) How various parts are related to the whole
(c) How one whole is related to other wholes
(d) How one part is related to other parts

36. On the keyboard of computer each character has an "ASCII" value which stands for
(a) American Stock Code for Information Interchange
(b) American Standard Code for Information Interchange
(c) African Standard Code for Information Interchange
(d) Adaptable Standard Code for Information Change

37. Which part of the Central Processing Unit (CPU) performs calculation and makes decisions
(a) Arithmetic Logic Unit
(b) Alternating Logic Unit
(c) Alternate Local Unit
(d) American Logic Unit

38. "Dpi" stands for
(a) Dots per inch
(b) Digits per unit
(c) Dots pixel inch
(d) Diagrams per inch

39. The process of laying out a document with text, graphics, headlines and photographs is involved in
(a) Deck Top Publishing
(b) Desk Top Printing
(c) Desk Top Publishing
(d) Deck Top Printing

40. Transfer of data from one application to another line is known as
(a) Dynamic Disk Exchange
(b) Dodgy Data Exchange
(c) Dogmatic Data Exchange
(d) Dynamic Data Exchange

41. Tsunami occurs due to
(a) Mild earthquakes and landslides in the oceans
(b) Strong earthquakes and landslides in the oceans
(c) Strong earthquakes and landslides in mountains
(d) Strong earthquakes and landslides in deserts

42. Which of the natural hazards have big effect on Indian people each year?
(a) Cyclones (b) Floods
(c) Earthquakes (d) Landslides

43. Comparative Environment Impact Assessment study is to be conducted for
(a) the whole year
(b) three seasons excluding monsoon
(c) any three seasons
(d) the worst season

44. Sea level rise results primarily due to
(a) Heavy rainfall
(b) Melting of glaciers
(c) Submarine volcanism
(d) Seafloor spreading

45. The plume rise in a coal-based power plant depends on
1. Buoyancy
2. Atmospheric stability
3. Momentum of exhaust gases

Identify the correct code

Codes:
(a) Both (1) and (2) (b) Both (2) and (3)
(c) Both (1) and (3) (d) (1), (2) and (3)

46. Value education makes a student
(a) Good citizen
(b) Successful businessman

(c) Popular teacher
(d) Efficient manager

47. Networking of libraries through electronic media is known as
(a) Inflibnet (b) Libinfnet
(c) Internet (d) HTML

48. The University which telecasts interactive educational programs through its own channel is
(a) B.R. Ambedkar Open University, Hyderabad
(b) I.G.N.O.U.
(c) University of Pune
(d) Annamalai University

49. The Government established the University Grants Commission by an Act of Parliament in the year
(a) 1980 (b) 1948
(c) 1950 (d) 1956

50. Universities having central campus for imparting education are called
(a) Central Universities
(b) Deemed Universities
(c) Residential Universities
(d) Open Universities

ANSWERS

1. (d)	2. (a)	3. (a)	4. (b)	5. (a)
6. (c)	7. (d)	8. (b)	9. (b)	10. (b)
11. (b)	12. (a)	13. (c)	14. (a)	15. (c)
16. (d)	17. (c)	18. (c)	19. (d)	20. (a)
21. (c)	22. (b)	23. (c)	24. (b)	25. (d)
26. (b)	27. (a)	28. (b)	29. (a)	30. (d)
31. (b)	32. (c)	33. (b)	34. (c)	35. (a)
36. (a)	37. (a)	38. (a)	39. (c)	40. (d)
41. (b)	42. (b)	43. (a)	44. (b)	45. (d)
46. (a)	47. (a)	48. (b)	49. (d)	50. (b)

PAPER–II

Note: This paper contains fifty (50) objective type questions, each question carrying two (2) marks. All questions are compulsory.

1. Who among the following first separated ethics from politics?
(a) Aristotle (b) Machiavelli
(c) Hobbes (d) Locke

2. Which one of the following concepts had been criticised as 'Paradox of Freedom'?
(a) Platonic 'Justice'
(b) Locke's 'Governmental Contract'
(c) Rousseau's 'General Will'
(d) Rawl's 'Distributive Justice'

3. "Politics is the process by which community of human beings deal with their problems"—Whose words are these?
(a) Aristotle (b) Gettel
(c) Harold Lasswell (d) Herbert J. Spiro

4. Who, among the following, had contributed to the growth of 'Comparative Politics' as a sub-discipline of Political Science?
(a) Arthur Bentley (b) Graham Wallas
(c) Harold Laski (d) R.T. Mckenzie

5. Which of the following countries has a federal form of government with dual citizenship?
(a) India (b) U.S.A.
(c) U.K. (d) Switzerland

6. According to Lucian Pye, which of the following are crisis of political development?
1. Crisis of identity
2. Crisis of legitimacy
3. Crisis of distribution
4. Crisis of corrupt political processes
Select the correct answer from the codes given below:

(a) (1), (2) and (4)
(b) (1), (2) and (3)
(c) (2), (3) and (4)
(d) (1), (2), (3) and (4)

7. "International peace and security" is referred to in the Indian Constitution in:
(a) The Preamble
(b) Fundamental Rights
(c) Directive Principles of State Policy
(d) Emergency provisions

8. Which Amendment of the Indian Constitution dealt with the reduction of number of Ministers in the Government?
(a) 85th Amendment
(b) 42nd Amendment
(c) 91st Amendment
(d) 52nd Amendment

9. Who among the following is the father of "Doctrine of Passive Resistance"?
(a) Mahatma Gandhi
(b) Aurobindo Ghosh
(c) Jawaharlal Nehru
(d) Rabindranath Tagore

10. Who defines Public Administration as consisting "of all those operations having for their purpose the fulfilment or enforcement of public policy"?
(a) D. Waldo (b) L.D. White
(c) L. Urwick (d) W.F. Willoughby

11. Who among the following called the classical principles of organisation 'proverbs'?
(a) Henri Fayol (b) L.D. White
(c) Herbert Simon (d) D. Waldo

12. Who defines civil service as "professional body of officials, permanent, paid and skilled"?
(a) Herman Finer
(b) Felix Nigro
(c) Max Weber
(d) O. Glenn Stahl

13. Survival of SAARC mainly depends on:
(a) Interest of weaker States
(b) Peace and Co-operation
(c) Unanimity of decisions
(d) Issues of Bilateral Relations

14. The 'Uniting For Peace' resolution was adopted by:
(a) NAM
(b) NATO
(c) UN
(d) Commonwealth of Nations

15. UNCTAD basically promoted:
(a) Peaceful settlement of disputes
(b) International Trade
(c) Prevention of war
(d) N.P.T.

Directions (16-25): The following ten questions consist of two statements one labelled as Assertion (A) and the other labelled as Reason (R). You are to examine these two statements carefully and decide if the Assertion (A) and the Reason (R) are individually true and if so whether the Reason is a correct explanation of the Assertion. Select your answers to these questions using the codes given below:
(a) Both (A) and (R) are true and R is the correct explanation of (A)
(b) Both (A) and (R) are true but (R) is not the correct explanation of (A)
(c) (A) is true but (R) is false
(d) (A) is false but (R) is true

16. **Assertion (A):** Scientific socialism explains history in terms of class struggle.
Reason (R): Class struggle takes place in the 'Superstructure' first.

17. **Assertion (A):** The idea of community is a major concern for the Western scholars in the late twentieth century.
Reason (R): The 'local' was lost and weakened.

18. **Assertion (A):** The structural-functional analysis revolves around the concepts of functions and structures.

Reason (R): A function is generally defined as the objective consequence of a pattern of action for the system.

19. **Assertion (A):** Elite Theory was first used in Central and Western European countries as a critique of democracy.
Reason (R): In every democratic society it is minority that rules.

20. **Assertion (A):** Since 1977 in India experimentation in consociational politics has survived.
Reason (R): One party dominant system has failed.

21. **Assertion (A):** Since 1970s in India, elites of every type have the same social character.
Reason (R): Language, religion and caste are being used for electoral purposes.

22. **Assertion (A):** Hierarchy leads to rigidity and affects human relationships in administration.
Reason (R): Hierarchy is a means to achieve coherence in the administrative organisation.

23. **Assertion (A):** Public Administration is not entirely devoid of profit motive.
Reason (R): The main aim of governmental activities is to promote societal welfare.

24. **Assertion (A):** NAM is still relevant in the post-cold war period.
Reason (R): Some of the developing countries will be in dominant position in the near future.

25. **Assertion (A):** Both China and India have paved the way for the establishment of a constructive and co-operative relationships for the 21st century.
Reason (R): China has opposed Pakistan's nuclear policy.

26. Identify the correct chronological order using the code given below in which the following concepts/theories appeared:
(i) Saptanga
(ii) Theory of Protection
(iii) Passive Resistance
(iv) Satyagraha
(a) (i), (ii), (iii), (iv) (b) (ii), (iii), (iv), (i)
(c) (ii), (i), (iv), (iii) (d) (iii), (ii), (iv), (i)

27. Identify the correct chronological order in which the following books were published:
(i) *A Grammar of Politics*
(ii) *Ideal of Human Unity*
(iii) *Multicultural Citizenship: A Liberal Theory of Minority Rights*
(iv) *Neo-Humanism*
Codes:
(a) (ii), (i), (iii), (iv) (b) (i), (iv), (ii), (iii)
(c) (ii), (iii), (i), (iv) (d) (i), (ii), (iv), (iii)

28. What is the correct sequence of the following four quantitative factors in Karl Deutsch's Communications Theory?
(i) Lag (ii) Load
(iii) Lead (iv) Gain
Select the correct answer from the codes given below:
Codes:
(a) (ii), (i), (iv) and (iii)
(b) (i), (ii), (iii) and (iv)
(c) (iii), (ii), (i) and (iv)
(d) (iv), (i), (ii) and (iii)

29. According to Kenneth Organski a developing society has to pass through the following four stages of political development:
(i) Political Unification
(ii) National Welfare
(iii) Industrialization
(iv) Abundance
What is the sequence in which they have been listed by Organski. Select the correct answer from the codes given below:
(a) (i), (ii), (iii) and (iv)
(b) (i), (iii), (ii) and (iv)
(c) (i), (iii), (iv) and (ii)
(d) (i), (ii), (iv) and (iii)

30. Identify the correct chronological order in which the following served the Lok Sabha as Speakers:
 (i) Sanjeeva Reddy
 (ii) Hukam Singh
 (iii) Som Nath Chatterjee
 (iv) P.A. Sangma
 (a) (iv), (i), (ii), (iii) (b) (iii), (iv), (ii), (i)
 (c) (ii), (i), (iv), (iii) (d) (i), (iii), (iv), (ii)

31. Identify the correct chronological order in which the following are placed in Indian Constitution:
 (i) Right to freedom of religion
 (ii) Changing the name of a State
 (iii) Imposition of President's rule in a State
 (iv) Reference of IAS and IPS
 (a) (iv), (ii), (iii), (i) (b) (ii), (i), (iv), (iii)
 (c) (iii), (iv), (ii), (i) (d) (i), (iii), (iv), (ii)

32. Consider the following steps in decision making:
 (i) Acquiring background information about the problem.
 (ii) Determining the problem.
 (iii) Evaluating the alternatives.
 (iv) Identifying the alternatives.
 What is the correct sequence of the above steps. Select the correct answer from codes given below:
 Codes:
 (a) (i), (ii), (iv) and (iii)
 (b) (ii), (i), (iv) and (iii)
 (c) (ii), (iii), (i) and (iv)
 (d) (i), (iii), (iv) and (ii)

33. Which one of the following is the correct sequence in which the following approaches to the study of Public Administration have evolved?
 (i) Classical Approach
 (ii) Behavioural Approach
 (iii) Human Relations Approach
 (iv) Policy Approach
 Select the correct answer from the codes given below:
 Codes:
 (a) (i), (iii), (ii) and (iv)
 (b) (i), (ii), (iii) and (iv)
 (c) (ii), (i), (iii) and (iv)
 (d) (i), (iii), (iv) and (ii)

34. Identify the correct chronological order of the following events in India-China relations:
 (i) Dalai Lama's entry into India
 (ii) India Recognising PRC
 (iii) Panchsheel Agreement
 (iv) Sino-India 50th Anniversary of Diplomatic Relations
 Select the correct answer from codes given below:
 (a) (iv), (i), (iii) and (ii)
 (b) (ii), (iii), (i) and (iv)
 (c) (i), (iv), (ii) and (iii)
 (d) (iii), (i), (iv) and (ii)

35. Identify the correct chronological order of the following:
 (i) Maastricht
 (ii) N.P.T.
 (iii) Belgrade Conference
 (iv) SALT
 Select the correct answer from codes given below:
 (a) (iv), (i), (iii), (ii) (b) (iii), (ii), (iv), (i)
 (c) (iii), (ii), (i), (iv) (d) (ii), (i), (iv), (iii)

36. Match List I with List II and select the correct answer from the codes given below:
 List I
 (A) 'Power'
 (B) 'Eternal Consciousness'
 (C) 'Authoritative allocation of values'
 (D) 'Prison Diary'
 List II
 (i) Green (ii) Easton
 (iii) Machiavelli (iv) Gramsci

Codes:	A	B	C	D
(a)	(iii)	(i)	(ii)	(iv)
(b)	(i)	(iii)	(ii)	(iv)
(c)	(iv)	(iii)	(i)	(ii)
(d)	(ii)	(iv)	(iii)	(i)

37. Match List I with List II and select the correct answer from the codes given below:

List I

(A) St. Augustine (B) Mao
(C) M.N. Roy (D) Aurobindo

List II

(i) 'Let hundred flowers bloom'
(ii) 'Colonial thesis'
(iii) 'Involution'
(iv) 'Two swords'

Codes:	A	B	C	D
(a)	(i)	(ii)	(iv)	(iii)
(b)	(ii)	(iii)	(i)	(iv)
(c)	(iv)	(i)	(ii)	(iii)
(d)	(iii)	(ii)	(i)	(iv)

38. Which one of the following pairs is not correctly matched?
(a) Robert Dahl : *Who Governs?*
(b) T.B. Bottomore : *Elites and Society*
(c) David Easton : *The Political System*
(d) Lucian Pye : *The Stages of Political Development*

39. Match List I with List II and select the correct answer from the codes given below:

List I

(A) Political Communication
(B) Dependency
(C) Mass mind
(D) Signs of political development at three different levels

List II

(i) A.G. Frank (ii) Lucian Pye
(iii) Roberto Michels (iv) Karl Deutsch

Select the correct answer from Codes given below:

Codes	A	B	C	D
(a)	(iv)	(i)	(iii)	(ii)
(b)	(i)	(ii)	(iii)	(iv)
(c)	(ii)	(i)	(iv)	(iii)
(d)	(iv)	(iii)	(ii)	(i)

40. Match List I with List II and select the correct answer from the code given below:

List I	List II
(A) Indian National Lok Dal	(i) West Bengal
(B) TMC	(ii) Bihar
(C) JD(U)	(iii) Andhra Pradesh
(D) TRS	(iv) Haryana

Codes:	A	B	C	D
(a)	(i)	(iii)	(iv)	(ii)
(b)	(ii)	(iii)	(i)	(iv)
(c)	(iv)	(i)	(ii)	(iii)
(d)	(iv)	(ii)	(iii)	(i)

41. Match List I with List II and select the correct answer from the code given below:

List I

(A) P.V. Narsimha Rao became the Prime Minister
(B) Babri Masjid was demolished
(C) Deve Gowda became the Prime Minister
(D) Nehru signed the Panchsheel with China

List II

(i) 1992 (ii) 1996
(iii) 1954 (iv) 1991

Codes:	A	B	C	D
(a)	(iii)	(iv)	(ii)	(i)
(b)	(i)	(iv)	(iii)	(ii)
(c)	(iv)	(i)	(ii)	(iii)
(d)	(iii)	(i)	(ii)	(iv)

42. Match List I with List II and select the correct answer from the codes given below:

List I

(A) An employee should receive orders from one superior only
(B) How many subordinates can an administrator direct personally?

(C) The superior-subordinate relationship through a number of levels of responsibility

(D) The orderly arrangement of group effort to provide unity of action in the pursuit of a common purpose

List II

(i) Span of Control
(ii) Unity of Command
(iii) Hierarchy
(iv) Co-ordination

Codes:	**A**	**B**	**C**	**D**
(a)	(i)	(ii)	(iv)	(iii)
(b)	(ii)	(iii)	(i)	(iv)
(c)	(iii)	(iv)	(ii)	(i)
(d)	(ii)	(i)	(iii)	(iv)

43. Which one of the following pairs is not correctly matched?
(a) Classical : Structure
(b) Human Relations : Informal Organisation
(c) Systems : Environment
(d) Scientific Management : Fourteen Principles of Organisation

44. Match List I with List II and select the correct answer from the codes given below:

List I

(A) Morgenthau (B) E.H. Carr
(C) Kenneth Waltz (D) Schelling T.

List II

(i) The Strategy of Conflict
(ii) Theory of International Politics
(iii) Politics among Nations
(iv) The Twenty Years Crisis

Codes:	**A**	**B**	**C**	**D**
(a)	(ii)	(iv)	(iii)	(i)
(b)	(iii)	(i)	(ii)	(iv)
(c)	(iii)	(iv)	(ii)	(i)
(d)	(iv)	(i)	(iii)	(ii)

45. Match List I with List II and select the correct match by using the codes given below:

List I

(A) GATT (B) SAARC
(C) NAFTA (D) TRIPS

List II

(i) South Asian Nations
(ii) Intellectual Property Rights
(iii) North American States
(iv) Agreement on Tariff and Trade

Codes:	**A**	**B**	**C**	**D**
(a)	(iii)	(ii)	(iv)	(i)
(b)	(ii)	(iv)	(iii)	(i)
(c)	(i)	(iii)	(iv)	(ii)
(d)	(iv)	(i)	(iii)	(ii)

Directions (46-50): Read the following passage and select the correct answers from the questions given below, on the basis of your understanding of the passage:

Individuals have a wide, indeed, potentially infinite range of interests; these are ranked in the most complicated manner—indeed, the ranking is so complicated that individuals themselves do not perceive what it is. Our interest in art, in food, in travel, in various social matters belongs to different 'areas' which we are rarely called to compare or contrast. Yet, if one wants to assess the power of an individual over another, one may have to take all these aspects into consideration. The comprehensive analysis of power thus makes us enter farther and farther fields. But in voting situations or in committee decisions, on the contrary, problems are narrowed down, because a decision has to be made between two or a small number of issues or candidates. The general preference process is, so to speak, operationalized into a choice mechanism which, however difficult it may be in many circumstances, is nonetheless markedly simplified by comparison with the theoretical choices which might be made. The proof of this drastic reduction of the ends is indeed given by the fact that many feel that voting decisions do not leave electors with a 'real' choice, that candidates or parties are too similar to each other, for instance, or that the issues are not-clear-cut enough. Be this as it may, that fact is that effective choice is constrained by the process of decision itself.

There is also simplification at the level of the means because of a number of rules which the democratic system of voting and of committee decision-making imposes. The reason why it is not very interesting to assess committee decision in this way if, for instance, someone like Stalin 'dominates' a committee is because Stalin would simply set aside the rules and threaten committee members if these were not to support his views. But a 'regular' democratic committee is one where a number of rules are scrupulously observed and where, in particular, great store is placed on rules relating to the ways in which issues are placed on the agenda, debated and voted on. The voting rules (majority voting, for instance) are of course those which are most conspicuous in restricting the freedom of members to act in an 'in egalitarian' manner, but the whole of the procedure also contributes in 'equalizing' the general framework. It becomes therefore both interesting and possible to analyse the effect of these rules on the decision-making process and specifically to examine the 'paradoxes' inherent in such a system as well as the ways in which one or more of the members can maximize their own interests in the context of the system.

46. The individual seems to be unaware of his interests because:
    (a) of their wide range
    (b) of difficult choices
    (c) of illiteracy
    (d) of dictatorial regimes

47. In voting behaviour problems have become simple because:
    (a) of the very 'process' of decision-making the voter is required to follow.
    (b) The theoretical issues are very limited
    (c) Voting has become mechanical
    (d) 'ends' are not important

48. Why is Stalin referred to?
    (a) Voting procedure is undemocratic
    (b) Ignoring rules and threatening opponents
    (c) Issues are limited
    (d) Candidates are few

49. Why are the voting rules undemocratic?
    (a) Because these give a lot of freedom to the voters
    (b) Because the choices of the voters are not restricted
    (c) Because these limit the freedom of the voters to take part in decision-making
    (d) Because they fail to promote the interests of the decision-makers

50. Which, among the following is important for assessing the power of an individual over another?
    (a) All interests of the individual and some other fields or areas
    (b) The individual's consciousness about the ranking of interests
    (c) The individual is constrained by the choice mechanism
    (d) Voting situations and committee decisions have been totally changed

ANSWERS

1. (a)	2. (c)	3. (c)	4. (a)	5. (b)
6. (b)	7. (c)	8. (c)	9. (b)	10. (a)
11. (c)	12. (a)	13. (c)	14. (c)	15. (b)
16. (b)	17. (b)	18. (a)	19. (b)	20. (b)
21. (b)	22. (a)	23. (b)	24. (b)	25. (c)
26. (a)	27. (c)	28. (a)	29. (a)	30. (c)
31. (b)	32. (a)	33. (a)	34. (b)	35. (a)
36. (b)	37. (c)	38. (d)	39. (a)	40. (b)
41. (c)	42. (c)	43. (a)	44. (b)	45. (d)
46. (a)	47. (a)	48. (b)	49. (c)	50. (c)

DECEMBER–2006

Note: This paper contains Fifty (50) multiple-choice questions, each question carrying two (2) marks. Attempt all of them.

PAPER–I

1. Which of the following is not instructional material?
   (a) Over Head Projector
   (b) Audio Casset
   (c) Printed Material
   (d) Transparency

2. Which of the following statement is not correct?
   (a) Lecture Method can develop reasoning
   (b) Lecture Method can develop knowledge
   (c) Lecture Method is one way process
   (d) During Lecture Method students are passive

3. The main objective of teaching at Higher Education Level is:
   (a) To prepare students to pass examination
   (b) To develop the capacity to take decisions
   (c) To give new information
   (d) To motivate students to ask questions during lecture

4. Which of the following statement is correct?
   (a) Reliability ensures validity
   (b) Validity ensures reliability
   (c) Reliability and validity are independent of each other
   (d) Reliability does not depend on objectivity

5. Which of the following indicates evaluation?
   (a) Ram got 45 marks out of 200
   (b) Mohan got 38 percent marks in English
   (c) Shyam got First Division in final examination
   (d) All the above

6. Research can be conducted by a person who:
   (a) has studied research methodology
   (b) holds a postgraduate degree
   (c) possesses thinking and reasoning ability
   (d) is a hard worker

7. Which of the following statements is correct?
   (a) Objectives of research are stated in first chapter of the thesis
   (b) Researcher must possess analytical ability
   (c) Variability is the source of problem
   (d) All the above

8. Which of the following is not the Method of Research?
   (a) Observation (b) Historical
   (c) Survey (d) Philosophical

9. Research can be classified as:
   (a) Basic, Applied and Action Research
   (b) Quantitative and Qualitative Research
   (c) Philosophical, Historical, Survey and Experimental Research
   (d) All the above

10. The first step of research is:
    (a) Selecting a problem
    (b) Searching a problem
    (c) Finding a problem
    (d) Identifying a problem

Read the following passage and answer the question nos. 11 to 15:

After almost three decades of contemplating Swarovski-encrusted navels on increasing flat abs, the Mumbai film industry is on a discovery of India and itself. With budgets of over 30 crore each, four soon to be released movies by premier directors are exploring the idea of who we are and redefining who the other is. It is a fundamental question which the bling-bling, glam-sham and dishamdisham tends to avoid. It is also a question which binds an audience when the lights go dim and the projector rolls : as a nation, who are we? As a people, where are we going?

The Germans coined a word for it, zeitgeist, which perhaps Yash Chopra would not care to pronounce. But at 72, he remains the person who can best capture it. After being the first to project the diasporic Indian on screen in *Lamhe* in 1991, he has returned to his roots in a new movie. *Veer Zaara*, set in 1986, where Pakistan, the traditional other, the part that got away, is the lover and the saviour. In Subhas Ghai's *Kisna*, set in 1947, the other is the English woman. She is not a memsahib, but a mehbooba. In Ketan Mehta's *The Rising*, the East India Englishman is not the evil oppressor of countless cardboard characterisations, which span the spectrum from *Jewel in the Crown* to *Kranti*, but an honourable friend.

This is Manoj Kumar's *Desh Ki Dharti* with a difference: there is culture, not contentious politics; balle balle, not bombs: no dooriyan (distance), only nazdeekiyan (closeness).

All four films are heralding a new hero and heroine. The new hero is fallible and vulnerable, committed to his dharma, but also not afraid of failure—less of a boy and more of a man. He even has a grown up name: Veer Pratap Singh in *Veer Zaara* and Mohan Bhargav in *Swades*. The new heroine is not a babe, but often a bebe, dressed in traditional Punjabi clothes, often with the stereotypical body type as well, as in *Bride and Prejudice* of Gurinder Chadha.

11. Which word Yash Chopra would not be able to pronounce?
    (a) Bling + bling (b) Zeitgeist
    (c) Montaz (d) Dooriyan

12. Who made *Lamhe* in 1991?
    (a) Subhash Ghai (b) Yash Chopra
    (c) Aditya Chopra (d) Sakti Samanta

13. Which movie is associated with Manoj Kumar?
    (a) *Jewel in the Crown*
    (b) *Kisna*
    (c) *Zaara*
    (d) *Desh Ki Dharti*

14. Which is the latest film by Yash Chopra?
    (a) *Deewar*
    (b) *Kabhi Kabhi*
    (c) *Dilwale Dulhaniya Le Jayenge*
    (d) *Veer Zaara*

15. Which is the dress of the heroine in *Veer Zaara*?
    (a) Traditional Gujarati Clothes
    (b) Traditional Bengali Clothes
    (c) Traditional Punjabi Clothes
    (d) Traditional Madrasi Clothes

16. Which one of the following can be termed as verbal communication?
    (a) Prof. Sharma delivered the lecture in the classroom.
    (b) Signal at the cross-road changed from green to orange.

(c) The child was crying to attract the attention of the mother.
(d) Dipak wrote a letter for leave application.

17. Which is the 24 hours English Business news channel in India?
(a) Zee News (b) NDTV 24×7
(c) CNBC (d) India News

18. Consider the following statements in communication:
(i) Hema Malini is the Chairperson of the Children's Film Society, India.
(ii) Yash Chopra is the Chairman of the Central Board of Film Certification of India.
(iii) Sharmila Tagore is the Chairperson of National Film Development Corporation.
(iv) Dilip Kumar, Raj Kapoor and Preeti Zinta have all been recipients of Dada Saheb Phalke Award.
Which of the statements given above is/are correct?
(a) (i) and (iii) (b) (ii) and (iii)
(c) (iv) only (d) (iii) only

19. Which of the following pair is not correctly matched?
(a) N. Ram : The Hindu
(b) Barkha Dutt : Zee News
(c) Pranay Roy : NDTV 24×7
(d) Prabhu Chawla : Aajtak

20. "Because you deserve to know" is the punchline used by:
(a) The Times of India
(b) The Hindu
(c) Indian Express
(d) Hindustan Times

21. In the sequence of numbers 8, 24, 12, X, 18, 54 the missing number X is:
(a) 26 (b) 24
(c) 36 (d) 32

22. If A stands for 5, B for 6, C for 7, D for 8 and so on, then the following numbers stand for 17, 19, 20, 9 and 8:
(a) PLANE (b) MOPED
(c) MOTOR (d) TONGA

23. The letters in the first set have certain relationship. On the basis of this relationship what is the right choice for the second set?
AST : BRU : : NQV : ?
(a) ORW (b) MPU
(c) MRW (d) OPW

24. In a certain code, PAN is written as 31 and PAR as 35. In this code PAT is written as:
(a) 30 (b) 37
(c) 38 (d) 39

25. The sides of a triangle are in the ratio of $\frac{1}{2}:\frac{1}{3}:\frac{1}{4}$. If its perimeter is 52 cm, the length of the smallest side is:
(a) 9 cm (b) 10 cm
(c) 11 cm (d) 12 cm

26. Which one of the following statements is completely non-sensical?
(a) He was a bachelor, but he married recently.
(b) He is a bachelor, but he married recently.
(c) When he married, he was not a bachelor.
(d) When he was a bachelor, he was not married.

27. Which of the following statements are mutually contradictory?
(i) All flowers are not fragrant.
(ii) Most flowers are not fragrant.
(iii) None of the flowers is fragrant.
(iv) Most flowers are fragrant.
Choose the correct answer from the code given below:
Code:
(a) (i) and (ii) (b) (i) and (iii)
(c) (ii) and (iii) (d) (iii) and (iv)

28. Which of the following statements say the same thing?
    (i) "I am a teacher" (said by Arvind)
    (ii) "I am a teacher" (said by Binod)
    (iii) "My son is a teacher" (said by Binod's father)
    (iv) "My brother is a teacher" (said by Binod's sister)
    (v) "My brother is a teacher" (said by Binod's only sister)
    (vi) "My sole enemy is a teacher" (said by Binod's only enemy)

    Choose the correct answer from the code given below:
    Codes:
    (a) (i) and (ii)
    (b) (ii), (iii), (iv) and (v)
    (c) (ii) and (vi)
    (d) (v) and (vi)

29. Which of the following are correct ways of arguing?
    (i) There can be no second husband without a second wife.
    (ii) Anil is a friend of Bob, Bob is a friend of Raj, hence Anil is a friend of Raj.
    (iii) A is equal to B, B is equal to C, hence A is equal to C.
    (iv) If everyone is a liar, then we cannot prove it.

    Choose the correct answer from the code given below:
    Codes:
    (a) (iii) and (iv)
    (b) (i), (iii) and (iv)
    (c) (ii), (iii) and (iv)
    (d) (i), (ii), (iii) and (iv)

30. Which of the following statement/s are always false?
    (i) The sun will not rise in the East some day.
    (ii) A wooden table is not a table.
    (iii) Delhi city will be drowned under water.
    (iv) Cars run on water as fuel.

    Choose the correct answer from the code given below:
    Codes:
    (a) (i), (iii) and (iv) (b) Only (iii)
    (c) (i), (ii) and (iii) (d) (ii) alone

Study the following graph and answer question numbers 31 to 33:

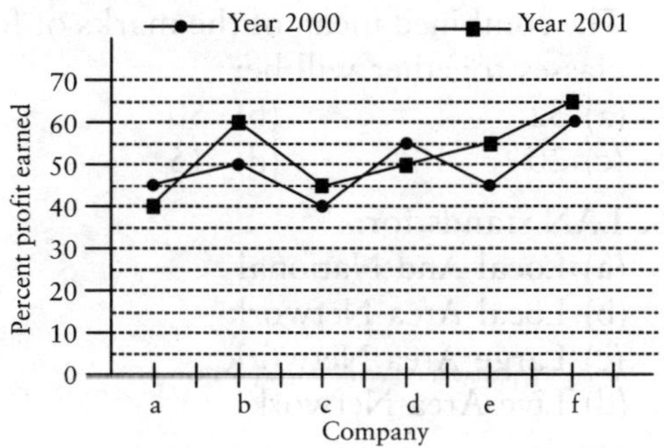

31. In the year 2000, which of the following Companies earned maximum percent profit?
    (a) a (b) b
    (c) d (d) f

32. In the year 2001, which of the following Companies earned minimum percent profit?
    (a) a (b) c
    (c) d (d) e

33. In the years 2000 and 2001, which of the following Companies earned maximum average percent profit?
    (a) f (b) e
    (c) d (d) b

34. Human Development Report for 'each' of the year at global level has been published by:
    (a) UNDP (b) WTO
    (c) IMF (d) World Bank

35. The number of students in four classes A, B, C, D and their respective mean marks obtained by each of the class are given below:

	Class A	Class B	Class C	Class D
Number of students	10	40	30	20
Arithmetic mean	20	30	50	15

The combined mean of the marks of four classes together will be:
(a) 32 (b) 50
(c) 20 (d) 15

36. LAN stands for:
(a) Local And National
(b) Local Area Network
(c) Large Area Network
(d) Live Area Network

37. Which of the following statement is correct?
(a) Modem is a software
(b) Modem helps in stabilizing the voltage
(c) Modem is the operating system
(d) Modem converts the analog signal into digital signal and vice-versa

38. Which of the following is the appropriate definition of a computer?
(a) Computer is a machine that can process information.
(b) Computer is an electronic device that can store, retrieve and process both qualitative and quantitative data quickly and accurately.
(c) Computer is an electronic device that can store, retrieve and quickly process only quantitative data.
(d) Computer is a machine that can store, retrieve and process quickly and accurately only qualitative information.

39. Information and Communication Technology includes:
(a) On line learning
(b) Learning through the use of EDUSAT
(c) Web Based Learning
(d) All the above

40. Which of the following is the appropriate format of URL of e-mail?
(a) www_mail.com
(b) www@mail.com
(c) WWW@mail.com
(d) www.mail.com

41. The most significant impact of volcanic erruption has been felt in the form of:
(a) change in weather
(b) sinking of islands
(c) loss of vegetation
(d) extinction of animals

42. With absorption and decomposition of CO_2 in ocean water beyond desired level, there will be:
(a) decrease in temperature
(b) increase in salinity
(c) growth of phyto plankton
(d) rise in sea level

43. Arrange column II in proper sequence so as to match it with column I and choose the correct answer from the code given below:

Column I Water Quality	Column II pH Value
(A) Neutral	(i) 5
(B) Moderately acidic	(ii) 7
(C) Alkaline	(iii) 4
(D) Injurious	(iv) 8

Code:	(A)	(B)	(C)	(D)
(a)	(ii)	(iii)	(i)	(iv)
(b)	(i)	(iii)	(ii)	(iv)
(c)	(ii)	(i)	(iv)	(iii)
(d)	(iv)	(ii)	(iii)	(i)

44. The maximum emission of pollutants from fuel sources in India is caused by:
(a) Coal
(b) Firewood
(c) Refuse burning
(d) Vegetable waste product

45. The urbanisation process accounts for the wind in the urban centres during nights to remain:
(a) faster than that in rural areas
(b) slower than that in rural areas
(c) the same as that in rural areas
(d) cooler than that in rural areas

46. The University Grants Commission was constituted on the recommendation of:
(a) Dr. Sarvapalli Radhakrishnan Commission
(b) Mudaliar Commission
(c) Sargent Commission
(d) Kothari Commission

47. Which one of the following Articles of the Constitution of India safeguards the rights of Minorities to establish and run educational institutions of their own liking?
(a) Article 19 (b) Article 29
(c) Article 30 (d) Article 31

48. Match List I (Institutions) with List II (Functions) and select the correct answer by using the code given below:

List I (Institutions)
(A) Parliament
(B) C. & A.G.
(C) Ministry of Finance
(D) Executing Departments

List II (Functions)
(i) Formulation of Budget
(ii) Enactment of Budget
(iii) Implementation of Budget
(iv) Legality of Expenditure
(v) Justification of Income

Codes:	**(A)**	**(B)**	**(C)**	**(D)**
(a)	(iii)	(iv)	(ii)	(i)
(b)	(ii)	(iv)	(i)	(iii)
(c)	(v)	(iii)	(iv)	(ii)
(d)	(iv)	(ii)	(iii)	(v)

49. Foundation training to the newly recruited IAS (Probationers) is imparted by:
(a) Indian Institute of Public Administration
(b) Administrative Staff College of India
(c) L.B.S. National Academy of Administration
(d) Centre for Advanced Studies

50. Electoral disputes arising out of Presidential and Vice-Presidential Elections are settled by:
(a) Election Commission of India
(b) Joint Committee of Parliament
(c) Supreme Court of India
(d) Central Election Tribunal.

ANSWERS

1. (d)	2. (a)	3. (b)	4. (b)	5. (d)
6. (c)	7. (d)	8. (b)	9. (d)	10. (d)
11. (b)	12. (b)	13. (d)	14. (d)	15. (c)
16. (c)	17. (c)	18. (d)	19. (b)	20. (d)
21. (c)	22. (b)	23. (d)	24. (b)	25. (d)
26. (b)	27. (b)	28. (b)	29. (a)	30. (d)
31. (d)	32. (a)	33. (a)	34. (a)	35. (a)
36. (b)	37. (d)	38. (b)	39. (d)	40. (b)
41. (a)	42. (c)	43. (c)	44. (c)	45. (b)
46. (a)	47. (c)	48. (b)	49. (c)	50. (c)

PAPER–II

1. The thinker who had accepted the fundamentals of Aristotle's political thought in the medieval period was:
(a) John of Salisbury
(b) St. Thomas Aquines
(c) Gregory
(d) Wycliffe

2. Who said, "Man is born free but everywhere he is in chains"?
(a) Locke (b) Rousseau
(c) Marx (d) Bentham

3. Match List I with List II and select the correct answer from the codes given below:

List I (Book)	List II (Author)
(A) *The Politics*	(i) Machiavelli
(B) *The Prince*	(ii) J.S. Mill
(C) *The Social Contract*	(iii) Rousseau
(D) *On Liberty*	(iv) Aristotle

Codes:	**A**	**B**	**C**	**D**
(a)	(iv)	(ii)	(i)	(iii)
(b)	(ii)	(iv)	(iii)	(i)
(c)	(iii)	(ii)	(iv)	(i)
(d)	(i)	(ii)	(iii)	(iv)

4. According to Aristotle, which of the following is the best form of government?
(a) Democracy (b) Oligarchy
(c) Polity (d) Tyranny

5. **Assertion (A):** According to Locke, the functions of government as well as its powers are limited.
Reason (R): Government exists, he says, to protect life, liberty and property.
(a) Both (A) and (R) are true, and (R) is the correct explanation.
(b) Both (A) and (R) are true, but (R) is not the correct explanation.
(c) (A) is true but (R) is false.
(d) (A) is false but (R) is true.

6. Match List I with List II and choose the correct answer from the codes given below:
List I (Concepts)
(A) General Will
(B) Absolute Sovereignty
(C) Limited Government
(D) New Political Science
List II (Thinkers)
(i) Machiavelli (ii) Locke
(iii) Hobbes (iv) Rousseau

Codes:	**A**	**B**	**C**	**D**
(a)	(ii)	(iii)	(iv)	(i)
(b)	(iii)	(iv)	(i)	(ii)
(c)	(iv)	(iii)	(ii)	(i)
(d)	(i)	(iv)	(iii)	(ii)

7. According to Plato, the most inferior type of the State is:
(a) Democracy (b) Oligarchy
(c) Tyranny (d) Timocracy

8. According to Aristotle, the best polity is that which is based on the principle of:
(a) Democracy (b) Oligarchy
(c) Mean (d) Quantity and quality

9. Who among the following can be put in the category of 'Anarchist'?
(a) M.N. Roy (b) Ambedkar
(c) Gandhi (d) Jai Prakash

10. Who examined the case of liberal democracy from the angle of 'possessive individualism'?
(a) J.J. Rousseau
(b) Anthony Downs
(c) C.B. Macpherson
(d) Robert Dahl

11. 'Bhoodan movement' in India was launched by:
(a) Jayaprakash Narayan
(b) The Communist Party of India
(c) Acharya Vinoba Bhave
(d) Acharya Narendra Dev

12. The author of the book *Politics of Scarcity*:
(a) Paul Brass (b) Myron Weiner
(c) Rajani Kothari (d) Morris Jones

13. In case of dispute between the two Houses of Indian Parliament over an Ordinary Bill the case is referred to:
(a) The President of India
(b) The Supreme Court of India
(c) Joint meeting of the Houses
(d) The Prime Minister of India

14. Decisions on questions about disqualification of members of the Lok Sabha are made by:

(a) The Minister for Parliamentary Affairs
(b) The Speaker
(c) Committee on Privileges
(d) The Prime Minister and the Council of Ministers

15. The right to constitutional remedy in the Indian Constitution is provided for under:
(a) Article 19 (b) Article 32
(c) Article 15 (d) Article 39

16. Which one of the following categories of Fundamental Rights incorporates 'Abolition of Untouchability'?
(a) Right to Freedom
(b) Right to Equality
(c) Right to Freedom of Religion
(d) Right against Exploitation

17. Which one among the following is not stipulated in the Constitution of India?
(a) Election Commission
(b) Union Public Service Commission
(c) Indian National Congress
(d) Council of Ministers

18. Sarkaria Commission was set up for reviewing the relations between:
(a) The President and the Prime Minister
(b) The Legislature and the Executive
(c) The Centre and the States
(d) The national and regional political parties

19. Nagar Palika Bill was first introduced in Parliament during the Prime Ministership of:
(a) Rajiv Gandhi (b) Narasimha Rao
(c) V.P. Singh (d) Indira Gandhi

20. Which one of the following parties has the highest percentage of its M.Ps with criminal cases registered against them?
(a) Bharatiya Janta Party
(b) Samajwadi Party
(c) Rashtriya Janta Dal
(d) National Congress Party

21. The scope of comparative politics include the study of:
(a) formal structures and their functions
(b) political processes
(c) extra-constitutional agencies
(d) All the three above

22. The general systems theory in social sciences was first developed in:
(i) Psychology (ii) Anthropology
(iii) Political Science (iv) Sociology
What is the correct chronological sequence of the above? Select the correct answer from the codes given below:
(a) (ii), (iv), (i) and (iii)
(b) (i), (ii), (iii) and (iv)
(c) (ii), (iv), (iii) and (i)
(d) (iii), (i), (ii) and (iv)

23. According to Almond, the input functions of a political system are:
(i) Interest-articulation
(ii) Interest-aggregation
(iii) Rule-making
(iv) Rule-application
Which of these are correct?
(a) (i) and (ii)
(b) (iii) and (iv)
(c) (i), (ii) and (iii)
(d) (i), (ii), (iii) and (iv)

24. Who among the following defines modernization as "a multifaceted process involving changes in all areas of human thought and activity"?
(a) Kenneth Organski
(b) Lucian Pye
(c) Almond and Powell
(d) Samuel Huntington

25. A constitutional government is:
(a) a limited government
(b) a government with a constitution
(c) a government headed by the President
(d) a government headed by the Prime Minister

26. Who among the following believed in the theory of circulation of elites?
(a) Max Weber and Bottomore
(b) Pareto and Mosca
(c) Mills and Max Weber
(d) Michels and Laski

27. The most powerful legislature in the world is:
(a) Indian Parliament
(b) British Parliament
(c) U.S. Congress
(d) French Parliament

28. Match List I with List II and select the correct answer from the codes given below:
List I
(A) Stages of Political Development
(B) Crises of Political Development
(C) Classification of Political Culture
(D) Classification of Political Parties
List II
(i) Lucian Pye
(ii) Kenneth Organski
(iii) Almond and Verba
(iv) La Palombara and Myron Weiner

Codes:	**A**	**B**	**C**	**D**
(a)	(ii)	(i)	(iii)	(iv)
(b)	(i)	(ii)	(iv)	(iii)
(c)	(iii)	(iv)	(ii)	(i)
(d)	(iv)	(i)	(ii)	(iii)

29. The 'procedure established by law' is a characteristic of the judicial system of:
(a) U.S.A. (b) U.K.
(c) India (d) China

30. Given below are two statements, one labelled as Assertion (A) and the other labelled as Reason (R):
Assertion (A): The Supreme Court of India cannot declare a bad law invalid.
Reason (R): The Supreme Court of India follows the 'due process of law'.
In the context of the two statements, which one of the following is correct?
(a) Both (A) and (R) are true and (R) is the correct explanation of (A).
(b) Both (A) and (R) are true but (R) is not the correct explanation of (A).
(c) (A) is true, but (R) is false.
(d) (A) is false, but (R) is true.

31. The Minnowbook Conference took place in the year:
(a) 1968 (b) 1969
(c) 1970 (d) 1972

32. Who among the following was the first to emphasise the need for a separate study of Public Administration?
(a) Frank J. Goodnow
(b) Woodrow Wilson
(c) D. Waldo
(d) Luther Gulick

33. The principles of Scientific Management developed by Taylor include:
(i) Incentive of high wages
(ii) Standardization of work methods
(iii) Esprit de Corps
(iv) Standardization of working conditions
Which of these are correct?
(a) (i), (ii) and (iii) (b) (i), (ii) and (iv)
(c) (ii), (iii) and (iv) (d) (i), (iii) and (iv)

34. Who among the following propounded the Fourteen principles of organization?
(a) Henri Fayol
(b) J.D. Mooney
(c) L.D. White
(d) Dimock and Dimock

35. Who among the following termed the 'auxiliary function' as the house-keeping function?
(a) W.F. Willoughby
(b) L.D. White
(c) Pfiffner and Presthus
(d) Dimock and Dimock

36. The word 'POSDCORB' was coined by:
(a) Luther Gulick (b) Marshal Dimock
(c) J.M. Pfiffner (d) D. Waldo

37. The following were associated with reforms in local government:
(i) Lord Ripon
(ii) Lord Mayo
(iii) Ashok Mehta
(iv) Balwant Rai Mehta
What is the correct chronological sequence of the above? Select the correct answer from the codes given below:
Codes:
(a) (ii), (i), (iv) and (iii)
(b) (i), (ii), (iii) and (iv)
(c) (ii), (iv), (iii) and (i)
(d) (iii), (iv), (ii) and (i)

38. The principle that every member of an organization should report to one and only one leader is called:
(a) Unity of Command
(b) Hierarchy
(c) Centralisation
(d) Delegation

39. Who is the author of the book *Administrative Behaviour*?
(a) Herbert Simon (b) L.D. White
(c) Henri Fayol (d) F.M. Taylor

40. Match List I with List II and select the correct answer from the codes given below:
List I
(A) Classical theory of organisation
(B) Functional foremanship
(C) Span of control
(D) Scalar process
List II
(i) J.D. Mooney (ii) V.A. Graicunas
(iii) Henri Fayol (iv) F.W. Taylor

Codes:	A	B	C	D
(a)	(iii)	(iv)	(ii)	(i)
(b)	(i)	(ii)	(iv)	(iii)
(c)	(ii)	(iv)	(i)	(iii)
(d)	(i)	(iii)	(iv)	(ii)

41. Realists construct the international system as:
(a) Co-operative (b) Ideal
(c) Anarchic (d) Non-functional

42. Power in international relations is:
(a) Absolute (b) Relative
(c) Infinite (d) Finite

43. The universal actor in Kaplan's Systems approach is:
(a) USA (b) UNO
(c) U K (d) WTO

44. Given below are two statements, one labelled as Assertion (A) and the other labelled as Reason (R).
Assertion (A): 'Collective security is a mirage'.
Reason (R): States do not have a common perception of threat.
Choose the correct answer from the given codes.
(a) Both (A) and (R) are true and (R) is the correct explanation of (A).
(b) Both (A) and (R) are true but (R) is not the correct explanation of (A).
(c) (A) is true, but (R) is false.
(d) (A) is false, but (R) is true.

45. 'Prisoner's dilemma' is a phenomenon' that fuels:
(a) Arms race (b) Arms control
(c) Disarmament (d) Peace

46. The military alliances are formed on the basic concept of:
(a) Collective defence
(b) Collective security
(c) Co-operative security
(d) Comprehensive security

47. International law in its application is:
(a) Universal (b) Partial
(c) Absolute (d) Relative

48. Identify the correct chronological sequence of the following events:
(a) Truman doctrine; Munroe doctrine; Brezhnev doctrine; Guam doctrine.

(b) Munroe doctrine; Truman doctrine; Brezhnev doctrine; Guam doctrine.
(c) Guam doctrine; Brezhnev doctrine; Truman doctrine; Munroe doctrine.
(d) Brezhnev doctrine; Truman doctrine; Guam doctrine; Munroe doctrine.

49. Match List I with List II and answer the correct match by using the codes given below:

List I

(A) Gentz (B) Norman Angell
(C) Kant (D) Woodrow Wilson

List II

(i) Collective security
(ii) Interdependence
(iii) Perpetual peace
(iv) Balance of power

Codes:	A	B	C	D
(a)	(iv)	(ii)	(iii)	(i)
(b)	(ii)	(i)	(iv)	(iii)
(c)	(iii)	(ii)	(i)	(iv)
(d)	(i)	(iii)	(iv)	(ii)

50. Identify the correct chronological sequence of the following events:
(a) Helsinki Summit; Congress of Vienna; Bay of pigs; Versailles Conference.
(b) Versailles Conference; Bay of pigs; Helsinki Summit; Congress of Vienna.
(c) Congress of Vienna; Versailles Conference; Bay of pigs; Helsinki Summit.
(d) Bay of pigs; Helsinki Summit; Congress of Vienna; Versailles Conference.

ANSWERS

1. (d)	2. (b)	3. (b)	4. (a)	5. (a)
6. (c)	7. (c)	8. (a)	9. (c)	10. (c)
11. (c)	12. (b)	13. (a)	14. (d)	15. (b)
16. (b)	17. (c)	18. (c)	19. (b)	20. (c)
21. (d)	22. (b)	23. (d)	24. (d)	25. (a)
26. (c)	27. (a)	28. (a)	29. (c)	30. (d)
31. (a)	32. (b)	33. (d)	34. (a)	35. (b)
36. (a)	37. (b)	38. (a)	39. (a)	40. (a)
41. (a)	42. (c)	43. (b)	44. (a)	45. (a)
46. (d)	47. (b)	48. (b)	49. (a)	50. (c)

JUNE–2006

Note: This paper contains fifty (50) objective type questions, each question carrying two (2) marks. All questions are compulsory.

PAPER–I

1. Which of the following comprise teaching skill:
   (a) Blackboard writing
   (b) Questioning
   (c) Explaining
   (d) All the above
2. Which of the following statements is most appropriate?
   (a) Teachers can teach.
   (b) Teachers help can create in a student a desire to learn.
   (c) Lecture Method can be used for developing thinking.
   (d) Teachers are born.
3. The first Indian chronicler of Indian history was :
   (a) Megasthanese (b) Fahiyan
   (c) Huan Tsang (d) Kalhan
4. Which of the following statements is correct?
   (a) Syllabus is a part of curriculum.
   (b) Syllabus is an annexure to curriculum.
   (c) Curriculum is the same in all educational institutions affiliated to a particular university.
   (d) Syllabus is not the same in all educational institutions affiliated to a particular university.
5. Which of the two given options is of the level of understanding?
   (I) Define noun.
   (II) Define noun in your own words.
   (a) Only I (b) Only II
   (c) Both I and II (d) Neither I nor II
6. Which of the following options are the main tasks of research in modern society?
   (I) To keep pace with the advancement in knowledge.
   (II) To discover new things.
   (III) To write a critique on the earlier writings.
   (IV) To systematically examine and critically analyse the investigations/ sources with objectivity.
   (a) IV, II and I (b) I, II and III
   (c) I and III (d) II, III and IV
7. Match List I (Interviews) with List II (Meanings) and select the correct answer from the code given below:
   List I (Interviews)
   (A) Structured interviews
   (B) Unstructured interviews
   (C) Focussed interviews
   (D) Clinical interviews
   List II (Meanings)
   (i) Greater flexibility approach
   (ii) Attention on the questions to be answered
   (iii) Individual life experience
   (iv) Pre-determined question
   (v) Non-directive

Codes:	A	B	C	D
(a)	(iv)	(i)	(ii)	(iii)
(b)	(ii)	(iv)	(i)	(iii)
(c)	(v)	(ii)	(iv)	(i)
(d)	(i)	(iii)	(v)	(iv)

8. What do you consider as the main aim of inter-disciplinary research?
   (a) To bring out holistic approach to research.
   (b) To reduce the emphasis of single subject in research domain.
   (c) To over simplify the problem of research.
   (d) To create a new trend in research methodology.

9. One of the aims of the scientific method in research is to:
   (a) improve data interpretation
   (b) eliminate spurious relations
   (c) confirm triangulation
   (d) introduce new variables

10. The depth of any research can be judged by:
   (a) title of the research.
   (b) objectives of the research.
   (c) total expenditure on the research.
   (d) duration of the research.

Read the following passage and answer the questions 11 to 15:

The superintendence, direction and control of preparation of electoral rolls for, and the conduct of, elections to Parliament and State Legislatures and elections to the offices of the President and the Vice-President of India are vested in the Election Commission of India. It is an independent constitutional authority.

Independence of the Election Commission and its insulation from executive interference is ensured by a specific provision under Article 324(5) of the Constitution that the chief Election Commissioner shall not be removed from his office except in like manner and on like grounds as a Judge of the Supreme Court and conditions of his service shall not be varied to his disadvantage after his appointment.

In C.W.P. No. 4912 of 1998 (Kushra Bharat Vs. Union of India and others), the Delhi High Court directed that information relating to Government dues owed by the candidates to the departments dealing with Government accommodation, electricity, water, telephone and transport etc. and any other dues should be furnished by the candidates and this information should be published by the election authorities under the commission.

11. The text of the passage reflects or raises certain questions:
   (a) The authority of the commission can not be challenged.
   (b) This would help in stopping the criminalization of Indian politics.
   (c) This would reduce substantially the number of contesting candidates.
   (d) This would ensure fair and free elections.

12. According to the passage, the Election Commission is an independent constitutional authority. This is under Article No.:
   (a) 324 (b) 356
   (c) 246 (d) 161

13. Independence of the Commission means:
   (a) have a constitutional status.
   (b) have legislative powers.
   (c) have judicial powers.
   (d) have political powers.

14. Fair and free election means:
   (a) transparency
   (b) to maintain law and order
   (c) regional considerations
   (d) role for pressure groups

15. The Chief Election Commissioner can be removed from his office under Article:
   (a) 125 (b) 352
   (c) 226 (d) 324

16. The function of mass communication of supplying information regarding the

processes, issues, events and societal developments is known as:
(a) Content supply (b) Surveillance
(c) Gratification (d) Correlation

17. The science of the study of feedback systems in humans, animals and machines is known as:
(a) cybernetics
(b) reverse communication
(c) selectivity study
(d) response analysis

18. Networked media exist in interconnected:
(a) social environments
(b) economic environments
(c) political environments
(d) technological environments

19. The combination of computing, telecommunications and media in a digital atmosphere is referred to as:
(a) online communication
(b) integrated media
(c) digital combine
(d) convergence

20. A dialogue between a human-being and a computer programme that occurs simultaneously in various forms is described as:
(a) man-machine speak
(b) binary chat
(c) digital talk
(d) interactivity

21. Insert the missing number:

$\frac{16}{32}, \frac{15}{33}, \frac{17}{31}, \frac{14}{34}$, ?

(a) $\frac{19}{35}$ (b) $\frac{19}{30}$
(c) $\frac{18}{35}$ (d) $\frac{18}{30}$

22. Monday falls on 20th March 1995. What was the day on 3rd November 1994?
(a) Thursday (b) Sunday
(c) Tuesday (d) Saturday

23. The average of four consecutive even numbers is 27. The largest of these numbers is
(a) 36 (b) 32
(c) 30 (d) 28

24. In a certain code, FHQK means GIRL. How will WOMEN be written in the same code?
(a) VNLDM (b) FHQKN
(c) XPNFO (d) VLNDM

25. At what time between 4 and 5 O'clock will the hands of a watch point in opposite directions?
(a) 45 min. past 4
(b) $40\frac{4}{11}$ min. past 4
(c) $50\frac{4}{11}$ min. past 4
(d) $54\frac{6}{11}$ min. past 4

26. Which of the following conclusions is logically valid based on statement given below ?
Statement: Most teachers are hard working.
Conclusions: (I) Some teachers are hard working.
(II) Some teachers are not hard working.
(a) Only (I) is implied
(b) Only (II) is implied
(c) Both (I) and (II) are implied
(d) Neither (I) nor (II) is implied

27. Who among the following can be asked to make a statement in Indian Parliament?
(a) Any MLA
(b) Chief of Army Staff

(c) Solicitor General of India
(d) Mayor of Delhi

28. Which of the following conclusions is logically valid based on statement given below ?

Statement : Most of the Indian states existed before independence.

Conclusions : (I) Some Indian States existed before independence.
(II) All Indian States did not exist before independence.

(a) Only (I) is implied
(b) Only (II) is implied
(c) Both (I) and (II) are implied
(d) Neither (I) nor (II) is implied

29. Water is always involved with landslides. This is because it:
(a) reduces the shear strength of rocks
(b) increases the weight of the overburden
(c) enhances chemical weathering
(d) is a universal solvent

30. Direction for this question:
Given below are two statements (A) and (B) followed by two conclusions (i) and (ii). Considering the statements to be true, indicate which of the following conclusions logically follow from the given statements by selecting one of the four response alternatives given below the conclusion:

Statements: (A) All businessmen are wealthy.
(B) All wealthy people are hard working.

Conclusions: (i) All businessmen are hard working.
(ii) All hardly working people are not wealthy.

(a) Only (i) follows
(b) Only (ii) follows
(c) Only (i) and (ii) follow
(d) Neither (i) nor (ii) follows

31. Using websites to pour out one's grievances is called:
(a) cyberventing (b) cyber ranting
(c) web hate (d) web plea

32. In web search, finding a large number of documents with very little relevant information is termed:
(a) poor recall
(b) web crawl
(c) poor precision rate
(d) poor web response

33. The concept of connect intelligence is derived from:
(a) virtual reality
(b) fuzzy logic
(c) bluetooth technology
(d) value added networks

34. Use of an ordinary telephone as an Internet applicance is called:
(a) voicenet (b) voice telephone
(c) voice line (d) voice portal

35. Video transmission over the Internet that looks like delayed livecasting is called:
(a) virtual video
(b) direct broadcast
(c) video shift
(d) real-time video

36. Which is the smallest North-east State in India?
(a) Tripura (b) Meghalaya
(c) Mizoram (d) Manipur

37. Tamil Nadu coastal belt has drinking water shortage due to:
(a) high evaporation
(b) sea water flooding due to tsunami
(c) over exploitation of ground water by tubewells
(d) seepage of sea water

38. While all rivers of Peninsular India flow into the Bay of Bengal, Narmada and

Tapti flow into the Arabian Sea because these two rivers:
(a) Follow the slope of these rift valleys
(b) The general slope of the Indian peninsula is from east to west
(c) The Indian peninsula north of the Satpura ranges, is tilted towards the west
(d) The Indian peninsula south of the Satpura ranges is tilted towards east

39. Soils in the Mahanadi delta are less fertile than those in the Godavari delta because of:
(a) erosion of top soils by annual floods
(b) inundation of land by sea water
(c) traditional agriculture practices
(d) the derivation of alluvial soil from red-soil hinterland

40. Which of the following institutions in the field of education is set up by the MHRD Government of India?
(a) Indian council of world Affair, New Delhi
(b) Mythic Society, Bangalore
(c) National Bal Bhawan, New Delhi
(d) India International Centre, New Delhi

41. **Assertion (A):** Aerosols have potential for modifying climate.
Reason (R): Aerosols interact with both short waves and radiation.
(a) Both (A) and (R) are true, and (R) is the correct explanation of (A)
(b) Both (A) and (R) are true, but (R) is not the correct explanation of (A)
(c) (A) is true, but (R) is false
(d) (A) is false, but (R) is true

42. 'SITE' stands for:
(a) System for International technology and Engineering
(b) Satellite Instructional Television Experiment
(c) South Indian Trade Estate
(d) State Institute of Technology and Engineering

43. What is the name of the Research station established by the Indian Government for 'Conducting Research at Antarctic'?
(a) Dakshin Gangotri
(b) Yamunotri
(c) Uttari Gangotri
(d) None of the above

44. Ministry of Human Resource Development (HRD) includes:
(a) Department of Elementary Education and Literacy
(b) Department of Secondary Education and Higher Education
(c) Department of Women and Child Development
(d) All the above

45. Parliament can legislate on matters listed in the State list:
(a) With the prior permission of the President.
(b) Only after the Constitution is amended suitably.
(c) In case of inconsistency among State legislatures.
(d) At the request of two or more States.

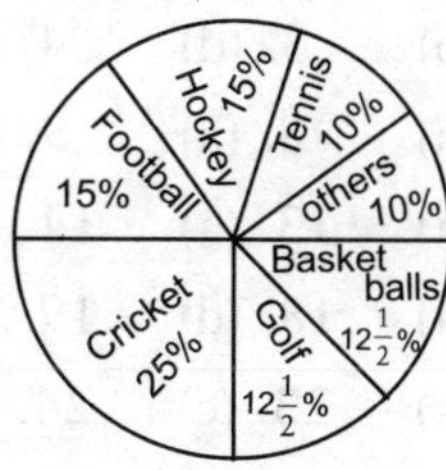

The following pie chart indicates the expenditure of a country on various sports during a particular year. Study the pie chart and answer it Question Numbers 46 to 50.

46. The ratio of the total expenditure on football to that of expenditure on hockey is:
(a) 1 : 15 (b) 1 : 1
(c) 15 : 1 (d) 3 : 20

47. If the total expenditure on sports during the year was Rs. 1,20,000,00 how much was spent on basket ball?
(a) Rs. 9,50,000 (b) Rs. 10,00,000
(c) Rs. 12,00,000 (d) Rs. 15,00,000

48. The chart shows that the most popular game of the country is:
(a) Hockey (b) Football
(c) Cricket (d) Tennis

49. Out of the following country's expenditure is the same on:
(a) Hockey and Tennis
(b) Golf and Basketball
(c) Cricket and Football
(d) Hockey and Golf

50. If the total expenditure on sport during the year was Rs. 1,50,00,000 the expenditure on cricket and hockey together was:
(a) Rs. 60,00,000 (b) Rs. 50,00,000
(c) Rs. 37,50,000 (d) Rs. 25,00,000

ANSWERS

1. (d)	2. (b)	3. (d)	4. (a)	5. (b)
6. (a)	7. (a)	8. (a)	9. (b)	10. (b)
11. (d)	12. (a)	13. (a)	14. (b)	15. (d)
16. (a)	17. (a)	18. (d)	19. (d)	20. (d)
21. (d)	22. (a)	23. (c)	24. (c)	25. (d)
26. (c)	27. (c)	28. (b)	29. (b)	30. (a)
31. (a)	32. (a)	33. (d)	34. (c)	35. (d)
36. (c)	37. (d)	38. (a)	39. (a)	40. (c)
41. (a)	42. (b)	43. (a)	44. (d)	45. (d)
46. (b)	47. (a)	48. (c)	49. (b)	50. (a)

PAPER–II

1. In his concept of Ideal state, Plato employs the term 'appetite' which refers to:
(a) Soldiers (b) Rulers
(c) Artisans (d) Individuals

2. The concept of 'best practicable state' is the contribution made by:
(a) Plato
(b) Cicero
(c) Aristotle
(d) Thomas Acquinas

3. Match the List I with List II and select the correct answer from the codes given below:

List I (Doctrine)
(A) Doctrine of Secularism
(B) Doctrine of Consent
(C) Doctrine of Individualism
(D) Doctrine of Freedom

List II (Thinker)
(i) Hobbes (ii) Rousseau
(iii) Machiavelli (iv) Locke

Codes:	A	B	C	D
(a)	(iii)	(ii)	(i)	(iv)
(b)	(iii)	(iv)	(i)	(ii)
(c)	(ii)	(iv)	(i)	(iii)
(d)	(iv)	(iii)	(ii)	(i)

4. Which one of the following pairs is not correctly matched?
(a) Idea of spiritualization of Politics—Mahatma Gandhi
(b) Concept of New Humanism—M.N. Roy
(c) Concept of Village Reorganization—J.P. Narayana
(d) Concept of spiritual determinism in history—B.R. Ambedkar

5. Who authored *Two Treatise on Civil Government*?
(a) Hobbes (b) Locke
(c) J.S. Mill (d) T.H. Green

6. Who among the following authors has written about 'Justice' based on 'Contracteuralism'?
(a) Lenin (b) Nozic
(c) Rawls (d) Rousseau

7. Which one of the following pairs is not correctly matched?
(a) Doctrine of Two Swords—John of Salisbury
(b) Theory of Distributive Justice—Rawls
(c) Idea of Contradictions—Mao
(d) Concept of New Humanism—Lenin

8. The ideology which has revolted against to prescriptive theory of politics is known as:
(a) Behaviouralism
(b) Post-behaviouralism
(c) Communitarianism
(d) Liberalism

9. 'The Government of the Church rests upon the consent of its members', this was upheld by:
(a) Renaissance
(b) Conciliar movement
(c) Age of Enlightenment
(d) Scholasticism

10. Given below are two statements, one is labelled as Assertion (A) and the other is labelled as Reason (R):
Assertion (A): The only rational governmental form for the present stage of historical development, Hegal says, is constitutional monarchy.
Reason (R): But for German temperament, monarchical absolutism alone is suitable.
In the context of the above two statements which one of the following is correct?
(a) Both (A) and (R) are true and (R) is the correct explanation of (A)
(b) Both (A) and (R) are true but (R) is not the correct explanation of (A)
(c) (A) is true but (R) is false
(d) (A) is false but (R) is true

11. The Chairman of the States Reorganisation Commission was:
(a) K.M. Panikkar
(b) Justice Fazal Ali
(c) H.N. Kunzru
(d) Justice Rajamannar

12. The first Indian Governor-General was:
(a) Rajendra Prasad
(b) Radhakrishnan
(c) C. Rajagopalachary
(d) Mavalankar

13. The Federal System of India is closer to the Federal System of:
(a) United States of America
(b) Canada
(c) Switzerland
(d) France

14. Which one of the following is not headed by the Prime Minister?
(a) National Development Council
(b) Union Council of Ministers
(c) Planning Commission
(d) Finance Commission

15. The Parliamentary system of India is not based on the principle of:
(a) Collective Responsibility
(b) Judicial Supremacy
(c) Separation of Powers
(d) Federalism

16. Under which Article(s) of the Constitution, the President of India could be impeached?
(a) Article 76
(b) Articles 56 and 61
(c) Article 75
(d) Article 79

17. Which of the following words were added to the Constitution of India through 42nd constitutional amendment?
(a) Democratic Federalism
(b) Secular and Socialist
(c) Indian Republic
(d) People of India

18. The duration of the Lok Sabha and the State Assemblies was increased from 5 to 6 years by:
(a) Forty-second Amendment
(b) Forty-fourth Amendment
(c) Forty-fifth Amendment
(d) Forty-sixth Amendment

19. The Ministers in the state could be prosecuted only with the approval of:
(a) Chief Minister
(b) Governor
(c) Council of Ministers
(d) Speaker of the Legislative Assembly

20. The Socially most advanced State in India is:
(a) Andhra Pradesh
(b) Punjab
(c) Kerala
(d) Rajasthan

21. "Who gets what, when and how" is the subject matter of politics. Who said this?
(a) Lasswell (b) Laski
(c) David Easton (d) Almond

22. The systems theory came to social sciences from:
(a) Biology through Anthropology and Sociology
(b) Physics through Mathematics and Economics
(c) Mathematics through Economics and Political Science
(d) Biology through Political Science and Sociology

23. The oldest second chamber in the world is:
(a) Rajya Sabha
(b) House of Lords
(c) US Senate
(d) Canadian Senate

24. According to Lucian Pye, the crises of political development are:
(i) Identity
(ii) Legitimacy
(iii) Urbanisation and Industrialisation
(iv) Participation
Which of these are correct?
(a) (i), (ii) and (iv) (b) (ii), (iii) and (iv)
(c) (i), (ii) and (iii) (d) (i), (iii) and (iv)

25. The important features of the western concept of constitutionalism are:
(i) Ideology
(ii) Rule of Law
(iii) Representative institutions
(iv) Strong public opinion
Which of these are correct?
(a) (i), (ii) and (iii) (b) (ii), (iii) and (iv)
(c) (i), (iii) and (iv) (d) (i), (ii) and (iv)

26. Who among the following believed that the governing elite rules by a mixture of force and cunning?
(a) Mosca (b) Pareto
(c) Mills (d) Michels

27. Which one of the following countries has a mix of parliamentary and presidential forms of government?
(a) India (b) U.S.A.
(c) United Kingdom (d) France

28. A simple three-fold classification of political parties into single party system two party system and multi party system has been made by:
(a) Duverger (b) La Palombara
(c) Jean Blondel (d) Alan Ball

29. Which one of the following countries has a separate constitution for each state?
(a) U.K. (b) U.S.A.
(c) France (d) India

30. Given below are two statements, one labelled as Assertion (A) and the other is labelled as Reason (R):
Assertion (A): Under Article 312 of the Indian Constitution, the Rajya Sabha

can create new All-India services in national interest.

Reason (R): The Rajya Sabha is better placed to define national interest.

In the context of the two statements, which one of the following is correct?

(a) Both (A) and (R) are true and (R) is the correct explanation of (A)
(b) Both (A) and (R) are true but (R) is not the correct explanation of (A)
(c) (A) is true but (R) is false
(d) (A) is false but (R) is true

31. The principle of balance of power aims at:
(a) Equilibrium (b) War
(c) Disequilibrium (d) Status quo-ante

32. 'Agenda for peace' proposal is associated with:
(a) League of Nations
(b) United Nations
(c) India
(d) Commonwealth of Nations

33. 'Objective laws of nature' is a principle of realism, enunciated by:
(a) E.H. Carr
(b) George F. Kennan
(c) Morgenthan
(d) Henry Kissinger

34. The Theory of 'Trading State' is enunciated by:
(a) Rosecrance (b) Adam Smith
(c) Robert Cox (d) Lenin

35. The meaning of realism revolves around power and:
(a) Security
(b) War
(c) Ideology
(d) National Interest

36. Idealism is based upon:
(a) Supremacy of Law
(b) Supremacy of Peace
(c) Supremacy of Reason
(d) Supremacy of Ethics

37. Given below are two statements, labelled as Assertion (A) and other as Reason (R). Choose the correct answer:

Assertion (A): 'Globalisation has undermined the relevance of nation state'.

Reason (R): No, Nation State is still relevant as nationalism continues to be a potent force.

Codes:
(a) Both (A) and (R) are true and (R) is the correct explanation of (A)
(b) Both (A) and (R) are true but (R) is not the correct explanation of (A)
(c) (A) is true and (R) is false
(d) (A) is false and (R) is true

38. Match the List I with List II and answer the correct match by using the codes given below:

List I
(A) P.V. Narasimha Rao
(B) Morarji Desai
(C) A.B. Vajapayee
(D) Rajiv Gandhi

List II
(i) Six-Nations disarmament conference
(ii) Pokhran-II
(iii) Look East policy
(iv) Genuine non-alignment

Codes:	A	B	C	D
(a)	(iv)	(iii)	(i)	(ii)
(b)	(ii)	(iv)	(iii)	(i)
(c)	(i)	(iii)	(ii)	(iv)
(d)	(iii)	(ii)	(iv)	(i)

39. Identify the correct chronological sequence of the following events:
(a) Teheran conference, Yalta conference, Potsdam conference, San Francisco peace treaty

(b) San Francisco peace treaty, Potsdam conference, Teheran conference, Yalta conference
(c) Yalta conference, Teheran conference, San Francisco peace treaty, Potsdam conference
(d) Potsdam conference, Yalta conference, San Francisco peace treaty, Teheran conference

40. Identify the correct chronological order of the following personalities, who held the office of the Secretary-General of the United Nations:
(a) Dag Hammerskjold, Tryque Lie, Uthant, Kurt Waldheim
(b) Tryque Lie, Uthant, Kurt Waldheim, Dag Hammerskjold
(c) Uthant, Kurt Waldheim, Dag Hammerskjold, Tryque Lie
(d) Tryque Lie, Dag Hammerskjold, Uthant, Kurt Waldheim

41. Public Administration as a discipline was born in:
(a) U.K. (b) U.S.A.
(c) France (d) India

42. The oldest approach to the study of Public Administration is:
(a) Legal Approach
(b) Philosophical Approach
(c) Historical Approach
(d) Behavioural Approach

43. Who among the following makes a clear distinction between public and private administration?
(a) Henri Fayol
(b) Mary P. Follet
(c) L. Urwick
(d) Paul H. Appleby

44. The first book on New Public Administration was edited by:
(a) Frank Marini
(b) D. Waldo
(c) James C. Charlesworth
(d) L.D. White

45. The Hawthorne experiments conducted by Elton Mayo and his colleagues gave rise to new thinking called:
(a) Scientific Management
(b) Classical Theory
(c) Bureaucratic Theory
(d) Human Relations Theory

46. Which one of the following is not the objective of Scientific Management?
(a) Informal group functioning
(b) Planning of daily work
(c) Standardization of working conditions
(d) Standardization of work methods

47. Who among the following classified staff into three types—general staff, technical staff and auxiliary staff?
(a) Pfiffner and Presthus
(b) L.D. White
(c) J.D. Mooney
(d) Albert Lepawsky

48. Superior-subordinate relationship through a number of levels of responsibility is called:
(a) Span of Control
(b) Hierarchy
(c) Delegation
(d) Unity of Command

49. In a democracy, a civil servant must be committed to:
(i) the execution of public policy
(ii) the goals of the Constitution
(iii) the common good
(iv) the ideology of the ruling party
Which of these are correct?
(a) (i), (ii) and (iii) (b) (i), (iii) and (iv)
(c) (ii), (iii) and (iv) (d) (i), (ii) and (iv)

50. Max Weber's three-fold classification of authority include:
(i) Hereditary authority
(ii) Traditional authority

(iii) Charismatic authority
(iv) Legal-Rational authority
Which of these are correct?
(a) (i), (ii) and (iii) (b) (ii), (iii) and (iv)
(c) (i), (iii) and (iv) (d) (i), (ii) and (iv)

ANSWERS

1. (b)	2. (c)	3. (b)	4. (a)	5. (b)
6. (c)	7. (d)	8. (a)	9. (b)	10. (b)
11. (b)	12. (c)	13. (a)	14. (d)	15. (c)
16. (b)	17. (b)	18. (b)	19. (b)	20. (c)
21. (a)	22. (c)	23. (c)	24. (c)	25. (a)
26. (b)	27. (d)	28. (d)	29. (b)	30. (b)
31. (d)	32. (b)	33. (c)	34. (a)	35. (c)
36. (d)	37. (b)	38. (c)	39. (a)	40. (d)
41. (b)	42. (b)	43. (b)	44. (b)	45. (d)
46. (b)	47. (d)	48. (b)	49. (d)	50. (d)

DECEMBER–2005

Note: This paper contains Fifty (50) objective type questions, each question carrying two (2) marks. All questions are compulsory.

PAPER–I

1. Team teaching has the potential to develop:
   (a) Competitive spirit
   (b) Cooperation
   (c) The habit of supplementing the teaching of each other
   (d) Highlighting the gaps in each other's teaching
2. Which of the following is the most important characteristic of Open Book Examination system?
   (a) Students become serious.
   (b) It improves attendance in the classroom.
   (c) It reduces examination anxiety amongst students.
   (d) It compels students to think.
3. Which of the following methods of teaching encourages the use of maximum senses?
   (a) Problem-solving method
   (b) Laboratory method
   (c) Self-study method
   (d) Team teaching method
4. Which of the following statement is correct?
   (a) Communicator should have fine senses
   (b) Communicator should have tolerance power
   (c) Communicator should be soft spoken
   (d) Communicator should have good personality
5. An effective teacher is one who can:
   (a) control the class
   (b) give more information in less time
   (c) motivate students to learn
   (d) correct the assignments carefully
6. One of the following is not a quality of researcher:
   (a) Unison with that of which he is in search
   (b) He must be of alert mind
   (c) Keenness in enquiry
   (d) His assertion to outstrip the evidence
7. A satisfactory statistical quantitative method should not possess one of the following qualities:
   (a) Appropriateness (b) Measurability
   (c) Comparability (d) Flexibility
8. Books and records are the primary sources of data in:
   (a) historical research
   (b) participatory research
   (c) clinical research
   (d) laboratory research
9. Which of the following statement is correct?
   (a) objectives should be pin-pointed
   (b) objectives can be written in statement or question form
   (c) another word for problem is variable
   (d) All the above
10. The important pre-requisites of a researcher in sciences, social sciences and humanities are:

(a) laboratory skills, records, supervisor, topic
(b) supervisor, topic, critical analysis, patience
(c) archives, supervisor, topic, flexibility in thinking
(d) topic, supervisor, good temperament, pre-conceived notions

Read the following passage and answer the questions 11 to 15:

Knowledge creation in many cases requires creativity and idea generation. This is especially important in generating alternative decision support solutions. Some people believe that an individual's creative ability stems primarily from personality traits such as inventiveness, independence, individuality, enthusiasm, and flexibility. However, several studies have found that creativity is not so much a function of individual traits as was once believed, and that individual creativity can be learned and improved. This understanding has led innovative companies to recognise that the key to fostering creativity may be the development of an idea-nurturing work environment. Idea-generation methods and techniques, to be used by individuals or in groups, are consequently being developed. Manual methods for supporting idea generation, such as brainstorming in a group, can be very successful in certain situations. However, in other situations, such an approach is either not economically feasible or not possible. For example, manual methods in group creativity sessions will not work or will not be effective when : (1) there is no time to conduct a proper idea-generation session; (2) there is a poor facilitator (or no facilitator at all); (3) it is too expensive to conduct an idea-generation session; (4) the subject matter is too sensitive for a face-to-face session; or (5) there are not enough participants, the mix of participants is not optimal, or there is no climate for idea generation. In such cases, computerised idea-generation methods have been tried, with frequent success.

Idea-generation software is designed to help stimulate a single user or a group to produce new ideas, options and choices. The user does all the work, but the software encourages and pushes, something like a personal trainer. Although idea-generation software is still relatively new, there are several packages on the market. Various approaches are used by idea-generating software to increase the flow of ideas to the user. Idea Fisher, for example, has an associate lexicon of the English language that cross-references words and phrases. These associative links, based on analogies and metaphors, make it easy for the user to be fed words related to a given theme. Some software packages use questions to prompt the user towards new, unexplored patterns of thought. This helps users to break out of cyclical thinking patterns, conquer mental blocks, or deal with bouts of procrastination.

11. The author, in this passage has focussed on
(a) knowledge creation
(b) idea-generation
(c) creativity
(d) individual traits

12. Fostering creativity needs an environment of
(a) decision support systems
(b) idea-nurturing
(c) decision support solutions
(d) alternative individual factors

13. Manual methods for the support of idea-generation, in certain occasions,
(a) are alternatively effective
(b) can be less expensive
(c) do not need a facilitator
(d) require a mix of optimal participants

14. Idea-generation software works as if it is a:
(a) stimulant
(b) knowledge package
(c) user-friendly trainer
(d) climate creator

15. Mental blocks, bouts of procrastination and cyclical thinking patterns can be won when:
(a) innovative companies employ electronic thinking methods
(b) idea-generation software prompts questions
(c) manual methods are removed
(d) individuals acquire a neutral attitude towards the software

16. Level C of the effectiveness of communication is defined as:
(a) channel noise
(b) semantic noise
(c) psychological noise
(d) source noise

17. Recording a television programme on a VCR is an example of:
(a) time-shifting
(b) content reference
(c) mechanical clarity
(d) media synchronisation

18. A good communicator is the one who offers to his audience:
(a) plentiful of information
(b) a good amount of statistics
(c) concise proof
(d) repetition of facts

19. The largest number of newspapers in India is published from the state of:
(a) Kerala (b) Maharashtra
(c) West Bengal (d) Uttar Pradesh

20. Insert the missing number:
8 24 1 2 ? 18 54
(a) 26 (b) 24
(c) 36 (d) 32

21. January 1, 1995 was Sunday. What day of the week lies on January 1, 1996?
(a) Sunday (b) Monday
(c) Saturday (d) None of these

22. The sum of a positive number and its reciprocal is twice the difference of the number and its reciprocal. The number is:
(a) $\sqrt{2}$ (b) $\frac{1}{\sqrt{2}}$
(c) $\sqrt{3}$ (d) $\frac{1}{\sqrt{3}}$

23. In a certain code, ROUNDS is written as RONUDS. How will PLEASE will be written in the same code:
(a) LPAESE (b) PLAESE
(c) LPAEES (d) PLASEE

24. At what time between 5.30 and 6.00 will the hands of a clock be at right angles?
(a) $43\frac{5}{11}$ min. past 5
(b) $43\frac{7}{11}$ min. past 5
(c) 40 min. past 5
(d) 45 min past 5

25. **Statements:** I All students are ambitious
II All ambitious persons are hard-working
Conclusions: (i) All students are hard-working
(ii) All hardly working people are not ambitious

Which of the following is correct?
(a) Only (i) is correct
(b) Only (ii) is correct
(c) Both (i) and (ii) are correct
(d) Neither (i) nor (ii) is correct

26. **Statement:** Most students are intelligent
Conclusions: (i) Some students are intelligent
(ii) All students are not intelligent

Which of the following is implied?
(a) Only (i) is implied
(b) Only (ii) is implied
(c) Both (i) and (ii) are implied
(d) Neither (i) nor (ii) is implied

27. **Statement:** Most labourers are poor
Conclusions: (i) Some labourers are poor
(ii) All labourers are not poor
Which of the following is implied?
(a) Only (i) is implied
(b) Only (ii) is implied
(c) Both (i) and (ii) are implied
(d) Neither (i) nor (ii) is implied

28. Line access and avoidance of collision are the main functions of:
(a) the CPU
(b) the monitor
(c) network protocols
(d) wide area networks

29. In the hypermedia database, information bits are stored in the form of:
(a) Signals (b) Cubes
(c) Nodes (d) Symbols

30. Communications bandwidth that has the highest capacity and is used by microwave, cable and fibre optics lines is known as:
(a) hyper-link (b) broadband
(c) bus width (d) carrier wave

31. An electronic bill board that has a short text or graphical advertising message is referred to as:
(a) Bulletin (b) Strap
(c) Bridge line (d) Banner

32. Which of the following is not the characteristic of a computer?
(a) computer is an electrical machine
(b) computer cannot think at its own
(c) computer processes information error free
(d) computer can hold data for any length of time

33. Bitumen is obtained from:
(a) Forests and plants
(b) Kerosene oil
(c) Crude oil
(d) underground mines

34. Malaria is caused by:
(a) bacterial infection
(b) viral infection
(c) parasitic infection
(d) fungal infection

35. The cloudy nights are warmer compared to clear nights (without clouds) during winter days. This is because:
(a) clouds radiate heat towards the earth
(b) clouds prevent cold wave from the sky, descend on earth
(c) clouds prevent escaping of the heat radiation from the earth
(d) clouds being at great height from earth absorb heat from the sun and send towards the earth

36. Largest soil group of India is:
(a) Red soil (b) Black soil
(c) Sandy soil (d) Mountain soil

37. Main pollutant of the Indian coastal water is:
(a) oil spill
(b) municipal sewage
(c) industrial effluents
(d) aerosols

38. Human ear is most sensitive to noise in the following frequency ranges:
(a) 1-2 kHz (b) 100-500 Hz
(c) 10-12 kHz (d) 13-16 kHz

39. Which species of chromium is toxic in water:

(a) Cr + 2 (b) Cr + 3
(c) Cr + 6 (d) Cr is non-toxic element

40. Match List I (Dams) with List II (River) in the following:

List I (Dams)	List II (River)
(A) Bhakra	(i) Krishna
(B) Nagarjunasagar	(ii) Damodar
(C) Panchet	(iii) Sutlej
(D) Hirakud	(iv) Bhagirathi
(E) Tehri	(v) Mahanadi

Codes:	A	B	C	D	E
(a)	v	iii	iv	ii	i
(b)	iii	i	ii	v	iv
(c)	i	ii	iv	iii	v
(d)	ii	iii	iv	i	v

41. A negative reaction to a mediated communication is described as:
(a) flak
(b) fragmented feedback
(c) passive response
(d) non-conformity

42. The launch of satellite channel by IGNOU on 26th January 2003 for technological education for the growth and development of distance education is:
(a) Eklavya channel
(b) Gyandarshan channel
(c) Rajrishi channel
(d) None of these

43. Match List I with List II and select the correct answer from the code given below:

List I (Institutions)
(A) The Indian Council of Historical Reasearch (ICHR)
(B) The Indian Institute of Advanced Studies (IIAS)
(C) The Indian Council of Philosophical Research (ICPR)
(D) The Central Institute of Coastal Engineering for fisheries

List II (Locations)
(i) Shimla (ii) New Delhi
(iii) Bangalore (iv) Lucknow

Codes:	A	B	C	D
(a)	ii	i	iv	iii
(b)	i	ii	iii	iv
(c)	ii	iv	i	iii
(d)	iv	iii	ii	i

44. Which of the following is not a Fundamental Right?
(a) Right to equality
(b) Right against exploitation
(c) Right to freedom of speech and expression
(d) Right of free compulsory education of all children upto the age of 14

45. The Lok Sabha can be dissolved before the expiry of its normal five year term by:
(a) The Prime Minister
(b) The Speaker of Lok Sabha
(c) The President on the recommendation of the Prime Minister
(d) None of the above

Study the following graph carefully and answer Q.No. 46 to 50 given below it:

EXPORT OF TINS

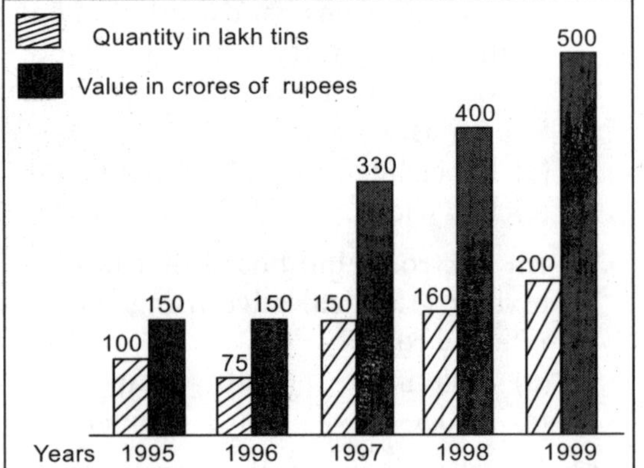

46. In which year the value per tin was minimum?
(a) 1995 (b) 1996
(c) 1998 (d) 1999

47. What was the difference between the tins exported in 1997 and 1998?
(a) 10 (b) 1000
(c) 100000 (d) 1000000

48. What was the approximate percentage increase in export value from 1995 to 1999?
(a) 350 (b) 330.3
(c) 433.3 (d) None of these

49. What was the percentage drop in export quantity from 1995 to 1996?
(a) 75 (b) 50
(c) 25 (d) None of these

50. If in 1998, the tins were exported at the same rate per tin as that in 1997, what would be the value (in crores of rupees) of export in 1998?
(a) 400 (b) 375
(c) 352 (d) 330

ANSWERS

1. (c)	2. (d)	3. (b)	4. (a)	5. (c)
6. (d)	7. (d)	8. (a)	9. (a)	10. (b)
11. (a)	12. (b)	13. (a)	14. (a)	15. (b)
16. (a)	17. (d)	18. (a)	19. (d)	20. (c)
21. (b)	22. (d)	23. (b)	24. (b)	25. (c)
26. (b)	27. (b)	28. (c)	29. (a)	30. (b)
31. (b)	32. (a)	33. (d)	34. (c)	35. (c)
36. (a)	37. (c)	38. (d)	39. (c)	40. (b)
41. (c)	42. (a)	43. (a)	44. (d)	45. (c)
46. (a)	47. (a)	48. (d)	49. (c)	50. (c)

PAPER–II

1. How many elements of the state are there in Kautilya's Theory?
(a) Eleven (b) Seven
(c) Ten (d) Five

2. Which one 'right' in the follwing includes two other rights according to Locke?
(a) Right to Property
(b) Right to Life
(c) Right to Liberty
(d) Right to Equality

3. Who among the following propounded the concept of 'organic intellectuals'?
(a) Rawls (b) Nozick
(c) Gramsci (d) Habermas

4. Who among the following wrote 'Life Divine':
(a) Gandhi (b) Savarkar
(c) Aurobindo (d) M.N. Roy

5. Given below are two statements, one labelled as Assertion (A) and the other labelled as Reason (R)
Assertion (A): Behaviouralism is value free.
Reason (R): Behaviouralism is intuitive.
In the context of the two statements which one of the following is correct?
(a) Both A and R are true and R is the correct explanation of A
(b) Both A and R are true but R is not the correct explanation of A
(c) A is true but R is false
(d) A is false but R is true

6. Given below are two statements, one labelled as Assertion (A) and the other labelled as Reason (R).
Assertion (A): Liberty without equality has no meaning.
Reason (R): Absolute liberty is not possible.
In the context of the two statements which one of the following is correct?
(a) Both A and R are true and R is the correct explanation of A
(b) Both A and R are true but R is not the correct explanation of A
(c) A is true but R is false
(d) A is false but R is true

7. Arrange the following books in order in which they appeared. Use the code given below:
   i. *Das Capital*
   ii. *The Laws*
   iii. *A Discourse on the Origin of Inequality*
   iv. *New Humanism: A Manifesto*

   Codes:
   (a) ii, iii, i, iv (b) i, ii, iii, iv
   (c) iii, i, ii, iv (d) iv, iii, ii, i

8. Arrange the following events/concepts in order in which they appeared. Use the code given below:
   i. Glorious Revolution
   ii. Proletariat Revolution
   iii. Total Revolution
   iv. Behavioural Revolution

   Codes:
   (a) ii, i, iii, iv (b) iii, iv, ii, i
   (c) iv, iii, i, ii (d) i, ii, iv, iii

9. Match List I with List II and select the correct answer from the codes given below:

List I (Thinkers)	**List II (Ideas)**
(A) Rawls	i. Hegemony
(B) Locke	ii. Distributive justice
(C) Gramsci	iii. Sovereignty
(D) Bodin	iv. Civil Society
	v. Separation of powers

Codes:	**A**	**B**	**C**	**D**
(a)	i	ii	iii	iv
(b)	ii	v	iv	iii
(c)	iii	i	iv	ii
(d)	ii	iv	i	iii

10. Match List I with List II and select the correct answer from the codes given below:

List I (Authors)	**List II (Books)**
(A) Gandhi	i. *Philosophy of Right*
(B) Aurobindo	ii. *The Statesman*
(C) Plato	iii. *India of my Dream*
(D) Hegel	iv. *Discovery of India*
	v. *The Human Cycle*

Codes:	**A**	**B**	**C**	**D**
(a)	i	ii	iv	iii
(b)	i	iii	ii	iv
(c)	iii	v	i	ii
(d)	iii	v	ii	i

11. Who among the following is considered to be the founder of comparative study of government?
    (a) Almond (b) Finer
    (c) Aristotle (d) Pye

12. When did Comparative Politics emerge as an autonomous discipline?
    (a) In the thirties of the 20th century
    (b) In the fifties of the 20th century
    (c) In the sixties of the 20th century
    (d) In the seventies of the 20th century

13. Which one of the following is considered to be a basic feature of a federal government?
    (a) Separation of Powers
    (b) Cabinet Dictatorship
    (c) Collective Responsibility
    (d) Division of powers between the centre and the units

14. Identify the concept associated with Political Communication:
    (a) Developmental Loop
    (b) Over-loading
    (c) Input-Function
    (d) Gate-Keepers

15. The essential feature of authority is:
    (a) Force (b) Legitimacy
    (c) Persuasion (d) Influence

16. Given below are two statements, one labelled as Assertion (A) and the other labelled as Reason (R)

    Assertion (A): Democracy has not succeeded in most of the developing countries.

Reason (R): Participant political culture is lacking in developing countries.

In the context of the two statements which one of the following is correct?

(a) Both A and R are true and R is the correct explanation of A
(b) Both A and R are true but R is not the correct explanation of A
(c) A is true but R is false
(d) A is false but R is true

17. Given below are two statements, one labelled as Assertion (A) and the other labelled as Reason (R):

Assertion (A): The American Senate is the strongest second chamber of the Legislature in the world.

Reason (R): The American Senate has equal powers as the House of Representatives.

In the context of the two statements which one of the following is correct?

(a) Both A and R are true and R is the correct explanation of A
(b) Both A and R are true but R is not the correct explanation of A
(c) A is true and R is false
(d) A is false and R is true

18. Arrange the following ideas/concepts in order in which they appeared. Use the code given below:

I. Feed-back loop
II. Rule of Law
III. Due Process of Law
IV. Democratic centralism

Codes:

(a) I, II, IV, III (b) III, II, IV, I
(c) II, IV, III, I (d) II, IV, I, III

19. Arrange the following books in order in which they appeared. Use the code given below:

I. 'The Politics of Developing Area'
II. 'Modern Politics and Government'
III. 'The Political Process'
IV. 'Aspects of Political Development'

Codes:

(a) IV, III, I, II (b) I, II, III, IV
(c) II, I, III, IV (d) III, II, I, IV

20. Match List I with List II and select the correct answer from the codes given below:

List I (Political Systems)

(A) Federal, Presidential, Republic
(B) Federal, Parliamentary, Republic
(C) Unitary, Parliamentary, Monarchy
(D) Presidential cum Parlimentary, Republic

List II (Countries)

i. India ii. U.K.
iii. Germany iv. U.S.A.
v. France

Codes:	A	B	C	D
(a)	iv	i	ii	v
(b)	iv	i	ii	iii
(c)	v	iv	iii	ii
(d)	v	ii	iii	iv

21. At which session, the Indian National Congress passed the resolution for Poorna Swaraj?

(a) Calcutta (b) Bombay
(c) Lahore (d) Madras

22. Doctrine of the Basic Structure of the Indian Constitution was enunciated by the Supreme Court in:

(a) Minerva Mills case
(b) Keshavanand Bharti case
(c) Golaknath case
(d) Shankari Prasad case

23. The function of Pro-Tem Speaker is:

(a) To conduct the proceedings in the absence of speaker.
(b) Officiate as speaker when speaker is unlikely to be elected.
(c) Swear in members and hold charge till a regular speaker is elected.
(d) Check if the election certificates of the members are in order.

24. Which of the following bodies is presided over by a non-member?
    (a) Lok Sabha
    (b) Rajya Sabha
    (c) Legislative Assembly
    (d) Legislative Council

25. Match List I with List II and select the correct answer from the code given below:

    List I

    (A) Article 14 (B) Article 39
    (C) Article 368 (D) Article 356

    List II

    i. Adequate means of livelihood
    ii. Right to equality
    iii. President's rule in a state
    iv. Amending procedure of the Indian Constitution

Codes:	A	B	C	D
(a)	ii	i	iii	iv
(b)	ii	i	iv	iii
(c)	i	ii	iv	iii
(d)	iv	iii	i	ii

26. Match List I of Functionaries with List II of Oath and select the correct answer from the codes given below:

    List I (Functionaries)

    (A) President of India
    (B) Judges of the Supreme Court
    (C) Members of Parliament
    (D) Ministers of the Union

    List II (Oath)

    i. Secrecy of office
    ii. Faithful discharge of duties
    iii. Faith and allegiance to the Constitution of India
    iv. Upholding the Constitution and the law

Codes:	A	B	C	D
(a)	i	ii	iv	iii
(b)	iv	iii	ii	i
(c)	iii	iv	ii	i
(d)	iii	iv	i	ii

27. Given below are two statements, one labelled as Assertion (A) and the other labelled as Reason (R). Choose the correct answer from the codes given below:

    Assertion (A): Rule of law finds expression in numerous Articles of the Indian Constitution.

    Reason (R): Rule of law does not form the part of the basic structure.

    Codes:

    (a) Both (A) and (R) are true and (R) is the correct explanation of (A)
    (b) Both (A) and (R) are but true (R) is not the correct explanation of (A)
    (c) (A) is true but (R) is false
    (d) (A) is false but (R) is true

28. Given below are two statements, one labelled as Assertion (A) and the other labelled as Reason (R). Choose the correct answer from the codes given below:

    Assertion (A): Directive Principles are not justiceable.

    Reason (R): Judicial pronouncements have made them part of the basic structure.

    Codes:

    (a) Both (A) and (R) are and true (R) is the correct explanation of (A)
    (b) Both (A) and (R) are true but (R) is not the correct explanation of (A)
    (c) (A) is true but (R) is false
    (d) (A) is false but (R) is true

29. Choose the correct chronological order of the concepts used in the Preamble of the Indian Constitution from the codes given below:

    i. Equality ii. Liberty
    iii. Fraternity iv. Justice

    Codes:

    (a) iv, iii, ii, i (b) iv, i, ii, iii
    (c) iv, ii, i, iii (d) ii, i, iii, iv

30. Identify the correct chronological order in which the following were elected as President of India:
    i. Fakhruddin Ali Ahmed
    ii. V.V. Giri
    iii. Zakir Hussain
    iv. Sanjeeva Reddy
    Codes:
    (a) ii, i, iii, iv (b) i, iii, iv, ii
    (c) iii, ii, i, iv (d) iv, ii, iii, i

31. Which one of the following organisational principles promotes motivation?
    (a) Hierarchy (b) Gangplank
    (c) Centralisation (d) Division of work

32. The Pendleton Act of 1883 was a major step towards reforms in civil services of:
    (a) U.K. (b) U.S.A.
    (c) France (d) Germany

33. According to Max Weber, some of the characteristics of fully developed bureaucratic form of organization are:
    i. Hiererchical order
    ii. Officials holding office by election
    iii. Promotion is by achivement alone
    iv. Selection on the basic of objective qualification
    Select the right answer from the codes given below:
    Codes:
    (a) i and ii (b) i and iii
    (c) ii and iv (d) i and iv

34. Identify the scholar who has remarked that 'The bureaucracy is a circle from which no one can escape, its hierarchy is a hiearchy of knowledge':
    (a) Frederick W. Riggs
    (b) Max Weber
    (c) Karl Marx
    (d) Morstein Marx

35. Identify the concept that is not associated with the 'Sala' Model of Riggs:
    (a) Bazar-canteen (b) Poly-normative
    (c) Clect (d) Industria

36. SAIL is:
    (a) A public corporation
    (b) A Departmental undertaking
    (c) A Holding company
    (d) A Private Limited company

37. Match List I and List II by using the codes given below:
    List I
    (A) W.F. Willoughby
    (B) L.D. White
    (C) L. Urwick
    (D) Dwight Waldo
    List II
    i. *Introduction to the Study of Public Administration*
    ii. *Principles of Public Administration*
    iii. *Idias and Issues in Public Administration*
    iv. *The Elements of Administration*

Codes:	A	B	C	D
(a)	iv	iii	ii	i
(b)	i	ii	iii	iv
(c)	iv	i	ii	iii
(d)	ii	i	iv	iii

38. Match List I and List II by using the codes given below:
    List I
    (A) Habeas Corpus (B) Mandamus
    (C) Certiorari (D) Quo Warranto
    List II
    i. By what warrant of authority
    ii. Quashing decision beyond legal
    iii. Command to perform
    iv. Produce the body of a person

Codes:	A	B	C	D
(a)	iii	iv	ii	i
(b)	iv	iii	ii	i
(c)	ii	i	iii	iv
(d)	i	ii	iv	iii

39. Arrange the following committees in order in which they appeared. Use the code given below:
   i. G.S. Bajpai committee
   ii. Santhanam committee
   iii. Ashok Mehta committee
   iv. Kothari committee

   Codes:
   (a) iv, i, ii, iii (b) iii, ii, i, iv
   (c) ii, iv, i, iii (d) i, ii, iii, iv

40. Given below are two statements, one labelled as Assertion (A) and the other labelled as Reason (R). Choose the correct answer:

   Assertion (A): Independence and Impartial character of Public Service Commission has been well ensured in the Constitution of India.

   Reason (R): The Consistution is the best only device to ensure integrity, and impartiality of the members of Public Service Commission.

   In the context of two statements which one of the following is correct?

   Codes:
   (a) Both (A) and (R) are true and (R) is the correct explanation of (A)
   (b) Both (A) and (R) are true but (R) is not a correct explanation of (A)
   (c) (A) is true but (R) is false
   (d) (A) is false but (R) is true

41. One of the following is the exponent of neo-realism:
   (a) Robert Cox
   (b) Fred Halliday
   (c) John Mearsheimer
   (d) David Campbell

42. The concept of circular error probability is associated with:
   (a) Chemical weapons
   (b) Nuclear weapons
   (c) Biological weapon
   (d) Conventional weapons

43. The primary explanation of state behaviour in neo-realism is the structure of:
   (a) International organisation
   (b) Nation state system
   (c) Non-state actors
   (d) Civil society

44. 'Agenda for peace' was proposed by:
   (a) Willy Brandt
   (b) Butros Butros Ghali
   (c) Kofi Annan
   (d) Kurt Waldheim

45. The SAARC Conference 2004 at Islamabad agreed upon the creation of:
   (a) Free Trade area in South Asia
   (b) United States of South Asia
   (c) Economic union of South Asia
   (d) Regional trading block

46. Given below are two statements, one labelled as Assertion (A) and the other labelled as Reason (R). Choose the correct answer from the codes given below:

   Assertion (A): Efforts at disarmament stop at arms control.

   Reason (R): With out arms states are vulnerable.

   Codes:
   (a) Both (A) and (R) are true and (R) is the correct explanation of (A)
   (b) Both (A) and (R) are true but (R) is not the correct explanation of (A)
   (c) (A) is true but (R) is false
   (d) (A) is false but (R) is true

47. Given below are two statements, one labelled as Assertion (A) and the other labelled as Reason (R). Choose the correct answer from the codes given below:

   Assertion (A): Krushchev proposed the principle of peaceful co-existence.

   Reason (R): Nuclear war is unwinnable

Codes:

(a) Both (A) and (R) are true and (R) is the correct explanation of (A)
(b) Both (A) and (R) are true but (R) is not the correct explanation of (A)
(c) (A) is true but (R) is false
(d) (A) is false but (R) is true

48. Identify the correct chronological order of the following regional organisations.

i. ASEAN	ii. OPEC
iii. APEC	iv. SAARC

Codes:

(a) i, iii, ii, iv	(b) iii, ii, iv, i
(c) ii, i, iv, iii	(d) iv, ii, iii, i

49. Match List I with List II and select the correct answer from the codes given below:

List I
(A) P.V. Narasimha Rao
(B) Morarji Desai
(C) A.B. Vajpayee
(D) Rajiv Gandhi

List II
i. Six-nation disarmament initiative
ii. Pokharan II
iii. Look East Policy
iv. Genuine non-alignment

Codes:	A	B	C	D
(a)	iii	i	iv	ii
(b)	iv	ii	i	iii
(c)	iii	iv	ii	i
(d)	ii	iii	iv	i

50. Match List I with List II and select the correct answer from the codes given below:

List I
(a) Karl Von Clansewitz
(b) Harold Mackinder
(c) Kenneth Waltz
(d) Thomos Schelling

List II
i. Heartland theory
ii. Conflict escalation
iii. War is the continuation action of politics by other means.
iv. Structured realism

Codes:	A	B	C	D
(a)	iii	i	iv	ii
(b)	ii	iii	iv	i
(c)	iii	iv	i	ii
(d)	iv	iii	ii	i

ANSWERS

1. (b)	2. (d)	3. (c)	4. (c)	5. (b)
6. (b)	7. (a)	8. (a)	9. (d)	10. (d)
11. (c)	12. (a)	13. (d)	14. (d)	15. (c)
16. (b)	17. (b)	18. (b)	19. (b)	20. (b)
21. (c)	22. (b)	23. (a)	24. (b)	25. (b)
26. (d)	27. (b)	28. (b)	29. (c)	30. (c)
31. (d)	32. (b)	33. (d)	34. (c)	35. (c)
36. (a)	37. (b)	38. (b)	39. (c)	40. (b)
41. (c)	42. (d)	43. (a)	44. (b)	45. (c)
46. (c)	47. (b)	48. (c)	49. (b)	50. (a)

JUNE–2005

Note: This paper contains fifty (50) objective type questions, each question carrying two (2) marks. All questions are compulsory.

PAPER–II

1. The central idea in Plato's *Republic* is:
   (a) Liberty (b) Equality
   (c) Harmony (d) Justice

2. Who, among the following, defined Liberty as 'a positive power or capacity of doing or enjoying something worth doing or enjoying'?
   (a) Bentham (b) Mill
   (c) Green (d) Barker

3. "The very essence of democracy is that a free person represents all the varied interests which compose the nation. It is true that it does not exclude and should not exclude special representation of special interests, but such representation is not its test".
   This statement was made by:
   (a) B.R. Ambedkar
   (b) M.K. Gandhi
   (c) J.L. Nehru
   (d) Jay Prakash Narain

4. The view that political theory is in a 'state of decline' was strongly opposed by:
   (a) David Easton (b) Cobban
   (c) Isaiah Berlin (d) Germino

5. Given below are two statements, one labelled as Assertion (A) and the other labelled as Reason (R):
   Assertion (A): Imperialism is the highest stage of capitalism.
   Reason (R): Imperialism leads to nationalist movements.
   In the context of the two statements which one of the following is correct?
   (a) Both (A) and (R) are true and (R) is the correct explanation of (A)
   (b) Both (A) and (R) are true, but (R) is not the correct explanation of (A)
   (c) (A) is true but (R) is false
   (d) (A) is false but (R) is true

6. Given below are two statements, one labelled as Assertion (A) and the other labelled as Reason (R).
   Assertion (A): It is better to be a Socrates dissatisfied than a fool satisfied.
   Reason (R): Quality of pleasure is no less important than quantity.
   In the context of the two statements, which one of the following is correct?
   (a) Both (A) and (R) are true and (R) is the correct explanation of (A)
   (b) Both (A) and (R) are true, but R is not the correct explanation of (A)
   (c) (A) is true but (R) is false
   (d) (A) is false but (R) is true

7. Arrange the following books in order in which they appeared. Use the code given below:
   I. 'The Prince'
   II. 'Leviathan'
   III. 'On Liberty'
   IV. 'A Theory of Justice'
   Codes:
   (a) I, III, IV, II (b) I, II, III, IV
   (c) II, I, IV, III (d) III, IV, I, II

8. Arrange the following concepts in order in which they appeared. Use the code given below:
   I. Surplus Value
   II. Mandal Theory of International Relations
   III. General Will
   IV. One-Dimensional Man

   Codes:
   (a) I, II, III, IV (b) III, II, IV, I
   (c) II, III, I, IV (d) IV, I, II, IIII

9. Match List I with List II and select the correct answer from the codes given below:

   List I (Ideas)
   (A) 'Forced to be free'
   (B) 'Base-superstructure'
   (C) 'Libertarianism'
   (D) 'Greatest happiness of the greatest number'

   List II (Thinkers)
   (i) Bentham (ii) J.S. Mill
   (iii) Rousseau (iv) Nozic
   (v) Marx

Codes:	A	B	C	D
(a)	(i)	(v)	(iv)	(ii)
(b)	(iii)	(v)	(iv)	(i)
(c)	(iii)	(i)	(iv)	(ii)
(d)	(ii)	(iii)	(i)	(iv)

10. Match List I with List II and select the correct answer from the codes given below:

    List I (Books)
    (A) *Human Nature in Politics*
    (B) *Modern Political Analysis*
    (C) *Contemporary Political Analysis*
    (D) *Political Theory: The Foundations of Twentieth Century Political Thought*

    List II (Authors)
    (i) Charlesworth (ii) David Easton
    (iii) Arnold Brecht (iv) Graham Wallas
    (v) Robert Dahl

Codes:	A	B	C	D
(a)	(iv)	(v)	(i)	(iii)
(b)	(iv)	(ii)	(i)	(iii)
(c)	(i)	(ii)	(iii)	(iv)
(d)	(ii)	(i)	(v)	(iv)

11. Which of the following approaches falls within traditional approach?
    (a) Marxist
    (b) Structural-Functional
    (c) Juristic
    (d) Systems

12. Which one of the following is not an element of Political Development?
    (a) Equality (b) Differentiation
    (c) Property (d) Capacity

13. Pareto is associated with:
    (a) Organizational theory of Elite
    (b) Economic theory of Elite
    (c) Psychological theory of Elite
    (d) Pluralist theory of Elite

14. 'Contradiction' as the cause of revolution is associated with:
    (a) Psychological theory of Revolution
    (b) Marxist theory of Revolution
    (c) Maoist theory of Revolution
    (d) Debray's theory of Revolution

15. Given below are two statements, one labelled as Assertion (A) and the other labelled as Reason (R).

    Assertion (A): The essential feature of constitutionalism is limited government.

    Reason (R): Government is limited by interest groups.

    In the context of the two statements which one of the following is correct?
    (a) Both (A) and (R) are true and (R) is the correct explanation of (A)
    (b) Both (A) and (R) are true, but (R) is not the correct explanation of (A)
    (c) (A) is true but (R) is false
    (d) (A) is false but (R) is true

16. Given below are two statements, one labelled as Assertion (A) and the other labelled as Reason (R).
    Assertion (A): U.K. has a plural executive.
    Reason (R): Head of state is different from Head of the government in U.K. In the context of the two statements which one of the following is correct?
    (a) Both (A) and (R) are true and (R) is the correct explanation of (A)
    (b) Both (A) and (R) are true, but (R) is not the correct explanation of (A)
    (c) (A) is true but (R) is false
    (d) (A) is false but (R) is true

17. Arrange the following ideas/concepts in order in which they appeared. Use the code given below.
    I. Class—in itself and class—for itself
    II. Encoding
    III. Circulation of Elites
    IV. Perestroika
    Codes:
    (a) I, II, III, IV (b) I, III, II, IV
    (c) II, I, III, IV (d) IV, III, II, I

18. Arrange the following books in order in which they appeared. Use the code given below.
    I. *Public Opinion and American Democracy*
    II. *Modern Democracies*
    III. *Fedral Government* (K.C. Wheare)
    IV. *Comparative Government* (Finer)
    Codes:
    (a) I, II, III, IV (b) III, II, IV, I
    (c) II, IV, I, III (d) II, IV, III, I

19. Match List I with List II and select the correct answer from the codes given below:
    List I
    (A) Political Development
    (B) Political Culture
    (C) Politics of Modernization
    (D) Political Decay
    List II
    (i) Huntington (ii) Apter
    (iii) Almond (iv) Verba
    (v) Riggs

Codes:	A	B	C	D
(a)	(iii)	(iv)	(i)	(ii)
(b)	(iv)	(iii)	(ii)	(i)
(c)	(ii)	(iii)	(i)	(v)
(d)	(iii)	(iv)	(ii)	(i)

20. Match List I with List II and select the correct answer from the codes given below:
    List I (Scholars)
    (A) Pareto (B) Lenin
    (C) Green (D) Eckstein
    List II (Concepts)
    (i) Pluralist theory of democracy
    (ii) Idealist theory of democracy
    (iii) Greek theory of democracy
    (iv) Elitist theory of democracy
    (v) Marxian theory of democracy

Codes:	A	B	C	D
(a)	(iv)	(iii)	(ii)	(i)
(b)	(iv)	(v)	(ii)	(i)
(c)	(v)	(iv)	(iii)	(ii)
(d)	(iii)	(iv)	(i)	(ii)

21. The author of *An Introduction to the Indian Constitution* is:
    (a) A.N. Palkhiwale
    (b) B. Shiva Rao
    (c) Dr. B.R. Ambedkar
    (d) D.D. Basu

22. In the context of State autonomy documents, identify the correct order from the codes given below:
    I. Akali Government Memorandum to Sarkaria Commission
    II. Rajamannar Committee Report
    III. Srinagar Conclave Resolutions
    IV. West Bengal Government Memorandum

Codes:

(a) II, III, IV, I (b) IV, II, III, I
(c) II, IV, III, I (d) II, IV, I, III

23. Given below are two statements, one labelled as Assertion (A) and the other labelled as Reason (R). Choose the correct answer from the codes given below:

Assertion (A): Equality before law is not applicable to the President of India.

Reason (R): The President of India enjoys special privileges under the Constitution of India.

Codes:

(a) Both (A) and (R) are true and (R) is the correct explanation of (A)
(b) Both (A) and (R) are true, but (R) is not the correct explanation of (A)
(c) (A) is true but (R) is false
(d) (A) is false but (R) is true

24. Given below are two statements, one labelled as Assertion (A) and the other labelled as Reason (R). Choose the correct answer from the codes given below:

Assertion (A): Indian Constitution is federal in name only.

Reason (R): Federalising process weakens the union and strengthens the states.

(a) Both (A) and (R) are true and (R) is the correct explanation of (A)
(b) Both (A) and (R) are true, but (R) is not the correct explanation of (A)
(c) (A) is false but (R) is true
(d) (A) is true but (R) is false

25. Match List I with List II and select the correct answer from the codes given below:

List I

(A) Government of India Act 1935
(B) Constitution of Britain
(C) Constitution of USA
(D) Constitution of Ireland

List II

(i) Rule of Law
(ii) Federal Scheme
(iii) Directive Principles of State Policy
(iv) Independence of Judiciary

Codes:	**A**	**B**	**C**	**D**
(a)	(ii)	(i)	(iii)	(iv)
(b)	(ii)	(i)	(iv)	(iii)
(c)	(ii)	(iv)	(iii)	(i)
(d)	(iv)	(iii)	(ii)	(i)

26. Match List I of states with List II of present leaders and select the correct answer from the codes given below:

List I

(A) Maharashtra (B) Uttar Pradesh
(C) Haryana (D) Punjab

List II

(i) Mahinder Singh Tikait
(ii) Ajmer Singh Lakhowal
(iii) Sharad Joshi
(iv) Ghasi Ram Nain

Codes:	**A**	**B**	**C**	**D**
(a)	(iii)	(iv)	(i)	(ii)
(b)	(iv)	(iii)	(ii)	(i)
(c)	(iii)	(i)	(ii)	(iv)
(d)	(iii)	(i)	(iv)	(ii)

27. The chief source of political power in India is:

(a) The Constitution
(b) The Parliament
(c) The People
(d) Parliament and the state legislatures

28. 'Drain of Wealth Theory' was propounded by:

(a) Feroz Shah Mehta
(b) M.N. Roy
(c) Dadabhoy Naoroji
(d) Surendranath Bannerjee

29. The present Constitution of India contains

(a) 395 Articles and 9 Schedules
(b) 395 Articles and 12 Schedules

(c) 372 Articles and 12 Schedules
(d) 370 Articles and 7 Schedules

30. Identify the correct chronological order in which the following states of India were created:

I. Maharashtra II. Andhra Pradesh
III. Punjab IV. Nagaland

(a) I, II, III, IV (b) I, II, IV, III
(c) II, I, III, IV (d) III, I, IV, II

31. The Human Relations Theory of organisation focuses on:
(a) Formal organisation
(b) Specialisation
(c) Informal Groups
(d) Red-Tapism

32. The Thinker who included intelligence design and choice activities in the decision-making process is:
(a) Dwight Waldo
(b) Herbert Simon
(c) Henri Fayol
(d) Chestar Barnard

33. The Fulton Committee Report of 1968 was concerned with reforms in the personnel administration of:
(a) France (b) Japan
(c) U.S.A. (d) United Kindgom

34. Max Weber's ideas on patrimonial bureauoracy are different from those of rational type in respect of:
(a) contractually appointed men
(b) officials appointed on merit basis
(c) unfree officials
(d) hierarchy of technical experts

35. The Estimates Committee of The Indian Parliament does not:
(a) Examine whether the money is well laid out within the limits of the policy.
(b) Examine that the money spent on the services on purposes for which it was made available on for which it was charged.
(c) Suggest economy and improvement in organisational efficiency.
(d) Suggest alternative policies for bringing efficiency and economy in administration.

36. The Institution of Ombudsman originated from:
(a) Denmark (b) Sweden
(c) U.K. (d) U.S.A.

37. Match List I with List II, by using the codes given below:

List I
(A) Max Weber (B) L. Urwick
(C) Martin Albrow (D) Micheal Crojier

List II
(i) The Elements of Administration
(ii) Economy and Society
(iii) The Bureaucratic Phenomenon
(iv) Bureaucracy

Codes:	A	B	C	D
(a)	(iv)	(iii)	(ii)	(i)
(b)	(i)	(ii)	(iii)	(iv)
(c)	(ii)	(i)	(iv)	(iii)
(d)	(iii)	(iv)	(i)	(ii)

38. Match List I with List II, by using the codes given below:

List I
(A) Human Relations Theory
(B) Theory of Scientific Management
(C) Decision Making Theory
(D) Communication Theory

List II
(i) F.W. Taylor (ii) Elton Mayo
(iii) Karl Deutseh (iv) Herbert Simon

Codes:	A	B	C	D
(a)	(i)	(ii)	(iii)	(iv)
(b)	(ii)	(i)	(iv)	(iii)
(c)	(iii)	(ii)	(i)	(iv)
(d)	(iv)	(i)	(ii)	(iii)

39. Arrange the following approaches in study of Public Administration in order

in which they appeared. Use the code given below:

I. Classical Approach
II. Behavioural Approach
III. Policy Approach
IV. Human Relations Approach

Codes:

(a) II, III, IV, I (b) I, IV, II, III
(c) IV, III, I, II (d) II, I, III, IV

40. Given below are two statements, one labelled as Assertion (A) and the other labelled as Reason (R).

Assertion (A): E-governance has facilitated good governance.

Reason (R): Transparency as virtue of good governance can be ensured through E-governance alone.

In the context of two statements, which one of the following is correct?

(a) Both (A) and (R) are true and (R) is the correct explanation of (A)
(b) Both (A) and (R) are true, but (R) is not the correct explanation of (A)
(c) (A) is true but (R) is false
(d) (A) is false but (R) is true

41. The theory of 'Trading State' is associated with:

(a) Adam Smith (b) Lenin
(c) Rosecrance (d) Robert-cox

42. The national interest of master class is the basis of:

(a) Realist theory
(b) Marxist theory
(c) Dependency theory
(d) Neo-realist theory

43. Brezhnev advocated the doctrine of:

(a) Limited Sovereignty
(b) Absolute Sovereignty
(c) Popular Sovereignty
(d) Defacto Sovereignty

44. The new member states of B I M S T E C are:

(a) Nepal and Bhutan
(b) Nepal and Pakistan
(c) Bhutan and Afghanistan
(d) Nepal and Laos

45. India's nuclear doctrine is based on:

(a) Credible minimum deterrence
(b) Nuclear Proliferation
(c) Mutually assured destruction
(d) First use strategy

46. Given below are two statements, one labelled as Assertion (A) and the other labelled as Reason (R). Choose the correct answer from the codes given below:

Assertion (A): Environment is a global problem.

Reason (R): "Earth Summit" has addressed the issues.

(a) Both (A) and (R) are true and (R) is the correct explanation of (A)
(b) Both (A) and (R) are true, but (R) is not the correct explanation of (A)
(c) (A) is true but (R) is false
(d) (A) is false but (R) is true

47. Given below are two statements, one labelled as Assertion (A) and the other labelled as Reason (R). Choose the correct answer from the codes given below:

Assertion (A): United Nations provides for the collective security of the member states.

Reason (R): States make their own arrangements for their security by entering into collective defence agreements.

(a) Both (A) and (R) are true and (R) is the correct explanation of (A)
(b) Both (A) and (R) are true, but (R) is not the correct explanation of (A)
(c) (A) is true but (R) is false
(d) (A) is false but (R) is true

48. Identify the correct chronological order of the following who held the office of Secretary General of the United Nations.

I. Kurt Waldhiem
II. Dag Hammarskjold
III. U. Thant
IV. Butros Butros Ghali

Codes:

(a) I, III, II, IV (b) III, IV, I, II
(c) II, III, I, IV (d) I, II, IV, III

49. Match List I with List II and select the correct answer from the codes given below:

List I

(A) Territorial Waters
(B) Exclusive Economic Zone
(C) Continental Shelf
(D) International Waters

List II

(i) Exploitation of resources upto 200 nautical miles
(ii) Exploitation of sea bed
(iii) Sovereignty
(iv) Waters beyond state boundary

Codes:	A	B	C	D
(a)	(iii)	(i)	(iv)	(ii)
(b)	(ii)	(iv)	(i)	(iii)
(c)	(iii)	(i)	(ii)	(iv)
(d)	(iv)	(iii)	(i)	(ii)

50. Match List I with List II and select the correct answer from the codes given below:

List I

(A) Wilson doctrine
(B) Carter doctrine
(C) Nixon doctrine
(D) Truman doctrine

List II

(i) Support to free people
(ii) Support to allies
(iii) Hegemony over Persian Gulf
(iv) Interventionist policies

Codes:	A	B	C	D
(a)	(ii)	(iv)	(i)	(iii)
(b)	(iv)	(iii)	(ii)	(i)
(c)	(i)	(ii)	(iv)	(iii)
(d)	(ii)	(iv)	(i)	(iii)

ANSWERS

1. (d)	2. (b)	3. (b)	4. (a)	5. (d)
6. (b)	7. (a)	8. (a)	9. (b)	10. (a)
11. (a)	12. (c)	13. (a)	14. (b)	15. (a)
16. (a)	17. (b)	18. (b)	19. (b)	20. (b)
21. (d)	22. (b)	23. (d)	24. (c)	25. (b)
26. (d)	27. (a)	28. (c)	29. (b)	30. (c)
31. (a)	32. (b)	33. (d)	34. (d)	35. (b)
36. (b)	37. (c)	38. (b)	39. (b)	40. (b)
41. (c)	42. (b)	43. (b)	44. (a)	45. (b)
46. (b)	47. (b)	48. (c)	49. (c)	50. (b)

PRACTICE PAPERS

MOCK TEST–1
PAPER–I

1. A teacher is called the leader of the class because
   (a) he is autocratic emperor of his class
   (b) he masters the art of oratory like a political leader
   (c) he is a maker of the future of his students
   (d) he belongs to a recognised teachers' union

2. The aim of introducing career courses in schools and colleges is to
   (a) increase G.K. in students
   (b) develop the ability to make the intelligent choice of jobs
   (c) provide professional knowledge to students
   (d) All of the above

3. The most effective attribute for a teacher is
   (a) Teaching skills (b) Knowledge
   (c) Feedback (d) Management

4. Those teachers are preferred most by students who
   (a) are themselves disciplined
   (b) give important questions before examination
   (c) dictate notes in the class
   (d) can clear their difficulties regarding subject-matter

5. The qualities of a teacher is/are:
   (i) He must not give any false promise
   (ii) He must not have any bad habits
   (iii) He should be mentally and physically fit
   (iv) He must not be superstitious about his class and students

   Codes:
   (a) (iii), (iv) and (ii)
   (b) (iv), (i) and (ii)
   (c) (i), (iii) and (iv)
   (d) All of the above

6. A teacher is more effective who can
   (a) motivate students to learn
   (b) control the class
   (c) correct the assignments carefully
   (d) give more information in less time

7. A teacher ought to know the problems prevalent in the field of education because
   (a) he can tell the government about it
   (b) with this knowledge, he can have information about education
   (c) he can tell about the same to another teacher
   (d) only he can do something about solving them

8. We can judge the quality of a research by the
   (a) experience of researcher
   (b) relevance of research
   (c) depth of the research
   (d) methodology followed in conducting the research

9. The theory or model developed through the fundamental research to the actual solution of the problems is applied in
   (a) educational research
   (b) action research
   (c) applied research
   (d) basic research

10. A write-up based on studies of the census data of a given area is called
    (a) Research paper (b) Article
    (c) Research report (d) Thesis

Direction: (11-16) Study the following passage and give answer to the questions based on it.

Knowledge creation in many cases requires creativity and idea generation. This is especially important in generating alternative decision support solutions. Some people believe that an individual's creative ability stems primarily from personality traits such as inventiveness, independence, individuality, enthusiasm, and flexibility. However, several studies have found that creativity is not so much a function of individual traits as was once believed, and that individual creativity can be learned and improved. This understanding has led innovative companies to recognise that the key to fostering creativity may be the development of an idea-nurturing work environment. Idea-generation methods and techniques, to be used by individuals or in groups, are consequently being developed. Manual methods for supporting idea generation such as brain-storming in a group, can be very successful in certain situations. However, in other situations, such an approach is either not economically feasible or not possible. For example, manual methods in group creativity sessions will not work or will not be effective when: (a) there is no time to conduct a proper idea-generation session; (b) there is a poor facilitator (or no facilitator at all); (c) it is too expensive to conduct an idea-generation session; (d) the subject-matter is too sensitive for a face-to-face session; or (e) there are not enough participants, the mix of participants is not optimal, or there is no climate for idea generation. In such cases, computerised idea-generation methods have been tried, with frequent success. Idea-generation software is designed to help stimulate a single user or a group to produce new ideas, options and choices. The user does all the work, but the software encourages and pushes, something like a personal trainer. Although idea-generation software is still relatively new, there are several packages on the market. Various approaches are used by idea-generating software to increase the flow of ideas to the user. Idea Fisher, for example, has an associate lexicon of the English language that cross-references words and phrases. These associative links, based on analogies and metaphors, make it easy for the user to be fed words related to a given theme. Some software packages use questions to prompt the user towards new, unexplored patterns of thought. This helps users to break out of cyclical thinking patterns, conquer mental blocks, or deal with bouts of procrastination.

11. The author, in this passage has focused on
    (a) individual traits
    (b) knowledge creation
    (c) creativity
    (d) idea-generation

12. Idea-generation software works as if it is a
    (a) user-friendly trainer
    (b) stimulant
    (c) climate creator
    (d) knowledge package

13. Which among the following personality traits is not believed to be a factor contributing to an individual's creative ability?
    (a) Flexibility (b) Individuality
    (c) Sophistication (d) Enthusiasm

14. In certain occasions, manual methods for the support of idea-generation
    (a) can be less expensive
    (b) do not need a facilitator
    (c) require a mix of optimal participants
    (d) are alternatively effective

15. Mental blocks, bouts of procrastination and cyclical thinking patterns can be won when
   (a) idea-generation software prompts questions
   (b) individuals acquire a neutral attitude towards the software
   (c) manual methods are removed
   (d) innovative companies employ electronic thinking methods
16. Fostering creativity needs an environment of
   (a) decision support systems
   (b) alternative individual factors
   (c) idea-nurturing
   (d) decision support solutions
17. For controlling noise in a classroom, the best method of communication is
   (a) remaining calm and just looking at student
   (b) saying 'don't talk'
   (c) continue teaching without caring for noise
   (d) raising one's voice above students voice
18. In India, Education TV was first introduced in the year
   (a) 1978 (b) 1959
   (c) 1987 (d) 1998
19. The failure of the teacher to communicate his ideas well to students may result into:
   I. Classroom indiscipline.
   II. Decrease in attendance in class.
   III. Loss of student's interest in class.
   Codes:
   (a) II only (b) III only
   (c) I only (d) All of these
20. Visualisation in the instructional process cannot increase
   (a) curiosity and concentration
   (b) interest and motivation
   (c) stress and boredom
   (d) retention and adaptation
21. Communication helps in
   (a) entertainment
   (b) integration of country
   (c) cultural promotion
   (d) All of these
22. "Because you deserve to know" is the punchline used by
   (a) *Hindustan Times*
   (b) *The Telegraph*
   (c) *The Times of India*
   (d) *India Today*
23. Find the odd man out from the following groups of letters.
   (a) UlmnE (b) AbcdE
   (c) ApqrL (d) IfghO
24. The ambitious computerisation program of the Government of India aimed at connecting 60,000 government schools through internet is known as
   (a) Vidya Vahini (b) Gyan Vahini
   (c) Kalpana project (d) Vidya Vani
25. Find the wrong number in the following sequence.
   225, 336, 447, 557, 669, 771
   (a) 669 (b) 557
   (c) 336 (d) 771
26. In this question two words are given which have certain relationship followed by four paired lettered words. Select the paired words, that has the same relation as original pair.
   ROOF : FOUNDATION
   (a) Plateau : Valley
   (b) Peak : Valley
   (c) Mountain : Grassland
   (d) Hill : Mountain
27. "Communication is a verbal process by which we understand each other and reduce uncertainty through the use of symbol." Who is the author of this statement?

(a) David K. Barlo
(b) Dance
(c) P.S.K. Serichavenko
(d) K.J. Newman

28. Find out the missing number:
8 24 12 ? 18 54
(a) 28 (b) 32
(c) 36 (d) 38

29. A D C F
C F E H
O R ? ?
(a) JK (b) RN
(c) SU (d) QT

30. 3, 12, 27, 48, 75, (?), 147.
(a) 111 (b) 108
(c) 117 (d) 122

31. In this question four words have been given, out of which three are alike in some manner and the fourth one is different. Choose the odd one out.
(a) Epigraphy (b) Ecology
(c) Archaeology (d) Palaeontology

32. Which of the following figures will represent the right relationship between, societies, societies who run schools, DPS society.

(a) 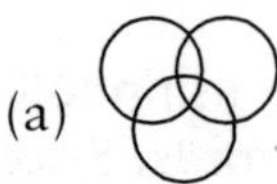 (b) 

(c) 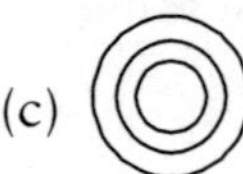 (d) 

33. **Statements:**
I. All students are ambitious.
II. All ambitious persons are hard-working.

Conclusions:
(i) All students are hard-working.
(ii) All hardly working people are not ambitious.

Which of the following is correct?
(a) Only (i) is correct
(b) Only (ii) is correct
(c) Both (i) and (ii) are correct
(d) Neither (i) nor (ii) is correct

34. In a certain code language:
'pit dit mit' means: 'Reena went to Delhi'.
'dit ket set' means: 'Delhi is closing'.
'mit set un' means: 'Reena' is educated.
Then what is the code for 'went'?
(a) dit (b) mit
(c) pit (d) None of these

35. EDITOR : MAGAZINE
Choose the pair from the answer choices that best expresses the relationship similar to that expressed by the question pair.
(a) Novel : Writer
(b) Director : Film
(c) Poem : Poet
(d) Chair : Carpenter

36. Should education in India be made free?
Arguments:
I. Yes, this is the only way to improve the level of literacy.
II. No, this would add already heavy burden on the exchequer.
(a) Only argument I is strong
(b) Only argument II is strong
(c) Both the arguments are strong
(d) None of these

Direction: (37-41) Study the table and answer the questions:

Export of Pulses and Import of Onion (in ₹ crores)

Year	Export of Pulses (in ₹ crores)	Import of Onion (in ₹ crores)
1998-99	44	58
1999-00	45	50
2000-01	60	54

2001-02	56	60
2002-03	92	68
2003-04	100	78
2004-05	68	60

37. During which year there was a maximum fall in export?
(a) 2004-05 (b) 2001-02
(c) 2003-04 (d) None of these

38. The percent of increase of imports in 2003-04 over 2002-03 is
(a) 14.9% (b) 14.7%
(c) 18.4% (d) 18.9%

39. In 1999-2000, the ratio of export to the import is
(a) 19:11 (b) 11:9
(c) 13:17 (d) 9:10

40. During which year there was maximum increase in import over its preceding year?
(a) 2003-04 (b) 2000-01
(c) 2001-02 (d) 2002-03

41. During which year there was minimum increase in import over its preceding year?
(a) 2003-04 (b) 2002-03
(c) 2001-02 (d) None of these

42. The sum of a positive number and its reciprocal is twice the difference of the number and its reciprocal. The number is
(a) $\sqrt{3}$ (b) $\sqrt{2}$
(c) $\frac{1}{\sqrt{2}}$ (d) $\frac{1}{\sqrt{3}}$

43. Which one of the following states has the maximum number of Wildlife Sanctuaries (National Park and Sanctuaries)?
(a) Madhya Pradesh
(b) Rajasthan
(c) Uttar Pradesh
(d) West Bengal

Direction: (44-48) Answer the following questions based on the graph given below:

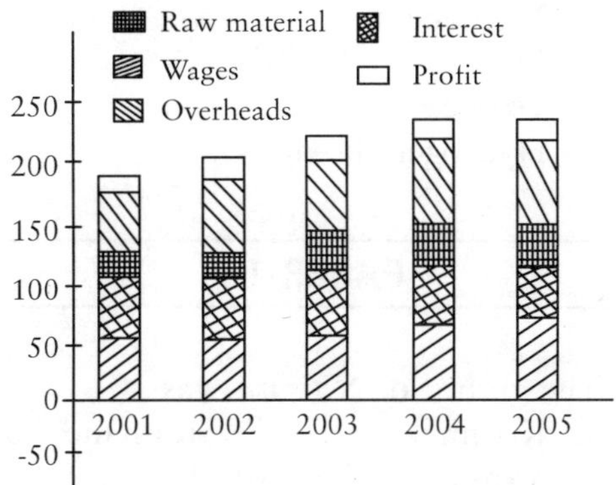

44. Which component of the cost of production has remained almost unchanged over the period 2001-2005?
(a) Wages (b) Interest
(c) Raw material (d) Overheads

45. In which year was the increase in raw material maximum?
(a) 2004 (b) 2002
(c) 2003 (d) 2001

46. What percent of costs did the profits from over the period?
(a) 7% (b) 5%
(c) 2% (d) 1%

47. In which period was the change in profit maximum?
(a) 2002-03 (b) 2001-02
(c) 2004-05 (d) 2003-04

48. If the interest component is not included in the total cost calculation, which year would show the maximum profit per unit cost?
(a) 2001 (b) 2002
(c) 2003 (d) 2005

49. How many types of emergencies have been envisaged by the Constitution?
(a) One (b) Two
(c) Three (d) Four

50. Photocopying and other electrical equipments produce
(a) Methane
(b) Ethane
(c) Ozone
(d) Hydrogen dioxide

PAPER–II

1. The author of *Nitisara* was
(a) Krishna (b) Kamandaka
(c) Vyasa (d) Kautilya

2. Which of the following is not included under shadgunya or six foreign policies of Kautilya?
(a) Samsraya (b) Vigraha
(c) Santhi (d) Vyavahara

3. Who was the doyen of the Pluralists?
(a) J.S. Mill (b) Bentham
(c) Laski (d) Leacock

4. The pluralists believe in
(a) nominal sovereignty.
(b) legal sovereignty.
(c) political sovereignty.
(d) None of the above.

5. Which discipline is generally regarded as the original fundamental social science?
(a) Sociology (b) Anthropology
(c) Politics (d) Philosophy

6. Max Weber in an attempt to distinguish political science from other social sciences made a departure and pointed out that the central idea of the subject must be
(a) Power (b) State
(c) Government (d) None of these

7. What is the main criticism against game theory and decision making theory?
(a) They are not scientific studies
(b) They are highly mechanistic and abstract in nature
(c) They are empirical in nature
(d) None of the above

8. Political realism maintains autonomy of
(a) social sphere
(b) political sphere
(c) national sphere
(d) international sphere

9. Which of the following is an important contribution to both political and administrative issues and ideas of the Western world?
(a) *Ramayana*
(b) *Mahabharata*
(c) *Arms and the Man*
(d) Aristotle's *Politics*

10. The scope of Public Administration depends on
(a) the goals of the political framework.
(b) the values of the political framework.
(c) Both (a) and (b).
(d) None of the above.

11. Which one of the following political theorists finds the concept of 'imagined community' inadequate to describe nationalism in post-colonial societies?
(a) Partha Chatterjee
(b) V.R. Mehta
(c) Hans Cohn
(d) Ernest Gellner

12. With growing power of bureaucracy it is said, "a new form of despotism has emerged". Who said it?
(a) Ramsay Muir
(b) Lord Hewart
(c) Harold Laski
(d) Sir William Beveridge

13. The important dynamic variable is
(a) organisational nature
(b) cultural variables
(c) superior's style and behaviour
(d) the task structure

14. The situational variables identified by Fiedler were
    (a) position power
    (b) leader-member relation
    (c) task structure
    (d) All of the above

15. "The greatest cause of revolutions is this, that while nations move onward, Csonstitutions stand still." Who said so?
    (a) Bryce (b) Woolsey
    (c) Gilchrist (d) Macaulay

16. The division of labour concept was advocated by
    (a) Adam Smith (b) Hansen
    (c) J.M. Keynes (d) Marshall

17. Who used the term "State" in modern sense for the first time?
    (a) Hobbes (b) T.H. Green
    (c) Gamer (d) Aristotle

18. Who defined justice as treating equals equally and unequals unequally?
    (a) T.H. Green (b) Bentham
    (c) J.S. Mill (d) Aristotle

19. Where is the headquarters of World Health Organisation situated?
    (a) Geneva (b) New York
    (c) London (d) New Delhi

20. The members of the Rajya Sabha are elected for a term of
    (a) six years (b) seven years
    (c) three years (d) five years

21. A non-money bill passed by the Parliament is returned by the President to Parliament for reconsideration. It is passed once again by the Parliament without any change. Now, the
    (a) Bill will be referred to the Supreme Court.
    (b) President will give his assent.
    (c) President can again withhold his assent.
    (d) Bill will automatically lapse.

22. The Organization of the Islamic Conference (OIC) consists of 56 Islamic states for the purpose of
    (a) promoting social and cultural cooperation.
    (b) promoting Islamic solidarity.
    (c) cooperation in economic and political affairs.
    (d) All of the above.

23. Which of the following is not an Islamic Organisation?
    (a) JKLF
    (b) LTTE
    (c) Hizbul Mujahideen
    (d) Hamas

24. The report of the Public Accounts Committee is presented to the
    (a) Rajya Sabha (b) Lok Sabha
    (c) President (d) Prime Minister

25. Rousseau believed that an ideal State should have
    (a) 10,000 persons (b) 25,000 persons
    (c) 50,000 persons (d) No fixed number

26. Which of the following are elements of Marxism?
    1. Dialectical materialism
    2. Economic interpretation of history
    3. Concept of surplus value
    4. Doctrine of class struggle

    Codes:
    (a) 1 and 2 (b) 1, 3 and 4
    (c) 2, 3 and 4 (d) 1, 2, 3 and 4

27. Consider the following statements about the organizational process model of decision making:
    1. Officials choose the action whose consequences best help to meet the state's established goals.
    2. Decisions result from routine administrative procedure.

    Codes:
    (a) 1 only (b) 2 only
    (c) Both 1 and 2 (d) Neither 1 nor 2

28. Arrange the following ideas/concepts in order in which they appeared.
    1. Class in itself and class for itself
    2. Encoding
    3. Circulation of Elites
    4. Perestroika

    Codes:
    (a) 1, 2, 3, 4 (b) 1, 3, 2, 4
    (c) 2, 1, 3, 4 (d) 4, 3, 2, 1

29. Consider the following statements about Civil Service in a developing society:
    1. It should act as an agent of change.
    2. It should have concern for social equity.
    3. It should have concern for vested interests.
    4. It should be politically neutral.

    Codes:
    (a) 1, 2 and 3 (b) 1, 2, and 4
    (c) 2, 3 and 4 (d) 1, 2, 3 and 4

30. In accordance to a growing consensus today, which of the following should freedom be inclusive of?
    1. Absence of certain physical and legal impediments.
    2. Presence of certain civil and political liberties.
    3. Social provisions of income, education and health.
    4. Protection of cultural identity.

    Codes:
    (a) 1 only (b) 2 and 3
    (c) 1, 2 and 3 (d) 1, 2, 3 and 4

31. Which of the following statements are correct?
    1. Merit system was introduced in India in 1853.
    2. Prussia was the first country to introduce merit system.
    3. Britain accepted merit system in 1854.
    4. Merit system replaced the spoils system.
    5. Civil Service Act of 1883 introduced merit system in the USA.

    Codes:
    (a) 1, 4 and 5 (b) 2, 3 and 4
    (c) 1, 2, 3 and 4 (d) 2, 3, 4 and 5

32. Match the two lists as per code.

List I (Saptanga)	List II (Reference)
A. Durga	1. Fortified Capital
B. Kosa	2. Army
C. Danda	3. Treasury
D. Mitra	4. Ally

Codes:	A	B	C	D
(a)	1	3	2	4
(b)	2	3	4	1
(c)	4	3	2	1
(d)	3	2	1	4

33. Match the two lists as per code.

    List I
    A. Karl von Clausewitz
    B. Harold Mackinder
    C. Kenneth Waltz
    D. Thomas Schelling

    List II
    1. Heartland Theory
    2. Conflict escalation
    3. War is the continuation of politics by other means
    4. Structured realism

Codes:	A	B	C	D
(a)	3	1	4	2
(b)	2	3	4	1
(c)	3	4	1	2
(d)	4	3	2	1

34. Match the two lists as per code.

    List I
    A. Will of a person could be enforced despite resistance.
    B. Exists as long as it is accepted and legitimised by the ruled.
    C. Power relationship between the rulers and the ruled.
    D. Administrative apparatus is very loose and unstable.

List II
1. Authority
2. Charismatic dominion
3. Power
4. Dominion

Codes:	**A**	**B**	**C**	**D**
(a)	4	1	3	2
(b)	1	3	4	2
(c)	3	1	4	2
(d)	3	1	2	4

35. Match the two lists as per code.

List I (Theories of Democracy)
A. Classical Theory
B. Neo-Liberal Theory
C. Elite Theory
D. Pluralist Theory

List II (Champions)
1. Giovanni Sartori
2. Abraham Lincoln
3. Robert A. Dahl
4. C. Wright Mills

Codes:	**A**	**B**	**C**	**D**
(a)	2	1	3	4
(b)	4	2	1	3
(c)	2	1	4	3
(d)	1	2	4	3

36. Match the two lists as per code.

List I
A. Architect of India's Foreign Policy
B. Russia
C. Panchsheel
D. INA

List II
1. S.C. Bose 2. China
3. Putin 4. Jawaharlal Nehru

Codes:	**A**	**B**	**C**	**D**
(a)	4	3	1	2
(b)	2	1	4	3
(c)	4	3	2	1
(d)	3	2	4	1

37. Match the two lists as per code.

List I (Commission/Committee)
A. K. Santhanam Committee
B. Shah Commission
C. S.R. Das Commission
D. N.N. Vohra Committee

List II (Subject)
1. Excesses Committed during Emergency
2. Criminalisation of Politics
3. Prevention of Corruption
4. Charges against Partap Singh Kairon
5. Arrest of M. Karunanidhi

Codes:	**A**	**B**	**C**	**D**
(a)	3	1	4	2
(b)	4	5	2	3
(c)	3	5	4	2
(d)	4	1	2	3

38. **Assertion (A):** Co-ordination can be achieved by establishing direct personal contacts with the people concerned.

Reason (R): Inter-personal communication facilitates quick resolution of differences.

Codes:
(a) Both (A) and (R) are true and (R) is the correct explanation.
(b) Both (A) and (R) are not true.
(c) (A) is true and (R) is false.
(d) (A) is false and (R) is true.

39. **Assertion (A):** Liberal democracy constitutes the basis of the growing internationalism today.

Reason (R): After the disintegration of the Soviet Union and Eastern Europe, there is no effective rival to liberal democracy in the world.

Codes:
(a) Both (A) and (R) are true and (R) is the correct explanation.
(b) Both (A) and (R) are not true.
(c) (A) is true and (R) is false.
(d) (A) is false and (R) is true.

40. **Assertion (A):** The act of the civil servant is in convention regarded as the act of his Minister.

Reason (R): It is a recognised rule of the Parliamentary practice that the criticism of administrative action must be framed as the criticism of the Minister.

Codes:

(a) Both (A) and (R) are true and (R) is the correct explanation.
(b) Both (A) and (R) are not true.
(c) (A) is true and (R) is false.
(d) (A) is false and (R) is true.

41. **Assertion (A):** Division between Line and Staff cannot be water tight.

Reason (R): Authority is more a matter of influence rather than of command.

Codes:

(a) Both (A) and (R) are true and (R) is the correct explanation.
(b) Both (A) and (R) are not true.
(c) (A) is true and (R) is false.
(d) (A) is false and (R) is true.

42. **Assertion (A):** Some of the developing societies have realised that their country is over-governed.

Reason (R): They feel that downsizing of government would be in everyone's interest.

Codes:

(a) Both (A) and (R) are true and (R) is the correct explanation.
(b) Both (A) and (R) are not true.
(c) (A) is true and (R) is false.
(d) (A) is false and (R) is true.

43. **Assertion (A):** Unity of command means the entire organisation has only one boss and one plan of action to promote efficiency and effectiveness.

Reason (R): The concept of unity of command is proposed as a substitute to the "Functional Foremanship."

Codes:

(a) Both (A) and (R) are true and (R) is the correct explanation.
(b) Both (A) and (R) are not true.
(c) (A) is true and (R) is false.
(d) (A) is false and (R) is true.

44. A non-money bill passes through the following stages which are jumbled up. Which of the given below responses gives the correct sequence of the passage of the bill through the Lok Sabha only
    1. The third reading
    2. Second reading
    3. Introduction and first reading
    4. The report stage
    5. Committee stage

Codes:

(a) 4, 5, 3, 2, 1 (b) 3, 2, 5, 4, 1
(c) 1, 4, 3, 2, 5 (d) 5, 2, 4, 1, 3

45. Consider the following statements:
    1. Since the sums required to meet expenditure described by the Constitution of India as expenditure charged upon the Consolidated Fund of India, are not submitted to the vote of Parliament, no House is competent to discuss these estimates.
    2. Annual Finance Bill provides the legal authority for the withdrawal of sums from the Consolidated Fund of India.

Codes:

(a) 1 only (b) 2 only
(c) Both 1 and 2 (d) Neither 1 nor 2

46. In a larger historical context, who argues that leadership consists in a gifted minority which has a vitality like morale and atmosphere?
(a) Arnold Toynbee
(b) Ralph Stogdill
(c) Chester Barnard
(d) Keith Davis

47. The Finance Commission makes recommendations about
(a) distribution of net proceeds of taxes between the Centre and the States.
(b) grants-in-aid including determination of the principles governing them.
(c) economy in expenditure.
(d) Both (b) and (c).

48. India had agreed to retain her membership of the Commonwealth
    (a) Contractually
    (b) Voluntarily
    (c) Conditionally
    (d) On the basis of Indian Independence Act 1947

49. Green Peace Movement has played a significant role in the field of
    (a) Regulating Sea Routes
    (b) Refugees Settlement
    (c) Water Management
    (d) Environment Protection

50. Who issues money from the Consolidated Fund of India?
    (a) The President
    (b) The Parliament
    (c) The Lok Sabha
    (d) The Comptroller and Auditor General

PAPER–III

1. Titular sovereign means
   (a) a person who is vested with all sovereign powers by the Constitution but whose powers are enjoyed by someone else.
   (b) a person who enjoys all the powers vested in him by the Constitution.
   (c) a person who enjoys absolute power and is not accountable to anyone.
   (d) a sovereign elected by Parliament.

2. Who is remembered as the pioneer of economic nationalism?
   (a) Gokhale
   (b) R.C. Dutt
   (c) Bipin Chandra Pal
   (d) Madan Mohan Malviya

3. In India, education is a
   (a) Fundamental Right
   (b) Class Privilege
   (c) Legal obligation
   (d) Qualification for political officer

4. The role of Public Administration is to execute the
   (a) programmes of political parties.
   (b) will of the states.
   (c) will of the people.
   (d) policies of the government.

5. The most important paradigm in Public Administration has been
   (a) the concept of human relationists.
   (b) the concept of Henri Fayol and others.
   (c) the Weberian concept of bureaucracy
   (d) None of the above.

6. The book *Economy and Society* has been authored by
   (a) Robert Merton
   (b) Max Weber
   (c) Victor Thompson
   (d) Ralph Hummel

7. Budget represents the plan of action for
   (a) Three years (b) Five years
   (c) Fiscal period (d) Two years

8. Railway Budget was separated from the General Budget in
   (a) 1951 (b) 1941
   (c) 1931 (d) 1921

9. Demands for grants can emanate only from
   (a) the Chairman of the Estimates Committee.
   (b) any member who is not a member of the ruling party.
   (c) the leader of the opposition.
   (d) the executive.

10. In the Indian budgetary system, pending the passage of Finance Bill in the Parliament, the provisional collection under Tax Act, 1931 empowers the government to collect taxes for a period of

(a) 75 days (b) 90 days
(c) 100 days (d) 120 days

11. In India, the Office of the Lokpal was suggested in 1966 on the basis of the recommendations of the
(a) Administrative Reforms Commission
(b) Planning Commission
(c) Law Commission
(d) Finance Commission

12. Realists regard the international system as
(a) Non-functional (b) Co-operative
(c) Anarchic (d) Ideal

13. Power in international relations is
(a) Absolute (b) Relative
(c) Infinite (d) Finite

14. India's nuclear doctrine is based on
(a) Credible minimum deterrence
(b) Nuclear Proliferation
(c) Mutually assured destruction
(d) First use strategy

15. UNRISD was established in
(a) 1985 (b) 1974
(c) 1963 (d) 1952

16. In ancient days Public Administration was confined itself to
(a) Some philanthropic functions
(b) Judicial functions
(c) Police functions
(d) All of the above

17. "Wherever many men are working together, the best results are secured when there is a division of labour among them". Who said this?
(a) Elton Mayo
(b) Luther Gulick
(c) F.W. Taylor
(d) None of the above

18. The normal tenure of the Mayor is
(a) Three years (b) Five years
(c) One year (d) Two years

19. Which one of the following would be counted as public opinion?
(a) Sum total of incoherent opinion held by different groups of citizens.
(b) Opinion held by effective majority based on reason and aiming at common good.
(c) Opinion of the majority of citizens.
(d) Unanimous opinion of all the citizens.

20. Superior-subordinate relationship through a number of levels of responsibility is called
(a) Span of Control
(b) Hierarchy
(c) Delegation
(d) Unity of Command

21. Match the two lists as per code.

List I (Bureaucracy)
A. Guardian B. Merit
C. Patronage D. Caste

List II (Feature)
1. Career open to talent
2. Has a class base
3. Prussian Civil Service 1640-1740
4. Indian Civil Service
5. Spoils system

Codes:	A	B	C	D
(a)	3	2	4	1
(b)	3	5	4	2
(c)	3	2	5	4
(d)	3	1	5	2

22. Match the two lists as per code.

List I
A. Appleby Report B. Gorwala Report
C. Assheton Report D. Fulton Report

List II
1. 1944 2. 1951
3. 1953 4. 1968

Codes:	A	B	C	D
(a)	2	3	4	1
(b)	2	3	1	4
(c)	3	2	1	4
(d)	3	2	4	1

23. Match the two lists as per code.

List I (Structure)

A. Flat Hierarchy
B. Linking-pin structure
C. Job-task Hierarchy
D. Project Matrix Structure

List II (Theory/Concept)

1. Concept of supportive relationships
2. Centralised direction and control
3. Self-direction and self-control
4. Decentralisation
5. Coequal authority

Codes:	**A**	**B**	**C**	**D**
(a)	4	1	2	3
(b)	1	2	4	5
(c)	1	5	2	4
(d)	3	1	4	2

24. Match the two lists as per code.

List I

A. Communal Award
B. JP's Bihar Movement
C. Giani Zail Singh's accession to Presidency
D. Vajpayee's first Prime Ministership

List II

1. 1996 2. 1982
3. 1932 4. 1974

Codes:	**A**	**B**	**C**	**D**
(a)	1	2	4	3
(b)	3	2	4	1
(c)	3	4	2	1
(d)	4	2	3	1

25. Match the two lists as per code.

List I (Writs)

A. Habeas Corpus B. Certiorari
C. Mandamus D. Quo Warranto

List II (Subject-matter)

1. A command to produce the body in person.
2. A command to a public authority to do its duty.
3. A proceeding to enquire into the legality of a claim of a person.
4. A directive to a lower court or judicial body not to exceed its limits.

Codes:	**A**	**B**	**C**	**D**
(a)	4	1	2	3
(b)	1	4	2	3
(c)	1	4	3	2
(d)	4	1	3	2

26. Match the two lists as per code.

List I (Books)

A. *Nerves of Government*
B. *The Idea of Development Administration*
C. *Development Administration*
D. *Politics of Modernization*

List II (Authors)

1. Irving Swerdlow 2. Karl Deutsch
3. F.W. Riggs 4. David Apter

Codes:	**A**	**B**	**C**	**D**
(a)	2	3	1	4
(b)	3	1	4	2
(c)	1	2	3	4
(d)	3	2	4	1

27. Consider the following statements about the post-World War II writings in Public Administration?

1. These seek to undertake cross-cultural studies.
2. These seek to evolve true science of administration based on inter-disciplinary approach.
3. These seek to develop appropriate methodology.
4. These seek to analyse all types of social phenomena.

Codes:

(a) 3 and 4 (b) 1 and 4
(c) 1 and 2 (d) 2 and 3

28. Which of the following are the ability tests?

1. Aptitude Test
2. Social Intelligence Test
3. Gottshchold Test
4. Achievement Test
5. General Intelligence Test

Codes:

(a) 2, 3 and 4 (b) 1, 2 and 3
(c) 1, 2 and 5 (d) 2, 3 and 5

29. Consider the following types of training programme:
   1. Induction
   2. Pre-selection
   3. Refresher
   4. Specialised
   5. In service

   The training programmes gone through by the IAS and IPS officers include

   Codes:

   (a) 2, 3, 4 and 5 (b) 1, 3, 4 and 5
   (c) 1, 2, 3 and 4 (d) 1, 2, 4 and 5

30. Which of the following factors could place limitations on the authority of a superior?
   1. Group behaviour
   2. Social relationships
   3. Organisational norms
   4. Bona fide instructions

   Codes:

   (a) 1 and 2 (b) 3 and 4
   (c) 1, 2 and 3 (d) 1, 2, 3 and 4

31. Consider the following features:
   1. A synonym of cabinet
   2. A branch of learning
   3. The art of management
   4. Sum-total of the activities undertaken to implement public policy/policies.

   Which of these are correct, in common parlance, about administration?

   Codes:

   (a) 2 and 3 (b) 3 and 4
   (c) 1, 3 and 4 (d) 1, 2, 3 and 4

32. Consider the following events:
   1. Inclusion of Ninth Schedule in the Constitution
   2. Passing of Anti-defection Bill
   3. First non-congress government at the Centre
   4. Reorganization of the State of Punjab

   The correct chronological sequence of these events

   Codes:

   (a) 1-2-3-4 (b) 4-3-2-1
   (c) 1-4-3-2 (d) 2-3-1-4

33. Which of the following are not necessarily the consequences of the proclamation of the President's rule in a state?
   1. Dissolution of the State Legislative Assembly.
   2. The removal of the Council of Ministers in the State.
   3. Dissolution of the local bodies.
   4. Takeover of the State administration by the Union Government.

   Codes:

   (a) 2 and 3 (b) 3 and 4
   (c) 2 and 4 (d) 1 and 3

34. Which of the following are the main jurisdictions of the High Court of a State?
   1. Original jurisdiction
   2. Appellate jurisdiction
   3. Supervisory jurisdiction
   4. Advisory jurisdiction

   Codes:

   (a) 1, 2 and 3 (b) 1, 2 and 4
   (c) 1, 3 and 4 (d) 2, 3 and 4

35. Consider the following statements regarding the Public Interest Litigation:
   1. In essence, a third party can bring before the courts, issues in the public interest.
   2. The Supreme Court may act on the receipt of a letter or postcard from a citizen requesting protection of his fundamental rights.
   3. It is also known as Social Action Litigation.
   4. Justices V.R. Krishna Iyer and P.N. Bhagwati were its proponents.

   Codes:

   (a) 1 and 2 (b) 2 and 3
   (c) 3 and 4 (d) 1, 2, 3 and 4

36. **Assertion (A):** In assessing power today, technology, education and economic growth are becoming more important than military might.
Reason (R): Source of powers are never static and are always in a state of flux.
Codes:
(a) Both (A) and (R) are true and (R) is the correct explanation.
(b) Both (A) and (R) are not true.
(c) (A) is true and (R) is false.
(d) (A) is false and (R) is true.

37. **Assertion (A):** Restrictions on political activities of public employees are in their own interests.
Reason (R): Neutrality of civil servants ensures that all of them are treated alike.
Codes:
(a) Both (A) and (R) are true and (R) is the correct explanation.
(b) Both (A) and (R) are not true.
(c) (A) is true and (R) is false.
(d) (A) is false and (R) is true.

38. **Assertion (A):** The Indian Councils Act of 1861 introduced a popular element in the governance of India.
Reason (R): The Governor General's Executive Councils, while transacting business as a Legislative Council, was to include non-official member.
Codes:
(a) Both (A) and (R) are true and (R) is the correct explanation.
(b) Both (A) and (R) are not true.
(c) (A) is true and (R) is false.
(d) (A) is false and (R) is true.

39. **Assertion (A):** Traditionally, the two-party system has been seen as one which allows for stable and effective democratic working.
Reason (R): A major function of political parties is the control and coordination of government.
Codes:
(a) Both (A) and (R) are true and (R) is the correct explanation.
(b) Both (A) and (R) are not true.
(c) (A) is true and (R) is false.
(d) (A) is false and (R) is true.

40. **Assertion (A):** The purpose of fundamental rights is to create an egalitarian society.
Reason (R): There is an inherent tendency among the individuals to dominate others.
Codes:
(a) Both (A) and (R) are true and (R) is the correct explanation.
(b) Both (A) and (R) are not true.
(c) (A) is true and (R) is false.
(d) (A) is false and (R) is true.

41. **Assertion (A):** The welfare state not only performs protective or police functions but also lays emphasis on welfare functions.
Reason (R): A modern welfare state does not regard itself as a mere tax collection agency or policeman.
Codes:
(a) Both (A) and (R) are true and (R) is the correct explanation.
(b) Both (A) and (R) are not true.
(c) (A) is true and (R) is false.
(d) (A) is false and (R) is true.

42. **Assertion (A):** State is not an anthropological necessity.
Reason (R): Society provides organisations to individuals and groups.
Codes:
(a) Both (A) and (R) are true and (R) is the correct explanation.
(b) Both (A) and (R) are not true.
(c) (A) is true and (R) is false.
(d) (A) is false and (R) is true.

43. **Assertion (A):** The British democracy has transformed itself from a parliamentary

system through a cabinet system to a prime ministerial system.

Reason (R): During the 1400 years of its constitutional development, the British Constitution has witnessed a substantial reduction in the powers of the Monarch and of the House of Lords.

Codes:

(a) Both (A) and (R) are true and (R) is the correct explanation.
(b) Both (A) and (R) are not true.
(c) (A) is true and (R) is false.
(d) (A) is false and (R) is true.

44. **Assertion (A):** The structural adjustment programme encourages state spending and budget deficit to spur growth.

Reason (R): The International Monetary Fund wants to ensure that money lent to a country is not spent for politically popular purposes but it is spent for purposes without economically profitable motives.

Codes:

(a) Both (A) and (R) are true and (R) is the correct explanation.
(b) Both (A) and (R) are not true.
(c) (A) is true and (R) is false.
(d) (A) is false and (R) is true.

45. Writings on organisation can be broadly classified into ______ basic categories.

(a) three (b) two
(c) ten (d) six

46. In all private organisations, principles of democratic control, public accountability and popular checks on administrative behaviour are followed on the basis of the concept of

(a) political promises.
(b) democratic welfare state.
(c) democratic state.
(d) constitutional promises.

47. Which one of the following cases prompted the Indian Parliament to enact 24th Constitution Amendment Bill?

(a) Golaknath case
(b) Shankari Prasad case
(c) Keshvananda Bharati case
(d) Shah Bano case

48. The supremacy of the Constitution is maintained by the

(a) Executive (b) Parliament
(c) Judiciary (d) All of the above

49. The purpose of which of the following types of training is to instruct the employees in some specialised technique or a complicated system of law or procedure?

(a) Central training
(b) Skill training
(c) Departmental training
(d) Background training

50. Which one of the following statements is correct?

(a) Socialism is nothing but Idealism minus its practicability.
(b) Socialism is a compromise between Communism and Idealism.
(c) Socialism is a compromise between Communism and Liberalism.
(d) Socialism is a half way house between Individualism and Idealism.

ANSWER SHEET

PAPER—I

1. (c)	2. (c)	3. (a)	4. (d)	5. (d)
6. (a)	7. (d)	8. (b)	9. (c)	10. (b)
11. (d)	12. (a)	13. (c)	14. (c)	15. (a)
16. (c)	17. (a)	18. (b)	19. (a)	20. (c)
21. (d)	22. (a)	23. (c)	24. (a)	25. (b)
26. (b)	27. (b)	28. (c)	29. (d)	30. (b)
31. (b)	32. (c)	33. (a)	34. (c)	35. (b)
36. (b)	37. (a)	38. (b)	39. (d)	40. (a)
41. (d)	42. (c)	43. (a)	44. (b)	45. (c)
46. (b)	47. (d)	48. (b)	49. (c)	50. (c)

PAPER—II

1. (b)	2. (d)	3. (c)	4. (c)	5. (a)
6. (a)	7. (b)	8. (b)	9. (d)	10. (b)
11. (a)	12. (b)	13. (c)	14. (d)	15. (d)
16. (a)	17. (d)	18. (d)	19. (a)	20. (a)
21. (d)	22. (d)	23. (b)	24. (b)	25. (a)
26. (d)	27. (a)	28. (b)	29. (b)	30. (d)
31. (a)	32. (a)	33. (a)	34. (c)	35. (c)
36. (c)	37. (a)	38. (b)	39. (a)	40. (d)
41. (b)	42. (b)	43. (c)	44. (b)	45. (c)
46. (a)	47. (d)	48. (b)	49. (d)	50. (b)

PAPER—III

1. (a)	2. (b)	3. (c)	4. (c)	5. (c)
6. (b)	7. (c)	8. (d)	9. (b)	10. (a)
11. (a)	12. (c)	13. (b)	14. (a)	15. (c)
16. (a)	17. (b)	18. (c)	19. (b)	20. (b)
21. (d)	22. (c)	23. (a)	24. (c)	25. (b)
26. (a)	27. (b)	28. (d)	29. (b)	30. (d)
31. (d)	32. (c)	33. (d)	34. (a)	35. (d)
36. (a)	37. (a)	38. (c)	39. (b)	40. (b)
41. (b)	42. (a)	43. (b)	44. (a)	45. (b)
46. (b)	47. (a)	48. (c)	49. (b)	50. (c)

MOCK TEST–2
PAPER–I

1. Minimum program of guidance includes
   (a) occupational information service
   (b) data collector service
   (c) counselling service
   (d) All of these

2. If majority of students in a class is weak, a teacher should
   (a) not care about intelligent students
   (b) keep his speed of teaching fast so that students comprehension level may increase
   (c) keep his teaching slow which can also be helpful to bright students
   (d) keep his teaching slow along with some extra guidance to bright students

3. If the principal of your institution is not satisfied with your performance and charge you with the act of negligence of duties, how would you behave with him?
   (a) You would neglect him
   (b) You would take revenge by giving physical and mental agony to him
   (c) You would keep yourself alert and make his efforts unfruitful
   (d) You would take a tough stand against the charges

4. What makes people to undertake research?
   (a) Desire to get intellectual joy of doing some creative work
   (b) Desire to get a research degree along with its consequential benefits
   (c) Desire to face the challenge in solving the unsolved problems
   (d) All of these

5. Which of the following aims at probing into the phenomenon to formulate a more precise research problem or to develop a new hypothesis?
   (a) Descriptive research
   (b) Conclusive research
   (c) Diagnostic research
   (d) Exploratory research

6. Which of the following is not instructional material?
   (a) Transparency
   (b) Overhead projector
   (c) Printed material
   (d) Audio cassette

7. Of great importance in determining the amount of transference that occurs in the process of learning is the

(a) knowledge of the teacher
(b) IQ of the teacher
(c) presence of identical elements
(d) use of appropriate elements

8. The characteristic(s) of hypothesis is/are:
   I. It can be tested.
   II. It must consist of known facts.
   III. It must be objective and specific.

   Codes:

   (a) I and III (b) I and II
   (c) I only (d) All of these

9. The guide for the research requires which of the following qualities?
   (a) Interdisciplinary expertise
   (b) Subject matter expertise
   (c) Methodological expertise
   (d) All of these

10. Which of the following indicates evaluation?
    (a) Seema got 195 marks out of 200
    (b) Sapna got 72 percent marks in English
    (c) Asha got First Division in final examination
    (d) All of the above

Direction: (11-16) Study the following passage and give answer to the questions based on it.

Much of the theoretical literature of archeology in the 1980s devotes considerable energy to bashing the 1970s, and the target often turns out to be the so-called New or Processual Archeology. While many of the attacks come from recent theorists who are attempting to replace it with post-processual archeology, some criticism comes from within what was New Archeology even from the hand of its original champion, Lewis Binford. If scholars from both outside and inside the theoretical developments of the 1970s are rejecting the New Archeology, why am I defending its importance to us today? The answer is very simple...for better or worse, it is us! As Alison Whylie has recently said the New Archeology of the 1960s quickly became everybody's archeology in the 1970s. Most of today's faculty members and senior archeologists were the people who, in one way or another, adopted the teachings of New Archeology. Although most archeologists did not claim to agree with all aspects of New Archeology nor could more than two or three people agree on what it was, virtually one rejected it outright. Typically, each one presented her or his version, often using a New Archeology text as a starting point for pedagogical purposes. Few wanted to be left out of the exciting new theoretical movement of those years, and New Archeology was passed on to the succeeding generation of students who reached maturity in the 1980s and are today's young professionals.

Criticisms now leveled against the New Archeology of the seventies do have merit, but by discounting that era as misguided, critics have overlooked its crucial importance. New Archeology has an important historical role in the developments of the field we have today and it has continuing importance because it is still guiding archeology's trajectory into the future. Equally troubling is that some critics ask us to reject the basic tenets of New Archeology and to replace them with a system often called post-processualist archeology. I believe this is rhetoric that not only misrepresents the achievements of the New Archeology of the seventies, but also does not successfully articulate the potential contributions of its own position.

To put the New Archeology of the seventies into perspective, it is important to review the decades leading up to its development. In the first years following World War II, archeology was still a small field, but by the fifties and the sixties, it was expanding rapidly and taking itself quite seriously. Since the launching of Sputnik in 1957 there had emerged a frenzy in the United States to make all disciplines more scientific. Great strides were made in bringing science into archeology through new dating techniques a multidisciplinary approach, early experiments with the use of statistics, and devoting substantial attention to increasing the precision of artifact classification. The sixties provided the nation with both the optimistic Kennedy years, with an emphasis on science and the conviction that we were capable of accomplishing wondrous; things, and the cynical Vietnam era. Coming on the heels of a decade of civil rights unrest, the widespread dissatisfaction with the Vietnam conflict in the late sixties molded a generation of young Americans who were distrustful of established authority. In academic life, there was an increasing emphasis on environment, other cultures, and people-oriented disciplines. Anthropology and archeology grew markedly because of these trends. Archeologists were urged to become concerned with sociological issues—the people behind the artifacts.

It was during these decades of rapid change that many of the core concepts of the New Archeology entered the literature. However, they were not, at first, assembled into a program for action that attracted a solid following. Water Taylor advocated the conjuctive approach with little effect, while Leslie White's evolutionism and Julian Styeward's cultural ecology attracted some attention, but largely among cultural anthropologists. Albert Spaulding led a one-man campaign to bring science and statistics into archeology. But the individual whose work catalyzed the New Archeology movement was Lewis Binford, who incorporated these earlier lines of thinking together with an explicit concern for scientific methods and field research designs. Much of Binford's thinking probably crystallised while he was at the University of Michigan, but was during his relatively few years at the University of Chicago that he changed the direction of modern archeology.

11. New Archeology refers to
    (a) newer techniques used in Archeology
    (b) newer inventions used in Archeology
    (c) newer theoretical foundations in Archeology
    (d) None of these

12. The author defends the Archeology of the 1970s because
    (a) he has a nostalgic feeling about it
    (b) it has research value
    (c) it paved the way for newer traditions
    (d) it has historical value

13. The author suggests that
    (a) We should respect new Archeology as a movement in Archeology
    (b) We should go back to the tenets of processual Archeology
    (c) We should treat tenets of new Archeology with respect
    (d) All of the above

14. The importance of Archeology arose from
    (a) the end of World War II
    (b) an increasing scientific outlook
    (c) the launch of Sputnik in 1957
    (d) All of these

15. Which one of the following is not an area of focus for Archeologist?
    (a) Study the interaction of people of small group
    (b) Studying cultures of other people
    (c) Study the social structure of the past societies
    (d) Study the man-environment relationship in the past

16. An Archeologist is concerned with
    (a) classification of artefacts
    (b) maintenance of museums
    (c) digging of ancient cities
    (d) All of these

17. Rhetorics means
    (a) study of the technique and rules for using language effectively
    (b) using language effectively to please or persuade
    (c) excessive use of verbal ornamentation
    (d) All of the above

18. If a receiver replying on 'hmm-mm' or 'I see'. This type of reply is known as
    (a) positive feedback
    (b) ambiguous feedback
    (c) negative feedback
    (d) None of these

19. Which of the following FM radio stations is owned by the Times of India group?
    (a) AIR
    (b) Radio Rainbow
    (c) Radio Mirchi
    (d) Red FM

20. Find the next number in the following sequence:
    9, 8, 25, 12, 49, 18, 121, 26, ?, ?
    (a) 142, 36 (b) 169, 36
    (c) 225, 36 (d) 196, 36

21. **Statement:** Should there be complete ban on pouched tobacco products (like Gutka) in India?
    Arguments:
    (i) Yes, it is the most important cause of mouth cancer and mouth ulcer in our country.
    (ii) No, there are many people employed in this industry right from manufacturing to retailing. This ban will hamper their livelihood.
    (a) Only argument (i) is strong
    (b) Only argument (ii) is strong
    (c) Both the arguments (i) and (ii) are strong
    (d) Neither (i) nor (ii) is strong

22. The relationship between animal, cows, dogs can be shown by

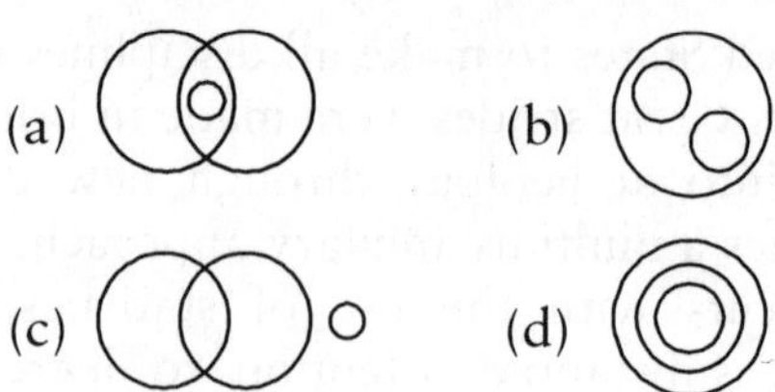

23. If in a certain code:
    'nso prt kli chn' means 'Sharma gets marriage gift'.
    'pit lnm wop chn' means 'wife gives marriage gift'. 'tti wop nhi' means 'he gives nothing'. What would mean gives:
    (a) kli (b) tti
    (c) wop (d) lnm

24. Characteristics of all informal and formal communications are
    (a) Same (b) Structured
    (c) Different (d) None of these

25. Three of the following four are alike in a certain way and so form a group. Find the one which doesn't belong to that group?
    (a) Dog (b) Tiger
    (c) Horse (d) Lion

26. What is research design?
    (a) The methods used in analysis and finding the final conclusion is known as research design
    (b) A researcher needs to prepare a plan of action for his study which is known as research design
    (c) The presentation of final data is known as research design
    (d) None of these

27. Recording a television program on a Set Top Box is an example of
    (a) content reference
    (b) time-shifting
    (c) media synchronisation
    (d) mechanical clarity

28. Which of the following statements say the same thing?

(i) "I am a teacher" (said by Arvind)
(ii) "I am a teacher" (said by Binod)
(iii) "My son is a teacher" (said by Binod's father)
(iv) "My brother is a teacher" (said by Binod's sister)
(v) "My brother is a teacher" (said by Binod's only sister)
(vi) "My sole enemy is a teacher" (said by Binod's only enemy)

Choose the correct answer from the codes given below:

Codes:
(a) (v) and (vi)
(b) (i) and (ii)
(c) (ii) and (vi)
(d) (ii), (iii), (iv) and (v)

29. In this question there are two statements followed by four conclusions numbered I, II, III and IV.

Statements:
A. All books are trees.
B. All trees are lions.

Conclusions:
I. All books are lions.
II. All lions are books.
III. All trees are books.
IV. Some lions are books.

Choose the correct answer.
(a) Only I and IV follow
(b) Only II and III follow
(c) None of conclusions follow
(d) All conclusion follows

Direction: (30-34) Answer the questions based on following table.

Machines X and Y can independently produce either product P or product Q. The time taken by machines X and Y (in minutes) to produce one unit of product P and Q are given in the table below. (Each machine works 8 hours per day.)

Product	X	Y
P	10	8
Q	6	6

30. If the number of units of P is to be three times that of Q, what is the maximum idle time to maximise total units manufactured?
(a) 8 minutes (b) 0 minute
(c) 12 minutes (d) None of these

31. If X works at half its normal efficiency, what is the maximum number of units produced, if at least one unit of each must be produced?
(a) 119 (b) 135
(c) 127 (d) 136

32. What is the maximum number of units that can be manufactured in one day?
(a) 250 (b) 160
(c) 270 (d) 195

33. If equal quantities of both are to be produced, then out of four choices given below the least efficient way would be
(a) 59 of each with 8 min. idle
(b) 71 of each with 9 min. idle
(c) 53 of each with 10 min. idle
(d) 48 of each with 4 min. idle

34. What is the least number of machine hours required to produce 30 pieces of P and 25 pieces of Q, respectively?
(a) 6 hr 30 min. (b) 9 hr 30 min.
(c) 6 hr 40 min. (d) 8 hr 30 min.

35. Telematic is a combination of
(a) Telecommunication and computer
(b) Telecommunication and information
(c) Television and computer
(d) All of the above

36. Following is a part of balance sheet of Timas Pvt. Ltd. Study the table and give answer to the question given below:

(All values in ₹ crore)

Year	Expenditure	Income
1990	3400	4000
1995	3800	4500
2000	4500	5400
2005	6400	8000

Which of the following conclusions is not true?
(a) There has been a steady growth in % profit of the company
(b) There is around 90% increase in expenditure of the firm from 1990 to 2005
(c) Income of the company is doubled in 15 years
(d) Percentage profit in 2000 was 18%

37. If EFGHUK is coded as VUTSRQ then LIMIT can be coded as
(a) KNRNC (b) ORNRG
(c) JKOKG (d) RSTSG

38. The more is 'Resolution Power' of a printer better is its
(a) Speed (b) Colour
(c) Memory (d) Quality

39. Laterite soil develops due to
(a) deposits of alluvial
(b) deposition of loess
(c) leaching
(d) continued vegetation cover

40. Line access and avoidance of collision are the main functions of
(a) network protocols
(b) wide area networks
(c) the CPU
(d) the monitor

41. Communication satellites are placed in
(a) Geostationary Orbit
(b) Polar Orbit
(c) Both (a) and (b)
(d) None of these

42. DLL stands for
(a) Data Deriving Language
(b) Data Definition Language
(c) Data Design Language
(d) All of the above

43. Transistors were first used in
(a) 2nd generation computers
(b) 3rd generation computers
(c) 4th generation computers
(d) None of these

44. Which of the following is not provided in the Constitution?
(a) Planning Commission
(b) Election Commission
(c) Finance Commission
(d) Public Service Commission

45. The first satellite launched in space was
(a) Early Bird (b) Sputnik-1
(c) Skylab (d) Aryabhatta-1

46. At what time between 5.30 and 6.00 will the hands of a clock be at right angles?
(a) 45 minutes past 5
(b) $43\frac{5}{11}$ minutes past 5
(c) $43\frac{7}{11}$ minutes past 5
(d) 40 minutes past 5

47. A person can be a member of Council of Ministers without being a member of Parliament for a maximum period of
(a) 45 days (b) 90 days
(c) 180 days (d) one year

48. Many engineers and architects use a different type of pen called a
(a) Pointer pen (b) Computer pen
(c) Light pen (d) Logical pen

49. Which of the following are wrongly matched?

Name of Volcano	Country
(a) Mt. Spur	USA
(b) Mt. Fuego	Guatemala
(c) Mt. Ag'ung	Indonesia
(d) Mt. Lascor	Equador

50. How many types of emergency can be declared by the President of India?
(a) 1 (b) 2
(c) 3 (d) 4

PAPER–II

1. A political party has been defined as "an association organised in support of some principles or policy which by constitutional means endeavours to make the determinant of government" by
   (a) Machiavelli (b) Bryce
   (c) Barker (d) MacIver
2. The concept of 'best practicable state' is the contribution made by
   (a) Plato (b) Cicero
   (c) Aristotle (d) Thomas Acquinas
3. The multinational corporations or the MNCs are replacing the national corporations because
   (a) MNCs have began to move the manufacturing plants overseas to meet the cost of competition in foreign markets.
   (b) the sales of these large corporations are geared to the global market.
   (c) A large portion of their revenues are generated from sales outside the countries where they are headquartered or originated.
   (d) All of the above.
4. Sir Henry Maine's theory of State was influenced by
   (a) Theory of Social Contract.
   (b) Hegelian idealism.
   (c) Benthamite Utilitarianism.
   (d) The theory of Social Evolution.
5. Duguit criticised the Austinian theory of sovereignty in the name of the
   (a) moral personality of corporations.
   (b) theory of natural law.
   (c) community's sense of right.
   (d) principle of social solidarity.
6. Authority should be commensurate with
   (a) degree of responsibility
   (b) degree of supervision
   (c) degree of coordination
   (d) position in the hierarchy
7. This type of training seeks to prepare future recruits for the service
   (a) Pre-entry training
   (b) Post-entry training
   (c) Formal training
   (d) Informal training
8. Which one of the following countries has/had single citizenship?
   (a) Former U.S.S.R. (b) U.S.A.
   (c) Australia (d) None of these
9. Which one of the following factors has not contributed to the strengthening of the Centre under a federal government?
   (a) Grants-in-aid by the Central government.
   (b) International rivalry and friction
   (c) Emergence of regional political parties
   (d) Centralised National Planning
10. Which one of the following was the first country-wide pressure group of the organized Indian working class?
    (a) All India Trade Union Congress
    (b) Indian National Trade Union Congress
    (c) Indian Mining Federation
    (d) Hind Mazdoor Sabha
11. Panchayati Raj system aims at
    (a) decentralisation of political power.
    (b) rural co-operation.
    (c) spreading political awareness among people.
    (d) improving the standard of living of rural people.
12. Non-security issues have taken priority over force, violence and military might because of
    (a) modernization of world political and communication systems.
    (b) modernization of world political and economic systems.

(c) trans-nationalization of world economic and political systems.
(d) decentralization of world economic and political systems.

13. According to classical school, 'the Science of Public Administration' was based on
(a) presence of scientific principles and methods of universal application.
(b) presence of empirical exact knowledge.
(c) absence of ethical or normative values.
(d) presence of codified principles and techniques.

14. Which theory is a part of the decision making approach in the field of mathematics and in behavioural sciences it has been incorporated into the models and experiments of both conflict and decision-making in a conflict-ridden situation?
(a) Neo-realist Theory
(b) Systems Theory
(c) Game Theory
(d) Coalition Theory

15. Which international organisation defined globalization as "the increasingly close international integration of markets both for goods and services and capital"?
(a) UNO (b) UNDP
(c) The World Bank (d) The IMF

16. According to Hobbes,
(a) individuals after the contract retain right to kill.
(b) individuals surrender no rights to create the state.
(c) individuals have all natural rights in the state.
(d) individuals have liberty and property rights in the state.

17. It is possible to levy the following types of tax without any sanction of the legislature.
(a) An indirect tax
(b) A direct tax
(c) A progressive tax
(d) An ad hoc levy

18. The Lok Sabha was first constituted in
(a) 1947 (b) 1950
(c) 1952 (d) 1951

19. Local government in recent times is regarded as
(a) Administrative line agencies
(b) People's voluntary agencies
(c) Subsidiary sovereign bodies
(d) Subsidiary law-making bodies

20. Which one of the following is not a function of the District Collector?
(a) Realisation of taquavi loans
(b) Maintenance of land records
(c) Hearing of appeals against the decisions of Nyaya Panchayats
(d) Collection of revenue

21. The fundamental theme of Sarvodaya is
(a) the realisation of the happiness and elevation of the elite.
(b) the realisation of the happiness and elevation of all.
(c) the realisation of the happiness and elevation of the downtrodden.
(d) None of the above.

22. Seats have been allotted on the basis of population for the States in the
(a) Lok Sabha
(b) Rajya Sabha
(c) Parliament
(d) Council of Ministers

23. The judgment delivered by the Supreme Court in what is known as Minerva Mills batch of cases in August 1980 has further reaffirmed the decision of the Supreme Court in
(a) Sajjan Singh case
(b) A.K. Gopalan case
(c) Golak Nath case
(d) Keshavananda Bharati case

24. Who among the following appoints the District Judge in a State?
    (a) The Governor of the State
    (b) The President of India
    (c) The Chief Minister of the State
    (d) Chief Justice of the High Court of the State

25. During financial emergency, the President of India can do the following things:
    1. Ask the State to reduce salaries of their employees including the judges of High Courts.
    2. Direct the States to reserve all their financial bills for his approval.
    3. Give directions to the States to observe certain canons of economy.
    4. Modify the provisions relating to the distribution of revenue between Centre and States.

    Codes:
    (a) 1 and 3 (b) 2 and 3
    (c) 1, 2 and 3 (d) 1, 3 and 4

26. Who among the following launched educational reform movements among Muslims in India?
    1. Sir Syed Ahmed Khan
    2. Sir W.W. Hunter
    3. Shah Waliullah
    4. Zakir Hussain

    Codes:
    (a) 1 and 3 (b) 1 and 4
    (c) 3 and 4 (d) 2, 3 and 4

27. Which of the following are the functions of coordination?
    1. It removes conflicts in administration.
    2. It encourages concentration on one aspect of work.
    3. It secures cooperation.
    4. It curbs the growing tendency towards empire building.

    Codes:
    (a) 1 and 4 (b) 1, 2 and 4
    (c) 1, 3 and 4 (d) 2, 3 and 4

28. Part XIV A inserted by the Constitution (Forty-second Amendment) Act, 1976 in the Constitution of India deals with which of the following?
    1. Administrative tribunals
    2. Adjudication or trial by tribunals in respect of enforcement of any tax
    3. Adjudication or trial by tribunals in respect of ceiling on urban properties
    4. Adjudication or trial by tribunals in respect of industrial and labour disputes

    Codes:
    (a) 1 and 4 (b) 3 and 4
    (c) 1, 2 and 3 (d) 1, 2, 3 and 4

29. Which of the following are the important features of 73rd Constitutional Amendment in respect of Panchayati Raj?
    1. Direct election of members at all levels.
    2. Mandatory provision of holding elections.
    3. Direct election of chairpersons at the village level.
    4. Indirect election of chairpersons at the intermediate and district levels.

    Codes:
    (a) 1, 2 and 4 (b) 1, 3 and 4
    (c) 1, 2 and 3 (d) 2, 3 and 4

30. Under the Panchayat Raj Amendment Act, which of the following have been provided?
    1. Direct elections to Panchayats at all three levels
    2. Direct election of Chairpersons of Panchayats at the village level
    3. Not less than one-third of the seats of Chairpersons at all three levels is reserved for women

    Codes:
    (a) 1 and 2 (b) 1 and 3
    (c) 2 and 3 (d) 1, 2 and 3

31. The main federal features of the Indian Constitution are
   1. Division of powers
   2. Supremacy of Constitution
   3. Dual citizenship
   4. Bi-cameral legislature

   Codes:
   (a) 2 and 3 (b) 1, 2 and 4
   (c) 1, 3 and 4 (d) 2, 3 and 4

32. President's Rule can be imposed in a State under the provision of which of the following Articles of the Constitution of India?
   1. Article 352 2. Article 356
   3. Article 360 4. Article 365

   Codes:
   (a) 2 only (b) 1 and 2
   (c) 1 and 3 (d) 1 and 4

33. Who among the following are not associated with Backward Caste Movements in India?
   1. Sri Narayan Guru
   2. B.R. Ambedkar
   3. Jyothibha Phule

   Codes:
   (a) 2 and 3 (b) 1, 2 and 3
   (c) 1 and 2 (d) 1 and 3

34. The Constitution of India has ensured independence of judiciary through which of the following?
   1. Providing single judiciary.
   2. Ensuring security of tenure to judges.
   3. Protecting salaries and service conditions of the judges.
   4. Prohibiting the judges from carrying on practice in the courts of law after retirement.

   Codes:
   (a) 1, 2 and 3 (b) 1, 3 and 4
   (c) 2, 3 and 4 (d) 1, 2, 3 and 4

35. Match the two lists as per code.

   List I
   A. Lord Hewart B. Ordway Tead
   C. Dwight Waldo D. Barnard

   List II
   1. The Functions of the Executive
   2. Ideas and Issues in Public Administration
   3. The new Despotism
   4. The Art of Administration

Codes:	**A**	**B**	**C**	**D**
(a)	4	2	1	3
(b)	3	4	2	1
(c)	3	2	1	4
(d)	4	1	3	2

36. In the second half of 19th century several peasant revolts took place in different parts of India. Match the revolt with its respective area
   A. Kuki Revolt 1. Punjab
   B. Kuka Revolt 2. Bengal
   C. Pabna Peasant Revolt 3. Bihar
   D. Birsa Munda's Revolt 4. Tripura

Codes:	**A**	**B**	**C**	**D**
(a)	2	3	1	4
(b)	4	1	3	2
(c)	4	1	2	3
(d)	4	2	1	3

37. Match the two lists as per code.

   List I (Source)
   A. Taxes levied by the Union but collected and appropriated by the State.
   B. Taxes levied, collected and retained by the Centre.
   C. Taxes levied and collected by the Centre but assigned to the States.
   D. Taxes levied and collected by the Centre and compulsorily distributed between the Union and the States.

List II (Tax)

1. Taxes on income other than agriculture
2. Stamp duties
3. Corporation Tax
4. Taxes on land and buildings
5. Taxes on railway fares and freights

Codes:	A	B	C	D
(a)	1	5	4	2
(b)	2	3	5	1
(c)	1	3	5	2
(d)	2	5	4	1

38. Match the two lists as per code.

List I

A. Madhya Pradesh B. West Bengal
C. Uttar Pradesh D. Gujarat

List II

1. Anchalik Parishad
2. Janapad Panchayat
3. Taluka Panchayat
4. Kshetra Samiti

Codes:	A	B	C	D
(a)	2	1	4	3
(b)	2	1	3	4
(c)	1	2	3	4
(d)	1	2	4	3

39. Match the two lists as per code.

List I (Provision)

A. Provisions concerning administration of Tribal Areas.
B. Language of the Union.
C. Trade and Commerce within India.
D. The Executive of the Union.

List II (Contained in)

1. Chapter I of Part V of the Constitution of India.
2. Part XIII of the Constitution of India.
3. Part XVII of the Constitution of India.
4. Sixth Schedule of the Constitution of India.

Codes:	A	B	C	D
(a)	2	1	4	3
(b)	4	3	2	1
(c)	2	3	4	1
(d)	4	1	2	3

40. Match the two lists as per code.

List I (Powers of the President)

A. Commutation B. Remission
C. Respite D. Reprieve

List II (Explanation)

1. Stay of execution of a sentence.
2. Reducing the amount of sentence without changing its character.
3. Awarding of a lesser sentence instead of the penalty prescribed.
4. Substituting one form of punishment for another of a lighter character.

Codes:	A	B	C	D
(a)	4	3	2	1
(b)	4	2	1	3
(c)	4	2	3	1
(d)	3	4	2	1

41. Match the two lists as per code.

List I (Constitutional Amendment)

A. 37th B. 49th
C. 58th D. 77th

List II (Effect)

1. Tripura in the sixth schedule
2. Legislature to some UTs
3. Publication of the Constitution in Hindi
4. National Capital status to Delhi
5. Reservation in promotions to SCs and STs

Codes:	A	B	C	D
(a)	2	1	3	5
(b)	3	4	2	1
(c)	2	4	3	1
(d)	3	1	2	5

42. Match the two lists as per code.

List I	List II
A. 1881	1. Abolition of import duty on cotton goods
B. 1883	2. The Factories Act

C. 1878 3. The Statutory Civil Service

D. 1879 4. The Famine Code

Codes:	**A**	**B**	**C**	**D**
(a)	4	2	3	1
(b)	2	1	4	3
(c)	1	2	3	4
(d)	2	4	1	3

43. Match the two lists as per code.

List I

A. Lord Curzon B. Lord Lytton

C. Rowlatt D. Ilbert

List II

1. Grand Durbar
2. Tenure System
3. Arrest without warrant
4. Indian Magistrate cannot be European

Codes:	**A**	**B**	**C**	**D**
(a)	1	4	3	2
(b)	2	1	3	4
(c)	4	1	2	3
(d)	3	1	4	2

44. **Assertion (A):** Rank classification facilitates lateral entry.

Reason (R): Rank classification facilitates transfers within the service.

Codes:

(a) Both (A) and (R) are true and (R) is the correct explanation.
(b) Both (A) and (R) are not true.
(c) (A) is true and (R) is false.
(d) (A) is false and (R) is true.

45. **Assertion (A):** Lack of promotion system has a marked retroactive effect on all process of personnel management.

Reason (R): Promotion system is vital for attracting and retaining talented persons in public services.

Codes:

(a) Both (A) and (R) are true and (R) is the correct explanation.
(b) Both (A) and (R) are not true.
(c) (A) is true and (R) is false.
(d) (A) is false and (R) is true.

46. **Assertion (A):** In systems approach, the process and the course of action is adopted to suit the requirements of the situation.

Reason (R): The organisation has a social purpose and is a part of the prevailing environment.

Codes:

(a) Both (A) and (R) are true and (R) is the correct explanation.
(b) Both (A) and (R) are not true.
(c) (A) is true and (R) is false.
(d) (A) is false and (R) is true.

47. **Assertion (A):** Development administration signifies action-oriented and target-oriented programmes suitable for developing countries.

Reason (R): The success of rural development plans acts as a strong impetus for initiating other developmental plans.

Codes:

(a) Both (A) and (R) are true and (R) is the correct explanation.
(b) Both (A) and (R) are not true.
(c) (A) is true and (R) is false.
(d) (A) is false and (R) is true.

48. **Assertion (A):** The appellate jurisdiction of the High Court is both civil and criminal.

Reason (R): On the civil side, an appeal to the High Court is either a First appeal or a Second appeal.

Codes:

(a) Both (A) and (R) are true and (R) is the correct explanation.
(b) Both (A) and (R) are not true.
(c) (A) is true and (R) is false.
(d) (A) is false and (R) is true.

49. **Assertion (A):** The Supreme Court as well as the High Court possesses an

extraordinary jurisdiction, under Articles 32 and 226 of the Constitution.

Reason (R): The 44th Amendment Act took away the jurisdiction of the High Courts over tribunals.

Codes:

(a) Both (A) and (R) are true and (R) is the correct explanation.
(b) Both (A) and (R) are not true.
(c) (A) is true and (R) is false.
(d) (A) is false and (R) is true.

50. **Assertion (A):** India is a Union of States and not a Federal State.

Reason (R): In the Indian Constitution, the Centre is given emergency powers which can convert the State into a Unitary State.

Codes:

(a) Both (A) and (R) are true and (R) is the correct explanation.
(b) Both (A) and (R) are not true.
(c) (A) is true and (R) is false.
(d) (A) is false and (R) is true.

PAPER–III

1. Who among the following described elites as "speculators" and "rentiers"?
   (a) Pareto (b) Mosca
   (c) Michels (d) Gasset

2. Residuary powers refers to those powers which are
   (a) bestowed on the States by the Parliament.
   (b) not included in any of the three lists in which the powers have been divided.
   (c) included in the Residuary List.
   (d) None of the above.

3. What is the difference between Indian Federalism and Canadian Federalism?
   (a) Indian Federation is centrally inclined, which is not with the Canadian Federation.
   (b) Indian Federation is evolved but Canadian Federation is a result of colonial legacy.
   (c) Indian Federation has written Constitution which is not with the Canadian.
   (d) None of the above.

4. The Supreme Court of India declares by issuing a writ that "the respondent was not entitled to an office he was holding or a privilege he was exercising." Which writ is that?
   (a) Quo Warranto (b) Certiorari
   (c) Habeas Corpus (d) Prohibition

5. Which one of the following statements regarding the exercise of judicial review in India is not correct?
   (a) Legislative enactments and executive orders may be struck down by the Supreme Court.
   (b) The power is implicit in the provisions of Article 13 of the Constitution.
   (c) A case must be brought before the Supreme Court regarding the validity of a law.
   (d) Unanimous opinion of all the judges is necessary for declaring a law null and void.

6. The Indian federation is a/an
   (a) destructible Union of indestructible States.
   (b) destructible Union of destructible States.
   (c) indestructible Union of indestructible States.
   (d) indestructible Union of destructible States.

7. Who among the following are involved in the Cauvery River dispute?
   (a) The Central Government and Karnataka.
   (b) The Central Government and Tamil Nadu.

(c) Karnataka and Tamil Nadu.
(d) Karnataka, Tamil Nadu, Kerala and Pondicherry.

8. The Constitution authorises the Parliament to increase any of the duties or taxes stipulated in Articles 269 and 270 by imposing surcharge. But the proceeds of the surcharge
   (a) must be deposited in the Contingency Fund of India to meet unforeseen expenses.
   (b) go to the Consolidated Fund of India.
   (c) must be equally shared by the Centre and the States.
   (d) must go to the States.

9. The main provision of the Sixth Schedule of the Constitution of India deals with
   (a) autonomy in administration in the tribal areas of north-east India.
   (b) reservation in educational institutions.
   (c) reservation in government jobs.
   (d) preservation of tribal lands.

10. The Constitutional Amendment Act which by far brought about the maximum changes in the Constitution was the
    (a) 42th Amendment Act
    (b) 44th Amendment Act
    (c) 72nd Amendment Act
    (d) 93rd Amendment Act

11. Which one of the following is a Constitutional Body?
    (a) National Commission for Scheduled Tribes
    (b) National Commission for Minorities
    (c) National Commission for Women
    (d) Planning Commission

12. Regarding the re-election of the Vice-President of India
    (a) The Constitution limits re-election to two terms.
    (b) The Constitution permits unlimited terms.
    (c) The Constitution is silent.
    (d) The Constitution does not allow it.

13. The quorum requirements in the Rajya Sabha is
    (a) 25 (b) 50
    (c) 100 (d) 125

14. For what period the life of the Lok Sabha can be extended at a time?
    (a) Three months (b) Six months
    (c) One year (d) Two years

15. In which of the following legislatures can a non-member be the Presiding Officer?
    (a) Rajya Sabha
    (b) Vidhan Parishad
    (c) Vidhan Sabha
    (d) None of the above

16. The object of the adjournment motion in Parliament is
    (a) collect information from the ministers
    (b) make a cut in the budget proposals
    (c) criticise a particular policy of the government
    (d) topple the government

17. Before giving any decision on questions as to disqualification of a member of either House of Parliament, the President of India shall obtain the opinion of which one of the following?
    (a) Supreme Court
    (b) Election Commission
    (c) Attorney General of India
    (d) Solicitor General of India

18. Which one of the following statements is correct?
    The Rajya Sabha has exclusive jurisdiction in
    (a) approving a Proclamation of Emergency.
    (b) the creation and abolition of States.
    (c) the election of the Vice-President.
    (d) authorizing the Parliament to legislate on a subject in the State List

19. Who declared, "The only hope for India is from the masses. The upper classes are physically and morally dead"?
(a) Mahatma Gandhi
(b) Swami Vivekanand
(c) Gopal Krishna Gokhale
(d) Bal Gangadhar Tilak

20. What were the Hindu counterparts to the movements of Tabligh and Tanzim?
(a) Self Respect movement
(b) Rashtriya Svayamsevak Sangh
(c) Satya Sodhak movement
(d) Shudhi and Sangathan

21. The Headquarters of the Ghadar Party was at
(a) San Francisco (b) Karachi
(c) Moscow (d) Berlin

22. Who strongly objected to the British Government's negotiating on terms of equality with the Seditious Fakir, i.e. Mahatma Gandhi in February-March 1931?
(a) Winston Churchill
(b) Lord Wavell
(c) Ramsay MacDonald
(d) Lord Linlithgow

23. The term 'equal protection of the law' used in Article 14 of the Indian Constitution was borrowed from
(a) USA (b) Germany
(c) Canada (d) Britain

24. Which Act abolished the Company's monopoly of trade with China?
(a) Indian Councils Act 1861
(b) Charter Act of 1833
(c) Charter Act of 1813
(d) None of the above

25. The Directive Principles of State Policy in Indian Constitution are ______ in their nature.
(a) non-justifiable (b) Gandhian
(c) democratic (d) collectivist

26. Who of the following was the Permanent Chairman of the Constituent Assembly?
(a) Pt. Jawaharlal Nehru
(b) Dr. Rajendra Prasad
(c) B.R. Ambedkar
(d) Sardar Patel

27. The phrase 'equality before law' used in Article 14 of the Constitution has been borrowed from
(a) U.S.A. (b) Britain
(c) France (d) None of these

28. Which of the following terms is not incorporated in the Constitution?
(a) Secular (b) Federal
(c) Democratic (d) Socialist

29. The idea of the Union giving directions to the States was adopted by the makers of the Indian Constitution from
(a) The Government of India Act, 1935
(b) The US Constitution
(c) The Soviet Constitution
(d) The Australian Constitution

30. Which of the following are termed as the privileges of the members of the Parliament?
1. Freedom of speech in Parliament.
2. Immunity to a member from any proceedings in any court in respect of anything said or any vote given by him in Parliament or any committee thereof.
3. Prohibition on the courts to inquire into proceedings of Parliament.
4. Freedom from arrest in civil cases during, forty days before and after, the parliamentary session.

Codes:
(a) 1 and 2 (b) 1, 2 and 3
(c) 2, 3 and 4 (d) 1, 2, 3 and 4

31. In the pluralist's view
1. the State is an association.
2. the State differs in no way from other associations.

3. the State is not distinct from the government.
4. there should be no concentration of authority in the State.

Codes:

(a) 1, 2 and 3 (b) 1, 3 and 4
(c) 2, 3 and 4 (d) 1, 2, 3 and 4

32. Which of the following are conservatism as a political ideology associated?
1. Burke 2. Hobbes
3. Hegel 4. Oakeshott

Codes:

(a) 1 and 3 (b) 2 and 4
(c) 1, 2 and 3 (d) 1, 3 and 4

33. Which of the following are envisaged by the Right against Exploitation in the Constitution of India?
1. Prohibition of traffic in human beings and forced labour.
2. Abolition of untouchability.
3. Protection of the interests of minorities.
4. Prohibition of employment of children in factories and mines.

Codes:

(a) 2 and 4 (b) 1 and 4
(c) 1 and 2 (d) 1 and 3

34. Consider the following events:
1. Pitt's India Act
2. Diwani Rights of the East India Company
3. Regulating Act
4. Appointment of Warren Hastings as Governor of Bengal

The correct chronological sequence of these events is

Codes:

(a) 2, 4, 1, 3 (b) 4, 2, 3, 1
(c) 2, 4, 3, 1 (d) 4, 2, 1, 3

35. What were the salient features of the Government of India Act, 1935?
1. Provincial Autonomy
2. Dyarchy at the Centre
3. Abolition of dyarchy in the States
4. Retention of Excluded Areas

Codes:

(a) 2 and 3 (b) 1, 2 and 4
(c) 1, 3 and 4 (d) 1, 2, 3 and 4

36. Give the correct chronological order
1. Communal Award
2. Simon Commission
3. First Round Table Conference
4. Gandhi-Irwin Pact

Codes:

(a) 2, 3, 1, 4 (b) 2, 3, 4, 1
(c) 1, 2, 3, 4 (d) 2, 1, 3, 4

37. Which is the correct chronological order of the following?
1. Cripps Mission,
2. Gandhi-Irwin pact,
3. Simon Commission,
4. Partition of the country

Codes:

(a) 1, 3, 2, 4 (b) 3, 2, 1, 4
(c) 3, 4, 1, 2 (d) 3, 1, 4, 2

38. What is the correct chronological sequence of the below. Choose the write answer from the codes.
1. Subhash as President of the Indian National Congress
2. Formation of Congress Socialist Party
3. Formation of Satyagraha Sabha by Gandhi
4. Communal Award

Codes:

(a) 4, 2, 3, 1 (b) 3, 4, 2, 1
(c) 2, 3, 4, 1 (d) 1, 3, 2, 4

39. The end of the Swadeshi Movement saw most of its established leadership disappear from the scene.

List I

A. Bal Gangadhar Tilak
B. Aurobindo Ghose

C. Bipin Chandra Pal
D. Lala Lajpat Rai

List II
1. Went abroad
2. Temporary retirement from politics
3. Revolutionary conspiracy case
4. Mandalay Jail

Codes:	A	B	C	D
(a)	1	3	4	2
(b)	2	3	1	4
(c)	2	4	3	1
(d)	4	3	2	1

40. Match the two lists as per code.

List I (Development Approaches)
A. Blue print approach
B. Learning process approach
C. Production centred approach
D. People centred approach

List II (Features)
1. Utilisation of capital resources over human resources
2. Cybernetic process with latitude for change according to needs
3. Planning in advance for development
4. Individual as an actor who defines the goal

Codes:	A	B	C	D
(a)	3	4	1	2
(b)	1	2	3	4
(c)	3	2	1	4
(d)	1	4	3	2

41. Match the two lists as per code.

List I
A. Theory of Masses
B. Iron Law of Oligarchy
C. Circulation of elites
D. Power elite

List II
1. Pareto
2. Michels
3. Ortega Gasset
4. Mills

Codes:	A	B	C	D
(a)	3	2	1	4
(b)	2	1	4	3
(c)	4	2	3	1
(d)	1	3	4	2

42. Match the two lists as per code.

List I (Stages in the emergence of political parties according to Max Weber)
A. Eighteenth century
B. Nineteenth century
C. Twentieth century

List II (Types of political parties according to Max Weber)
1. Parties of notables
2. Pure following of the aristocracy
3. Highly structured party machines
4. Parties of clerics

Codes:	A	B	C
(a)	1	2	3
(b)	2	4	1
(c)	2	1	3
(d)	3	1	4

43. Match the two lists as per code.

List I	**List II**
A. India	1. Socialism
B. Brunei	2. Democracy
C. Erstwhile U.S.S.R.	3. Theocracy
D. Iran	4. Monarchy
	5. Fascism

Codes:	A	B	C	D
(a)	2	4	1	3
(b)	5	4	3	1
(c)	1	2	3	4
(d)	4	5	3	1

44. Match the two lists as per code.

List I (Countries)
A. China
B. Germany
C. France
D. South Africa

List II (Types of Political System)
1. Federal, Representative, Democratic, Republic
2. Sovereign, Democratic, Republic
3. People's Democratic Socialist Republic
4. Indivisible, Secular, Democratic, Republic

Codes:	A	B	C	D
(a)	2	1	3	4
(b)	3	1	4	2
(c)	4	3	2	1
(d)	3	4	1	2

45. **Assertion (A):** According to T.H. Green, the self is a social self.
Reason (R): Bosanquet believes that there is mutuality of relationship between individual and social community of which he is a member.
Codes:
(a) Both (A) and (R) are true and (R) is the correct explanation.
(b) Both (A) and (R) are not true.
(c) (A) is true and (R) is false.
(d) (A) is false and (R) is true.

46. **Assertion (A):** According to Article 256, the executive power of every State is to be exercised in such a way to ensure compliance with the laws made by Parliament.
Reason (R): The idea of the Union giving directions to the States is foreign to most federations.
Codes:
(a) Both (A) and (R) are true and (R) is the correct explanation.
(b) Both (A) and (R) are not true.
(c) (A) is true and (R) is false.
(d) (A) is false and (R) is true.

47. **Assertion (A):** The Council of Ministers is a composite body.
Reason (R): The number of members of the Council of Ministers is specified in the Constitution.
Codes:
(a) Both (A) and (R) are true and (R) is the correct explanation.
(b) Both (A) and (R) are not true.
(c) (A) is true and (R) is false.
(d) (A) is false and (R) is true.

48. **Assertion (A):** After three Round Table Conferences, the British Government published a white paper in March 1933 containing an outline of a new Constitution.
Reason (R): The Scheme contained provisions for a federal set-up and provincial autonomy.
Codes:
(a) Both (A) and (R) are true and (R) is the correct explanation.
(b) Both (A) and (R) are not true.
(c) (A) is true and (R) is false.
(d) (A) is false and (R) is true.

49. **Assertion (A):** Power signifies the capacity to affect the behaviour of others by some form of sanction.
Reason (R): Increase in power can be measured by the frequency of sanctions.
Codes:
(a) Both (A) and (R) are true and (R) is the correct explanation.
(b) Both (A) and (R) are not true.
(c) (A) is true and (R) is false.
(d) (A) is false and (R) is true.

50. **Assertion (A):** Guild Socialism aims at placing authority in the hands of consumers as they are in majority.
Reason (R): Public Authority in representative democracy is constituted on the principle of majority.
Codes:
(a) Both (A) and (R) are true and (R) is the correct explanation.
(b) Both (A) and (R) are not true.
(c) (A) is true and (R) is false.
(d) (A) is false and (R) is true.

ANSWER SHEET

PAPER—I

1. (d)	2. (d)	3. (c)	4. (d)	5. (d)
6. (a)	7. (b)	8. (d)	9. (d)	10. (d)
11. (d)	12. (c)	13. (c)	14. (b)	15. (a)

16. (d) 17. (d) 18. (b) 19. (c) 20. (b)
21. (a) 22. (b) 23. (c) 24. (c) 25. (c)
26. (b) 27. (b) 28. (c) 29. (b) 30. (b)
31. (a) 32. (b) 33. (c) 34. (a) 35. (b)
36. (d) 37. (b) 38. (d) 39. (c) 40. (a)
41. (a) 42. (b) 43. (a) 44. (a) 45. (b)
46. (c) 47. (c) 48. (c) 49. (d) 50. (c)

PAPER—II

1. (d) 2. (b) 3. (d) 4. (d) 5. (d)
6. (a) 7. (a) 8. (a) 9. (c) 10. (a)
11. (a) 12. (b) 13. (a) 14. (c) 15. (d)
16. (d) 17. (d) 18. (c) 19. (d) 20. (c)
21. (b) 22. (c) 23. (d) 24. (a) 25. (c)
26. (b) 27. (c) 28. (d) 29. (c) 30. (d)
31. (b) 32. (b) 33. (c) 34. (c) 35. (b)
36. (c) 37. (b) 38. (b) 39. (b) 40. (c)
41. (a) 42. (d) 43. (b) 44. (d) 45. (a)
46. (b) 47. (b) 48. (b) 49. (c) 50. (a)

PAPER—III

1. (d) 2. (b) 3. (b) 4. (a) 5. (a)
6. (d) 7. (d) 8. (b) 9. (a) 10. (a)
11. (a) 12. (a) 13. (a) 14. (c) 15. (a)
16. (c) 17. (b) 18. (d) 19. (b) 20. (d)
21. (a) 22. (a) 23. (d) 24. (b) 25. (a)
26. (b) 27. (b) 28. (b) 29. (a) 30. (d)
31. (b) 32. (d) 33. (b) 34. (c) 35. (d)
36. (b) 37. (b) 38. (b) 39. (d) 40. (c)
41. (a) 42. (c) 43. (a) 44. (b) 45. (b)
46. (b) 47. (c) 48. (a) 49. (b) 50. (b)

MOCK TEST–3

PAPER–I

1. Which among the following gives more freedom to the learner to interact?
(a) Small group discussion
(b) Lectures by experts
(c) Use of film
(d) Viewing country-wide classroom program on TV

2. While designing communication strategy feed-forward studies are conducted by
(a) Media (b) Audience
(c) Communicator (d) Satellite

3. A theory is correct because
(a) its derivations match with most observations
(b) its advocate has written a big volume to establish it
(c) it is supported by a large number of scholars
(d) it has a large number of followers

4. Which of the following are true about the concepts?
I. Concepts have different meanings in different contents.
II. Concepts are the blocks from which theories are built.
III. Concepts are ideas, abstractions, that do not have meaning in themselves.
Codes:
(a) II only (b) I and III
(c) I and II (d) All of these

5. The most sensible idea about teaching and research is that
(a) they interfere with each other
(b) they are two entirely different kinds of activities
(c) they cannot go together
(d) they are two sides of the same coin

6. Which of the following is quality of a teacher?
   (a) He should know the child psychology
   (b) He should evoke curiosity of the pupils by presenting the subject-matter in an effective manner with clear explaining leading to better understanding of the matter
   (c) He should be trained in various teaching methodologies
   (d) All of these
7. Which of the following are true about research?
   (i) Gives emphasis to the development of theories, principles and generalisation, which are very helpful in accurate prediction regarding the variable understudy.
   (ii) It is always directed towards the solution of a problem.
   (iii) It is always based upon empirical or observable evidences.

   Codes:
   (a) Both (i) and (ii)
   (b) Both (i) and (iii)
   (c) Both (ii) and (iii)
   (d) All of the above
8. Which of the following methods of teaching encourages the use of maximum senses?
   (a) Team teaching method
   (b) Problem-solving method
   (c) Laboratory method
   (d) Self-study method
9. A non-fictional literary composition that forms an independent part of a publication, as a newspaper or magazine is known as
   (a) Symposium (b) Paper
   (c) Article (d) None of these
10. Photo bleeding means
   (a) Photo placement
   (b) Photo cropping
   (c) Photo colour adjustment
   (d) Photo cutting
11. Attitudes, concepts, skills and knowledge are products of
   (a) Explanation (b) Learning
   (c) Research (d) Heredity
12. To study the relationship of family size with income a researcher classifies his population into different income slabs and then takes a random sample from each slab. Which technique of sampling does he adopt?
   (a) Systematic Sampling
   (b) Random Sampling
   (c) Stratified Random Sampling
   (d) Cluster Sampling
13. In business communication, the major obstacles arise because of the
   (a) psychological barriers
   (b) physical barriers
   (c) organisational barriers
   (d) mechanical barriers
14. The most important question that a researcher is interested to use statistical techniques in his problem then he has to see
   (a) whether worthwhile inferences could be drawn
   (b) whether the data could be quantified
   (c) whether appropriate statistical techniques are available
   (d) whether analysis of data would be possible
15. How can the objectivity of the research be enhanced?
   (a) Through its validity
   (b) Through its impartiality
   (c) Through its reliability
   (d) All of these
16. Which one of the following is not correct? A belief becomes a scientific truth when it

(a) can be replicated
(b) is established experimentally
(c) is arrived by logically
(d) is accepted by many people

17. **Statement:** All cars are ducks. All ducks are birds.

Conclusions:
(i) All birds are cars.
(ii) All cars are birds.
Choose the correct one.
(a) Only conclusion (i) follows
(b) Only conclusion (ii) follows
(c) Both (i) and (ii) follow
(d) Neither (i) nor (ii) follows

18. Research can be conducted by a person who
(a) is a hard worker
(b) has studied research methodology
(c) holds a postgraduate degree
(d) possesses thinking and reasoning ability

19. Action-research is
(a) A longitudinal research
(b) An applied research
(c) A research carried out to solve immediate problems
(d) All of the above

Read the following passage and answer the questions 20 to 24:

The genesis of service tax emanates from the ongoing structural transformation of the Indian economy, whereby presently more than one-half of GDP originates from the services sector. Despite the growing presence of the services sector in the Indian economy it remained out of the tax net prior to 1994-95, leading to a steady deterioration in tax-GDP ratio. The service tax was introduced in 1994-95 on a select category of services at a low rate of five percent. While the service tax rate and the coverage of services being taxed have increased ever since, the combined tax-GDP ratio of the Centre and States, nevertheless, deteriorated from 16.4 percent in 1985-86 to 14.1 percent in 1999-2000. It may be noted that between 1990-91 and 1998-99, the share of industrial sector in GDP dropped by 6.4 percentage points whereas almost 64 percent of the tax revenue was generated by indirect taxes for which industrial sector continues to be the principal tax base. On the other hand, during the same period, the share of services sector in GDP has increased by 10 percentage points and this sector has still remained poorly taxed.

The rationale for service tax, therefore, lies not only in arresting the falling tax-GDP ratio but also in *ipso facto* improving allocative efficiency in the economy as well as promoting equity. Against this backdrop, the service tax needs to be designed taking into account the fact that (i) the share of services in GDP is expanding; (ii) failure to tax services distorts consumer choices and encourages spending on services at the expense of goods; (iii) untaxed service traders are unable to claim Value Added Tax (VAT) on service inputs, which encourages businesses to develop in-house services, creating further distortions; and (iv) most services that are likely to become taxable are positively correlated with expenditure of high-income households and, therefore, service tax improves equity.

In the Indian context, taxation of services assumes importance in the wake of the need for improving the revenue system, ensuring a measure of neutrality in taxation between goods and services and eventually helping to evolve an efficient system of domestic trade taxes, both at the Central and the State levels.

20. What, according to the passage, was the impact of exclusion of service tax till the first half of the last decade of the past century?

(a) Service sector used to flourish exorbitantly
(b) There was no impact as there was no service tax
(c) There was a steady deterioration in the GDP
(d) Tax-GDP ratio had steadily and gradually aggravated

21. Levying service tax is most likely to achieve which of the following?
(i) Promoting equity.
(ii) Check on reducing tax-GDP ratio.
(iii) Enhancement in allocative efficiency.
Codes:
(a) Both (ii) and (iii)
(b) Both (i) and (iii)
(c) Both (i) and (ii)
(d) All the three

22. The origin of service tax is attributed to
(a) metamorphosis of our country's economy
(b) increase in Gross Domestic Product (GDP)
(c) existence of service sector
(d) tax of the future

23. Which of the following factors helps service tax to improve fairness across different economic strata of society?
(a) It improves revenue system
(b) Taxable services are mostly those that are utilised by the rich
(c) Untaxed service traders are prevented from claiming value added tax
(d) Encouragement to in-house services is effected

24. Which of the following is most likely to provide neutrality to various economic activities?
(a) Consistency in tax structure and revenue buoyancy
(b) Increase in revenue buoyancy
(c) fairness in tax administration
(d) Equity and efficiency in various activities

25. Which of the following is classified in the category of the developmental research?
(a) Descriptive research
(b) Philosophical research
(c) Action research
(d) All the above

26. The education aims at the fullest realisation of all the potentialities of children. It implies that
I. it is necessary that their attitudes are helpful, encouraging and sympathetic.
II. teacher and parents must know what children are capable of and what potentialities they possess.
III. they should provide suitable opportunities and favourable environmental facilities which are conducive to the maximum growth of children.

Choose the correct one.
Codes:
(a) II and III (b) I and III
(c) I and II (d) All of them

27. How many times has the Preamble of Indian Constitution been amended so far?
(a) Once (b) Twice
(c) Thrice (d) Never

28. The relationship between earth, mountains and forests can be represented as

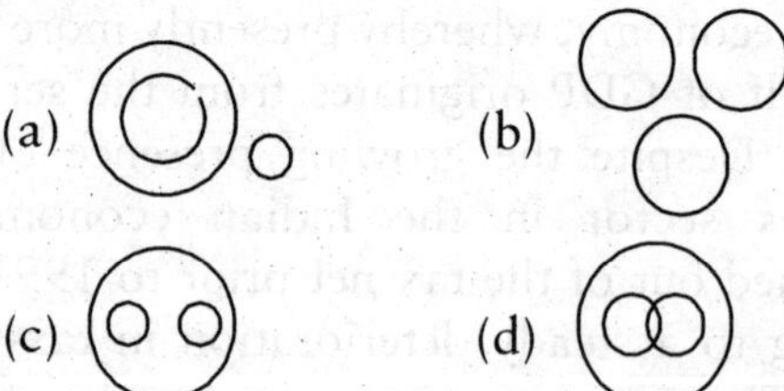

29. Central Fuel Research Institute is situated in
(a) Pune (b) Jadugoda
(c) Lucknow (d) Kolkata

30. The letters in the first set have certain relationship. On the basis of this relationship what is the right choice for the second set?
AST : BRU :: NQV : ?
(a) OPW (b) ORW
(c) MPU (d) MRW

31. The number of students in four classes A, B, C, D and their respective mean marks obtained by each of the class are given below:

	Class A	Class B	Class C	Class D
Number of students	10	40	30	20
Arithmetic mean	20	30	50	15

The combined mean of the marks of four classes together will be
(a) 15 (b) 32
(c) 50 (d) 20

32. Communication with oneself is known as
(a) Organisational communication
(b) Interpersonal communication
(c) Intrapersonal communication
(d) Grapevine communication

33. The number system which is not a positional notation system is
(a) Binary (b) Octal
(c) Roman (d) Decimal

34. Which of the following options will complete the series?
AZ, GT, MN, ?, YB.
(a) TS (b) KF
(c) RX (d) SH

35. If '367' means 'I am happy'; '748' means 'You are sad' and '469' means 'Happy and sad' in a given code, then which of the following represents 'and' in that code?
(a) 4 (b) 6
(c) 3 (d) 9

36. What is the excess 3 code?
(a) self-algebraic code
(b) cyclic complimenting code
(c) cyclic algebraic code
(d) self-complimenting code

37. Which of the following is not created by the Act of Parliament?
(a) Railway Board
(b) Atomic Energy Commission
(c) Backward Class Commission
(d) University Grants Commission

38. Which of the following is radioactive pollutant?
(a) Nickel (b) Iron
(c) Chlorine (d) Thorium

39. The first Indian experimental geostationary communication satellite was
(a) Skylab (b) Apple
(c) INSAT-1A (d) INSAT-1B

40. Which one of the following is a research tool?
(a) Diagram (b) Questionnaire
(c) Graph (d) Illustration

41. Which article of the Constitution provides safeguards to Naga Customary and their social practices against any act of Parliament?
(a) Article 371B (b) Article 371A
(c) Article 263 (d) Article 371C

42. **Statement:** Although the city was under kneedeep water for a week in this monsoon, there is no outbreak of any water borne disease.
Assumptions:
(i) Waterborne disease usually spreads in monsoon.
(ii) Water concentration at a place leads to waterborne disease.

Choose the correct option.
(a) Only assumption (i) is implicit
(b) Only assumption (ii) is implicit
(c) Both (i) and (ii) are implicit
(d) Neither (i) nor (ii) is implicit

43. Books and records are the primary sources of data in
(a) laboratory research
(b) historical research
(c) participatory research
(d) clinical research

44. The Kothari Commission's report was entitled on
(a) Learning to be adventure
(b) Education and National Development
(c) Education and socialisation in democracy
(d) Diversification of Education

45. What is the term used for a half byte?
(a) Word (b) Bit
(c) Nibble (d) Bug

46. C-band transponder in satellites uses the frequency range
(a) 12 GHz to 14 GHz
(b) 4 GHz to 6 GHz
(c) 2 GHz to 4 GHz
(d) None of these

47. Which of the following water pollutants is the cause of sterility in human beings?
(a) Manganese (b) Mercury
(c) Arsenic (d) None of these

48. Match List I with List II and select the correct answer using the codes given below.
List I (Institutes)
A. Central Arid Zone Institute
B. Space Application Centre
C. Indian Institute of Public Administration
D. Headquarters of Indian Science Congress
List II (Cities)
1. Kolkata 2. New Delhi
3. Ahmedabad 4. Jodhpur

Codes:	A	B	C	D
(a)	4	3	2	1
(b)	4	2	1	3
(c)	3	1	2	4
(d)	1	2	4	3

The total CO_2 emissions from various sectors are 5 mmt. In the Pie Chart given below, the percentage contribution to CO_2 emissions from various sectors is indicated.

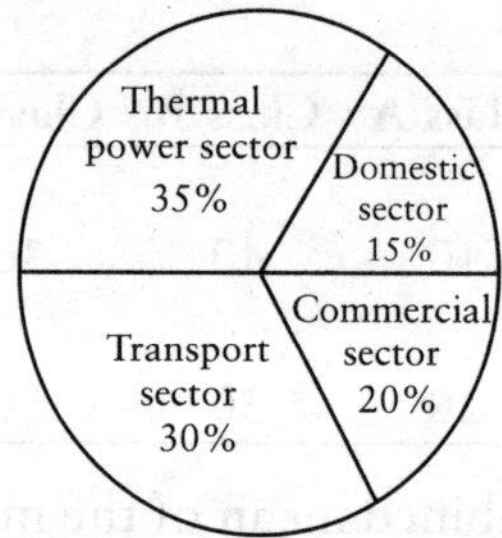

49. What is the absolute CO_2 emission from domestic sector?
(a) 1.75 mmt (b) 0.75 mmt
(c) 1.5 mmt (d) 2.5 mmt

50. What is the absolute CO_2 emission for combined thermal power and transport sectors?
(a) 1.5 mmt (b) 3.25 mmt
(c) 4 mmt (d) 2.5 mmt

PAPER–II

1. In which year five districts and four tribal administered agencies were taken away from Punjab to create the North-West Frontier Province?
(a) 1901 (b) 1911
(c) 1914 (d) 1915

2. Who among the following exercised great influence on the use of the concept of system in political analysis?

(a) Robert K. Merton
(b) Talcott Parsons
(c) Antonio Gramsci
(d) Both (a) and (b)

3. Karl Popper has advocated
(a) rational reconstruction of entire socio-political system on scientific principles.
(b) piecemeal social engineering.
(c) historicists view of social evolution.
(d) democratic planning.

4. Which one of the following indicates a relationship between inputs and outputs of a political system?
(a) Extractive capability
(b) Regulative capability
(c) Distributive capability
(d) Responsive capability

5. In the Marxian political discourse, ideology signifies
(a) political ideals of the proletariat.
(b) false consciousness.
(c) the universal principles of justice.
(d) any system of ideas, beliefs, values and aspirations that inform a social system.

6. The traditional approaches to the study of comparative politics neglected the
(a) comparison of constitutions.
(b) empirical investigations.
(c) study of governments.
(d) description of institutions.

7. The Federal Council of Switzerland consists of
(a) 9 members (b) 8 members
(c) 7 members (d) 6 members

8. Which one of the following statements is not correct?
In the American Federal System,
(a) the Federal government can change the name and territory of any constituent state.
(b) the residuary powers are vested in the states.
(c) the power of states are undefined but they are not unlimited.
(d) all states possess equal rights and equal representation in the Senate.

9. Presidential system of government is
(a) neither responsible nor representative.
(b) responsible without being representative.
(c) representative without being responsible.
(d) None of the above.

10. 'Constitutional Government' means
(a) Government according to the Constitution
(b) Government by the consent of the people
(c) Representative government
(d) Limited government

11. In a federal system,
(a) The Union is indestructible.
(b) The Union and State are indestructible.
(c) The Union is dissolvable.
(d) The States can secede from the union.

12. In the U.S.A., residuary power or reserve powers are
(a) left to the federal government.
(b) left to the States.
(c) not defined properly.
(d) given to local government.

13. Which one of the following countries has a separate constitution for each State?
(a) U.K. (b) U.S.A.
(c) France (d) India

14. Which one of the following statements is not correct?
(a) British Parliament is sovereign.
(b) The monarchy is rooted in Britain.
(c) Separation of powers is the essential principle of the British system of government.
(d) The Cabinet is the most powerful body in Britain.

15. What is not correct in respect to India and WTO?
    (a) India joined WTO in 1995.
    (b) India obliged all terms and conditions of WTO.
    (c) India has some reservations on agricultural areas.
    (d) All of the above.

16. The idea that the sovereign must receive habitual obedience from the bulk of the community in order to qualify as sovereign was rejected by
    (a) T.H. Green
    (b) Hans Kelsen
    (c) Sir Henry Maine
    (d) John Austin

17. One of the criticisms of the theory of Natural Rights is that it
    (a) believes that rights are the creation of the sovereign.
    (b) puts too much emphasis on social recognition of rights.
    (c) places social interests above individual interests.
    (d) assumes that rights exist prior to society.

18. Who among the following thinkers is connected with the concept of 'General Will'?
    (a) Rousseau (b) Locke
    (c) Laski (d) Hobbes

19. Who said "workers of the world unite; you have nothing to lose, except your chains"?
    (a) Mao Tse Tung (b) Lenin
    (c) Stalin (d) Marx

20. The three sources of Marx's thought are
    (a) German Philosophy, British Economics and French Socialism.
    (b) Utopian Socialism, French Revolution and Tsarist Autonomy.
    (c) German Philosophy, French Economy and British Socialism.
    (d) German Philosophy, Russian Anarchism and French Socialism.

21. The term "territorial water" means
    (a) water supplied to other countries.
    (b) water of the sea, close to coast of the country.
    (c) water inside the country.
    (d) water secured from other countries.

22. The political communication approach studies how one segment of a system affects another part by transmitting messages or sending information. Which political scientist developed this approach?
    (a) Karl Deutsch
    (b) Charles Merriam
    (c) Dr. Gallup
    (d) None of the above

23. Arrange the following federal systems in the chronological order in which they were formed.
    1. USA 2. Canada
    3. Nigeria 4. Australia
    Codes:
    (a) 2, 4, 1, 3 (b) 2, 4, 3, 1
    (c) 1, 3, 2, 4 (d) 1, 2, 4, 3

24. Which of the following indicators were emphasized on a development approach by the World Bank report in the 1990s?
    1. Subsidies
    2. Structural change inbuilt with competition
    3. Good governance
    4. An open system
    Codes:
    (a) 1, 2 and 3 (b) 1, 3 and 4
    (c) 2, 3 and 4 (d) 1, 2, 3 and 4

25. Which of the following characteristics are essential to Federal Government?
    1. A supreme and written Constitution.
    2. Separation of powers and the system of checks and balances.

3. Distribution of powers between the Centre and States in a manner that each is independent of the other.
4. Fundamental rights guaranteed to citizens.

Codes:

(a) 1 and 2 (b) 2 and 3
(c) 1, 2 and 3 (d) 2, 3 and 4

26. Consider the following statements in respect of the constitutional features of Germany:
1. Specified human rights can be changed only by a Constitutional amendment.
2. Any proposal to change the provisions, concerning the federal structure or powers of the States (Lander) is inadmissible.

Codes:

(a) 1 only (b) 2 only
(c) Both 1 and 2 (d) Neither 1 nor 2

27. Consider the following International Women's Conferences:
1. Nairobi 2. Mexico
3. Copenhagen 4. Beijing

What is the correct chronological sequence of the above Conferences?

Codes:

(a) 3, 2, 4 and 1 (b) 2, 1, 3 and 4
(c) 4, 3, 1 and 2 (d) 2, 3, 1 and 4

28. Which of the following statements were suggested by Robert Dahl?
1. Science is value free but administration is not.
2. Universal principle cannot be based on limited examples.
3. Administration involves human beings.
4. Social framework does not differ from country to country.

Codes:

(a) 1, 3 and 4 (b) 1, 2 and 3
(c) 1, 2 and 4 (d) 2, 3 and 4

29. Which of the following were the original objectives of SAARC?
1. Promotion of the welfare of people of South Asia through acceleration of economic growth, social progress and cultural development.
2. Strengthening cooperation with other developing states.
3. Strengthening cooperation with other regional organizations.
4. Promotion of regional peace and security.

Codes:

(a) 4 only (b) 1 and 4
(c) 1, 2 and 3 (d) 1, 2, 3 and 4

30. What is the correct sequence of the following four quantitative factors in Karl Deutsch's Communications Theory?
1. Lag 2. Load
3. Lead 4. Gain

Codes:

(a) 2, 1, 4 and 3 (b) 1, 2, 3 and 4
(c) 3, 2, 1 and 4 (d) 4, 1, 2 and 3

31. Match the two lists as per code.

List I (Political Scientists)

A. Rajni Kothari
B. Bhikhu Parikh
C. Iqbal Narain
D. Partha Chatterjee

List II (Subjects)

1. Multiculturalism
2. Party system in India
3. Indian nationalism
4. State politics in India

Codes:	**A**	**B**	**C**	**D**
(a)	3	4	1	2
(b)	2	4	1	3
(c)	3	1	4	2
(d)	2	1	4	3

32. Match the two lists as per code.

List I	**List II**
A. *Polis*	1. Teutons
B. *Civitas*	2. Greeks

C. *Status* 3. Plato
D. *Republic* 4. Romans

Codes:	A	B	C	D
(a)	1	2	4	3
(b)	2	1	4	3
(c)	2	4	1	3
(d)	1	2	3	4

33. Match the two lists as per code.

List I (Books)
A. *A Preface to Economic Democracy*
B. *The Life and Times of Liberal Democracy*
C. *Participation and Democratic Theory*
D. *Capitalism, Socialism and Democracy*

List II (Authors)
1. C.B. Macpherson 2. J. Schumpeter
3. Robert Dahl 4. C. Pateman

Codes:	A	B	C	D
(a)	3	1	4	2
(b)	1	3	2	4
(c)	1	2	4	3
(d)	2	3	1	4

34. Match the two lists as per code.

List I
A. Hierarchy
B. Span of control
C. Delegation
D. Unity of command

List II
1. Flow of Authority
2. One single boss
3. Through proper channel
4. Supervision

Codes:	A	B	C	D
(a)	4	3	2	1
(b)	2	1	3	4
(c)	4	2	1	3
(d)	3	4	1	2

35. Match the two lists as per code.

List I
A. Classical theory of organisation
B. Functional foremanship
C. Span of control
D. Scalar process

List II
1. J.D. Mooney 2. V.A. Graicunas
3. Henri Fayol 4. F.W. Taylor

Codes:	A	B	C	D
(a)	3	4	2	1
(b)	1	2	4	3
(c)	2	4	1	3
(d)	1	3	4	2

36. Match the two lists as per code.

List I
A. *Political System*
B. *Modern Democracies*
C. *New Aspects of Politics*
D. *The Nature of the State*

List II
1. Charles Merriam
2. David Easton
3. Wested Willoughby
4. James Bryce

Codes:	A	B	C	D
(a)	2	4	3	1
(b)	4	3	1	2
(c)	2	4	1	3
(d)	1	2	4	3

37. Match the two lists as per code.

List I
A. State upholds University
B. State upholds dominant interest
C. State has the monopoly of coercive power
D. State is an evil to be immediately and outrightly rejected

List II
1. Marx 2. Hegel
3. Bakunia 4. Weber

Codes:	A	B	C	D
(a)	4	1	2	3
(b)	2	3	4	1
(c)	1	2	3	4
(d)	2	1	4	3

38. **Assertion (A):** Interest groups can bring pressure to bear in a number of ways.
Reason (R): From a pluralistic perspective, political parties and interest groups are cornerstones of democracy.
Codes:
(a) Both (A) and (R) are true and (R) is the correct explanation.
(b) Both (A) and (R) are not true.
(c) (A) is true and (R) is false.
(d) (A) is false and (R) is true.

39. **Assertion (A):** In 1975, a new Constitution of China was inaugurated and it replaced the Constitution of 1954.
Reason (R): The Chinese Constitution of 1954 had a chapter on Fundamental Rights as well as Duties, which the citizens were expected to perform.
Codes:
(a) Both (A) and (R) are true and (R) is the correct explanation.
(b) Both (A) and (R) are not true.
(c) (A) is true and (R) is false.
(d) (A) is false and (R) is true.

40. **Assertion (A):** The State is neither the handiwork of God, nor the result of superior physical force, nor the creation of resolution or convention, nor a mere expansion of the family.
Reason (R): The State emerged imperceptibly, supported by various influences and conditions. It is an institution of natural growth.
Codes:
(a) Both (A) and (R) are true and (R) is the correct explanation.
(b) Both (A) and (R) are not true.
(c) (A) is true and (R) is false.
(d) (A) is false and (R) is true.

41. **Assertion (A):** Fascism could not conceive of any sphere of human activity remaining immune from intervention by the State.
Reason (R): Fascism strove to unify the world by appealing to shared traditions of humankind.
Codes:
(a) Both (A) and (R) are true and (R) is the correct explanation.
(b) Both (A) and (R) are not true.
(c) (A) is true and (R) is false.
(d) (A) is false and (R) is true.

42. **Assertion (A):** The interdependence and flows guaranteed by globalisation have severely restricted the powers and scope of nation-states.
Reason (R): World Trade continues to be confined among the developed states in the world.
Codes:
(a) Both (A) and (R) are true and (R) is the correct explanation.
(b) Both (A) and (R) are not true.
(c) (A) is true and (R) is false.
(d) (A) is false and (R) is true.

43. **Assertion (A):** A 'Secular State' means a State which observes neutrality and impartiality towards all religions.
Reason (R): A secular State is founded on the idea that the State views the relation between man and God as a matter of individual and private choice.
Codes:
(a) Both (A) and (R) are true and (R) is the correct explanation.
(b) Both (A) and (R) are not true.
(c) (A) is true and (R) is false.
(d) (A) is false and (R) is true.

44. In India, generally, Public Administration has been defined to include the
(a) Judiciary branch only
(b) Legislative branch only
(c) Executive branch only
(d) All of the above

45. The emergence of "New Public Administration" was initially associated with

(a) American Society of Public Administration
(b) Comparative Administration Group
(c) Minnowbrook Conference
(d) Indian Institute of Public Administration

46. In Mahabharata, Bhisma explained the principles of righteousness to be the essence of kingship which involve
(a) his selection of qualified ministers.
(b) high moral qualification.
(c) protection of the subjects.
(d) All of the above.

47. Who among the following authored one of the major books in the area of Games Theory: *The Theory of Games and Economic Behaviour*?
(a) John Nash
(b) Von Neumann and Oskar Morgenstern
(c) Anthony Downs
(d) Jeffrey S. Banks

48. The term 'political system' refers to
(a) all structures within politics.
(b) the study of government in its empirical dimensions.
(c) the study based on a strictly inter-disciplinary approach.
(d) All of the above.

49. Which of the following are the types of authority attributed to the President of India?
(a) Political and Nominal
(b) Constitutional and Nominal
(c) Real and Popular
(d) Titular and *De facto*

50. Which one of the following is not a proper function of political parties in a democratic country?
(a) To establish proper relation between the public and the government
(b) To form the government
(c) To propagate the ideology and policies of the party
(d) To appoint officials for the running of the government administration.

PAPER–III

1. Who among the following made a systematic study of pressure groups in the first decade of the twentieth century?
(a) David Truman (b) Arthur Bentley
(c) Duverger (d) La Palombara

2. "A partyless regime is a conservative regime, an anti-party regime is a reactionary regime." Who made this statement?
(a) K.C. Wheare
(b) Carl J. Friedrich
(c) Giovanni Sartori
(d) Samuel Huntington

3. Which political thinker advocated 'plural voting' to the higher educated citizens?
(a) J. Bentham (b) J.J. Rousseau
(c) J.S. Mill (d) T.H. Green

4. The entrepreneur can survive only in
(a) conditions where the state regulates the economy.
(b) conditions of equilibrium.
(c) conditions of free markets and free economy.
(d) socialistic pattern of society.

5. Who is not a proponent of liberal theory of development?
(a) Inkles
(b) Smith
(c) Wilbert E. Moore
(d) Billwarm

6. The judgement in the *S.R. Bommai* v. *Union of India* case pertained broadly to which Article of the Constitution of India?
(a) Article 29 (b) Article 32
(c) Article 353 (d) Article 356

7. The theory of Utilitarianism is associated with the name of
   (a) Green (b) Locke
   (c) Bentham (d) Hegel

8. Under Article 21(3), the Governor of a State is empowered to
   (a) appoint a Judge of the State High Court.
   (b) exercise his emergency powers.
   (c) exercise discretionary powers.
   (d) promulagate ordinances during the recess of the Legislature.

9. The President can assign any function in relation to any matter to which the executive power of the Union extends to the States. But this has to be with the consent of the
   (a) Parliament
   (b) State Governor
   (c) State Government
   (d) Chief Justice of India

10. To whom are the Ministers individually responsible?
    (a) The President
    (b) The Prime Minister
    (c) The Lok Sabha
    (d) The people

11. In which year the provisions pertaining to financial emergency were invoked for the first time?
    (a) 1971 (b) 1992
    (c) 1995 (d) None of these

12. "Polity (in the modern sense of democracy) is more stable and gives less occasion for revolution". This statement is attributed to
    (a) Cicero (b) Plato
    (c) Polybius (d) Aristotle

13. The view that the State is "the self-realizing and the self-actualising individual" was propounded by
    (a) Bosanquet (b) Hegel
    (c) Laski (d) Kant

14. J.S. Mill dealt with many political issues in his
    (a) *On Liberty*
    (b) *Utilitarianism*
    (c) *The Principles of Political Economy*
    (d) *War Expenditure*

15. Who did not consider territory as an essential element of State?
    (a) Seeley (b) Laski
    (c) Aristotle (d) Hobbes

16. In political sphere, the Fascists stood for
    (a) bi-party system.
    (b) multi-party system.
    (c) partyless government.
    (d) single-party government.

17. The philosopher who has transformed classical liberalism into a kind of welfarism in modern times is
    (a) Rawls (b) Nozick
    (c) MacPherson (d) Hayek

18. Who among the following, besides the three leading contractualists, favoured the theory of natural rights and who denied it, respectively?
    (a) J.S. Mill and J. Bentham
    (b) T. Panine and J. Bentham
    (c) T. Paine and J.S. Mill
    (d) T.H. Green and J.S. Mill.

19. In Rawls' theory, rights are based on which of the following principles?
    (a) Deontologism (b) Hedonism
    (c) Pragmatism (d) Idealism

20. The *Politics* of Aristotle treated _____ as the art of managing household that constituted an inseparable part of his political philosophy.
    (a) economics (b) sociology
    (c) psychology (d) None of these

21. The theory which holds that the State and living organisms are structurally and functionally similar is known as the

(a) Organisational Theory.
(b) Organic Theory.
(c) Structural Theory.
(d) Functional Theory.

22. The structural-functional approach and the input-output approach have been derived from
(a) the general systems theory approach.
(b) the sociological approach.
(c) the political simulation approach.
(d) the quantitative approach.

23. Which of the following are the features of the List System of Voting?
1. The constituencies are both single and multi-member ones.
2. The constituencies are only multi-member ones.
3. The voters vote for the individuals.
4. Parties put up a panel of candidates for the constituency.

Codes:
(a) 1 and 2 (b) 1 and 4
(c) 2 and 3 (d) 2 and 4

24. Consider the following statements about conservatism:
1. Conservatism is opposed to revolutionary change.
2. For conservatives, traditions, customs and usages are sources of rights.
3. Conservatives are invariably committed to religious practices.
4. Conservatives are opposed to universal adult franchise.

Codes:
(a) 1 and 2 (b) 1 and 3
(c) 3 and 4 (d) 1, 2, 3 and 4

25. What is the correct order of primacy of the following layers of social structure according to the Materialistic Interpretation of History?
1. Relations of production
2. Ideology
3. Forces of production
4. Legal and Political organisation

Codes:
(a) 2, 3, 4, 1 (b) 3, 4, 1, 2
(c) 3, 1, 4, 2 (d) 1, 3, 2, 4

26. Identity the two among these who sought to define underdevelopment in terms of neocolonial dependency mode:
1. A.G. Frank 2. Celso Furtado
3. E.W. Weidner 4. Gunnar Myrdal

Codes:
(a) 1 and 2 (b) 1 and 3
(c) 2 and 3 (d) 1 and 4

27. The President has the right to address
1. Lok Sabha
2. either House of the Parliament
3. a joint sitting of the Parliament

Codes:
(a) 2 only (b) 1 and 2
(c) 1 and 3 (d) 2 and 3

28. Consider the following statements: Under Article 200 of the Constitution of India, the Governor may
1. withhold his assent to a Bill passed by the State legislature.
2. reserve the Bill passed by the State legislature for the consideration of the President.
3. return a Bill, other than a money Bill, for reconsideration of the legislature.

Codes:
(a) 1 and 2 (b) 1 and 3
(c) 2 and 3 (d) 1, 2 and 3

29. According to the Constitution of India, for introduction of which of these Bills, previous sanction or recommendation of the President of India is required?
1. Bills for the formation of new States or reorganisation of State boundaries.
2. Money Bills.
3. State Bills imposing restrictions upon the freedom of trade.
4. Bills involving expenditure from the Consolidated Fund of India.

Codes:

(a) 1 only (b) 2 and 3
(c) 1, 2 and 3 (d) 1, 2, 3 and 4

30. Consider the following developments:
    1. Outsourcing of services
    2. Shrinking of geographical distance
    3. Rise of ethnic identity
    4. Emergence of regional associations

    Which of the above developments are associated with globalization?

    Codes:

    (a) 1 and 2 (b) 2 and 3
    (c) 1, 3 and 4 (d) 1, 2, 3 and 4

31. Match the two lists as per code.

    List I

    A. Division B. Guillotine
    C. Motion D. Point of order

    List II
    1. Bring the debate to a close.
    2. Formal proposal made by a member to the House.
    3. Relates to interpretation or enforcement of the rules of procedure or Constitution.
    4. Concludes discussion on demand for grants.
    5. Mode of arriving at a decision.

Codes:	**A**	**B**	**C**	**D**
(a)	4	5	1	2
(b)	5	4	1	3
(c)	5	4	2	3
(d)	4	5	2	1

32. Match the two lists as per code.

    List I (Disciplines)

    A. Philosophy B. Sociology
    C. Economics D. Political Science

    List II (Theme)

    1. Stratification 2. Mind
    3. Power 4. Trade

Codes:	**A**	**B**	**C**	**D**
(a)	4	3	2	1
(b)	2	1	4	3
(c)	4	1	2	3
(d)	2	3	4	1

33. Match the two lists as per code.

    List I (Concepts/Theories)

    A. Proletarian internationalism
    B. Political realism
    C. Complex interdependence
    D. Hegemonic stability theory

    List II (Scholars)
    1. Charles Kindleberger
    2. Hans Morgenthau
    3. V.I. Lenin
    4. Keohane and Nye

Codes:	**A**	**B**	**C**	**D**
(a)	1	2	4	3
(b)	3	4	2	1
(c)	1	4	2	3
(d)	3	2	4	1

34. Match the two lists as per code.

    List I

    A. Gentz B. Norman Angell
    C. Kant D. Woodrow Wilson

    List II
    1. Collective security
    2. Interdependence
    3. Perpetual peace
    4. Balance of power

Codes:	**A**	**B**	**C**	**D**
(a)	4	2	3	1
(b)	2	1	4	3
(c)	3	2	1	4
(d)	1	3	4	2

35. Match the two lists as per code.

    List I (Constitution Amendment Acts)

    A. 52nd Amendment Act
    B. 57th Amendment Act
    C. 61st Amendment Act
    D. 65th Amendment Act

    List II (Broad Subjects)
    1. National Commission for Scheduled Castes and Scheduled Tribes
    2. Voting age reduction

3. Reservation of seats for Scheduled Tribes of Nagaland, Meghalaya, Mizoram and Arunachal Pradesh in the Lok Sabha
4. Anti-defection law
5. Municipalities

Codes:	A	B	C	D
(a)	4	1	2	3
(b)	2	3	5	1
(c)	4	3	2	1
(d)	2	1	5	3

36. Match the two lists as per code.

List I (Concepts)

A. General Will
B. Absolute Sovereignty
C. Limited Government
D. New Political Science

List II (Thinkers)

1. Machiavelli
2. Locke
3. Hobbes
4. Rousseau

Codes:	A	B	C	D
(a)	2	3	4	1
(b)	3	4	1	2
(c)	4	3	2	1
(d)	1	4	3	2

37. Match the two lists as per code.

List I

A. The only sovereignty is the sovereignty of law
B. Law is independent of, and superior and anterior to political organisation
C. The State has the essential character of a corporation
D. 'The home of my soul is in the State'

List II

1. Krabbe
2. Duguit
3. MacIver
4. M.P. Follett

Codes:	A	B	C	D
(a)	1	2	3	4
(b)	3	4	1	2
(c)	4	3	2	1
(d)	2	1	3	4

38. Match the two lists as per code.

List I (Thinkers)

A. Edmund Burke
B. Mussolini
C. Hegel
D. Locke

List II (Statements)

1. "It is not the nation which generates the state. Rather it is the state which creates the nation."
2. "State is a partnership in all science; a partnership in all art; a partnership in every virtue and in all perfection."
3. "The state is a divine will, in the sense that it is mind present on earth, unfolding itself to be the actual shape and organisation of a world."
4. "The state acts as a nightwatchman whose services are only called upon when orderly existence is threatened."

Codes:	A	B	C	D
(a)	2	1	3	4
(b)	3	4	2	1
(c)	2	4	3	1
(d)	3	1	2	4

39. **Assertion (A):** The President has the power to legislate by ordinance, at a time when it is not possible to have a parliamentary enactment on the subject, immediately.

Reason (R): The ambit of the ordinance-making power of the President is different from the legislative powers of Parliament.

Codes:

(a) Both (A) and (R) are true and (R) is the correct explanation.
(b) Both (A) and (R) are not true.
(c) (A) is true and (R) is false.
(d) (A) is false and (R) is true.

40. **Assertion (A):** According to Kautilya, four wings of the army—elephants, cavalry, chariots and infantry—should be placed under different officers.

Reason (R): The officers do not fall prey to the enemy's intrigues.

Codes:
(a) Both (A) and (R) are true and (R) is the correct explanation of (A).
(b) Both (A) and (R) are true but (R) is not the correct explanation of (A).
(c) (A) is true but (R) is false.
(d) (A) is false but (R) is true.

41. **Assertion (A):** Public opinion thrives in a democratic society.
Reason (R): There is freedom of the press.
Codes:
(a) Both (A) and (R) are true and (R) is the correct explanation of (A).
(b) Both (A) and (R) are true but (R) is not the correct explanation of (A).
(c) (A) is true but (R) is false.
(d) (A) is false but (R) is true.

42. **Assertion (A):** The Supreme Court of India cannot declare a bad law invalid.
Reason (R): The Supreme Court of India follows the 'due process of law'.
Codes:
(a) Both (A) and (R) are true and (R) is the correct explanation of (A).
(b) Both (A) and (R) are true but (R) is not the correct explanation of (A).
(c) (A) is true but (R) is false.
(d) (A) is false but (R) is true.

43. **Assertion (A):** Equality before law is not applicable to the President of India.
Reason (R): The President of India enjoys special privileges under the Constitution of India.
Codes:
(a) Both (A) and (R) are true and (R) is the correct explanation of (A).
(b) Both (A) and (R) are true but (R) is not the correct explanation of (A).
(c) (A) is true but (R) is false.
(d) (A) is false but (R) is true.

44. **Assertion (A):** Since 1977 in India experimentation in colocational politics has survived.
Reason (R): One party dominant system has failed.
Codes:
(a) Both (A) and (R) are true and (R) is the correct explanation of (A).
(b) Both (A) and (R) are true but (R) is not the correct explanation of (A).
(c) (A) is true but (R) is false.
(d) (A) is false but (R) is true.

45. **Assertion (A):** In the changed world scenario, non-alignment in its traditional form is not relevant.
Reason (R): India can be considered as an upcoming economic power.
Codes:
(a) Both (A) and (R) are true and (R) is the correct explanation of (A).
(b) Both (A) and (R) are true but (R) is not the correct explanation of (A).
(c) (A) is true but (R) is false.
(d) (A) is false but (R) is true.

46. Alliances are essential components of
(a) Balance of power
(b) Collective Security System
(c) UN's peace keeping operations
(d) Multilateral Agreements

47. Generally in a federal state the units are given equal representation. But in one of the following states, the units have not been accorded equal representation.
(a) Canada (b) USA
(c) Australia (d) Nigeria

48. The American Senate is the strongest of all the Upper Houses in the world today. In the light of this statement, which one of the following is relevant?
(a) Powers of the House of Representatives can be curtailed by the Senate.
(b) All political appointments at federal level made by the President are to be approved by the Senate.
(c) Treaties signed by the President must be approved by the Senate.
(d) None of the above.

49. Which one of the following statements aptly describes the basis of the cabinet system of government?
    (a) The cabinet government is a majority government.
    (b) The cabinet government is a party government.
    (c) The cabinet works on the system of collective responsibility.
    (d) The cabinet is responsible to the people.
50. Which one of the following principles distinguishes the cabinet system from the Presidential system?
    (a) The relationship of the legislature with the executive.
    (b) The concentration or division of governmental powers.
    (c) Fixed tenure of government.
    (d) Judicial review.

ANSWER SHEET

PAPER—I

1. (a)	2. (c)	3. (a)	4. (d)	5. (d)
6. (d)	7. (d)	8. (c)	9. (b)	10. (c)
11. (b)	12. (c)	13. (c)	14. (b)	15. (d)
16. (b)	17. (a)	18. (d)	19. (c)	20. (d)
21. (d)	22. (a)	23. (b)	24. (a)	25. (d)
26. (d)	27. (a)	28. (d)	29. (b)	30. (a)
31. (b)	32. (c)	33. (c)	34. (d)	35. (d)
36. (d)	37. (a)	38. (d)	39. (b)	40. (b)
41. (b)	42. (c)	43. (b)	44. (b)	45. (c)
46. (b)	47. (a)	48. (a)	49. (b)	50. (b)

PAPER—II

1. (a)	2. (d)	3. (b)	4. (d)	5. (b)
6. (b)	7. (c)	8. (a)	9. (c)	10. (a)
11. (b)	12. (b)	13. (b)	14. (c)	15. (b)
16. (c)	17. (d)	18. (a)	19. (d)	20. (a)
21. (b)	22. (a)	23. (d)	24. (c)	25. (a)
26. (c)	27. (d)	28. (d)	29. (c)	30. (a)
31. (d)	32. (c)	33. (a)	34. (d)	35. (a)
36. (c)	37. (d)	38. (b)	39. (b)	40. (a)
41. (b)	42. (c)	43. (a)	44. (d)	45. (c)
46. (d)	47. (b)	48. (a)	49. (b)	50. (d)

PAPER—III

1. (b)	2. (d)	3. (c)	4. (c)	5. (a)
6. (d)	7. (c)	8. (d)	9. (c)	10. (a)
11. (d)	12. (d)	13. (b)	14. (c)	15. (a)
16. (d)	17. (c)	18. (b)	19. (c)	20. (a)
21. (b)	22. (a)	23. (d)	24. (d)	25. (c)
26. (a)	27. (d)	28. (d)	29. (d)	30. (a)
31. (c)	32. (b)	33. (d)	34. (a)	35. (a)
36. (c)	37. (a)	38. (a)	39. (c)	40. (c)
41. (a)	42. (a)	43. (a)	44. (a)	45. (b)
46. (b)	47. (a)	48. (a)	49. (a)	50. (a)

MOCK TEST–4
PAPER–I

1. Chlorophyll is related to chloroplast in the same way as vulture is related to
   (a) Air (b) Flesh
   (c) Birds (d) Wings
2. In which language the newspapers have highest circulation?
   (a) Hindi (b) English
   (c) Malyalam (d) Bengali
3. Factorial Analysis is used
   (a) to test the hypothesis
   (b) to know the difference between two variables

(c) to know the difference among the many variables
(d) to know the relationship between two variables

4. Which of the following statements is correct?
(a) Variability is the source of problem
(b) Objectives of research are stated in first chapter of the thesis
(c) Researcher must possess analytical ability
(d) All of the above

5. The best way for a teacher to introduce a new subject is by
(a) relating it to previously studied subject or course material
(b) giving a broad outline of the subject
(c) relating it to daily life situation
(d) Any of these

6. The most important function of education is
(a) Human resource development
(b) Political development
(c) Industrial development
(d) Economic development

7. Which one of the following Telephonic Conferencing with a radio link is very popular throughout the world?
(a) Telepresence
(b) TPS
(c) Video teletext
(d) Video conference

8. If a researcher does not get a satisfactory explanation to certain occurrences
(a) he would not be at rest until he gets an appropriate explanation
(b) he should give a damn to it perhaps it is not worth knowing
(c) he would wait until he comes across a right person who may explain it to him
(d) he would visit a nearby research institute to find out whether an answer could be obtained

9. Which of the following is characteristic of a hypothesis?
(a) It can be tested
(b) It must be clear in concept
(c) It must consists of known fact
(d) All of these

10. The main objective of FM station in radio is
(a) Tourism, Interaction and Entertainment
(b) Entertainment only
(c) Entertainment, Information and Interaction
(d) Information, Entertainment and Tourism

11. Inductive logic studies the way in which a premise may
(a) not support but entail a conclusion
(b) support and entail a conclusion
(c) support a conclusion without entailing it
(d) neither support nor entail a conclusion

12. The Prime Minister is the chairman of
(a) Minorities Commission
(b) Planning Commission
(c) Finance Commission
(d) None of these

13. One of the following is not a quality of researcher.
(a) His assertion to outstrip the evidence
(b) Unison with that of which he is in search
(c) He must be of alert mind
(d) Keenness in enquiry

14. Which of the following pollutants is not emitted from the transport sector?
(a) Carbon monoxide
(b) Oxides of nitrogen

(c) Chlorofluorocarbons
(d) Poly aromatic hydrocarbons

15. Ozone layer is present in the
(a) Troposphere (b) Ionosphere
(c) Mesosphere (d) Stratosphere

16. A journalist need to be _____ while covering an event.
(a) impartial (b) partial
(c) meticulous (d) None of these

17. How many types of political units existed in India at the time of independence?
(a) 1 (b) 2
(c) 3 (d) 4

18. Ecological footprint represents
(a) CO_2 emissions per person
(b) forest cover
(c) energy consumption
(d) area of productive land and water to meet the resources requirement

19. The aim of value education to include in students is
(a) the social values
(b) the political values
(c) the moral values
(d) the economic values

Read the following passage and answer the questions 20 to 24:

At one time it would have been impossible to imagine the integration of different religious thoughts, ideas and ideals. That is because of the closed society, the lack of any communication or interdependence on other nations. People were happy and content amongst themselves; they did not need any more. The physical distance and cultural barriers prevented any exchange of thoughts and beliefs. But such is not the case today. Today, the world has become a much smaller place, thanks to the adventures and miracles of science. Foreign nations have become our next-door neighbours. Mingling of population is bringing about an interchange of thought. We are slowly realising that the world is a single cooperative group. Other religions have become forces with which we have to reckon and we are seeking for ways and means by which we can live together in peace and harmony. We cannot have religious unity and peace so long as we assert that we are in possession of the light and all others are groping in the darkness. That very assertion is a challenge to a fight. The political ideal of the world is not so much a single empire with a homogeneous civilisation and single communal group as a brotherhood of free nations differing profoundly in life and mind, habits and institutions, existing side by side in peace and order, harmony and cooperation and each contributing to the world its own unique and specific best, which is irreducible to the terms of the others.

The cosmopolitanism of the eighteenth century and the nationalism of the nineteenth are combined in our ideal of a world commonwealth, which allows every branch of the human family to find freedom, security and self-realisation in the larger life of mankind. I see no hope for the religious future of the world, if this ideal is not extended to the religious sphere also. When two or three different systems claim that they contain the revelation of the very core and centre of truth and the acceptance of it is the exclusive pathway to heaven, conflicts are inevitable. In such conflicts, one religion will not allow others to steal a march over it and no one can gain ascendancy until the world is reduced to dust and ashes. To obliterate every other religion than one's own is a sort of Bolshevism in religion which we must try to prevent. We can do so only if we accept something like the Indian solution, which seeks the unity of religion not in a common creed but in a common quest. Let us believe in the unity of spirit and not of organisation, a unity which secures ample liberty not only for every individual but for every type of organised life which has proved itself effective.

20. According to the passage, the political ideal of the contemporary world is to
    (a) create a world commonwealth preserving religious diversity of all the nations
    (b) create a single empire with a homogeneous civilisation
    (c) foster the unity of all the religions of the world
    (d) None of these

21. According to the passage, religious unity and peace can be obtained if
    (a) we believe that truth does matter and will prevail
    (b) we believe that the world is a single co-operative group
    (c) we do not assert that we alone are in possession of the real knowledge
    (d) we believe in a unity of spirit and not of organisation

22. Which of the following is most opposite in meaning of the word "profoundly" as used in the passage?
    (a) Marginally (b) Meagerly
    (c) Hardly (d) Scarcely

23. Which of the following, according to the passage, is the 'Indian solution'? Unity of religions in a common
    (a) Creed (b) Belief
    (c) Organisation (d) Search

24. According to the passage, what is Bolshevism in religion?
    (a) To make changes in a religion so that it becomes more acceptable
    (b) To ridicule the views sincerely held by others
    (c) To accept others' religious beliefs and doctrines to be as authentic as ours
    (d) To adhere to rigid dogmatism in religion

25. Which is not 24 hours news channel?
    (a) Aajtak
    (b) Zee News
    (c) Lok Sabha channel
    (d) NDTV 24×7

26. Which of the following is not a source of pollution in soil?
    (a) Hydropower plants
    (b) Transport sector
    (c) Agriculture sector
    (d) Thermal power plants

27. Which institution brought co-ordination and co-operation between Union and States in the field of education?
    (a) CCCE (Council for Co-ordination and Cooperation on Education)
    (b) NCERT (National Council for Educational Research and Training)
    (c) CABE (Central Advisory Board of Education)
    (d) None of these

28. In this question four words are given, out of which three are alike and fourth one is different. Choose the odd one out.
    (a) Spectacle (b) Pageant
    (c) View (d) Display

29. Which of the following is not a natural hazard?
    (a) Tsunami
    (b) Flash floods
    (c) Nuclear accident
    (d) Earthquake

30. **Statement:** Should all electronic goods be exempted from the custom duty?
    Arguments:
    I. No, it will reduce the income of the government and development activities will be adversely affected.
    II. No, local manufacturers will be unable to compete with technology of foreign manufacturers.
    (a) Only I is strong
    (b) Only II is strong

(c) Both are strong
(d) None of them is strong

31. The Minimata disease of Japan in 1953 was caused by eating fish contaminated by
(a) Nickel (b) Cadmium
(c) Lead (d) Mercury

32. Kishanganga power project has now become the new sour point in Indo-Pak relations. This project is situated on which of the following rivers?
(a) Indus (b) Chenab
(c) Bias (d) Jhelum

33. In a certain code, ROUNDS is written as RONUDS. How will PLEASE will be written in the same code?
(a) PLASEE (b) LPAESE
(c) PLAESE (d) LPAEES

34. **Statement:** Most labourers are poor.
Conclusions:
(i) Some labourers are poor.
(ii) All labourers are not poor.
Which of the following is implied?
(a) Only (i) is implied
(b) Only (ii) is implied
(c) Both (i) and (ii) are implied
(d) Neither (i) nor (ii) is implied

35. One-rupee currency note in India bears the signature of
(a) Finance Minister of India
(b) Finance Secretary of Government of India
(c) The President of India
(d) Governor, Reserve Bank of India

36. Name the kind of pen used to draw directly on the digitizing tablet.
(a) Computer Pen (b) Puck/stylus
(c) Light Pen (d) None of these

37. FERA was changed to FEMA in 1998, FEMA stands for
(a) Foreign Exchange Monitoring Act
(b) Foreign Exchange Management Administration
(c) Foreign Exchange Management Act
(d) Foreign Exchange Maintenance Act

38. The Lok Sabha can be dissolved before the expiry of its normal five-year term by
(a) The Speaker of Lok Sabha
(b) The Prime Minister
(c) The President on the recommendation of the Prime Minister
(d) None of the above

39. Match the List I with the List II and select the correct answer from the codes given below:
List I (Commissions and Committees)
A. First Administrative Reforms Commission.
B. Paul H. Appleby Committee I.
C. K. Santhanam Committee.
D. Second Administrative Reforms Commission.
List II (Years)
1. 2005
2. 1962
3. 1966
4. 1953

Codes:	A	B	C	D
(a)	1	3	2	4
(b)	3	4	2	1
(c)	4	2	3	1
(d)	2	1	4	3

40. Internet is
(a) a commercial information service run by Zift Davis Co. in United States of America.
(b) a network owned and run by US Government.
(c) a network for education, news and entertainment run by United Nations and owned by the people of world.
(d) a network not owned by any body but used by all including governments agencies, universities, United Nations, etc. all round the globe.

41. Which of the following was created for the co-ordination and maintenance of standards in higher education?

(a) SCERT
(b) UGC
(c) NCERT
(d) Higher Education Information System Project

42. In communication chatting in Internet is
(a) Non-verbal communication
(b) Verbal communication
(c) Parallel communication
(d) Grapevine communication

43. The unit kIPS (thousand instruction per second) is used to measure the speed of
(a) Tape drive (b) Processor
(c) Disk drive (d) Printer

44. Data (information) is stored in computers as
(a) Matter (b) Files
(c) Directories (d) Floppies

45. Laser Scanners are capable of scanning bar codes upto a distance of
(a) 35 cm (b) 8 cm
(c) 25 cm (d) 45 cm

46. The coldest place on earth is
(a) Siachin (b) Halifex
(c) Verkhoyansk (d) Chicago

47. Memory unit is one part of
(a) Central Processing Unit
(b) Input device
(c) Control unit
(d) Output device

Study the following graph carefully and answer questions 48 to 50.

Export of Engineering Goods

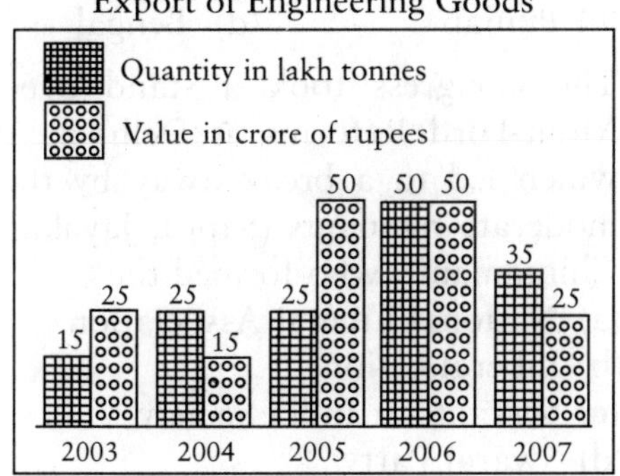

48. In which year the quantity of engineering goods' exports was maximum?
(a) 2006 (b) 2005
(c) 2007 (d) 2003

49. In which year the quantity of exports was 100 percent higher than the quantity of previous year?
(a) 2003 (b) 2007
(c) 2006 (d) 2005

50. In which year the value of engineering goods decreased by 50 percent compared to the previous year?
(a) 2006 (b) 2004
(c) 2007 (d) 2005

PAPER–II

1. The statement "it brings about a chasm between executive sources of knowledge and legislative centres of their application" applies to
(a) the Presidential system of government.
(b) the practice of delegated legislation.
(c) dictatorship of the Cabinet.
(d) the relationship between ministers and civil servants.

2. Which one of the following is not a characteristics of a "Theocratic State"?
(a) The religious authority should prevail over political authority.
(b) Government posts are filled up on the basis of one's position in the religious hierarchy.
(c) Religious rules and precepts take precedence over political rules and regulations.
(d) Its authority is based on popular consent.

3. Which of the following shows a greater political tolerance for pressure group activity?
(a) European liberal democracies
(b) Nigerian political system

(c) British political system
(d) American political system.

4. The basis for acquiring citizenship through naturalization is
(a) Birth (b) Choice
(c) Coercion (d) Descent

5. Elite Theory was first developed by
(a) Indian sociologists
(b) Italian sociologists
(c) American sociologists
(d) French sociologists

6. Which one of the following is not included in Max Weber's threefold classification of authority?
(a) Charismatic (b) Moral
(c) Legal-rational (d) Traditional

7. The neo-classical theorists believed that
(a) wages would decline if there was surplus population.
(b) wages should be fixed by the capitalists.
(c) the wages were determined by the supply and demand of labour.
(d) wages should be fixed through mutual agreements between workers and the capitalists.

8. Most of the Third World States are
(a) rich in natural resources
(b) economically self-reliant
(c) ethnically and culturally divided
(d) linguistically homogeneous

9. Which aspect of imperialism does the dependency theory emphasize?
(a) Economic (b) Political
(c) Cultural (d) Strategic

10. Fabian Economic Theory is based on
(a) Laissez-faire theory.
(b) Theory of mixed economy.
(c) Ricardian theory of rent.
(d) Labour theory of value.

11. "Guild Socialism is based on the idea of partnership between the producers and the state in the control of industry". This was said by
(a) Hobson (b) G.D.H. Cole
(c) Laidler (d) Orange

12. The statement that "property is theft" is attributed to
(a) Engels (b) Lassalle
(c) Marx (d) Proudhon

13. What amongst the following is the main thrust of neo-liberalism?
(a) To place market efficiencies as foundation for political freedom and to argue for a limited role for the state
(b) Commitment to an autonomous attitude to state, society and individual
(c) To accord priority to the will of the majority
(d) To extend power of a state beyond its borders.

14. Which one of the following is not a tenet of liberalism?
(a) Limited government
(b) Social classes as basic social units
(c) Upholding rights
(d) Separation of powers.

15. Swaraj Party took part in the election in
(a) 1920, 1926 (b) 1919, 1920
(c) 1923, 1926 (d) 1919, 1923

16. Some of the regional bases of militant nationalism during 1907-19 are given below. Find the odd one out.
(a) Maharashtra (b) Gujarat
(c) Punjab (d) Bengal

17. The Congress took a stand over the Mont-Ford Reforms at Delhi in 1918, which led to a break away by the old moderate remnants (Sapru, Jayakar and Chintamani), who formed the
(a) National Liberal Association
(b) Liberal Union
(c) Servants of India Society
(d) Swaraj Party

18. 'Pant Resolution' passed at Tripuri Congress, 1939 is significant because
   (a) it was a vote of censure against Subhas Chandra Bose.
   (b) it reiterated the Congress faith in Gandhian policies.
   (c) following it, P. Sitaramayya defeated Subhas Chandra Bose as the candidate for Presidentship.
   (d) None of the above.

19. The most outstanding event of the year 1919 which had a profound impact on the course of national movement was
   (a) Formation of Muslim League
   (b) Introduction of communal electorates
   (c) Jallianwala Bagh massacre
   (d) None of the above

20. The British for the first time conceded the demand for partition of India into two parts under
   (a) Cabinet Mission Plan
   (b) Cripps Mission Plan
   (c) Mountbatten Plan of June, 1947
   (d) None of the above

21. The system of dyarchy at the Centre was introduced under the
   (a) Government of India Act, 1935
   (b) Montague-Chelmsford Reforms Act, 1919
   (c) Morley-Minto Reforms Act, 1909
   (d) None of the above

22. The Directive Principles of State Policy aim at
   (a) establishing a social and economic base for the political democracy in the country.
   (b) establishing a genuine political democracy.
   (c) establishing a free society.
   (d) None of the above.

23. Which of the following are the grounds on which discrimination of citizens for admission into educational institutions is constitutionally prohibited?
   1. Religion and Race
   2. Sex and Place of Birth
   3. Nationality and Colour
   4. Age and Nativity

   Codes:
   (a) 1 and 2 (b) 1, 2 and 3
   (c) 1, 2 and 4 (d) 1, 2, 3 and 4

24. Identify the correct chronological order of the following events:
   1. Camp David
   2. My-lai Massacre
   3. Iraq's invasion of Kuwait
   4. G-8 summit in St. Petersburg

   Codes:
   (a) 3, 4, 2, 1 (b) 2, 3, 4, 1
   (c) 2, 1, 3, 4 (d) 1, 3, 4, 2

25. According to the Structural-Functional perspective of Political Development. Who among the following may act as a dynamic instrument of change?
   1. Scientists 2. Technocrats
   3. Agronomists 4. Political Leaders

   Codes:
   (a) 1, 2 and 3 (b) 4 only
   (c) 2 and 3 (d) 1, 2, 3 and 4

26. American and Indian federal systems differ in which of the following respects?
   1. Possession of separate Constitutions by the states.
   2. Double judicial system.
   3. Rigidity of the Constitution.
   4. Independent judiciary which acts as the guardian of the Constitution.

   Codes:
   (a) 2 and 4 (b) 1, 2 and 3
   (c) 1, 3 and 4 (d) 2, 3 and 4

27. While ancient Greek political thought equated State with society, modern political scientists do not consider the two terms identical. What are the factors that differentiate State from society?

1. The State was an earlier creation than society.
2. The State generally operates through coercion and compulsion; society works through moral pressure and persuasion.
3. The functions of State are much more limited than those of society.
4. The State is a functional institution created by society.
5. Society consists of many forms and forces that do not owe their origin to the State.

Codes:

(a) 1 and 4 (b) 2, 3 and 5
(c) 1, 2, 3 and 4 (d) 2, 3, 4 and 5

28. Belief in which of the following is cardinal to totalitarianism?
   1. Utility of democratic institutions
   2. Moral values in politics
   3. Sovereignty and omnipotence of the state
   4. Complete control over the individual's life

   Codes:

   (a) 1 and 2 (b) 2 and 3
   (c) 3 and 4 (d) 1 and 4

29. Consider the following statements:
   The major functions of political parties are
   1. Rule making
   2. Interest aggregation
   3. Political socialization
   4. Regulation of the behaviour of the people

   Codes:

   (a) 1 and 2 (b) 2 and 3
   (c) 1 and 4 (d) 3 and 4

30. Consider the following:
   1. Orientation to problem solving
   2. Orientation to collective action
   3. Orientation to the political system
   4. Orientation to other people

   Who among the following has listed the above as the salient features of political culture?
   (a) Robert Dahl
   (b) John Locke
   (c) Jeremy Bentham
   (d) John Stuart Mill

31. Which of the following features are present in the Indian Constitution?
   1. Multiple procedures for amendment.
   2. States are not empowered to initiate amendment.
   3. Certain amendments have to be passed just by State Legislatures.
   4. Joint-sittings of Parliament to solve disputes regarding Constitutional amendments.

   Codes:

   (a) 1 and 4 (b) 1, 2 and 4
   (c) 1, 3 and 4 (d) 2, 3 and 4

32. Match the two lists as per code.

   List I
   A. Govt. of India Act, 1919
   B. Govt. of India Act, 1935
   C. Morley-Minto Reforms, 1909
   D. Indian Councils Act, 1861

   List II
   1. Dynarchy in provinces
   2. Provincial autonomy
   3. Legislative councils for provinces
   4. Introduction of communal electorate

Codes:	A	B	C	D
(a)	1	4	3	2
(b)	1	2	4	3
(c)	2	1	4	3
(d)	1	3	2	4

33. Match the two lists as per code.

   List I
   A. 1883 B. 1884
   C. 1877 D. 1905

   List II
   1. Full codification of the Indian system of law and procedure.
   2. Imperial *darbar* at Delhi.

3. Partition of Bengal.
4. Indian magistrates got the right to try Europeans in criminal cases.

Codes:	A	B	C	D
(a)	1	4	3	2
(b)	4	2	1	3
(c)	2	4	1	3
(d)	1	4	2	3

34. Match the two lists as per code.

List I

A. Abul Kalam Azad
B. Maulana Mazharul Haque
C. Madan Mohan Malviya
D. Pherozeshah Mehta

List II

1. *The Motherland*
2. *Hindustan*
3. *Al Hilal*
4. *Bombay Chronicle*

Codes:	A	B	C	D
(a)	4	2	1	3
(b)	3	1	2	4
(c)	3	2	1	4
(d)	4	1	2	3

35. Match the two lists as per code.

List I

A. Mulraj
B. The First Anglo-Sikh War
C. Lord Dalhousie
D. Annexation of Avadh
E. Greased cartridges

List II

1. Doctrine of Lapse
2. Revolt of 1857
3. 1845-46
4. 1856
5. Governor of Multan

Codes:	A	B	C	D	E
(a)	3	2	1	5	4
(b)	2	1	3	4	5
(c)	5	3	1	4	2
(d)	4	2	5	3	1

36. Match the two lists as per code.

List I

A. Sanitation, Fire fighting, Public safety
B. Art galleries, Museums, Public parks, Zoos
C. Roads and bridges, Public Utility Services
D. Education, Hospitals, Libraries

List II

1. Cultural Services
2. Welfare Services
3. Physical Services
4. Protective Services

Codes:	A	B	C	D
(a)	4	1	3	2
(b)	4	1	2	3
(c)	1	4	3	2
(d)	1	4	2	3

37. Match the two lists as per code.

List I

A. "Liberty consists the power to do anything which inflicts no injury on one's neighbour."
B. "The state of war shows the omnipotence of the state in its individuality."
C. "The state is the supreme expression of the general will."
D. "Will, not force, is the basis of the state."

List II

1. Kant 2. Hegel
3. Bosanquet 4. Green

Codes:	A	B	C	D
(a)	3	1	4	2
(b)	1	2	3	4
(c)	4	3	2	1
(d)	2	4	3	1

38. Match the two lists as per code.

List I

A. Justice as a virtue of soul
B. Justice as individual rights

C. Justice as an irrational notion
D. Justice as proportionate equality

List II

1. Aristotle 2. Kelsen
3. Nozick 4. Plato

Codes:	A	B	C	D
(a)	4	3	2	1
(b)	3	4	2	1
(c)	4	3	1	2
(d)	3	4	1	2

39. **Assertion (A):** Free and independent press is associated with democracy.
Reason (R): Liberty is possible only under a democratic set-up.
Codes:
(a) Both (A) and (R) are true and (R) is the correct explanation of (A).
(b) Both (A) and (R) are true but (R) is not the correct explanation of (A).
(c) (A) is true but (R) is false.
(d) (A) is false but (R) is true.

40. **Assertion (A):** Rule of law is a precondition for a free society.
Reason (R): When those wielding power can use force in anyway they like, everyone is at the mercy of the rulers.
Codes:
(a) Both (A) and (R) are true and (R) is the correct explanation of (A).
(b) Both (A) and (R) are true but (R) is not the correct explanation of (A).
(c) (A) is true but (R) is false.
(d) (A) is false but (R) is true.

41. **Assertion (A):** The anarchists and the syndicalists are mistaken in thinking that liberty can be enjoyed by people without authority and restraints.
Reason (R): Liberty means absolute freedom.
Codes:
(a) Both (A) and (R) are true and (R) is the correct explanation of (A).
(b) Both (A) and (R) are true but (R) is not the correct explanation of (A).
(c) (A) is true but (R) is false.
(d) (A) is false but (R) is true.

42. **Assertion (A):** Preferential policies need not always violate the principle of fairness.
Reason (R): Treating citizens as equals may require treating them differently.
Codes:
(a) Both (A) and (R) are true and (R) is the correct explanation of (A).
(b) (A) is true but (R) is false.
(c) Both (A) and (R) are true but (R) is not the correct explanation of (A).
(d) (A) is false but (R) is true.

43. **Assertion (A):** Rousseau disapproved representative democracy.
Reason (R): Sovereignty resided in General Will.
Codes:
(a) Both (A) and (R) are true and (R) is the correct explanation of (A).
(b) Both (A) and (R) are true but (R) is not the correct explanation of (A).
(c) (A) is true but (R) is false.
(d) (A) is false but (R) is true.

44. **Assertion (A):** Hobbes was inclined towards absolutism.
Reason (R): Hobbes was an Englishman who lived in the days of the Civil War.
Codes:
(a) Both (A) and (R) are true and (R) is the correct explanation of (A).
(b) Both (A) and (R) are true but (R) is not the correct explanation of (A).
(c) (A) is true but (R) is false.
(d) (A) is false but (R) is true.

45. Which one of the following pairs is not correctly matched?
(a) J.J. Rousseau: Sovereignty resides in the general will
(b) Jeremy Bentham: Laws are the commands of the sovereign

(c) Hegel: Sovereign power is subject to Divine and Natural Laws
(d) Hugo Grotius: Sovereign power is limited by the laws of God, Nature and Nations.

46. Who has regarded Locke's theory of the state as the manifestation of 'possessive individualism'?
(a) Hayek (b) Macpherson
(c) Oakeshott (d) Rawls

47. Who among the following propounded the Functional Theory of Rights?
(a) E. Barker (b) A.D. Lindsay
(c) H.J. Laski (d) J.S. Mill

48. Who among the following denied the existence of rights before the development of society?
(a) T. Hobbes (b) J. Locke
(c) J. Rousseau (d) T.H. Green

49. Which one is not a characteristic of sovereignty?
(a) Indivisibility (b) Inclusiveness
(c) Permanence (d) Absoluteness

50. Classical liberalism grew out of the struggle between
(a) middle class and the downtrodden.
(b) aristocracy and commoners.
(c) labour and bourgeoisie.
(d) capitalists and feudalists.

PAPER–III

1. According to the pluralist theory of democracy
(a) the politics of consensus is not feasible.
(b) the power of individuals should be organised into syndicates and guilds to counter State power.
(c) political power is shared by the State and non-political associations and interest groups.
(d) people participate in politics with the express aim of overcoming their alienation from the groups to which they belong.

2. The system of proportional representation as an electoral mechanism ensures
(a) Common political thinking
(b) Minority representation
(c) Majority rule
(d) Stability in government

3. The general opinion at present is in favour of
(a) Right to property within certain limitations.
(b) Abolition of all private property.
(c) Absolute right to property.
(d) None of the above.

4. Which one of the following would promote economic justice?
(a) A system of graded taxation
(b) A policy of incentives
(c) A policy of free trade
(d) The existence of monopolies

5. Which one of the following is not generally considered as a part of the right to equality?
(a) Equality of right to satisfaction of basic needs of all.
(b) Equality of treatment in all circumstances.
(c) Equal protection under law.
(d) Equality of opportunity for all.

6. In India, generally, Public Administration has been defined to include the
(a) Judiciary branch only
(b) Legislative branch only
(c) Executive branch only
(d) All of the above

7. In this style, the leader is authoritarian, task-oriented lives power from his authority position and levels his team in instructions and discipline.

This leadership style is known as
(a) High-high management style
(b) Low-low management style
(c) High-low management style
(d) Low-high management style

8. "Personnel recruitment for the second half of the twentieth century will have to be geared to a nuclear physical world in which the solutions of human problems will demand the utmost in human competence." This is the quote of
(a) Donald Kingsley
(b) S.K. Bailey
(c) P.H. Douglas
(d) Pfiffner and Presthus

9. The system of recruitment through competitive examination first came into vogue in the
(a) 2nd century B.C.
(b) 5th century B.C.
(c) 10th century B.C.
(d) 20th century B.C.

10. Lal Bahadur Shastri Academy of Musoorie is an illustration of
(a) Background training
(b) Departmental training
(c) Skill training
(d) Central training

11. Which one of the following is not a correct statement?
(a) Seniority principle helps in building up the morale and efficiency of public services.
(b) Seniority is a matter of a fact which cannot be denied.
(c) The principle of seniority gives certainty of promotion of employees.
(d) Greater experience is a greater qualification for promotion.

12. Which of the following is not a staff agency?
(a) Commerce and industry
(b) Cabinet committees
(c) Cabinet Secretariat
(d) Prime Minister's Office

13. The 'Balance Principle' is related to
(a) Victor Thompson
(b) Donald Smithburg
(c) Chester Barnard
(d) Herbert Simon

14. The principle of the span of control has been elaborated by
(a) Graicunas (b) H. Simon
(c) Peter Blau (d) L.D. White

15. Which of the following is true in case of India?
(a) Public sector reigns supreme over private sector.
(b) Growing interaction between the public and private sectors.
(c) No link between public and private sectors.
(d) Private sector is not concerned about public sector.

16. The word 'POSDCORB' was coined by
(a) Luther Gulick (b) Marshal Dimock
(c) J.M. Pfiffner (d) D. Waldo

17. Who among the following uses the term bureaucracy in this sense: "Bureaucracy is a systematic organisation of tasks and individuals into a pattern which can most effectively achieve the ends of collective efforts"?
(a) Laski (b) Finer
(c) Pfiffner (d) Gladden

18. Which one of the following is not a characteristic feature of the bureaucratic authority?
(a) Hierarchy
(b) Role-segmentation
(c) Continuous organisation
(d) Democratisation

19. Which of the following forms of disciplinary action are enumerated in the Indian Civil Services Rules?

(a) Removal from services, dismissal, etc.
(b) Censure of withholding of increments of promotion.
(c) Supervision, reduction to lower post or time scale.
(d) All of the above.

20. The type of bureaucracy that is committed to the programmes of the party in power is
(a) Committed bureaucracy
(b) Fully politicised bureaucracy
(c) Depoliticised bureaucracy
(d) Semi-politicised bureaucracy

21. The type of communication which helps greater understanding, teamwork and mutual trust among inter-disciplinary and inter-departmental functionaries is
(a) horizontal communication
(b) crosswise communication
(c) from up downward communication
(d) from down upward communication

22. Salary is
(a) a self-actualization
(b) a hygiene factor
(c) a motivator
(d) None of the above

23. Which of the following statements are correct?
1. Legal sovereignty always exists in a human being, not an organisation.
2. All rights emanate from the legal sovereign.
3. By a popular sovereign one means members of parliament.
4. *De facto* sovereignty has its foundation in force rather than in law.

Codes:
(a) 1 and 3 (b) 2 and 4
(c) 1, 2 and 4 (d) 2, 3 and 4

24. Consider the following statements:
1. Liberal democratic tradition views equality primarily as "equality of opportunity" and "equality of conditions".
2. "Equality of conditions" seeks to ensure that equality of results is achieved regardless of natural ability.

Codes:
(a) 1 only (b) 2 only
(c) Both 1 and 2 (d) Neither 1 nor 2

25. Which of the following factors contributed to the rise of nationalism in India?
1. Socio-cultural renaissance of the eighteenth and nineteenth centuries.
2. Impact of Western culture.
3. Policy of racial discrimination pursued by the British.
4. The Bolshevik Revolution of 1917.

Codes:
(a) 1 and 4 (b) 2 and 3
(c) 1, 2 and 3 (d) 2, 3 and 4

26. The methods advocated by the moderate nationalists for the attainment of their objectives were
1. Resolutions 2. Petitions
3. Representations 4. Demonstrations

Codes:
(a) 2 and 3 (b) 3 and 4
(c) 1, 2 and 3 (d) 1, 2 and 4

27. Which of following are the features of Indian and Canadian federal system?
1. Division of powers between the centre and the units.
2. Residuary powers vested in the Centre.
3. Existence of the nominal and real Executive.

Codes:
(a) 1 and 2 (b) 1 and 3
(c) 2 and 3 (d) 1, 2 and 3

28. Which of the following are true of socialism?
1. Socialism aims at the elimination of capitalism.

2. Socialism stands for the subordination of the interests of the society to the higher interests of the individuals.
3. Socialism stands for justice, fairplay and liberty. It aims at adding to the sum total of social welfare.
4. Socialism stands for the elimination of competition where there is much economic waste.

Codes:

(a) 2, 3 and 4 (b) 1, 2 and 4
(c) 1, 3 and 4 (d) 1, 2 and 3

29. Consider the following statements:
    1. Political power is the organised power of one-class for oppressing another.
    2. The existence of the state is bound up with class conflict in society.
    3. The state is not a power imposed on society from without; it is actually a product of society at a particular stage of its development.
    4. The state is independent of civil society.

Codes:

(a) 1 and 2 (b) 1 and 4
(c) 1, 2 and 3 (d) 2, 3 and 4

30. Which of the following reflect supervision?
    1. Watching the work of the subordinate.
    2. Ensuring proper and efficient performance.
    3. Guiding subordinates for efficient performance.
    4. Finding fault with the work of the subordinates.

Codes:

(a) 3 and 4 (b) 1, 2 and 3
(c) 2, 3 and 4 (d) 1, 2 and 4

31. Match the two lists as per code.

List I

A. "Land, Bread, Peace"
B. "Liberty, Equality, Fraternity"
C. "Nationalism, Democracy, Livelihood"
D. "No taxation without representation"

List II

1. Chinese Revolution
2. French Revolution
3. Russian Revolution
4. American Revolution
5. Glorious Revolution

Codes:	**A**	**B**	**C**	**D**
(a)	3	1	2	5
(b)	3	2	1	4
(c)	2	3	1	4
(d)	2	1	4	3

32. Match the two lists as per code.

List I (Views about Legal Theory of Sovereignty)

A. The theory of sovereign State has broken down
B. It would be of lasting benefit to Political Science if the whole concept of sovereignty were surrendered
C. A sovereign power is the centre of gravity in a mass of matter
D. The State in the sense of an absolute super-entity has never existed

List II (Thinkers)

1. H.J. Laski 2. J.N. Figgis
3. Sir H. Maine 4. A.D. Lindsay

Codes:	**A**	**B**	**C**	**D**
(a)	3	2	4	1
(b)	3	1	4	2
(c)	4	2	3	1
(d)	4	1	3	2

33. Match the two lists as per code.

List I

A. Aristotle B. Bentham
C. Marx D. Ruskin

List II

1. *Unto This Last*
2. From each according to his ability to each according to his needs

3. Greatest happiness of the greatest number
4. Treat equals equally and unequals unequally

Codes:	A	B	C	D
(a)	3	2	1	4
(b)	4	2	3	1
(c)	1	2	3	4
(d)	4	3	2	1

34. Match the two lists as per code.

List I (Theories of Function of State)

A. Marxian View B. Liberal View
C. Fascist View D. Fabian View

List II (Thinkers)

1. Herbert Spencer
2. Rosa Luxemberg
3. G.B. Shaw
4. Giovanni Gentile

Codes:	A	B	C	D
(a)	1	2	3	4
(b)	2	1	4	3
(c)	1	2	4	3
(d)	2	1	3	4

35. Match the two lists as per code.

List I (Theorists)

A. Duguit B. Locke
C. MacIver D. Austin

List II (Statements)

1. "Where there is no law, there is no freedom."
2. "Law is the command of the Sovereign."
3. "It is not the State which creates law but it is the law which creates the State. Laws are merely the expressions of social reality."
4. "The State is both the child and the parent of law."

Codes:	A	B	C	D
(a)	4	1	3	2
(b)	3	2	4	1
(c)	4	2	3	1
(d)	3	1	4	2

36. Match the two lists as per code.

List I (Views on Property)

A. Capitalist form of property is historically more developed than feudal form of property.
B. Right to property is a natural right of the individual.
C. Property is theft.
D. The right to property must involve a theory of industrial organisation not less than a theory of reward.

List II (Thinkers)

1. Joseph Proudhon 2. John Locke
3. H.J. Laski 4. Karl Marx

Codes:	A	B	C	D
(a)	1	2	4	3
(b)	4	2	1	3
(c)	3	2	1	4
(d)	4	1	3	2

37. Match the two lists as per code.

List I (Groups)

A. NGOs B. Pressure groups
C. Political parties D. Elites

List II (Concerns/Distinctiveness)

1. To promote interests of their members and to influence politics
2. A group of eminent persons in their chosen field
3. Concerned with some public issues/problems
4. Seek political power

Codes:	A	B	C	D
(a)	3	1	4	2
(b)	4	2	3	1
(c)	4	1	3	2
(d)	3	2	4	1

38. Match the two lists as per code.

List I

A. Green B. Bradley
C. Machiavelli D. Hobbes

List II

1. *The Prince*
2. *Leviathan*

3. *Lectures on the Principles of Political Obligation*
4. *Ethical Studies*
5. *On Liberty*

Codes:	A	B	C	D
(a)	3	4	1	2
(b)	3	5	4	2
(c)	4	2	1	3
(d)	2	4	3	1

39. **Assertion (A):** The system of Proportional Representation may solve the problem of minority representatives to some extent.
Reason (R): The system of Proportional Representation enables due representation to all types of groups based on ethnicity, gender interests and ideologies.
Codes:
(a) Both (A) and (R) are true and (R) is the correct explanation of (A).
(b) Both (A) and (R) are true but (R) is not the correct explanation of (A).
(c) (A) is true but (R) is false.
(d) (A) is false but (R) is true.

40. **Assertion (A):** Modern dictatorship abolishes all opposition parties.
Reason (R): It is impossible to perpetually maintain an atmosphere of fear and suspicion through coercion and terrorism.
Codes:
(a) Both (A) and (R) are true and (R) is the correct explanation of (A).
(b) Both (A) and (R) are true but (R) is not the correct explanation of (A).
(c) (A) is true but (R) is false.
(d) (A) is false but (R) is true

41. **Assertion (A):** The American Senate is the strongest second chamber of the Legislature in the world.
Reason (R): The American Senate has equal powers as the House of Representatives.
Codes:
(a) Both (A) and (R) are true and (R) is the correct explanation of (A).
(b) Both (A) and (R) are true but (R) is not the correct explanation of (A).
(c) (A) is true but (R) is false.
(d) (A) is false but (R) is true

42. **Assertion (A):** The President of India occupies almost the same position as the King or Queen of England.
Reason (R): The President is ultimately bound to act in accordance with the advice given by the Council of Ministers.
Codes:
(a) Both (A) and (R) are true and (R) is the correct explanation of (A).
(b) Both (A) and (R) are true but (R) is not the correct explanation of (A).
(c) (A) is true but (R) is false.
(d) (A) is false but (R) is true

43. **Assertion (A):** U.K. has a plural executive.
Reason (R): Head of state is different from Head of the government in U.K.
Codes:
(a) Both (A) and (R) are true and (R) is the correct explanation of (A).
(b) Both (A) and (R) are true but (R) is not the correct explanation of (A).
(c) (A) is true but (R) is false.
(d) (A) is false but (R) is true

44. **Assertion (A):** The central issue in International Politics is the inability of our present global political system to adequately meet the problems created by globalization.
Reason (R): Westphalia system has failed to satisfy the long term conditions for sustainability.
Codes:
(a) Both (A) and (R) are true and (R) is the correct explanation of (A).

(b) Both (A) and (R) are true but (R) is not the correct explanation of (A).
(c) (A) is true but (R) is false.
(d) (A) is false but (R) is true.

45. According to Barnard, administrator should be encouraged to gain experience in leadership.
(a) Within the organization
(b) Outside the organization
(c) Both within and outside the organization
(d) None of the above

46. The contemporary approach to communication has been greatly influenced by
(a) scientific school of management
(b) cybernetics
(c) human relations scholars
(d) None of the above

47. Leader member relation refers to
(a) leader's relation with the members of his group.
(b) the authority and power status of the leaders' position.
(c) the structure characteristics of the group task.
(d) None of the above.

48. In Weber's view, which one of the following further stimulated the growth of bureaucratisation?
(a) Pressures of democratisation
(b) Influence of socialism
(c) Emergence of welfare state
(d) Rise of authoritarianism

49. Executive control over Budget could be exercised
(a) when the estimates are prepared.
(b) when expenditure is incurred.
(c) when the estimates are prepared and when expenditure is incurred.
(d) None of the above.

50. The budget goes through _____ stages before it is passed finally by Parliament or State Legislature as the case may be.
(a) five (b) six
(c) two (d) three

ANSWER SHEET

PAPER—I

1. (c)	2. (b)	3. (c)	4. (d)	5. (d)
6. (a)	7. (a)	8. (a)	9. (d)	10. (c)
11. (c)	12. (b)	13. (a)	14. (c)	15. (d)
16. (b)	17. (b)	18. (d)	19. (c)	20. (d)
21. (c)	22. (a)	23. (d)	24. (b)	25. (c)
26. (a)	27. (c)	28. (c)	29. (c)	30. (a)
31. (d)	32. (a)	33. (c)	34. (c)	35. (b)
36. (b)	37. (b)	38. (c)	39. (b)	40. (d)
41. (b)	42. (a)	43. (b)	44. (b)	45. (c)
46. (c)	47. (a)	48. (a)	49. (c)	50. (c)

PAPER—II

1. (a)	2. (d)	3. (d)	4. (b)	5. (b)
6. (b)	7. (a)	8. (c)	9. (a)	10. (c)
11. (b)	12. (d)	13. (a)	14. (b)	15. (c)
16. (b)	17. (a)	18. (c)	19. (c)	20. (c)
21. (a)	22. (a)	23. (a)	24. (c)	25. (b)
26. (b)	27. (d)	28. (c)	29. (b)	30. (a)
31. (a)	32. (b)	33. (d)	34. (b)	35. (c)
36. (b)	37. (b)	38. (a)	39. (b)	40. (b)
41. (c)	42. (c)	43. (b)	44. (b)	45. (b)
46. (b)	47. (d)	48. (a)	49. (b)	50. (a)

PAPER—III

1. (c)	2. (b)	3. (a)	4. (a)	5. (a)
6. (d)	7. (c)	8. (d)	9. (a)	10. (d)
11. (c)	12. (a)	13. (c)	14. (a)	15. (b)
16. (a)	17. (c)	18. (b)	19. (d)	20. (a)
21. (a)	22. (b)	23. (b)	24. (b)	25. (c)
26. (c)	27. (d)	28. (c)	29. (c)	30. (b)
31. (b)	32. (d)	33. (d)	34. (b)	35. (d)
36. (b)	37. (a)	38. (a)	39. (a)	40. (b)
41. (d)	42. (b)	43. (d)	44. (a)	45. (b)
46. (b)	47. (a)	48. (d)	49. (c)	50. (a)

MOCK TEST–5
PAPER–I

1. Dewry defines education as a
   (a) theoretical need
   (b) social need
   (c) personal need
   (d) psychological need
2. All of the following statements about a teacher are correct except the one.
   (a) A teacher changes his/her attitudes and behaviour according to the need of the society
   (b) A teacher is a friend, guide and philosopher
   (c) A teacher distinguishes between students
   (d) A teacher is the leader in the class
3. A person cannot be an effective teacher if he
   (a) teaches moral values
   (b) is a strict disciplinarian
   (c) knows his subject well
   (d) has no interest in teaching
4. The most important single factor in underlying the success of a teacher is
   (a) organisational ability
   (b) scholarship
   (c) communicative ability
   (d) personality and his ability to relate to the class and to the pupils
5. If you are irritated and show rashness because of the inadequate behaviour of another teacher, what do you think about your own behaviour?
   (a) Your behaviour is also a sign of maladjustment and so try to control yourself when you are maltreated
   (b) It is justified because behaviours are choice
   (c) Your behaviour is not good because elders have the right to behave you in this way
   (d) All of the above
6. The term 'SITE' stands for
   (a) Satellite Instructional Teachers Education
   (b) Satellite International Television Experiment
   (c) Satellite Instructional Television Experiment
   (d) Satellite Indian Television Experiment
7. Team teaching has the potential to develop
   (a) highlighting the gaps in each other's teaching
   (b) competitive spirit
   (c) cooperation
   (d) the habit of supplementing the teaching of each other
8. In any research, one should
   (a) not try out anything blindly but wait until a sudden flash appears in his mind
   (b) know everything in the area without bothering to learn the details of any
   (c) know more and more about less and less in certain specific sub-area
   (d) None of these
9. Determine the nature of the following definition:

'Poor' means having an annual income of ₹ 10,000.
(a) Lexical (b) Persuasive
(c) Precising (d) Stipulative

10. Which of the following methods implies the collection of information by way of investigators own examination without interviewing the respondents?
(a) Random probability sampling
(b) Observation
(c) Posting questionnaire
(d) Schedule method

11. Why do teachers use teaching aid?
(a) For students' attention
(b) To make teaching fun-filled
(c) To make students attentive
(d) To teach within understanding level of students

12. On which of the following statements there is consensus among educators?
(a) Disciplinary cases should be totally neglected in the class
(b) Disciplinary cases should be sent to the principal only when other means have failed
(c) Disciplinary cases should never be sent to principal's office
(d) None of these

13. Good evaluation of written material should not be based on
(a) Logical presentation
(b) Comprehension of subject
(c) Linguistic expression
(d) Ability to reproduce whatever is read

14. A good researcher lays his hands on
(a) any area as long as manpower and fundings are available in plenty
(b) a specific area and tries to understand in minute details
(c) several areas and tries to understand them at fundamental level
(d) None of these

15. The basis on which assumptions are formulated
(a) Universities
(b) Cultural background of the country
(c) Specific characteristics of the castes
(d) All of these

Read the following passage and answer the questions 16 to 20:

India is dedicated to free institutions and principles of democracy. We are striving to give everyone an opportunity and raise the standard of living for all. A democracy is one where people have the right to live their own lives and develop themselves in their own way under the guidance of their chosen representatives. If our political democracy is to succeed, it is essential that it be buttressed by steps towards economic equality or what has been referred to as the 'socialistic pattern of society'. Poverty and unemployment hold the biggest threat to the successful working of our democratic system.

16. One may infer from the paragraph that in a socialistic pattern of society
(a) to provide employment to all is the greatest problem
(b) the socialist party dominates
(c) all the inhabitants are treated equal
(d) None of these

17. The successful working of Indian democratic system is under a threat of
(a) economic inequality
(b) poverty
(c) unemployment
(d) All the above

18. In a democratic system,
(a) commodities are freely bought and sold
(b) government serves the people
(c) the government is run by the people themselves
(d) people do not have political freedom

19. The word buttressed in the paragraph means
    (a) Supported (b) Dictating
    (c) Declared (d) Guided
20. Democracy can fail if there is
    (a) opportunity for development
    (b) a weak government
    (c) economic inequality
    (d) unemployment
21. Aspect ratio of TV screen is
    (a) 4:3 (b) 3:4
    (c) 2:3 (d) 2:4
22. Which of the following is not a product of learning?
    (a) Knowledge (b) Attitudes
    (c) Maturation (d) Concepts
23. The first paper for the human beings was developed by
    (a) The Aryans
    (b) The Babilonians
    (c) The Chinese
    (d) The Sumerians
24. Which sequence in turn will lead one to face the west direction from which one starts turning?
    (a) Right, right, left, right, left right
    (b) Left, right, left, left, right, right
    (c) Right, right left, left, right, right
    (d) Left, left, right, left, right, left
25. Fill in the blank with the most appropriate choice.
    _____ is the supreme medium to express yesterday, today and tomorrow with its own unique language.
    (a) Television (b) Cinema
    (c) Radio (d) Newspaper
26. In which language the newspapers have highest circulation?
    (a) Tamil (b) English
    (c) Bengali (d) Hindi
27. Amit is the son of Rahul. Sarika, Rahul's sister has a son Sonu and a daughter Rita. Raja is the maternal uncle of Sonu. How is Rita related to Raja.
    (a) Aunt (b) Sister
    (c) Daughter (d) Niece
28. **Statement:** A man must be wise to be a good wrangler. Good wrangler's are all talkative and boring.
    Conclusions:
    I. All the wise persons are boring.
    II. All the wise persons are good wranglers.
    Choose the correct option.
    (a) Only conclusion I follows
    (b) Only conclusion II follows
    (c) Both I and II follow
    (d) None of these
29. What is the number that comes next in the sequence?
    2, 5, 9, 19, 37, ...
    (a) 74 (b) 75
    (c) 76 (d) 78
30. Match List I with List II and select the correct answer using the codes given below:

List I	List II
A. Pandit Jasraj	1. Hindustani vocalist
B. Kishan Maharaj	2. Sitar
C. Ravi Shankar	3. Tabla
D. Udai Shankar	4. Dance

Codes:	A	B	C	D
(a)	1	2	3	4
(b)	1	3	4	2
(c)	1	3	2	4
(d)	3	2	1	4

31. Who developed the ability to speak?
    (a) Aryans (b) Neanderthal
    (c) Cro-Magnon (d) Dravidians
32. In what way does communication in small group differ from that in the large group?

(a) Large group communication provides better feedback
(b) Small group provides far more interaction among the participants
(c) Interaction in small group is more restrictive
(d) Small group takes less time to convey the message

33. What is the main aim and objective of provision for feedback in communication system?
(a) Understand more about the content
(b) To make communication better by adjusting at both ends of Encoder and Decoder
(c) Identify the defect of communication
(d) Make necessary modification in communication system

34. Communications bandwidth that has the highest capacity and is used by microwave, cable and fibre optics lines is known as
(a) Carrier wave (b) Hyper-link
(c) Broadband (d) Bus width

35. In a certain code, CLOCK is written as KCOLC. How would STEPS be written in that code?
(a) SPETS (b) SPEST
(c) SPSET (d) SEPTS

36. Which one of the following is not an argument?
(a) Ram is not at home, so he must have gone to town
(b) Ram insulted me so I punched him in the nose
(c) If today is Tuesday, tomorrow will be Wednesday
(d) Since today is Tuesday, tomorrow will be Wednesday.

Direction: (37-41) Study the following pie chart and answer the questions based on it. Following pie chart represents the investment done by Timas Finance Ltd. in the various sectors. (All investments are in ₹ crores)

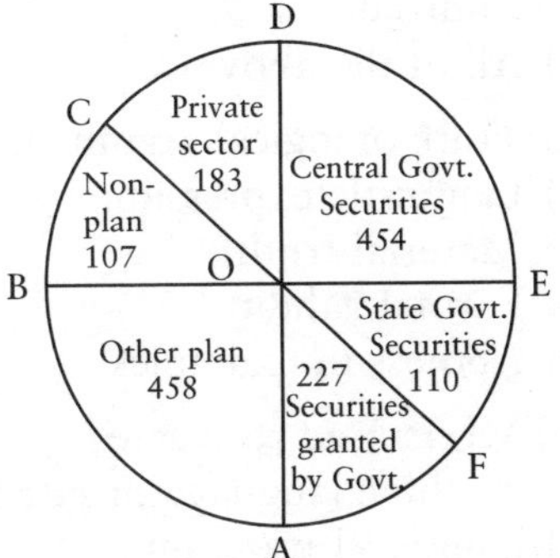

37. The percentage or gross investment in state government securities is nearly
(a) 7.1% (b) 9.2%
(c) 8.6% (d) 7.8%

38. The investment in plan and non-plan sector together is more or less than the investment in government securities (Central and State) by
(a) less, 106 crores (b) more, 4 crores
(c) more, 1 crores (d) more, 111 crores

39. The magnitude of ∠AOC is nearly
(a) 132° (b) 123°
(c) 126° (d) 115°

40. The ratio of area of the circle above ∠COF to the area of the circle below it is about
(a) 1 (b) 0.92
(c) 0.94 (d) 0.96

41. The investment in private sector is nearly what percent higher than the investment in State Government Security?
(a) 44% (b) 66%
(c) 54% (d) 46%

42. How many numbers between 100 and 300 begin or end with 2?
(a) 120 (b) 110
(c) 100 (d) 180

43. Which of the following operating system is used on mobile phones?

(a) Windows XP
(b) Windows Vista
(c) Android
(d) All of the above

44. Structure of logical argument is based on
(a) Linguistic expression
(b) Material truth
(c) Formal validity
(d) Aptness of examples

45. HTML is used to create
(a) machine language program
(b) high level program
(c) web page
(d) web server

46. Which of the following pollutants affects the respiratory tract in humans?
(a) Aerosols
(b) Sulphur dioxide
(c) Nitric oxide
(d) Carbon monoxide

47. Which of the following sources of energy has the maximum potential in India?
(a) Wind energy
(b) Solar energy
(c) Ocean thermal energy
(d) Tidal energy

48. In a deductive argument conclusion is
(a) Additional to the premises
(b) Entailed by the premises
(c) Summing up of the premises
(d) Not necessarily based on premises

49. What is the range of the numbers which can be stored in an eight bit register?
(a) −127 to + 128 (b) −127 to + 127
(c) −128 to + 128 (d) −128 to + 127

50. Universal Product Code (UPC), a pattern of bars printed on merchandise can be read by
(a) Product Code Reader
(b) Bar Code Reader
(c) Code Reader
(d) Card Reader

PAPER–II

1. Which part of the Mahabharata deals with the theory of government?
(a) Adi Parva (b) Sabha Parva
(c) Yuddha Parva (d) Shanti Parva

2. The definition of State that it is an 'association of families and villages' was given by
(a) Jean Bodin (b) Aristotle
(c) Rousseau (d) Kant

3. The modern concept of sovereignty was first analysed by
(a) Grotius (b) Rousseau
(c) Bodin (d) Beaumanoir

4. According to Bodin, "Sovereignty is the supreme power over citizens and subjects unrestained by law."
In the above definition, the term 'law' refers to
(a) Divine law
(b) Positive law
(c) Salic law of France
(d) Natural law

5. The Principle of 'Survival of the Fittest' was advocated by
(a) Herbert Spencer (b) Charles Darwin
(c) J.S. Mill (d) Adam Smith

6. Who proposed the Preamble before the drafting committee of the Constitution?
(a) B.N. Rau
(b) Mahatma Gandhi
(c) Jawaharlal Nehru
(d) B.R. Ambedkar

7. Which one of the following Acts created the office of the Governor-General of Bengal?
(a) Pitt's India Act, 1784
(b) Regulating Act, 1773
(c) Charter Act of 1813
(d) None of the above

8. The Governor-General of Bengal was designated as Governor-General of India under
   (a) Indian Councils Act, 1861
   (b) Charter Act of 1853
   (c) Charter Act of 1833
   (d) None of the above
9. Which of the following features were borrowed by the Indian Constitution from the British Constitution?
   (a) Idea of Concurrent List
   (b) Independence of judiciary
   (c) Law-making procedure
   (d) Parliamentary system
10. How many members were included in the Drafting Committee?
    (a) Eleven (b) Thirteen
    (c) Seven (d) Nine
11. Fundamental Rights guaranteed in the Indian Constitution can be suspended only by
    (a) a proclamation of national emergency.
    (b) an Act passed by the Parliament.
    (c) an amendment of the Constitution.
    (d) the judicial decisions of the Supreme Court.
12. Which of the following rights is availabe only to citizens?
    (a) Right to freedom of movement
    (b) Right against exploitation
    (c) Right to freedom of religion
    (d) Right to life and liberty
13. According to the Cabinet Mission Plan, which one of the following was the method of electing the Constituent Assembly?
    (a) Universal Adult Franchise
    (b) Party elected by the Provincial Assemblies and partly nominated by the Governor General
    (c) Nominated by the Princely States
    (d) Partly elected by the Provincial Assemblies and partly nominated by the Princes
14. In which chapter of the Indian Constitution there is a mention of uniform civil code?
    (a) Preamble
    (b) Directive Principles of State Policy
    (c) Fundamental Duties
    (d) Judiciary
15. The Liberal thinkers of the nineteenth century considered the state as
    (a) a check on liberty.
    (b) an instrument of exploitation.
    (c) an imposition on the citizens by the ruling elites.
    (d) a necessary evil.
16. Liberal Democracy means
    (a) government in the interest of the people.
    (b) limited majority rule.
    (c) government by majority.
    (d) government by the people.
17. Which of the following thinkers considered liberty and equality as complementary?
    (a) Machiavelli (b) De Tocqueville
    (c) Lord Acton (d) MacIver
18. Which of the following is a feature of rights?
    (a) Rights are unlimited
    (b) Rights are indispensable
    (c) Rights are static
    (d) Rights are anti-state
19. Apart from India, in which other federal country can the Central Government appoint the Governors of the States?
    (a) Canada (b) USA
    (c) Australia (d) None of these
20. In which year was the Canadian Federation established?

(a) 1950 (b) 1945
(c) 1869 (d) 1867

21. The essence of the Presidential system of government is that in such a system
    (a) it has a written and rigid Constitution.
    (b) the Supreme Court has power of judicial review.
    (c) the executive is independent of the legislature.
    (d) the President is elected directly by the people.

22. Which of the following statements were suggested by Robert Dahl?
    1. Science is value free but administration is not.
    2. Universal principle cannot be based on limited examples.
    3. Administration involves human beings.
    4. Social framework does not differ from country to country.

    Codes:
    (a) 1, 3 and 4 (b) 1, 2 and 3
    (c) 1, 2 and 4 (d) 2, 3 and 4

23. Consider the following statements:
    1. Coordination and cooperation are synonyms.
    2. Coordination is of the work of subordinates by a superior officer.
    3. Cooperation is inter-personal relationship between two or more similar individuals or units.
    4. Coordination and cooperation are not the same thing.

    Codes:
    (a) 1 and 3 (b) 2, 3 and 4
    (c) 1 and 2 (d) 2 and 4

24. The principles of Scientific Management developed by Taylor include
    1. Incentive of high wages
    2. Standardization of work methods
    3. Esprit de Corps
    4. Standardization of working conditions

    Codes:
    (a) 1, 2 and 3 (b) 1, 2 and 4
    (c) 2, 3 and 4 (d) 1, 3 and 4

25. Arrange the following approaches in study of Public Administration in order in which they appeared.
    1. Classical Approach
    2. Behavioural Approach
    3. Policy Approach
    4. Human Relations Approach

    Codes:
    (a) 2, 3, 4, 1 (b) 1, 4, 2, 3
    (c) 4, 3, 1, 2 (d) 2, 1, 3, 4

26. In which of the following countries have the states been given an equal representation in the upper house of the federal legislature?
    1. USA 2. Nigeria
    3. Australia 4. India

    Codes:
    (a) 1 and 2 (b) 3 and 4
    (c) 1, 2 and 3 (d) 2, 3 and 4

27. Which of the following are glorified by the Fascists?
    1. Violence 2. War
    3. Leader 4. Individual

    Codes:
    (a) 1, 3 and 4 (b) 2 and 4
    (c) 1, 2 and 3 (d) 2, 3 and 4

28. Which of the following were the ideas of Roman Empire?
    1. Unity 2. Order
    3. Cosmopolitanism

    Codes:
    (a) 1 and 2 (b) 1 and 3
    (c) 2 and 3 (d) 1, 2 and 3

29. Consider the following statements:
    For Gramsci, civil society is the arena of
    1. consent over coercion
    2. hegemony over domination
    3. leadership over power
    4. reconciliation over struggle

Codes:

(a) 4 only	(b) 1 and 2
(c) 1, 2 and 3	(d) 1, 2, 3 and 4

30. In which of the following federations does the Second Chamber have equal representation of the States?
    1. U.S.A. 2. India
    3. Australia 4. Canada

    Codes:

(a) 1 and 2	(b) 1 and 3
(c) 1 and 4	(d) 2 and 3

31. Match the two lists as per code.

    List I

    A. "The concept of unity of command requires that every member of an organisation should report to one, and only one leader."
    B. "In no case is there adaptation of the social organism to dual command."
    C. "The old concept of one single boss for each person is seldom found in fact in complex governmental situations."
    D. "The concept of unity of command needs to be reconciled with a recognition that supervision of any activity may be dual—technical and administrative."

    List II

    1. Henri Fayol
    2. John D. Millet
    3. Pfiffner and Presthus
    4. Seckler-Hudson
    5. F.W. Taylor

Codes:	**A**	**B**	**C**	**D**
(a)	4	3	5	1
(b)	3	4	1	2
(c)	4	2	1	5
(d)	3	1	4	2

32. Match the two lists as per code.

    List I

    A. An employee should receive orders from one superior only.
    B. How many subordinates can an administrator direct personally?
    C. The superior-subordinate relationship through a number of levels of responsibility.
    D. The orderly arrangement of group effort to provide unity of action in the pursuit of a common purpose.

    List II

    1. Span of Control
    2. Unity of command
    3. Hierarchy
    4. Co-ordination

Codes:	**A**	**B**	**C**	**D**
(a)	1	2	4	3
(b)	2	3	1	4
(c)	3	4	2	1
(d)	2	1	3	4

33. Match the two lists as per code.

    List I (Books)

    A. *The American Presidency*
    B. *Democracy in America*
    C. *The American Commonwealth*
    D. *Congressional Government*

    List II (Authors)

    1. Woodrow Wilson
    2. Harold Laski
    3. James Bryce
    4. de Tocqueville

Codes:	**A**	**B**	**C**	**D**
(a)	2	4	3	1
(b)	2	4	1	3
(c)	4	2	3	1
(d)	4	2	1	3

34. Match the two lists as per code.

    List I (Types of Constitution)

    A. Parliamentary, Federal, Republican
    B. Presidential Federal, Republican
    C. Parliamentary, Unitary, Monarchical
    D. Parliamentary-cum-Presidential Unitary, Republican

    List II (Names of the Country)

    1. United Kingdom
    2. France
    3. United States of America

4. India
5. Nigeria

Codes:	A	B	C	D
(a)	4	3	1	2
(b)	4	3	2	1
(c)	3	4	1	5
(d)	3	5	4	1

35. Match the two lists as per code.

List I	List II
A. Libertarianism	1. Bentham
B. Utilitarianism	2. Gandhi
C. Civil Society	3. Nozick
D. Swaraj	4. Hegel

Codes:	A	B	C	D
(a)	3	1	4	2
(b)	1	3	2	4
(c)	2	1	3	4
(d)	4	1	2	3

36. Match the two lists as per code.

List I

A. St. Augustine B. Mao
C. M.N. Roy D. Aurobindo

List II

1. "Let hundred flowers bloom"
2. "Colonial thesis"
3. "Involution"
4. "Two swords"

Codes:	A	B	C	D
(a)	1	2	4	3
(b)	2	3	1	4
(c)	4	1	2	3
(d)	3	2	1	4

37. Match the two lists as per code.

List I

A. "Rights and duties are conditions of social welfare."
B. "Rights are those conditions of social life without which no man can seek, in general, to be himself at his best."
C. "We have a right to the means that are necessary to the development of our lives."
D. "The fundamental right of every one is self-preservation."

List II

1. Laski 2. Hobhouse
3. Bosanquet 4. Hobbes

Codes:	A	B	C	D
(a)	4	3	2	1
(b)	3	4	1	2
(c)	2	1	3	4
(d)	1	2	4	3

38. Match the two lists as per code.

List I (Authors)

A. F.A. Hayek
B. Johan Rawls
C. C.B. Macpherson
D. Milton Friedman

List II (Books)

1. *Political Liberalisation*
2. *The Constitution of Liberty*
3. *The Real World of Democracy*
4. *Capitalism and Freedom*

Codes:	A	B	C	D
(a)	2	1	3	4
(b)	4	3	1	2
(c)	2	3	1	4
(d)	4	1	3	2

39. **Assertion (A):** Staff is indispensable to the chief executive in the performance of his multifarious tasks.

Reason (R): It is thus, obvious that the staff agency personnel must be intellectually virile and possess a sense of evaluating a problem in the context of the total needs of the administration.

Codes:

(a) Both (A) and (R) are true and (R) is the correct explanation of (A).
(b) Both (A) and (R) are true but (R) is not the correct explanation of (A).
(c) (A) is true but (R) is false.
(d) (A) is false but (R) is true.

40. **Assertion (A):** A hierarchical organisation does not necessarily involve superior subordinate relationship.

Reason (R): Delegation of authority is possible in hierarchial organisation.

Codes:

(a) Both (A) and (R) are true and (R) is the correct explanation of (A).
(b) Both (A) and (R) are true but (R) is not the correct explanation of (A).
(c) (A) is true but (R) is false.
(d) (A) is false but (R) is true.

41. **Assertion (A):** The auxiliary function, or the house-keeping function is undertaken to enable the line agency to perform its primary function.

Reason (R): But this is not a secondary function.

Codes:

(a) Both (A) and (R) are true and (R) is the correct explanation of (A).
(b) Both (A) and (R) are true but (R) is not the correct explanation of (A).
(c) (A) is true but (R) is false.
(d) (A) is false but (R) is true.

42. **Assertion (A):** Line and Staff agencies are so inextricably intermingled in practice that many scholars and practitioners of management do not even attempt to clarify a Line and Staff concept.

Reason (R): Many ministries such as Finance and Education are neither purely Line agencies nor purely Staff agencies.

Codes:

(a) Both (A) and (R) are true and (R) is the correct explanation of (A).
(b) Both (A) and (R) are true but (R) is not the correct explanation of (A).
(c) (A) is true but (R) is false.
(d) (A) is false but (R) is true.

43. **Assertion (A):** The essential element in decentralisation is the delegation of decision-making functions.

Reason (R): Decentralisation may be political or administrative.

Codes:

(a) Both (A) and (R) are true and (R) is the correct explanation of (A).
(b) Both (A) and (R) are true but (R) is not the correct explanation of (A).
(c) (A) is true but (R) is false.
(d) (A) is false but (R) is true.

44. **Assertion (A):** Dual citizenship is a usual feature that goes with the dual form of government established under a federation.

Reason (R): As a result, each member-State has the right to grant its citizens or residents certain rights which it may deny, or grant on more difficult terms, to non-residents.

Codes:

(a) Both (A) and (R) are true and (R) is the correct explanation of (A).
(b) Both (A) and (R) are true but (R) is not the correct explanation of (A).
(c) (A) is true but (R) is false.
(d) (A) is false but (R) is true.

45. In which one of the following systems of government is bi-cameralism an essential feature?

(a) Federal system
(b) Unitary system
(c) Presidential system
(d) Parliamentary system

46. The weakest second chamber of the Federal Legislature exists in

(a) Nigeria (b) U.S.S.R.
(c) Canada (d) U.S.A.

47. The Federal System of India is closer to the Federal System of

(a) United States of America
(b) Canada
(c) Switzerland
(d) France

48. Who among the following said, "Federalism seeks to reconcile unity with multiplicity, centralisation with

decentralisation and nationalism with localism"?
(a) K.C. Wheare (b) W.H. Riker
(c) Daniel J. Elazar (d) A.V. Dicey

49. Duguit criticised the Austinian theory of sovereignty in the name of the
(a) community's sense of right.
(b) principle of social solidarity.
(c) moral personalityof corporations.
(d) theory of natural law.

50. Which one of the following political philosophers is an advocate of positive liberty?
(a) Isaiah Berlin
(b) Iris Marion Young
(c) John Stuart Mill
(d) T.H. Green

PAPER–III

1. Which one of the following statements can be attributed to T.H. Green?
(a) "Nature has made men equal."
(b) "There can be no identity of treatment and identity of reward so long as men differ in their needs and capacities."
(c) "The passion for equality makes vain the hope of freedom."
(d) "Equality, far from being inimical to liberty, is absolutely essential for its preservation."

2. Which one of the following is not a characteristic of Socialism?
(a) It is a protest against an economic and social system based on profit.
(b) It strives for the abolition of the State.
(c) It is a reaction to the social and economic injustice of the capitalist system.
(d) It is a revolt against the exploitation of man by man.

3. Who among the following championed the cause of socialist ideas in the Indian National Congress before independence?
(a) Dr. Pattabhi Sitaramayya
(b) Pt. Jawaharlal Nehru
(c) Sardar Vallabhbhai Patel
(d) Jamnalal Bajaj

4. Terms such as 'Purna Swaraj', 'Ramarajya' 'Sarvodaya' and 'Panchayat Raj' were used by M.K. Gandhi to indicate
(a) citizenship.
(b) a blissful state in the past.
(c) political obligation.
(d) an ideal political order.

5. Gandhian concept of Satyagraha is a
(a) Political weapon (b) Social weapon
(c) Legal weapon (d) Moral weapon

6. Early socialists who confused capitalism with industrialism and wanted to retain only agricultural labour included
(a) Proudhon, Fourier and Cabet.
(b) Jefferson, Proudhon and Cabet.
(c) Fourier and Cabet.
(d) Fourier and Proudhon.

7. The function of the State is not to promote morality but remove obstacles from the way of good life. The above view is attributed to
(a) New-idealists (b) Fascists
(c) Utilitarians (d) Anarchists

8. The difference principle in the Rawlsian theory of liberal-welfare state is derived from
(a) sympathy for the worst off in society.
(b) moral duty to help the least advantaged.
(c) the principle of maximization of utilities.
(d) the maxmin principle.

9. The earlier known example of 'direct democracy' is found in

(a) Athens (b) Sparta
(c) Corinth (d) Syracuse

10. The concept of 'legal sovereignty' was for the first time put forward by
(a) Bentham (b) Machiavelli
(c) Hobbes (d) Locke

11. Which one of the following statements is correct?
(a) Socialist state is characterised by waste and injustice.
(b) A socialist state aims at economic equality for all.
(c) In a socialist state production is carried on for the good of the producing class.
(d) In a socialist state there is wide gulf between the haves and have-nots.

12. Marx views history as
(a) a faithful record of the past events.
(b) a waste of time.
(c) a mere record of the wars between the various peoples.
(d) a succession of struggle between the oppressor and the oppressed classes.

13. "Each to count for one and no one for more than one" was the principle propounded by
(a) Jeremy Bentham
(b) Lord Bryce
(c) Abraham Lincoln
(d) John S. Mill

14. "His social contract represents the triumph of reason rather than hard necessity." This statement is true of
(a) Rousseau (b) Locke
(c) Hooker (d) Hobbes

15. Which of the following is rejected by Hobbes as the founder of the state?
(a) The view that might is right
(b) Individualism
(c) Concept of authorization
(d) Rational self-preservation as the ground for social contract.

16. Who among the following thinkers made a distinction between Real Will and Actual Will?
(a) Rousseau (b) Green
(c) Bosanquet (d) Kant

17. J. Rousseau's concept of general will avows which one of the following?
(a) Parliamentary sovereignty
(b) Popular sovereignty
(c) Sovereignty of the constitution
(d) *de jure* sovereignty.

18. Who said, "Man is born free everywhere he is in chains"?
(a) Locke (b) Rousseau
(c) Marx (d) Bentham

19. What is the correct sequence of States in terms of descending order of percentage of Scheduled Caste population to the total population of the concerned State?
(a) Punjab-Uttar Pradesh-Maharashtra.
(b) Tamil Nadu-West Bengal-Uttar Pradesh.
(c) Uttar Pradesh-Karnataka-Tamil Nadu.
(d) Andhra Pradesh-West Bengal-Kerala.

20. The best form of federalism suited for countries like India is
(a) Centralised federalism
(b) Bargaining federalism
(c) Cooperative federalism
(d) Conflicting federalism

21. What all are the characteristic of state, according to Bentham?
1. To promote social good.
2. To remove all restriction for the freedom of individual.
3. Maximise possible individual freedom should be promoted.

Codes:
(a) 2 only (b) 1 and 2
(c) 2 and 3 (d) 1, 2 and 3

22. Identify the correct chronological order using the code given below in which the following concepts/theories appeared:
    1. Saptanga
    2. Theory of Protection
    3. Passive Resistance
    4. Satyagraha

    Codes:
    (a) 1, 2, 3, 4 (b) 2, 3, 4, 1
    (c) 2, 1, 4, 3 (d) 3, 2, 4, 1

23. Which of the following are true functions of the electoral process in a democracy?
    1. To keep government responsive to the popular will.
    2. To bring together citizens to choose public decision-makers.
    3. To change the government periodically if necessary.
    4. To support a competitive party system.

    Codes:
    (a) 1, 3 and 4 (b) 2, 3 and 4
    (c) 1, 2 and 4 (d) 1, 2 and 3

24. Freedom of press includes
    1. right to print and publish news.
    2. distribution and circulation of printed matter.
    3. criticism of public affairs.

    Codes:
    (a) 1 and 2 (b) 1 and 3
    (c) 2 and 3 (d) 1, 2 and 3

25. Which of the following were the principal features of the Government of India Act, 1919?
    1. Introduction of dyarchy in the Provinces.
    2. Introduction of separate communal electorates for Muslims.
    3. Devolution of legislative authority by the Centre to the provinces.
    4. Expansion and reconstitution of Central and Province Legislatures.

    Codes:
    (a) 1, 2 and 4 (b) 1, 3 and 4
    (c) 1, 2 and 3 (d) 2, 3 and 4

26. According to Granville Austin, which of the following are the conscience of the Constitution of India?
    1. Preamble
    2. Fundamental Rights
    3. Directive Principles of State Policy
    4. Fundamental Duties

    Codes:
    (a) 1 and 2 (b) 2 and 3
    (c) 1 and 4 (d) 1, 2 and 3

27. Consider the following statements about secularism:
    1. It promotes religious philosophy.
    2. It separates religion from politics.
    3. It denies state support to religious organizations.
    4. It opposes religious ideas and ideology.

    Codes:
    (a) 2 only (b) 1 and 3
    (c) 2 and 3 (d) 1, 2, 3 and 4

28. Consider the following statements:
    1. Jeremy Bentham preserved the individualist notion of moral autonomy.
    2. Jeremy Bentham supported the idea that division of power secured and protected constitutional liberty.

    Codes:
    (a) 1 only (b) 2 only
    (c) Both 1 and 2 (d) Neither 1 nor 2

29. Match the two lists as per code.

    List I (Theorists)
    A. John Stuart Mill B. Karl Marx
    C. Isaiah Berlin D. John Locke

    List II (Ideas)
    1. Alienation
    2. Positive and negative liberty

3. Equality for women
4. Toleration

Codes:	A	B	C	D
(a)	2	4	3	1
(b)	3	1	2	4
(c)	2	1	3	4
(d)	3	4	2	1

30. Match the two lists as per code.

List I (Doctrines)

A. Doctrine of Secularism
B. Doctrine of Consent
C. Doctrine of Individualism
D. Doctrine of Freedom

List II (Thinkers)

1. Hobbes 2. Rousseau
3. Machiavelli 4. Locke

Codes:	A	B	C	D
(a)	3	2	1	4
(b)	3	4	1	2
(c)	2	4	1	3
(d)	4	3	2	1

31. Match the two lists as per code.

List I

A. The state comes into existence for sake of life, but continues to exist for good life.
B. The state is a march of God on Earth.
C. The state is a Joint Stock Protection Company for mutual assurance.
D. The state is nothing more than a machine for oppression of one class by another.

List II

1. J.S. Mill 2. Aristotle
3. Herbert Spencer 4. Marx
5. Hegel

Codes:	A	B	C	D
(a)	2	5	3	4
(b)	1	2	5	3
(c)	3	1	4	5
(d)	5	4	3	2

32. Match the two lists as per code.

List I

A. Article 5 B. Article 12
C. Article 14 D. Article 19

List II

1. Fundamental Rights
2. Equality before law
3. Citizenship
4. Right to freedom
5. Judicial Review

Codes:	A	B	C	D
(a)	3	1	2	4
(b)	3	1	2	5
(c)	1	3	2	5
(d)	3	5	4	1

33. Match the two lists as per code.

List I (Directives)

A. Equitable distribution of wealth
B. Organisation of Village Panchayats
C. Provision for free and compulsory education for children
D. Provision for living wages

List II (Principles)

1. Gandhian
2. Socialist
3. Western Liberal
4. International Understanding

Codes:	A	B	C	D
(a)	3	2	1	4
(b)	1	2	3	4
(c)	4	1	3	2
(d)	2	1	3	4

34. Match the two lists as per code.

List I

A. Democratic Decentralization
B. Nagar Panchayats
C. Panchayati Raj Elections
D. Two-tier System

List II

1. 73rd Amendment
2. 74th Amendment
3. B.R. Mehta Committee
4. Ashok Mehta Committee

Codes:	A	B	C	D
(a)	3	1	2	4
(b)	4	1	2	3
(c)	4	2	1	3
(d)	3	2	1	4

35. **Assertion (A):** Lenin wanted the Indian Communists to support the bourgeois democratic movement in their country.

Reason (R): Lenin wanted to merge the Communist movement with Democratic movement.

Codes:

(a) Both (A) and (R) are true and (R) is the correct explanation of (A).
(b) Both (A) and (R) are true but (R) is not the correct explanation of (A).
(c) (A) is true but (R) is false.
(d) (A) is false but (R) is true

36. **Assertion (A):** Kautilya's account of the state law is an improvement upon that of his predecessors.

Reason (R): Kautilya includes two new sources of law and lays down two rules of interpretation in the case of conflict of laws.

Codes:

(a) Both (A) and (R) are true and (R) is the correct explanation of (A).
(b) Both (A) and (R) are true but (R) is not the correct explanation of (A).
(c) (A) is true but (R) is false.
(d) (A) is false but (R) is true.

37. **Assertion (A):** According to Aristotle, Political Science is a master science.

Reason (R): It imparted knowledge to the rulers and provided principles for regulating public life.

Codes:

(a) Both (A) and (R) are true and (R) is the correct explanation of (A).
(b) Both (A) and (R) are true but (R) is not the correct explanation of (A).
(c) (A) is true but (R) is false.
(d) (A) is false but (R) is true.

38. **Assertion (A):** Parliamentary system of government is based on the principle of collective responsibility.

Reason (R): A Parliamentary defeat is not necessarily a sufficient cause for resignation of the Ministry.

Codes:

(a) Both (A) and (R) are true and (R) is the correct explanation of (A).
(b) Both (A) and (R) are true but (R) is not the correct explanation of (A).
(c) (A) is true but (R) is false.
(d) (A) is false but (R) is true.

39. **Assertion (A):** In his colonial thesis, Lenin argued that there is a close bond between national liberation movements and working class movement worldwide.

Reason (R): Both the working class movement and national movements in the colonies are directed against a common enemy, i.e. imperialism.

Codes:

(a) Both (A) and (R) are true and (R) is the correct explanation of (A).
(b) Both (A) and (R) are true but (R) is not the correct explanation of (A).
(c) (A) is true but (R) is false.
(d) (A) is false but (R) is true.

40. **Assertion (A):** Federal government is a political mechanism for reconciling national unity and power with the maintenance of States' rights.

Reason (R): Autonomous States with contiguous territory having certain common affinities and historical interests crave for unity by means of a National Government.

Codes:

(a) Both (A) and (R) are true and (R) is the correct explanation of (A).
(b) Both (A) and (R) are true but (R) is not the correct explanation of (A).

(c) (A) is true but (R) is false.
(d) (A) is false but (R) is true.

41. It would be obligatory to appoint Ward Committees in case of a Municipality of a population of
(a) Ten lakhs (b) Twenty lakhs
(c) One lakhs (d) Three lakhs

42. The first Municipal Corporation that was established in India was at
(a) Bombay (b) Calcutta
(c) Madras (d) Delhi

43. In 1989, the 64th and 65th Amendment Bills (Nagarpalikas and Panchayats) were not passed and the Amendment Act could not come in force at that time because
(a) Lok Sabha was dissolved in November, 1989
(b) Lok Sabha could not pass the Bill for lack of required majority
(c) Rajya Sabha could not pass the Bill due to lack of the required majority
(d) The President sent the Bill for reconsideration.

44. Perhaps, the oldest approach to the public administration is the
(a) Legal approach
(b) Philosophical approach
(c) Historical approach
(d) Behavioural approach

45. Who among the following agrees that Public Administration is different from Private Administration?
(a) Mary P. Follet (b) L. Urwick
(c) Paul H. Appleby (d) Henri Fayol

46. Which of the following is not emphasised by Gerald Caiden about public administration?
(a) Politicisation
(b) Humanisation
(c) Decentralisation
(d) Democratisation

47. India recognised Bangladesh as a sovereign and independent state on
(a) 6 September 1971
(b) 6 December 1971
(c) 6 April 1972
(d) 6 August 1972

48. Which day every year is celebrated as the U.N.O. Day?
(a) October 24 (b) November 26
(c) July 18 (d) August 20

49. Which one of the following is not a part of the European Union?
(a) European Commission
(b) European Territorial Commission
(c) European Parliament
(d) European Central Bank

50. Who among the following does not agree on the central importance of the state in international relations?
(a) Pluralists
(b) Realists
(c) Neo-realists
(d) Structural realists

ANSWER SHEET

PAPER—I

1. (b)	2. (c)	3. (d)	4. (d)	5. (a)
6. (c)	7. (d)	8. (c)	9. (c)	10. (b)
11. (b)	12. (b)	13. (a)	14. (b)	15. (b)
16. (c)	17. (d)	18. (b)	19. (a)	20. (c)
21. (a)	22. (c)	23. (c)	24. (b)	25. (b)
26. (b)	27. (d)	28. (d)	29. (b)	30. (c)
31. (c)	32. (b)	33. (b)	34. (c)	35. (a)
36. (b)	37. (a)	38. (c)	39. (a)	40. (c)
41. (b)	42. (b)	43. (c)	44. (b)	45. (c)
46. (c)	47. (b)	48. (b)	49. (d)	50. (b)

PAPER—II

1. (d)	2. (b)	3. (c)	4. (b)	5. (b)
6. (c)	7. (b)	8. (c)	9. (c)	10. (c)
11. (b)	12. (a)	13. (d)	14. (b)	15. (d)
16. (b)	17. (d)	18. (b)	19. (a)	20. (d)
21. (c)	22. (d)	23. (b)	24. (c)	25. (b)
26. (c)	27. (c)	28. (d)	29. (b)	30. (b)
31. (d)	32. (d)	33. (a)	34. (a)	35. (a)
36. (c)	37. (c)	38. (a)	39. (a)	40. (d)
41. (c)	42. (d)	43. (b)	44. (a)	45. (a)
46. (d)	47. (b)	48. (d)	49. (b)	50. (d)

PAPER—III

1. (d)	2. (b)	3. (b)	4. (d)	5. (a)
6. (b)	7. (a)	8. (c)	9. (a)	10. (c)
11. (c)	12. (d)	13. (a)	14. (d)	15. (b)
16. (a)	17. (b)	18. (b)	19. (a)	20. (c)
21. (b)	22. (a)	23. (a)	24. (d)	25. (b)
26. (d)	27. (c)	28. (b)	29. (b)	30. (b)
31. (a)	32. (a)	33. (c)	34. (d)	35. (b)
36. (a)	37. (a)	38. (c)	39. (a)	40. (b)
41. (c)	42. (c)	43. (c)	44. (b)	45. (c)
46. (a)	47. (b)	48. (a)	49. (b)	50. (a)